Media, Society, World

To Louise

Media, Society, World

Social Theory and Digital Media Practice

Nick Couldry

polity

First published in 2012 by Polity Press

Reprinted 2012, 2013

Polity Press
65 Bridge Street
Cambridge CB2 1UR, UK

Polity Press
350 Main Street
Malden, MA 02148, USA

ISBN-13: 978-0-7456-3920-8
ISBN-13: 978-0-7456-3921-5(pb)

A catalogue record for this book is available from the British Library
.
Typeset in 10.5 on 12 pt Times
by Toppan Best-set Premedia Limited
Printed and bound in Great Britain by MPG Books Group Limited

The publisher has used its best endeavours to ensure that the URLs for external websites referred to in this book are correct and active at the time of going to press. However, the publisher has no responsibility for the websites and can make no guarantee that a site will remain live or that the content is or will remain appropriate.

Every effort has been made to trace all copyright holders, but if any have been inadvertently overlooked the publisher will be pleased to include any necessary credits in any subsequent reprint or edition.

For further information on Polity, visit our website: www.politybooks.com

The quotation on p. 33 is taken from Brian Larkin, *Signal and Noise*: *Media, Infrastructure and Urban Culture in Nigeria*, © 2008 Duke University Press. All rights reserved. Reprinted by permission of the publisher.

Contents

Figures and Text Boxes

The axis of reference of our examination must be rotated, but around the fixed point of our real need.

Wittgenstein, *Philosophical Investigations*, 1978 [1953]: 46

Preface

This book is about media's contribution to social organization and to our sense of living in a world. The book's main title needs unpacking. *Society* remains the usual word for the containers of social organization within which we live, even though the boundaries of national societies no longer contain all the processes that make up our sense of living 'together' and even though some important groups (stateless people, those who migrate regularly across state boundaries to earn enough to eat) do not live simply in one 'society'. *World* refers to the environments which make sense to us as spaces for living, up to and including the scale of the planet. *Media* as a term is intended to be narrower than 'communication', but much wider than the media that have made up traditional media (newspapers, radio, television, film). By 'media', I mean to cover all institutionalized structures, forms, formats and interfaces for disseminating symbolic content. When virtually all symbolic content is *digital* and many platforms carry both mass produced content and interpersonal communication, the old research divide between 'mass media' and general 'communication' becomes blurred, but I retain the word 'media' to signal that it is the *institutionalized* forms of, and platforms for, producing, disseminating and receiving content that are this book's primary focus. Media in this sense are inescapably entangled with power relations.

In my subtitle, I signal two wrong turns in understanding the relations between media, society and world that I wish to avoid. As many writers argue,[1] media commentary about media is a poor guide to understanding what is going on with media, and for a number of reasons. Mass media production is directly influenced by marketing practice, particularly the push of those who want to promote new products, interfaces and platforms and claim some hold on 'the future of media'. Media commentators on media (and their sources) are often part of a technophiliac elite, and so their interpretations of what's happening with media are tied up with their own strategies of distinction. Media institutions' underlying interests in sustaining their position as a 'central' social infrastructure (as the place we go to find out 'what's going on') influence the accounts that media outlets give of the difference media make to social life. To avoid the trap of following media hype, research must remain close to what people – all people, not just a technophiliac elite – are doing with media. You will not therefore find much attention given in this book to early adopters: I am more interested in habits of media use across wider populations. It is only in everyday media *practice* and everyday *assumptions* about how to get things done through media, where to get information and images from, what can be circulated and how, that we get a grip on media's relations to society and world. Some of those assumptions have been changing rapidly in the past fifteen years or so.

Talking about media's relations to 'society' and 'world' means, whether explicitly or not, taking a view on what 'there is' in the social world, that is, adopting a social ontology: what types of things, relations and processes *are* there in the spaces we call 'social'? At some level, this involves drawing on *social theory*. But here we must avoid a more subtle trap: drawing on a version of social theory that constrains how we understand what is going on with media.

Three types of problem have contributed to this. First, until at least the early 1990s, most sociology and social theory neglected to say anything about media. This only began to be reversed with Anthony Giddens's work on modernity, John Thompson's work on media and modernity and Manuel Castells's work on the rise of 'the network society', which followed on, although not directly, from important work on the social adaptation and domestication of communications and other technology in the 1980s.[2] The same blind spot,[3] incidentally, has characterized political theory and taken even longer to be noticed. Second, these crucial interventions in understanding how media alter the possibilities of social organization did not inspire a broader set of investigations, for example about how media change sociology's other terms of reference (class, group formation and so on). As a result, there is, as yet, no comprehensive account of how media change social ontology, and this book cannot fill that huge gap. Third, some sociologists have started to make media their priority, and particularly the technological base of media, but within a version of social theory that is unhelpful for understanding media and media's role in social life. Such work is influenced sometimes by a turn towards 'non-representational theory', or more broadly towards a rejection of any notion of social order, preferring instead an exclusive language of 'affect', 'intensities' and even 'pure immanence'. Leaving aside broader philosophical objections,[4] such approaches are analytically unhelpful in grasping how media represent the world, and, in particular, how they represent the social and its processes of ordering, since representing the social is one of the main things media institutions do. They are also politically unhelpful because they seem to turn their back on media's role in the production of social knowledge and media's failures to represent the increasingly unequal worlds in which we live.

In thinking about media, I will draw on, and develop, a version of social theory that takes seriously the role that representations, power over representations and how we interact with technologies of representation, play in the possibility of something like 'social order'. Social order is not a given or natural state; it is constructed practically and represented symbolically, and media representations of the 'order' of social life help enact and perform that order. At the level of social theory, the book starts out in chapters 1 and 2 with *ontology* (what there is in the social and media world). I move on in chapters 3 and 4 to *divisions and categorizations* (how media divide up the social world, and also claim to bring it together). In chapters 5 and 6, I turn to *accumulation* – the gathering of social resources for building or opposing power – and the systemic complexities that arise from accumulation and competition. Chapters 7 and 8 move on to questions of *evaluation*: the needs that shape how individual groups and cultures select from the infinite variety of media and our broader frameworks for assessing whether media contribute to a life together that we can value and that is just. What binds together these themes is a concern to understand better media's contribution to our possibilities for knowledge, agency and ethics.

Three other points about this book's approach to media: first, it is not media-centric. I do *not* assume media are the most important things in people's lives; a problem with media studies is that it often seems to assume this. Instead, my approach is grounded in the analysis of everyday action and habit. The social grounding of media analysis is particularly important when the forms and technological basis of media outputs are changing fast. From this broader starting point, difficult questions arise: can there be a separate *media* sociology or *media* studies? Does the exponential growth of media and communication networks across borders render a sociology focused on national *societies* redundant? Has the nature of *power* itself been fundamentally transformed by these processes? How are media changing the *phenomenology* and *ethics* of everyday life? Second, my approach is focused primarily not on the production of media outputs, interfaces and platforms but on what people do with them once produced. This book is therefore intended to *complement* the political economy research which has transformed our understanding of how media get made and circulated, and of the economic forces that shape such production and circulation.[5] This is because my own work comes originally out of audience research. However, a simple boundary between researching media production or researching consumption is now unsustainable: political economy must consider the production work of consumers or audiences, while this book strays at times into considering logics of production. Some division of labour between 'political economy' and 'audience' research remains necessary, given the sheer size of each domain. Third, the book is intended as a toolkit for thinking about everyday practice in relation to digital media through the lens of social theory. While chapters 1 and 2 lay some foundations (an overall perspective on current transformations in media and on the varieties of practice), readers may choose their own path through the remaining chapters, depending on the particular questions in which they are most interested.

In pursuing the many paths that led to this book, I owe a deep debt to two key mentors: David Morley, my MA and PhD supervisor, who saw some research potential in a man in his thirties on a media masters; and the late Roger Silverstone, an examiner of my PhD thesis and, at the London School of Economics, the founder of Media@LSE and then the new Department of Media and Communications, exciting developments of which I was proud to be part.

Thanks to students on the option course on 'Media Rituals' that I taught at LSE between 2002 and 2005 and at Goldsmiths since 2006. Their insights and scepticism kept me on track, even as the 'common sense' about media changed hugely during the 2000s. Various colleagues and friends, in person or through their writing, have been important interlocutors as I developed these ideas: Sarah Banet-Weiser, Rod Benson, Göran Bolin, Richard Butsch, Jessica Clark, Paul Frosh, Jeremy Gilbert, Jonathan Gray, Melissa Gregg, James Hay, Dave Hesmondhalgh, Marwan Kraidy, Sonia Livingstone, Mirca Madianou, Robin Mansell, Divya McMillin, Toby Miller, Laurie Ouellette, Jack Qiu, Paddy Scannell, Johanna Sumiala, Joe Turow, Bruce Williams and Liesbet van Zoonen. Special thanks to Andreas Hepp, James Curran and Polity's anonymous reviewers for their comments on draft chapters. Thanks also to Andreas Hepp, Matt Hills, Stewart Hoover, Sebastian Kubitschko, Mia Løvheim, Scott Rodgers, Jeffrey Wimmer and my MA students, Harris MacLeod, Sujin Oh and Yingxi Ziang, for suggesting useful references.

Particular thanks to Andrea Drugan who since 2005 has been an inspiring (and patient!) editor at Polity Press.

Thanks also to: Anglia Ruskin University where I presented a version of chapter 5 at the Platform Politics conference in May 2011; Bremen University where I gave a version of chapter 6 at the Mediatized Worlds conference in April 2011; JMK, Stockholm University where, as Albert Bonnier Visiting Professor, I gave talks based on chapters 6 and 7 in May 2011; and Warwick University where I gave a keynote based on chapter 7 to their fifth interdisciplinary postgraduate conference in March 2011. I am grateful to fellow members of the NSF-funded CultureDigitally symposium, and especially to Tarleton Gillespie (Cornell) and Hector Postigo (Temple), its leaders, for stimulating discussions, and to Gail Ferguson, Polity's copy-editor, who saved me from many errors and infelicities.

This book has gestated for years but actually been written in the midst of an extremely busy time. Only one person knows how difficult this has been, my wife Louise Edwards. Above all, I want to thank Louise for her love, support and belief throughout, and long before, this book's work. For her, only the old Latin tag will do. *Sine qua non*: without whom, not.

Nick Couldry
London, September 2011

1

Introduction: Digital Media and Social Theory

Media suffuse our sense – our various senses – of living in a world: a social world, an imaginative world, the world of global politics and confrontation. Until the end of the fifteenth century, wrote historian Fernand Braudel, the life of mankind was divided into 'different planets', each occupying regions of the earth's surface, but out of effective contact with each other.[1] Many factors (economic, political, military) and many processes (trade, transport, measurement) contributed to the making of the world we take for granted today, but it is media that instal that world as 'fact' into everyday routines, and in ever-changing ways. News of US President Lincoln's assassination took twelve days to cross the Atlantic in 1865,[2] but in early 2011, world audiences could spend their lunch breaks following a live political crisis in Arab states fuelled, in part, by transnational TV coverage and online social networks.

Half a century ago, Paul Lazarsfeld and Robert Merton asked what were 'the effects of the existence of media in our society'.[3] They had in mind a national society, and nation-states remain of crucial importance to many questions, from control over the movement of people to legal capacity and the regulation of telecommunications. But 'society' can no longer be confined within national boundaries. Indeed, the concept of 'society' – the 'whole' of which, as social beings, we regard ourselves as part – has in recent years been rethought: societies are no longer, as Anthony Giddens put it, 'wholes', but levels of relative 'systemness' which emerge against the background of many other flows and relationships that cross or ignore national borders.[4] Media's social consequences must therefore be examined in relation to both society *and* world.

This book uses social theory to think about everyday experiences of media in the early twenty-first century. Such experience is inevitably marked by big media whose history has been so important to modernity's shared worlds, but it is not limited to them; indeed, the increasing interface between person-to-person media and what formerly were called 'mass' media is possibly the most radical change now under way. Behind this huge change lies an even bigger transformation of human action. If *all* media are 'spaces of action' that 'attempt ... to connect what is separated' (Siegfried Zielinski), then the internet extends this feature. The internet's global connectivity creates a sense of the world as, for the first time in history, 'a single social and cultural setting'.[5]

Media, as a term, is ambiguous. 'Media' refers to institutions and infrastructures that make and distribute particular contents in forms that are more or less fixed and carry their context with them, but 'media' are also those contents themselves. Either way, the term links fundamentally to the institutional dimensions of communication, whether as infrastructure or content, production or circulation.[6] Digital media comprise merely the latest phase of media's contribution to modernity, but the most complex of all, a complexity illustrated by the nature of the internet as a network of networks that connects all types of communication from one-to-one to many-to-many into a wider 'space' of communication.[7] Media have become flexible and interconnected enough to make our only starting point the 'media environment', not specific media considered in isolation.[8]

The internet is the institutionally sustained space of interaction and information storage developed since the early 1960s. The internet only became an everyday phenomenon through the World Wide Web protocols that link hypertext documents into a working system that were conceived first by Tim Berners-Lee in 1989, launched in 1991, but only began to enter everyday use in 1993–4. The internet's fundamental property is an end-to-end architecture neatly summarized by Clay Shirky: 'the internet is just a set of agreements about how to move data between two points,'[9] that is, any two points in *information* space. With the advent of mobile internet access, those points can be accessible by social actors anywhere in *physical* space. The internet's consequences for social theory are therefore radical. Online connection changes the space of social action, since it is interactive, draws on reports of interactions elsewhere and puts them to use in still further interactions. In this way, the internet creates an effectively infinite *reserve* for human action whose existence changes the possibilities of social organization in space everywhere.[10] Action at any site can link prospectively to action elsewhere, drawing, in turn, on actions committed anywhere else; and all those connections are open to commentary and new connections from other points in space. As US religious scholar David Morgan notes, the photos of torture by US army personnel in Abu Ghraib prison in 2004 were one of the most extraordinary recent examples of the expanded social circulation that digital media make possible.[11] Performances and perceptions of the social acquire a new *elasticity*, even if the consequences that flow from this are highly conditioned still by local contexts and resources. Media today are a key part of how agents 'grasp . . . environment as reality'.[12]

Canadian communication theorist Harold Innis once distinguished between 'space-biased' and 'time-biased' media.[13] The internet is certainly space-biased because it changes communications' movement across space not just by extension, but in terms of complexity: the folding of internet information-space into everyday action-space requires a different understanding of what can be done where and by whom. If so, then Innis's contrasting notion of 'time-biased media' (the inscription, the papyrus) recedes into inaccessibility in a world where both space and time are transformed by the reserve of the internet.

Metaphors of media change

Media's importance for society and world cannot be grasped as linear development.[14] When media are embedded in wider cultural and social processes, tensions and contradictions result. Marcel Proust, in his great novel *In Search of Lost Time*, describes his narrator's first telephone call but folds into the description the memory of many later calls:

> as soon as our call has rung out . . . a tiny sound, an abstract sound – the sound of distance overcome – and the voice of the dear one speaks to us . . . But how far away it is! How often I have been unable to listen without anguish, as though . . . I felt more clearly the illusoriness in the appearance of the most tender proximity, and at what distance we may be from the persons we love at the moment it seems that we have only to stretch out our hands to seize and hold them. A real presence, perhaps, that voice that seemed so near – in actual separation![15]

In this account of private pain enacted through a communication technology, Proust captures an ambiguity inherent to media's role in everyday life – 'a real presence . . . in actual separation!' – even if, now the telephone has been transformed almost beyond recognition, we no longer feel that tension the way Proust did.[16] Raymond Williams also had a sense of modern media's ambiguities: 'much of the content of modern communications ... is a form of unevenly shared consciousness of persistently external events. It is what appears to happen, in these powerfully transmitted and mediated ways, in a world with which we have no other perceptible connections but which we feel is at once central and marginal to our lives.'[17]

There is no way back to a world before the transformations that Proust and Williams discuss: those transformations are built into our assumptions about what, and how, the world is. And yet the results of what we now call 'traditional' (mid-twentieth century) media remained puzzling long after they had become the background of daily life. One way of reading Don DeLillo's 1999 epic novel *Underworld* is as a series of meditations on television and radio's role in sustaining, and troubling, the myth of American society.[18]

Many further transformations have occurred since DeLillo wrote. First of all, the sheer proliferation of television and other images themselves: 'life experience has become an experience in the presence of media'. Then, the rise of continuous mobile communication on a second-to-second basis, the overlaying online of broadcast and interpersonal communications, the ability of anyone to make and distribute media contents through what Manuel Castells calls 'mass self-communication'. We are still trying to understand how these recent transformations will be integrated into everyday habit.[19]

Media transform the smallest details of individual actions *and* the largest spaces in which we are involved. Take search engines, now the focus of one of the world's largest businesses, yet an unknown social form fifteen years ago. Google articulates for us 'what there is': it provides us routinely via its browser with what John Tomlinson calls 'the instant and infinite availability of the world's informational resources'. The positive side of this transformation is banally familiar: we 'look things up' very often not in books or directories, but by 'googling it'. A lawyer friend tells me in passing that 'the law is now on Google'; people check their children's illness symptoms by typing them into Google; the director of the once familiar UK phone directory Yellow Pages admits that 'nobody under 25 knows who we are'.[20]

One particular story captures this transformation more vividly than any other. Five years ago, the scandal of a man's faked death and his fraudulent escape with his wife gripped the UK press. A decisive moment came when a *Daily Mirror* reader proved the man's 'posthumous' presence with his wife in Panama by typing 'John and Mary and Panama' into Google. Her comment was interesting: 'I'm a sceptic. Nobody can simply vanish in this day and age, there has to be something, some sign.'[21] This enterprising Google user captured the now familiar ambiguity of the internet: as means for individual discovery, collective contact and guaranteed mutual surveillance.

But how to grasp the impact of this and other parallel changes when embedded in daily life on *every* scale? Metaphors may help. One metaphor of the difference media make to the world is, following Roger Silverstone, a 'dialectic'.[22] The word 'dialectic' derives from the Greek for conversation and so captures how any conversation's components remain separate from, though informed by, each other. All of us – individuals and groups – contribute something to this dialectic, through our media-informed assumptions about 'what there is' and 'what can be done'; those contributions are not acts of individual choice, but shaped by largescale infrastructural changes, themselves driven by economic and other forces. A dialectical approach brings out the flexibility of how humans negotiate the differences that media make, and the traffic *between* media we have come to call 'remediation'.[23]

Does 'dialectic' capture the cumulative *volume* of media, and media's resulting *systemic* impact on everyday life? Perhaps for that we need another metaphor: Todd Gitlin's image of media as 'torrent', a 'supersaturated' flow of visuals and text that overwhelms us daily. A few years after Gitlin wrote, his image became integrated into the brand name Bit-Torrent, the software that allows large media files (TV programmes, films) to be shredded into bits and sent in countless parallel streams over the internet. But we do not grow accustomed to media's wider 'torrent' because its scale and depth *go on* growing: even people's comments about media now add to the flow through blogs, digg-it recommendations, YouTube mashups and tweets, all postdating Gitlin's analysis. So the metaphor of a media 'torrent' only takes us so far, and this without even considering the saturation of today's consumer environment by data sources and modes of information transmission such as RFID chips.[24]

Here, the technical meaning of the term 'supersaturated' is significant. Supersaturation refers in chemistry and thermodynamics to a solution that contains more of a material dissolved within it 'than could be dissolved by the solvent under normal circumstances'.[25] Supersaturation therefore names an *unstable* state, a deviation from the equilibrium state of the dissolved and solvent materials in question. This unstable state occurs only as a result of particular changes, for example, temperature change or pressure change. The supersaturation of *society* by media would mean the unstable, non-equilibrium state when social life is filled with media contents at every level owing to particular pressures (spatial – the boundaries of a particular broadcasting territory; temporal – a particular event-cycle such as a global political crisis). There are limits to using even this more precise sense of the term 'supersaturated' to capture the density of media in contemporary societies: social life is based on interpretations, but a liquid does not 'interpret' the bubbles of gas inserted within it! But at least the supersaturation metaphor allows us to appreciate the phase shifts in social life when media saturation reaches a certain point: changes to the *possibilities of order* within the social. At this point, it becomes clear we need to connect with social theory.

Towards a socially oriented media theory

I want in this book to develop some mid-range conceptual tools for understanding the difference media make in our lives: it is a work of media theory. But what *sort* of media theory?

There can be no 'pure' theory of media, since media are always particular, historically embedded ways of communicating information and meaning. Even the most abstract theories of communication, such as Shannon and Weaver's self-styled 'mathematical theory of communication', could only emerge as salient in a particular historical context, in the dawning age of computers and television when codes for converting complex information into simple common forms were invented.[26] What for convenience I am calling media theory involves particular choices about the data on which it draws and the types of analysis it prefers. Let me explain.

For simplicity, we might think of media research as a pyramid with four apexes. We can turn the pyramid four ways up, with the type of research we want to prioritize at the top, while others form the pyramid base. No way of turning the pyramid is 'right', or 'better', since the apexes name different priorities for research: media *texts*; the *political economy* of media production, distribution and reception; the *technical properties* of each medium; and the *social uses* to which media technologies and media contents are put.

Any of these research priorities *can* generate theory, that is, mid-range concepts to make broader sense of their field of inquiry, and each type of theory will need to draw on research (and theory) from the other points of the pyramid. But whether and how far research at any apex actually develops into theory depends on intellectual fashion and how disciplines change. In the 1970s and 1980s, general theory about media content, particularly its ideological properties, was all the rage (the screen theory that dominated film studies and

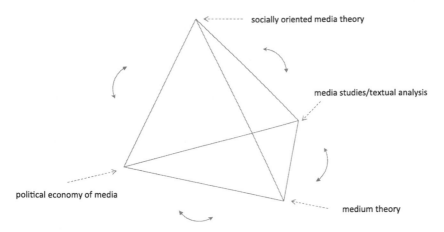

Figure 1.1 What kind of media theory?

to a lesser degree television studies), but its influence largely faded
in the 1990s. Political economy has generated important theory about
the distinctive features of media and cultural production and, in its
broadest versions, is concerned not just with media ownership but
with power inequalities across social life.[27]

Perhaps the most celebrated form of media theory recently has
been 'medium theory', whose most well-known exponents have been
the early Canadian theorists Marshall McLuhan and Harold Innis
and the German theorist Friedrich Kittler, who died in October 2011.
Kittler provided some brilliant insights into what media do, and specifically how particular techniques and inventions emerged as 'media',
and so how media extended, indeed gave new form to, our senses and
perceptual capacities.[28] Some of Kittler's insights have implications
for sociology of media, but Kittler's real interest was understanding
the distinctive 'technical' contribution made to our extended faculties
by each medium *at the point of its emergence*. Only this explains how
he could devote just a few pages at the end of *Optical Media* to the
computer which, in its triumphant 'liquidation of . . . the [pre-media]
imaginary', *completed* his history of media as the extension of human
senses. This focus on the technical 'essence' of each medium means,
as Kittler himself noted, 'to *forget* humans, language and sense', and
to dismiss a 'trivial content-based approach to media', or the study
of 'popular films and television programmes'. It even means dismissing sociology itself, since Kittler showed no interest in how media
such as the computer are *put to use*: he offered, as John Durham

Peters notes, 'a media studies without people', a media/medium theory with its back turned away from sociology.[29]

By contrast with Kittler, I offer in this book a media theory turned *towards* sociology and social theory. This fourth possibility for media theory foregrounds how media are put to use in, and help shape, social life and how the meanings circulated through media have social consequences. This type of media theory lacks a ready name, so let me call it, slightly awkwardly, *socially oriented media theory*: that is, theory focusing on the social processes that media constitute and enable. Its disciplinary connections are primarily with sociology,[30] not literature, economics or the history of technology and visual communication.

Already 'new' media, like traditional media before them, have become ordinary contents of everyday life, a 'taken-for-granted part of our infrastructure'.[31] That makes understanding the consequences of media for society and world difficult. Grasping how media shape contemporary social life requires *social* theory. If we want to unravel the complex interdependencies of the digital world, we need to recall German sociologist Norbert Elias's work on 'figurations' in his classic account of the 'civilizing process'; if curious about the local patterns of order and resource concentration emerging in production and everyday life online, then we would do well to consult French sociologist Pierre Bourdieu's theory of 'fields' of cultural production; if we want to ask, simply, what difference do the countless messages circulated online make to the social world, we need to draw on classical French sociologist Emile Durkheim's account of the ready-made distinctions and hierarchies – 'categories' in his term – into which our representations of the world get condensed.[32] To grasp media in their contemporary complexity, we need not just *any* social theory; we need social theory that addresses the construction, representation and contestation *of* the social.

A socially oriented approach to media theory is concerned fundamentally with action. Media provide an entry point for understanding the organization of human action. Our starting point is the open-endedness of practice and the embedding of practice in wider relations of power. This approach has much more in common with a critical sociology of power[33] than with a history of technological discovery. Socially oriented media theory, however, shares two important things with medium theory. First, it is concerned with media, that is, organized mechanisms and infrastructures for channelling communication rather than 'communication' in some general sense.[34] The other, more surprising, overlap is with a less well-known representative of medium theory, Siegfried Zielinski, who, far from espousing a linear model of media development, opposes 'the economy of adjusting and shaping [media] that is committed to the paradigm of productivity'. Zielinski's stance impels him into an '*an*archaeological' approach to media history that celebrates heterogeneity and diversity in media's past.[35] Translate such scepticism into the sociological challenges of understanding media's present, and you get a socially oriented media theory concerned to *deconstruct* the tremendous forces that interpret media products and systems as 'natural' or seamless outcomes of economic, social and political rationalization.

Any media theory or media analysis today, however, must confront some crucial uncertainties that I will now, rather schematically, explore.

The digital revolution and its uncertainties

Most commentators believe that we are in the middle of a media revolution, centring on the internet's connection and transmission capacities and the countless digital media devices and infrastructures that have grown up around them. But the long history of 'myth-making' about technology should make us cautious.[36] New communications technologies in particular have generated endless myths (of democratization, political harmony, world peace), most recently the myth that information, and particularly digital information, is free.[37]

It is worth looking back to some features that the great historian of print, Elizabeth Eisenstein, saw as characterizing 'the print revolution' between the fifteenth and seventeenth centuries in Europe. Print involved the shift in cultural production from unique texts made by individual scribes to distinct products made for multiple readers' convenience, and the creation of a distribution mechanism (the book market) whereby 'identical images, maps and diagrams could be viewed *simultaneously* by scattered readers'.[38] As a result, the number of texts increased massively, so that a seventeenth-century scholar could read more books in a few months – just by sitting in his study – than earlier scholars would have seen in a lifetime of travelling. Other implications followed: the immense new data-recording and archiving capacities of print; new notions of individual rather than collective authorship.[39] This was indeed a revolution in how communication was *socially* organized, whose first precondition was the technology of the printed book, but it took place over a long time. As two other historians of print, Febvre and Martin, note, the early printers were nomads who physically transported their technology around with them: the result was an unimaginably slow (to us) diffusion of printing across Western Europe 'over a period of 300 years'.[40]

Today's media and information revolution, while it has its scep-tics,[41] is comparable in depth to, even if massively faster than, the print revolution. It has happened in less than two decades and with few geographical boundaries, overlaying previous important shifts in media infrastructure (satellite and cable TV). In Iraq in the early 1990s, the requirement that *typewriters* be registered with the authori-ties was still a plausible means of state censorship, and television channels were few and heavily influenced by the state; by 2009, 470 Arabic-language satellite TV channels were available in the Arab world,[42] and the recent spread of Web-enabled mobile phones has made state censorship still more difficult. The internet has brought a shift in information production from a limited number of discrete forms (books, pamphlets, letters, reports, lists) to information units of any form and size whatsoever (websites), provided they confirm to some basic criteria of standard text or image format, and identifiable location (url).[43] Collections of such information units – websites, data-bases – are now accessible with few restrictions on what types or volumes of media can be brought together in such collections. The result has been an exponential growth in data volume and archiving capacity, new forms of both collective authorship (Wikipedia) and individual authorship (blogs, vlogs, etc.), and a space, as the creator of the World Wide Web, Tim Berners-Lee, put it, for us to 'interact on all scales'. Many commentators in the academy and industry believe that whole sectors of public and professional life are being radically transformed by the information revolution.[44]

Three immediate qualifications, however, are necessary. The first is that a high proportion of the digital world's information-processing capacity is in private hands via corporate intranets and proprietary systems, and Lawrence Lessig has famously argued that the internet's open end-to-end architecture is becoming a thing of the past.[45] Fears over whether 'net neutrality' can be preserved continue; the trade-offs between the everyday convenience of search-engine use and corporate Google's resulting ability to do side-deals, for example, with US phone-provider Verizon over the openness of the wireless internet, apparently beyond the reach of the Federal Communica-tions Commission, are troubling; Google's market dominance is now facing legal challenges by the US Federal Trade Commission and the European Competition Commissioner.[46] So we cannot treat the 'space' of the internet as simply free and available to all.

The second qualification is that within the apparently infinite expansion of global connectivity, new hidden forms of *disconnection* are emerging. The issue of the digital divide has been prominent since the late 1990s. In some countries – the USA, Denmark, South Korea, for example – levels of internet access are so high that the online world is seemingly a universal reference point. But the UK government has made no such assumption. Disconnection becomes even more acute when we look outside the West, where the percentage of annual monthly salary necessary to buy a computer varies widely; in many parts of the world, a personally owned computer remains out of the reach of all but a small minority.[47] Meanwhile, gender stratifies internet access *within* nations, for example in the Middle East, as do class and ethnicity. As US scholar Ellen Seiter puts it, 'the children of elite and urban professionals experience new technologies in a qualitatively different way from poor children'. The 'virtuous circle' of easy access to computers, related skills and social support, entails *a vicious circle* for those who lack those things: these inequalities are likely to extend into the world of social networking.[48]

Consider, third, the internet's huge geographical expansion, and the resulting shift from an English language-dominated internet to an internet where many languages have hegemony over mutually inaccessible territories of users (Arabic, Chinese, Japanese and so on). The internet may already be too large for any one research frame to grasp: there are 420 million internet users in China alone, of whom 364 million have broadband and 115 million live rurally. One key point however is indisputable, disrupting any easy generalization: that nations and parts of the world vary in terms of their inhabitants' likely status as voices in the global internet. As James Curran points out, if your native or mastered second language is English, then your chances of a wide readership are many times higher than if it is Marathi. There is, in other words, no single 'world' of digital media and, to the extent that there appears to be, this is an illusion based on global rhetoric fuelled by the very inequalities that this illusion masks.[49]

When we consider the social consequences of digital media, predictions of a positive 'revolution' become even more complex. Having one's own personal computer is not the only route into internet use where internet access is socially coordinated. The internet revolution cannot therefore be understood exclusively via statistics on individual internet access; meanwhile cross-border movements of labour, driven by global patterns of inequality, shape both resources and needs for such social coordination. Second, there is a big difference between the basic possibilities for using technology and how it comes to be *used in practice*. As Regis Debray puts it, 'usage is more archaic than the tool . . . if the medium is "new", the milieu [of its use] is "old", by definition.'[50] Indeed, histories of the book's long-term social consequences bring out *how many* factors combined to produce over time the reading habits standard in late nineteenth-century and early twentieth-century Europe: institutional contexts and associations for reading; new cultural conventions; the increased leisure time of the growing bourgeoisie; even the increased availability in the home of light after sunset.[51] An accelerator in the 'internet revolution' has been the ability of not just content but software (in other words, infrastructure) to be distributed through the same medium. The book was a great leap forward in disseminating innovation, since it enabled the transmission of diagrams and other technical descriptions,[52] but today the software infrastructure on which important communication innovations rely can be globally disseminated online without any person or object having to move physically! Think of the open-editing system of Indymedia sites, invented in Australia but first used in Seattle around the protests at the 1999 WTO meetings; or the Usha-hidi website template available for disaster reporting across Africa.[53]

To sum up: for all its excitement, the non-linear world of contem-porary media transformation is marked by intense *uncertainty*. Predictions based on the so-called 'digital generation' substitute mar-keting hype for serious analysis, and risk the basic error of confusing life-stage behaviours with genuine historical change.[54] Similarly, while we undoubtedly live in an era when media outputs are converging on common platforms, claims that we inhabit something as singular as 'convergence culture' should be treated with suspicion.[55] Clay Shirky recently suggested that 'the bigger the opportunity offered by new tools, the less completely anyone can extrapolate the future from the previous shape of society.' It is exactly the wider interface between media and the distribution of social power that is most uncertain. Proust had it right when he commented on the fallacy of judging 'what [is] kept secret . . . in the light of what [has been] revealed'.[56]

More specifically, any media theory today must address six types of uncertainty which, while linked to broader processes of differentiation and reflexivity within late modernity,[57] are best under-stood in terms of the specific dynamics of media institutions and technologies.

What, who and where are media?

Contemporary digital media are in crucial ways 'underdetermined'.[58] A decade and a half ago, the key elements of media research (texts, the political economy of production, the study of audiences) were in place. While the mini-revolution of audience studies raised new ques-tions – how exactly do texts work with audiences and audiences work with texts? – those questions appeared containable. Technological

innovations (home video recording, the multiplication of TV channels via satellite and cable) had not, in spite of predictions to the
contrary, fundamentally altered the object of study. The audience –
my own particular interest – seemed securely positioned within a
largely national landscape of media offerings. And we had by the
early 1980s begun to understand media's role in sustaining nations.[59]

Over the next decade, media research expanded laterally. We started
to appreciate the many things audiences do besides watching, reading
or listening to a text, with fandom studies just one important new
area; media came to be seen not as a closed circuit of production–
distribution–reception, but as a larger process of 'mediation' stretched
out across space. A slow rapprochement between media studies and
media-related work in anthropology began.[60] The internet, World Wide
Web and mobile phones pushed computer-related communication
and mobile media to the forefront of research,[61] with uncertainties
emerging over whether the centralized power of traditional media
institutions would be replaced by a more dispersed space of online
production and consumption.[62] Yet in 2005 the landscape of media
research remained basically unchanged.

The years since 2005 have seen a more fundamental disruption to
media and media research. Digital media convergence has accelerated hugely. Circulating your photos and videos online has become
commonplace; so too has commenting on other people's blogs,
mashups and online self-presentations. The increased availability of
mobile phones with fast internet access has increased (exponentially)
people's capacities to be receivers *and* circulators of media. The fast
growth of social networking sites (Facebook in the UK, USA and
many other countries, Orkut in Brazil and India, RenRen in China,
Mixi in Japan, Cyworld in South Korea) has added an entirely new
dimension. The things we call 'media', and the rules that govern their
combinations, have hugely expanded: the *what* of media research has
changed. The *Economist* was right to ask in 2006: 'what *is* a media
company?'[63]

Beware of attributing these changes to technology alone. Changes
in the communication infrastructure we call 'media' have always
resulted from the *intersections* between technological, economic, social
and political forces. In the pre-digital era, 'media' were productions
that radiated outwards from a limited number of production/
distribution points and were received by members of a separate, larger
'mass', the 'audience'. But this was not through technological necessity,
as the early history of radio demonstrates: in the USA, the
possibility of radio as a one-to-one or many-to-many medium was
actively developed before and after the end of the First World War,

while in France and the UK the possibility of radio operating through a decentred, inclusive, 'community' model of production was explored.[64] That such non-mass models fell away – to the point of being largely written out of media history – reflects the efforts that went into developing the commercial and political opportunities of one-to-many radio: high capital was required for national-scale media production/distribution, and the resulting capital-intensive mass media fitted well with the increasingly centralized organization of the modern state.[65]

Now a different type of transformation is under way, again not attributable to simple technological possibility. We are familiar with the idea of the 'constant TV' household. But today, even in a moderately well-equipped country like the UK, 74 per cent of the population have broadband and 50 per cent of 16- to 24-year-olds have internet-enabled phones.[66] As substantial internet use has become routine in many countries, new media actors have emerged: the producers of *jihadist* videos online or indeed any self-produced clips uploaded to YouTube; celebrities tweeting from their phones; demonstrators, camera-phone upheld, in a crowd. Not just the 'what' but the '*who*' of media is changing, complicating what John Thompson called mass communications' 'fundamental break between the producer and the consumer'. Today, the internet gives individuals a capacity to reach large audiences that recalls the early use of phone wires by individuals to sing and play music to 'the world',[67] although this time both the range and infrastructural constraints are quite different. Specialist media producers/distributors invest not just in their own content but in stimulating and managing 'user-generated content', while media consumers or audience members have endless opportunities to contribute to or comment upon institutional media production, although who exactly takes up these opportunities remains uncertain. Some celebrate the interactive communities around newspaper websites, while others are more sceptical.[68] Some discern even more fundamental shifts: the Web's shift from 'a publishing medium' to a 'communication medium', video's shift from a centrally distributed cultural medium to 'an extension of . . . interpersonalized networks'.[69] Could we be seeing the disaggregation of media outputs, the withering away of 'the mass media'? Or does this underestimate the interest of today's new media corporations such as Google in *sustaining* a quality media environment across which its search engines will crawl?[70]

The leading *commercial* media players are arguably today not programme makers, news agencies or film companies, but Google (including YouTube, which they own), Facebook and Apple. They make and sell the devices, platforms and search engines on which media interfaces rely: it is those players who *link up* the many streams of media usage into practical 'wholes'. As Tarleton Gillespie notes, 'platform' is a much-used term within industry circles to capture this linking capacity: the quest for new platforms is incessant so, writing in summer 2011, I wait to see if Microsoft's acquisition of Skype for US$8.5 billion will enable it to join the pantheon of dominant media players.[71] Such transformations work at two levels. First, there is the level of *what is conveyed* across platforms and the resulting changes in *where* particular content-types are standardly consumed: Premium VOD (video-on-demand), planned by leading film producers (Warner Bros, Twentieth-Century Fox), may shift film demand decisively towards home settings, while Google is simultaneously exploring the possibility of launching new film releases via YouTube, available on people's smartphones. Meanwhile, the era of 'cloud gaming' takes once-individualized media practices (gaming via a separate console) and ensures they increasingly depend on an *online* infrastructure that connects huge groups of players.[72] Second, there is a transformation at the level of *how the conveying is done*. We get information increasingly through embedded 'apps' that draw us into proprietary regions of the internet not reachable by simple search: this is Chris Anderson and Michael Wolff's vision that the open-access 'Web is dead'.[73]

We must, however, tread cautiously. Some media institutions remain constant, in spite of new delivery possibilities: radio has in part moved online, but its soundworld still forms part of the routine background of many people's lives. Or take television: in the early 2000s, it was commonplace to proclaim the 'end of television'.[74] Undoubtedly, the nature of television has changed from being a box in the corner of the living room to what one writer called 'an ensemble of non-site specific screens', from being a 'push' medium available only in one form (broadcast or distributed by cable or satellite to a television set) to 'a matrix medium' that offers, in connection with other digital media platforms and contents, 'an increasingly flexible and dynamic mode of communication'.[75] We can no longer take for granted the single entity of 'TV', produced by separate television companies; 'television' is now a space where huge *multi*media conglomerates compete.[76] Strange new entrants stray into this space: newspapers showcase their own video material on their websites (*Sun, New York Times*), or warehouse others' self-produced videos (*Guardian*). Yet, although the size of prime-time audiences has in many countries declined, television *continues* to be watched and in large numbers, while 'television is still the most widespread and influential medium in China today'.[77] As William Uricchio argues, television may now be returning to the 'pluriformity' that characterized television before the mass television audience.[78] Clearly, we cannot grasp our expanding media environment by thinking of how new media (the internet?) substitute for old media (television? radio?).

Wave upon wave of newly saturating media has flowed over inhabitants of richer countries:

1   the move from a limited number of terrestrial television channels to hundreds of cable or satellite channels;
2   increasingly fast and continuous access to the internet and World Wide Web;
3   media access from transportable or 'mobile' phones;
4   radio and the press's move online through digitalization and newspaper websites;
5   the massive growth in online content delivery networks for both top-down distribution and horizontal exchange of photos, film, television and music;
6   social networking sites such as Facebook as a new interface for linking to any of the above, or simply for contacting our friends and mobilizing our supporters;
7   many-to-many interfaces for continuous broadcasting in time and space, such as Twitter;
8   media applications ('apps') for iPhones, android phones, blackberries and other mobile devices.

These recent waves of media saturation are cumulative, making the term 'saturation' inadequate. Media has the type of sedimented complexity that a landscape does. But *how* saturated by media each person's world is – how actively people *select* from the media landscape available to them – remains uncertain.[79]

Select from or use *what exactly*? Built on top of what Henry Jenkins notes is a still limited range of basic media,[80] we now experience a *media manifold*, comprising a complex web of delivery platforms, behind which lies the effectively infinite reserve of the internet. The media manifold is something we can all imagine, even if its actuality is uneven, because all media are already – or are on the way to becoming – digital, convertible into information bits of basically the same type. The installation of internet access as a basic capacity of many devices (fixed and portable) means that we increasingly use a connected range of media rather than single media in isolation. Anthropologists Madianou and Miller designate this plurality 'polymedia',[81] but the term risks signifying a mere plurality, rather than the linked *configuration* of media that is crucial. So I will retain here the term media manifold. That manifold can seem to be everywhere and nowhere in particular: we are just embedded in it to varying degrees.

At this point, generalities about media interfaces become inadequate. Habits of use are crucial, and habit is more than just repetition: any habit is stabilized through multiple practices that construct new ways of living, whether in the home or in everyday culture more generally. This takes us to a second area of uncertainty: use.

What do we do with media?

Describing what people do with media used to be simple: watching a documentary programme; following a radio serial; reading weekly magazines or daily newspapers; going to the cinema to see a film; turning the pages of a book. Well-established changes complicated this basic landscape: time-shifting by VCR and, more recently, by digital recorders with hard disks. Remediation within the digital media environment goes much further. True, some media bundles have always involved indeterminacy: we have never known systematically about how different people consume a newspaper (do they start with the sports pages, fashion pages or front-page news?). But uncertainties as to the size, order and context of media consumption are now *inherent to* all media consumption within the unbounded hypertext of the Web.

Once more, this destabilization is not simply a matter of technology. As Lisa Gitelman insists, media technologies' 'protocols of use' are important.[82] A factor in stabilizing media consumption for decades has been the sheer convenience – for use – of the information and entertainment bundles that media industries evolved: the prime-time news bulletin, the newspaper delivered or collected every morning, the daily or weekly instalments of a soap opera. Scarcity was once a key factor in the shaping of convenience: there were a limited number of television and radio stations and newspapers, making media sources relatively scarce. But in an era of information plenty, convenience works differently: what is convenient may now be not large media packages (with dedicated advertising built into them) but the glance past online news headlines ten times a day.[83] The practical convergence of older habits of media consumption – the way people could assume others were doing much the same as them, when they switched on the TV or the radio (and the way producers could make parallel assumptions) – no longer holds, or at least not as simply as before. Convenience must be understood within the changing organization of work, family and leisure. New grids of habit are forming, so far only partly mapped. We start out then from the *heterogeneity* of what people now do with media: posting family photos onto Facebook for relatives in different countries, watching an old film on a film channel, surfing the weather on the other side of the planet.

Some decisive trends have occurred, for example the decline in hard-copy newspaper consumption, especially amongst younger users in the UK and USA. I turn to the economic context of this shortly, but note there are countries, for example in Scandinavia, where youth newspaper consumption remains strong, and free newspapers handed out on urban transit systems may prove a viable basis for something like a press.[84] With other media, things are even more complex. The acknowledged network news decline in the USA, as Amanda Lotz notes, is at most the beginnings of the long-term 'death of the network newscast', *not* the death of network news itself. The penetration of online news, even in the USA, is in any case exaggerated: as ABC World News executive Jon Banner puts it, 'our [TV] broadcast dwarfs any audience that we get on the Web, and probably will continue to do so for the foreseeable future.'[85] Even in the USA, time spent consuming TV news has still changed little since 1996, well before the internet's main growth, while in the UK and Germany many times more people use television as their main news source than the internet. Television news remains the main news source even in a country with high internet penetration like Denmark; so too, as a recent survey showed, among European Arab migrants.[86]

Hard-copy newspapers and television news are the most favourable case for predictions of drastic change in the media landscape. But if we look at television consumption overall, actual statistical trends are dramatically at odds with media hype about the death of old media. US television viewing was higher in 2005 than in 1995 (that is, before the rise of regularly available internet access) and continued to rise in 2008, while UK TV viewing was unchanged between 2002 and 2007, increasing in 2008, 2009 and 2010; in Germany, overall TV viewing also rose during 2002–7.[87] For every case where programme content is dominated by the follow-on Web audience (e.g., MTV's *The Hills*), we can find, as Toby Miller notes, another programme where the immediate TV audience dominated (e.g., the US version of *The Office*).[88] One reason for this is the many ways in which the guaranteed simultaneity of 'push' television fits routine desires: the need to keep up with the flow of a daily soap, to have a familiar background to dull domestic tasks, to watch, not just read about, sporting events live.[89] In spite, then, of dire contradictions to the contrary, *television* is likely to remain most people's primary medium for the foreseeable future, however delivered and with whatever Web-based enhancements.[90] That is the assumption on which UK media regulator Ofcom now bases its policy. Yet when back in 2006 Sonia Livingstone, Tim Markham and I reached that conclusion in our 'Public Connection' research, we contradicted received wisdom![91]

There are good reasons why media hype and actual media use diverge. We can easily miss key forms of *dis*articulation, including many people's active choice *not* to buy or use a technology, a neglected area of media research until now.[92] Media reports based on the latest offers of media technology regularly mislead us as to the pace of change because they underplay the inertia of *habit*: habit is not news. Yes, more people are now multi-tasking between multiple media; yes, the ability to communicate socially and with loved ones across multiple platforms is becoming basic for many, rich and poor. But complexity is difficult to handle, and new ways of *simplifying* media use online are also becoming habitual. Philip Napoli discerns the growing 'massification' of the internet whereby most online activity converges around rather fewer sites than we would first expect.[93] Iconic new devices, such as the iPhone, simplify our interface with the media manifold. More broadly, our media practice changes only because media technologies within everyday contexts mesh with our wider habits, our ways of 'getting by'. The power of phone 'apps' is their capacity to reconfigure our basic habits of interacting with media. The implications for wider power dynamics are potentially profound: as Susan Halpern puts it, 'once there is an app for everything, it's Apple's Web, not the Wide World's'.[94]

Such meshing of media practice and world cannot be predicted from the standpoint of technology alone. When media interfaces and uses are changing fast, it is especially difficult to grasp such articulations and disarticulations. Raymond Williams's well-known discussion of technologies of 'mobile privatization' was an early insight here: on the one hand, increased mobility (of goods, people, information), made feasible by the self-sufficient 'private' site of the home where TV was watched and from which people set out in their cars; on the other hand, new disarticulations between the home and older forms of shared public space. New visions of changing media production – such as *Guardian* editor Alan Rusbridger's theory of the 'mutualization' of the news – tend to say more about new articulations than about *dis*articulations.[95]

Habits of media use change in line with the wider bundles of habits from which our daily practice is made up. Much is made of the use of social media in, say, times of political protest, but political upheavals are poor guides to wider change, since they are precisely exceptional. Entertainment and the basic necessities of 'holding things together' may be a much more useful guide. If, as Jonathan

Crary points out, societies and cultures' 'regimes of attention' (and inattention) are historically variable, then the shift to entertainment in global media agendas may be the biggest change under way every day in media use.[96] This takes us to underlying uncertainties over the economics of media production.

Are media operations economically viable any more?

This book is not primarily concerned with media economics, but we cannot ignore shifts in media's economic viability that, potentially, challenge what media *can* exist and in what forms.

First, the good news. The internet's open 'end-to-end' structure,[97] its hypertextuality and low production costs, lead, according to Yochai Benkler, to a massive stimulation of cultural production.[98] But, from the perspective of mainstream media, things look different. Consider the economic models on which the funding of long-established media formats is based. Leaving aside public service broadcasting, which is subject to supervening political pressures, media that depend on advertising are currently facing intense pressures due to the increasing shift of advertising revenues online (Craigslist, eBay, online holiday booking sites). Changes in audience practice, even if less dramatic than hyped, may lead to changed business perceptions that transform particular media's income base, especially if reinforced by a perception that the exclusive future trend of advertising is to move online, or by business models within larger corporate groups which make few concessions to the distinctive features of media businesses (take the *Los Angeles Times*'s shrinkage in recent years as an example).[99]

The case of the hard-copy newspaper is particularly striking. In the UK and US newspaper industries, the loss of advertising income is real and linked to falling readerships; for the local press in particular, there has been a near collapse of its classified advertisement market due to convenient online alternatives. Paul Starr sums this up from a US perspective: 'the Internet has undermined the newspaper's role as market intermediary.'[100] And what if news production has *never* been independently profitable without cross-subsidy from other more entertaining parts of media offerings (sport, gossip, celebrity news)? If so, the disaggregation of the newspaper 'bundle' into a mass of hypertext links poses a fundamental challenge to news production's viability.[101] Meanwhile, Terhi Rantanen suggests that the constant availability of news-*like* 'information', wherever we are, whatever the time, makes it 'more and more difficult to make a profit from general news services'. If so, will the discrete packages of modern news die and be replaced by undifferentiated 'new stories' told by multiple tellers, recalling the era before modern news institutions? As yet, it is entirely uncertain whether new forms of subsidy will emerge to counterbalance newspapers' declining economic viability.[102]

Yet there is no single direction of travel for media advertising. In March 2011, the UK's regulatory authority for media, Ofcom, announced a review of the television advertising market in response to its growth in 2010, while the global television advertising market is also growing.[103] Meanwhile, the jury is out on whether a workable general model for *online* advertising can be found.

There are, however, deeper factors reconfiguring media economics. The increasing unknowability of the media audience in the digital age is a challenge for those trying to buy its attention: the advertisers who have always been a driving force in the media environment.[104] What if, through the convergence of once separate media, people's trajectories across the media landscape become so varied that neither producers nor advertisers can assume a pattern any more? As Joseph Turow's pioneering work on the audience selling process shows, the shifting terrain of the audience has begun to have profound impacts on how media industries (whether television or the new converged platforms) *think of* the audience. Their focus now is on the targeted search for individual high-value consumers not through specific media packages (programmes or series in which advertising can be placed) but via continuous online tracking which targets them *individually and continuously*, as they move around online. Will this erode the idea of a general audience and with it media producers' sense of responsibility for a shared public world? Non-target audiences are of declining value to media institutions, while the differential value of niche audiences matters much more. A similar argument can be developed for the long-term consequences of segmented marketing on the political audience.[105]

And yet the tastes of individual consumers, even the most wealthy, need to be grounded in some wider web of belief.[106] So the overall implications of Turow's analysis are still uncertain; indeed this leads us to a different uncertainty, the changing status of media as social institutions.

How is the social/political status of media institutions changing?

Media institutions, indeed all media producers, make representations: they re-present worlds (possible, imaginary, desirable, actual). Media make truth claims, explicit or implicit: the gaps and repetitions in media representations, if systematic enough, can distort people's sense of *what there is to see* in the social and political domains. Modernity's key processes of centralization (economic, social, political, cultural) themselves have relied on media as infrastructures of communication.[107] An insight of James Beniger's great book, *The Control Revolution*, was to identify the 'crisis of control' in mid-nineteenth century industrializing societies, such as the USA and the UK, and the role of information and media production in resolving that crisis.[108] The twinning of modern media institutions with modern social organization is not specific to the West. It is under way, under distinct conditions, in contemporary India and China, Iran and Brazil.

It is the *apparently* necessary role of media in the social fabric that underlies what I have called elsewhere 'the myth of the mediated centre'.[109] I say 'apparently' because there are always historical alternatives (there is no teleology to history, *pace* Hegel). There are the contingencies of how particular techniques and inventions became adopted as 'media' (which Kittler brilliantly uncovers), but also the radical contingency of all processes of 'modernization' and 'centralization'.[110] 'Centres', still less 'mediated centres', are not necessary features of social organization: rather, over time, things have been progressively organized so that, to borrow a phrase of Pierre Bourdieu, *everything goes on as if* they are necessary. Our very notion of 'the media' is an example:[111] out of the disparate dynamics of multiple media industries, something emerged as general and as mythical as '*the* media'. This notion is reproduced by an everyday social functionalism. We cannot ignore the claims to and on behalf of social 'order' which saturate media discourse, whether in Europe and North America or in historic projects for expansion of state authority in Africa.[112]

But what if the changing dynamics of media's production, consumption and economics are *undermining* the myth of the mediated centre? What if the very idea of '*the* media' is imploding, as the interfaces we call 'media' are transformed? Once again, the disruptive dynamics are *not* technological per se: the internet's distinctive ability to link up previously separate contexts (think of YouTube) arguably makes it *easier,* not harder, to sustain 'the media' as a common reference point. Disruption derives from how technological possibilities are meshed with wider economic, social and political forces. Turow's analysis of the media industry's decreasing interest in the general audience identifies an economic dynamic of disruption. However, if basic consumer demand – for fashion, music, sport – is to be sustained at all, it requires 'the media' to provide *common* reference points towards which we turn to see what's going on, what's cool. Indeed media corporations are increasingly looking for the 'water-cooler moment' that will *drive* multiple individual users to follow content across platforms so that income can be generated along the way.[113] As Graeme Turner argues, the decline of mass media is not the same as a decline of media's 'centrality'. In the multiple-outlet digital media era, 'centrality' becomes an even more important claim for media institutions to make, as they seek to justify the wider 'value' they provide.[114] The ability to speak for, and link audiences to, the 'mediated centre' becomes all the more important, even as its reference points in social and political reality become more tenuous; for similar reasons, the increasing difficulties of centrally controlling celebrity production motivate not a reduction but 'a frenzy' of celebrity stories. Many forms of audience interactivity, far from being democratizing, provide media producers with key market information while intensifying audience identification with particular products.[115]

Arguments for change in media's underlying *social* dynamics are equally ambiguous. For decades, the word 'liveness' has captured our sense that we must switch on centrally transmitted media to check 'what's going on'.[116] Such social impulses do not suddenly disappear. But what if new forms of 'liveness' are now emerging that are primarily interpersonal? Is there emerging (on social networking sites, through everyday use of smartphones and organizers) a sense of *social* 'liveness', what Ken Hillis calls a 'distributed social centrality' – mediated, but not by central media institutions?[117] What if social networking sites induce a shift in our sense of what news is – from public politics to social flow – a change as fundamental perhaps as the birth of 'news' itself in the sixteenth and seventeenth centuries?[118]

Dialectical analysis again works better than linear analysis. At the very least, YouTube is a helpful mediating mechanism between audience members and media corporations. Media institutions (BBC, NBC, music majors, commercial brands) are building profiles in social networking sites (SNS) whose personalized data are of great interest to marketers and of crucial financial value to those who control such access (Google, Facebook). Twitter has become an increasingly important stage for celebrity promotion: in May 2011, news agency WENN signed exclusive rights to distribute photos posted by celebrities on Twitter.[119] The intensity of feedback loops on SNS make them particularly well suited to create a 'buzz' around both niche and general products, feeding back into mainstream media. Far from SNS focusing an alternative 'centre', the centring processes of SNS and mainstream media may well become increasingly intertwined like the strands of a *double helix* in a world where marketing itself strives increasingly to be like 'conversation' and to 'mobilize consumer agency'.[120] But there is little evidence so far that this double helix works to amplify general *news* consumption. This is not to deny that social media can take on a political role under conditions of conflict. Meanwhile, media institutions' connection with 'social media' is one way they can claim to stay socially relevant, so it is no surprise that news referrals on social media get quickly amplified by mainstream media (see chapter 5). But there is little evidence as yet *anywhere* in the world that demand for national broadcasters is declining. The reasons for watching state media can be complex, as with this Chinese viewer: 'we know that TV only shows us what the Government wants us to see, but that doesn't mean it's not worth watching ... I can always go to the internet, if I want to get a different perspective.'[121] But those reasons do not disappear.

More broadly, media's relations to 'the social' are intertwined with the fate of national politics, indeed *any* politics. It is now a truism of political science that politics is fundamentally mediated, so the picture of politics that media circulate is not 'just another' narrative: it underwrites contemporary politics' *space of appearances*.[122] States have not disappeared; indeed their projects of social surveillance and border defence have, if anything, grown more ambitious.[123] Governments must engage intensely with 'the media's' fate, hence their pursuit of new political audiences via social networking sites prominent first in President Obama's use of SNS in his 2008 campaign. But here the underlying interests of large political, and large media, institutions – in sustaining their authority *through* the construction of a mediated centre – converge. The *Guardian* and the BBC were happy to act as warehouses of protester videos from the 1 April 2009 G20 London summit, including the videos that challenged police narratives of their fatal confrontation with a bystander, Ian Tomlinson. Media corporations' *uses* of user-generated content to bolster *their own* position as leading social storytellers repeat, under new conditions, a strategy Barbie Zelizer first noticed in television coverage of the assassination of John F. Kennedy and its aftermath. A short BBC website report on the Egyptian revolution read: 'social media has played a crucial role in the ongoing unrest *and* people have been sending their messages to the BBC.'[124]

If a mediated centre is sustained, it may be at the price of entertainment dislodging politics from its core, fitting Douglas Kellner's wider claim that 'entertainment is shaping every domain of life from the Internet to politics.'[125] The dominance of entertainment (a less costly investment than investigative journalism) suits the bottom-line economics of weak media institutions, but is compatible with *many*

political contexts and outcomes: post-socialist competitive nationalism in former Yugoslavia; the socialist/market hybrid politics of
China; the fragile democratic politics of post-dictatorship Philippines.
And sometimes, as in today's Arab world or the USA of President
George W. Bush, entertainment may be the most effective way for
voices and questions that challenge traditional and elite discourse to
break through.[126]

Cutting across all these questions about media institutions' social
valence, are, however, broader uncertainties of scale.

On what scale do media have consequences?

One of the most important ways in which media have consequences
is in terms of social, economic and political scale: the scale implied
by media representations of space and place (on which, see chapter
4), and the scale enabled by the distribution of media and mediated
connections in space, on which I concentrate here.

Media are processes in space. Media operations 'in space', because
of the organization of content and communication that they enable,
create spaces 'in media', what Manuel Castells calls 'a space of flows'.[127]
Media enable social, economic and political processes to be coordinated over large scales. Media literally change the scale on which we
can speak of societies at all, but building *inequalities* into this very
process (above all, inequalities of visibility).[128] It is through media
that we have a sense of living in a world, a horizon of world events;
it is through communication also that capitalism on a global scale is
sustained, so enabling a potential new global scale of rebellion against
capital.[129] Yet globalization itself masks considerable complexity: if,
according to globalization's leading theorists, its key features are the
'extensity of networks' and the 'intensity of interconnectedness', such
features always leave other places uncovered, less connected.[130]

There is a long history of wonder at media's role in transforming
social scale. In the early twentieth century, it was the *newspaper* that
astounded Gabriel Tarde: 'even if the book made all who read
it ... feel their philological identity, it was not concerned with questions both current and simultaneously exciting to everybody ... it is
the newspaper that fires national life, stirs up united movements of
minds and wills'.[131] But the early twentieth century's configuration of
scale through media was very different from today's. How remote to
us now seems Polish writer Bruno Schulz's sentiment, in a letter to a
friend in March 1938, as Germany invaded Austria in the fateful
build-up to World War II:

Don't be angry if I didn't reply at once. Spatial remoteness causes the written word to seem too weak, ineffective, powerless to hit its target. And the target itself, the person who gets our words at the end of that road through space, seems only half-real, of uncertain existence, like a character in a novel. This discourages writing, robs it of topical timeliness, makes it seem – in the face of the onrush of nearby reality – ... a gesture of dubious impact.[132]

Now in a world of email and Skype, we live with – and alongside – each other in a communication space whose intensity and speed were unimaginable a few years ago. Scott McQuire invents the term 'relational space' to capture media's role in shifting the 'contours' of everyday experience and social space.[133]

The resulting 'time–space distanciation'[134] is reinforced by everyday *assumptions* of transnational, even global, connectivity which are, in large part, grounded in the experience of digital media. Striking new examples of connection and flow occur regularly. In June 2009, phone video images of a demonstrator, Neda Agha-Soltan, dying in the streets of Tehran, were sent to a Twitter account, evading Iran's general internet clampdown; after wide circulation outside Iran, they reemerged on a banner held the next day on the very same street where the demonstrator had died.[135] In January 2007, a furore over Jade Goody's racist comments against a Bollywood actress in *Celebrity Big Brother* – circulated within hours to Indian audiences via YouTube – generated a political crisis for British ministers then visiting India. Parallel examples can be found from the pre-digital age, for example a dispute about racist comments in a US television boxing commentary during the 1988 Olympics which infuriated South Korean audiences who saw US television signals that leaked from one of South Korea's US military bases.[136] But in that older example, the cultural flow was accidental; in the *Celebrity Big Brother* case, it was doubly motivated: the footage was passed on through networks of diasporic affinity and that circulation reflected how YouTube connects media and audiences across cultural borders. As a result, we must recalibrate the scale on which anything shown in media comes to matter.

Globalization of media flows increases the internal complexity of 'the national' and the causal complexity of interactions between national and international politics and culture. But it is a mistake to see such changes in terms of the abolition of space.[137] All space, however interconnected, has 'texture' (in André Jansson's term): patterns of order and hierarchy that are based on social representations and undermine notions that contemporary life is 'liquid' or 'free-flowing'.[138] Nor does the Web's decentralized connectivity mean that the internet's effects are derritorialized. As Saskia Sassen notes, there are 'material conditions' to processes of apparent 'de-materialization', conditions which are unevenly distributed across territories and power structures. Accordingly, media do not abolish hierarchies of scale so much as generate *rescaling* effects. Media, and the continuing struggles over the myth of the mediated centre, are part of what Sassen calls the 'multiple partial normative orders' of a globalized world. Meanwhile, national media still dominate as a percentage of what people consume.[139]

Media's relationship to scale connects to an area of social theory so far relatively absent from debates on media: Actor-Network Theory. ANT grew out of sociology of science and ethnomethodology, informed by a suspicion towards inherited languages of description, and a profound belief in the malleability of human practice. Reflecting back on ANT's first two decades, Latour rejected all the elements of the name ('actor', 'network', 'theory', and the hyphen!) and insisted that 'ANT' was simply a method for following the circulation across space of people and objects as actors make up their worlds. Latour rejects conventional understandings of scale (the micro–macro distinction): 'in the social domain there is no change of scale [between micro and macro]. [Scale] is so to speak always flat and folded . . . each locus can be seen as framing and summing up.' So for Latour there is no natural 'scale' of the social, no 'largeness' or 'smallness'; there is just extension, and therefore no characteristic scale where 'the social' typically takes place.[140] This usefully challenges any natural association between media and either 'macro' or 'micro' scales; it explains, for example, why what Innis calls the 'space-biased' medium of the telephone can operate to reinforce physically *proximate* networks, whatever the distances over which phones interconnect us.[141] But along with the insight there is also a problem: Latour loses sight of the accumulated, sedimented contexts of action. Similarly, John Urry's call for a sociology of 'mobilities' captures how ordinary social life has folded into it various 'mobilities' tied to work, family, imagination and infrastructural systems but ignores the reference points that *connect* those mobilities: the home, the workplace, the social or civic meeting points and the local accumulation of resources and routines *between which* those mobilities are sustained.[142]

A more sophisticated understanding of social scale does not mean giving up on what French social theorist Danilo Martuccelli calls 'the ontological nature of social life': the spatially specific *accumulations* of 'constraints' and 'coercions' on action that flow from human life being lived in coordination or competition with others.[143] I return shortly to one key implication of this for media theory. For now it takes us to one final uncertainty concerning contemporary media: ethics.

How can we live well with media?

Media's transformations of the scale of human life have major implications for ethics. The philosopher Hans Jonas pointed out how new understandings of the earth as a vast environmental system transformed our ethical insight into how, as human beings,[144] we act in the world: we came to see our small-scale environmental actions as having cumulative effects on a larger scale. But this transformation of the scale of ethical reflection – a direct consequence of what Ulrich Beck calls the global 'risk society' – applies to other domains than the environment. The implications of media's global scale for an ethics of media have recently become clear.[145]

There is no agreed starting point for answering the question: what is it to live ethically with, and through, media? And yet the fact that our lives are supersaturated with media makes it increasingly difficult to be satisfied with an ethics that is not, in part, an ethics *of media*. The global scale relevant to that ethics follows directly from the implicitly global scale on which all mediated communications can now circulate.[146] But the ethical issues of the local – the spaces of family, friendship, institutions – are also entangled in, and transformed by, the flows of media on all scales.

In chapter 8, we will explore some starting points for thinking more systematically about the ethics of media. We will also look there at the related question of justice, as it applies to media operations. Media justice, while not completely unfamiliar as a term, is an area whose details have hardly begun to be explored. And yet the question of what it would be for media resources to be justly distributed are central to understanding how media are changing the world.

A toolkit and some guiding principles

If you have followed me so far, you will realize that this book does not map out a straightforward journey. The six lines of uncertainty intersect, but there is no point on the horizon where they neatly converge and the accumulating uncertainties get resolved. Understanding today's relations between media, society and world is not a matter of analysing *this* Web interface, *that* technological innovation. Instead we need a whole set of mid-range concepts for grasping the *types of* order – and disorder – that result from media's deep embedding in social space. This book aims to provide that toolkit.

In chapter 2, we make a basic but important step: to take media seriously as a heterogeneous bundle of practices for acting in the world. All later chapters are predicated on this first move. In chapter 3, we look closely at media institutions' claims to be a privileged window on the social world, and the resulting rituals and myths that, under many varied conditions across the world, still dominate much of our experience of media. Chapter 4 looks at one of the consequences of those myths and rituals, that is, the hidden shaping of the social through media processes, including the hidden injuries and symbolic violence done to some individuals and groups as a result of the practices of large-scale media institutions.

The next four chapters turn more directly to media's consequences for social and political change. Chapter 5 examines the frequently made claims that new forms of media have transformed the possibilities of social formation and political action: such claims are often incomplete or insufficiently grounded in knowledge about the resources that sustain particular types of social and political practice. Chapter 6 looks to the long-term impacts of media saturation for particular fields of practice far from media – education, medicine, law – as well as those now obviously saturated with media, such as politics. This in turn enables us to revisit some classic sociological concepts (authority, capital) from a new direction. Chapter 7 turns to the global scale, looking at the underlying dynamics which shape the diversity of media cultures. Finally, chapter 8 addresses the issues of ethics and justice that our contemporary ways of living with, and through, media generate.

Underlying this toolkit are three principles that emerge from the approach to media theory and social theory outlined in this chapter. The first was formulated at the opening of the chapter: *the principle of non-linearity*.[147] In developing a broader account of media's role in social change, we must always be suspicious of linear accounts of how media change, how people respond to those technologies and how effects flow from those responses. Contradictions, tensions and ambiguities affect media's social workings at all scales. A sociological account of media must therefore balance two registers: accounts of how *power* is sustained across space, cutting through the complexities of the individual point of view; and accounts of how everyday encounters with, and through, media *feel* to each of us, informing our strategies within the world. A media phenomenology not grounded in political economy is blind, but a political economy of media that ignores the phenomenology of media use is radically incomplete.

Two further principles connect with this. One is that media research must *analyse media as practice*, as an open-ended set of things people do in the world. The world is not a text but a vast weaving together of particular practices and resources, including practices of making and interpreting texts; reading the social world as if it were a text is deeply misguided.[148] Grasping this in the 1980s was a fundamental contribution of media audience studies and technology studies to wider social science. Without what Claude Fischer called a 'user heuristic', accounts of technology development risk simply repeating the claims of technologies' own marketing.[149]

A third principle, which requires more detailed unpacking, is *the materiality of representations*. Representations matter. Representations are a material site for the exercise of, and struggle over, power. Put most simply, our sense of 'what there is' is always the result of social and political struggle, always a site where power has been at work.[150] But fully grasping this in relation to media is difficult: *because* the role of media institutions is to tell us 'what there is' – or at least what there is that is 'new' – media's work involves *covering over* its daily entanglement in that site of power. Media aim to focus populations' attention in a particular direction, on common sites of social and political knowledge. Media institutions' embedding as the central focus of modern societies is the result of a *history* of institutional struggle that is becoming more, not less, intense in the digital media era. It is essential to deconstruct the apparently natural media 'order' of contemporary societies. Raymond Williams put the choice well: 'the real question, whether the social order actually serves our needs, cannot be asked when our social thinking is determined by the assumption that it is from the order that we must start.'[151]

Rather than starting our exploration of media, society and world from the supposed 'fact' that media give us our world as it is, I prefer, following Luc Boltanski, to foreground such media claims as *a particular and continuous institutional construction* whose workings and consequences must continually be unpacked: that is what earlier I called the 'myth of the mediated centre'.[152] We need a materialist account of how such social constructions work, which starts out from a pluralist social ontology but is alive also to the ways in which a plural social world can, effectively, be *reduced* through acts of simplification which are themselves key forms of power. By contrast with an earlier (Marxist, Lacanian) view of ideology, this argument does not depend on claiming that there really is one underlying structure of ideology, desire or drive, let alone one institutional crucible of value ('the media'). Domination is plural; it possesses an economic dimension but always also a symbolic dimension, what Boltanski calls 'the field of determining what is' (*le champ de détermination de ce qui est*). This lends particular importance in social analysis to 'the instruments for *totalizing and representing what is*, or at least what's given as relevant for the collective': they are the institutions that shape 'how things stand with what is' (*ce qu'il en est de ce qui est*).[153] And so, without mentioning media institutions explicitly, Boltanski reveals why a critical understanding of media is crucial to any understanding of the contemporary social world.

This approach to media, because it is rooted in the concerns of social theory, avoids the 'mediacentrism' often noted as a danger in media research.[154] It also starts out from a distinctive territory within social theory itself. By emphasizing the role of representations in the attempted ordering of the social world, this approach rejects the recent turn against representation in social theory. While some elements of 'non-representational theory' are helpful (its emphasis on play, the precognitive, the variability of practice: see chapter 2), its most basic move – ignoring or discounting representational acts and contents – is deeply unhelpful for studying media. When Nigel Thrift, the leading proponent of 'non-representational theory', discusses media, he does so only in terms of affect or emotional charge:[155] what about news? This move is not accidental; it is motivated by a belief that 'contours and content of what happens continually change,' so that 'there is no stable "human" experience' and the human 'sensorium' is continually being extended.[156] Yet this radicalizing of medium theory is at odds with power's actual work in stabilizing representations of 'what there is'. Indeed like Actor-Network Theory which it closely follows, non-representational theory has no account of how representational contents and interpretations get embedded in the world.[157]

Behind this apparently strange rejection of representation lies an important debate about sociology's empirical basis. In the best analysis of that debate, Scott Lash argues sociology should turn away from the 'rationalism' of classical social theory – based, in Kant's terms, on the empirical a priori (particularly Durkheim's notion of social 'facts', such as the bond that underlies social life, intuited in those moments that we come together in large groups) – and turn instead towards a different type of empirical: the empirical a posteriori which registers a 'social process [that] rarely stands still long enough to congeal into "facts"'. The choice Lash sees is stark: an older sociology that asks 'how is [social] order possible?' versus a new approach that asks, simply, 'what is this social stuff we are experiencing?'[158] Lash claims that the intensity of our embedding in technological systems means 'there is no time, no space . . . for reflection' and so no role for representation within our social ontology. Indeed, for Lash 'the dualism of epistemology and ontology is flattened into the radical monism of technology.'[159] My own emphasis on the myth of the mediated centre shares Lash's scepticism about the inherited language of social order but also marks an important difference. Even if there is no natural social order focused on social 'centres' such as the nation, systematic *attempts* to order the social continue and are consequential: all is not chaos. Social functionalism – the claim that the social world is fully ordered, its parts fully interdependent like those of a body or organism – remains an important force *within* the social, and bears (ironically) the marks of earlier sociological discourse![160] Since media institutions are active in promoting – indeed representing – their supposedly natural role in such order, a media theory that ignores such claims lacks a crucial tool.[161]

So our choices in social theory make a difference to whether or not we have the tools to understand what media do in the world, particularly at a time of intense and multidimensional change. This book sets out from a view of the social that is pluralistic, not totalizing; that acknowledges the role of media and other technologies in the practical constitution of the social[162] but also the role of social representations made through those technologies. The mobility and fluidity of practice certainly exceeds the attempts to impose order on it by governments, institutions and sociologists, but practice itself depends on processes of ordering and categorization (in which media are involved). Everyday life is not the space of pure invention that some recent theory might suggest.[163] That is, at bottom, what I mean by a 'socially oriented media theory': I want to take seriously the social as a site of material constraint and possibility, and media's role in its construction. This is a key principle to hold on to, as we review (particularly in chapter 7, but regularly throughout the book) the huge transnational variety of how today we live with media.

2

Media as Practice

'What media are needs to be interrogated, not presumed.'

Brian Larkin[1]

The uncertainties reviewed in chapter 1 about media's relation to society might seem daunting. To move forward, we need a simple point of departure and, as Ludwig Wittgenstein once noted, friction.[2] The concept of 'practice' provides both. By looking at media as practice, as 'something human beings do ... a form of action',[3] we find both a vast array of things to explore and a useful source of tension with the instinct to theorize about media in the abstract. Before I look at the background to the recent 'practice' paradigm in sociology and media research, let me explain four basic advantages of looking at media as practice.

First of all, practice is concerned with *regularity*, that is, regularity of *action*.[4] Sociology itself is interested in regularities, not chance or incidental occurrences. Media sociology is concerned with the specific regularities in our actions related to media and the regularities of context and resource that make certain types of media-related actions possible or impossible, likely or unlikely. We cannot act in the world except on the basis of many levels of regularity and order. Indeed, our sense of living *in* a 'world' is built *on* such background order. The articulation of our media-related practices with other practices into larger combinations (our daily 'routine', 'schedule', 'lifestyle') is part of whatever order we find and rely upon in the world.

Second, practice is *social*. Behind the recent turn to 'practice' in social theory lies an interest in Wittgenstein's later philosophy of language. This involved a key move to understanding language as action in the world, by contrast with an older view of language as the expression of meanings that must somehow 'correspond' to the world. Wittgenstein thus sought to challenge any overarching theory of language 'as a whole' and replace it with a view of language as toolkit: 'think of the tools in a tool box: there is a hammer, pliers, a saw, a screwdriver, a rule, a glue-pot, glue, nails and screws – the functions of words are as diverse as the functions of these objects.' Note the implicit social context in which Wittgenstein formulates his new action-based approach to language: Wittgenstein's term for that inherent social dimension was 'form of life'. Forms of life point to things that humans regularly do, without any need to codify or legislate for them: as Wittgenstein puts it, '[where] human beings agree in the language they use ... that is no agreement in opinions but in forms of life.'[5] On this view, language is an open-ended set of practices embedded in convention. Many have seen in this a jumping-off point for thinking about other types of practice. A difficulty in Wittgenstein's own formulations is uncertainty over whether 'forms of life' are limited to universal human practices or encompass more contingent, culturally shaped practices that acquire the force of convention.[6] Wittgenstein's social emphasis – the interlocking interdependencies that enable a toolkit – is clear, and converges for example with Weber's founding of sociology in the study of social action, that is, action oriented to others.[7] Practices are not bundles of individual idiosyncrasies; they are social constructions that carry with them a whole world of capacities, constraints and power.

Third, practice points to things that we do because they relate to human *needs*. That does not imply a fixed set of human needs defined by reference to a universal human nature: even if, for example, we see human life as always requiring coordination of some sort, the nature of coordinating activities depends, as we consider later, on the background of interdependencies that in particular times and places characterize social life more generally, including those underpinned by media. In this chapter, we explore how practices related to media are shaped by basic needs for coordination, interaction, community, trust and freedom. Needless to say, there is no simple mapping of 'needs' onto practices, but, in what follows, you should keep in mind the needs that shape the variety we uncover.

Fourth, practice's link to action provides a distinctive and important basis for thinking *normatively* about media via the question of how we should live with media. From Aristotle onwards, a long tradition of ethics has understood value by reference not merely to abstract thought but to action, actual or potential: as Aristotle puts it, 'the good for man is an *activity* of the soul in accordance with virtue.'[8] So the best starting point for an inquiry into how we should live with media is to think about media as practice: we build on this in chapter 8.

In all these ways, a practice approach to media frames its questions by reference, not to media considered as objects, texts, apparatuses of perception or production processes, but to what people are doing in relation to media in the contexts in which they act. Such a media sociology is interested in actions that are *directly oriented* to media, actions that *involve* media without necessarily having media as their aim or object; and actions whose possibility is *conditioned by* the prior existence, presence or functioning of media. We can combine those interests into a single, apparently naive question that will be our reference point for the rest of this book: *what are people doing that is related to media?*

This requires a wide definition of 'media' (see chapter 1), encompassing not just traditional media (television, radio, press, film) but all the other media platforms, mobile or fixed, through which content of any sort – both institutionally and individually produced – is now accessible or transmissible. The 'systemness' of media that shapes action can, as Friedrich Krotz notes, take many forms.[9]

Our questions about media-related practice should not be limited by the immediate concerns of media industries or media history. Indeed, some interesting questions about media may be inspired by very different histories. Take the development of memory and mnemonics.[10] In the pre-modern era, the scarcity of information storage and flows put a premium on the arts of memory and retrieval, but does today's over-abundance of information put a premium on new arts of *selection* and *combination*? Media hype about the universality of change in media, captured in crude notions of 'the net generation' or loose distinctions between young 'digital natives' and older generations of digital immigrants, is unhelpful.[11] As Susan Herring points out, the 'net generation' is an *adult* construct which obscures our grasp of how communication needs, and their solutions, are (or are *not*) changing, and if changing, how fast and against what resistance.[12] That is not to deny important shifts are going on: for younger people in many countries, computers are now part of the social infrastructure.[13] Equally, no one could deny that cultural production and dissemination have been radically transformed in the past fifteen years, yet there are significant numbers even in countries such as the UK and USA for whom even basic access to the online world is still not guaranteed. If those who create online content, even in the USA, are stratified by gender and class, then the heralded transition from a 'read-only culture' to a 'read/write culture' is not assured.[14] In this controversial terrain, an approach open to the *varieties* of practice is useful.

The background in media research

A great deal of media studies has focused on analysing media texts. But a practice approach to media *decentres* the media text for a reason: to sidestep insoluble problems over how to prove 'media effects': how can we ever know that a particular media text changed the behaviour of audiences in particular ways? Hidden assumptions about 'media effects' still abound in media analysis and in everyday talk about media. Indeed, they are hard to avoid if we start our analysis from the consumption of media texts themselves. Outside literary approaches which regard the text as of value in itself, why treat a media text as your primary research focus unless you know its details make a difference to wider social processes? But it is exactly this that is normally difficult to show.[15]

A popular alternative has been to start from the institutional structures that produce media, as in the political economy and (more recently) cultural economy traditions.[16] The analysis of industrial and market structures in the media and cultural sectors is important in its own right and vital to understanding the pressures which limit participation in those sectors and constrain the outputs they produce. But media production cannot be the exclusive starting point for media *sociology* or *socially* related media theory, even though that is where media products start their life. Why? Because the structures of media production, and particularly the dynamics of concentration and conglomeration, do not of themselves tell us anything about the *uses* to which media products are put in social life generally.

The problem of media 'effects' – which in political economy is displaced but not resolved – is a challenge for many approaches to media: whether Marxist theories of 'dominant ideology',[17] or recent and much less sophisticated popular accounts of the difference that celebrity narratives make in everyday life.[18] 'Medium theory' faces distinctive problems when it makes claims about media's social effects. An example is Matt Fuller's attempt to develop a materialist account of media 'systems' and media 'objects' via the concept of 'media ecologies'. Fuller's term 'media ecology' is designed 'to indicate the massive and dynamic interrelation of processes and objects, beings and things, patterns and matter'.[19] Clearly, there is scope for looking in this way at the 'systemness' of media's contribution to daily life; indeed, as discussed in chapter 4, there are long-term consequences of the 'representations' built into software interfaces and search engines; we can take this even deeper to the criterion of programmability on which such interfaces ultimately depend, as Lev Manovich pointed out a decade ago.[20] But we still need to know how differences at the level of 'programmability' generate important differences at the level of everyday practice. Similarly Fuller's definition of 'ecology' allows no account of patterns of use or interpretation. So Fuller ends up assuming, at a system level, the very social 'effects' that the connective concept of ecology is designed to address. The problem with this approach to digital media – and other approaches that privilege software – is they bypass the role that representations play in explicit practices of social ordering.

The philosophical route beyond this impasse is through an account of everyday life *as practice*, as the interweaving of multiple 'forms of life', including practices *of* representation, interpretation and reflection. For Wittgenstein, representation and intersubjectivity are practically constituted, and as such are irreducible components of human life.[21] No less radical than Deleuze's move beyond Kantian philosophy,[22] this Wittgenstinian move involves much less violence to everyday language and understanding.

A practice approach starts not with media texts or media institutions but from media-related practice in all its looseness and openness. It asks quite simply: *what are people* (individuals, groups, institutions) *doing in relation to media* across a whole range of situations and contexts?[23] How is people's media-related practice related, in turn, to their wider agency? The outcome, potentially, is a new paradigm for media research.[24]

The basic question ('what [do] people do with media?') was originally asked by Elihu Katz in the 1950s,[25] but the Uses and Gratifications approach that followed focused on *individual usage* of bounded objects called 'media'. The practice approach to media discussed here differs in its social emphasis and in its emphasis on relations not limited to use, but was itself foreshadowed in media research of the 1980s and 1990s. Early audience research emphasized that consumption is itself a 'determinate moment' in the production of meaning through media texts. From this developed important research on the whole range of domestic practices in which television viewing was inserted, overlapping with early work on computer-mediated communication.[26] In time, researchers started to move beyond the specific contexts of media consumption. Ien Ang asked: 'what [does] it mean . . . to live in a media-saturated world'?[27] My own research considered 'what it means to live in a society dominated by

large-scale media institutions'.[28] Meanwhile a so-called 'third generation' of audience research aimed to 'get a grasp on our contemporary
"media culture"', looking, for example, at the open-ended processes
of identity construction linked to media.[29] Whether this research still
needed the concept of an 'audience' for a specific text was by now
less clear. A little later, in film and screen studies, a welcome shift
towards studying audiences emphasized 'film consumption as an
activity', organized in space and time.[30] Other media researchers
searched for a broader term to capture our wider engagement with
texts in circulation, whether 'mediation' or 'mediatization': we return
to those terms in chapter 6.

By now, audience research was becoming difficult to distinguish
from the interest in media emerging within *anthropology*. In the
early 1980s, anthropologist Eric Michaels in his PhD thesis on
'TV Tribes' recalled his own 1979 study of Protestants in Amarillo,
Texas which had uncovered huge variation in people's assessments
of media.[31] A decade later, Faye Ginsburg defined a distinctively
anthropological approach to 'mass media' in terms that read like a
prediction of where the whole field of media research was heading:
'Our work is marked by the centrality of people and their social
relations – as opposed to media texts or technology – to the empirical
and theoretical questions being posed in the analysis of media as a
social form.'[32]

A decade further on, an anthropologist specializing in media, Liz
Bird, wrote that 'we cannot really isolate the role of media in culture,
because the media are firmly anchored into the web of culture,
although articulated by individuals in different ways...The "audience" is everywhere and nowhere.' Note this is different from bland
statements that we live in a 'media-saturated' culture, since Bird
insists that *'as individuals* we are not [media-saturated], or at least
not in any predictable, uniform way.'[33] A further debate emerged
from research on how religious families regulate their media consumption, including their practices of *avoiding or selecting out* certain
media inputs.[34] Already, then, we see how an approach focused on
practice can complicate general understandings about contemporary
media culture.

By the mid-2000s, media research had started to shake itself loose
from the constraining origin of the text and to focus on the diversity
of practice related to media. Meanwhile, as discussed in chapter 1,
the whole landscape of media practice began to expand and transform rapidly. By happy coincidence, a way of making sense of these
changes in both media research and everyday media was emerging
within broader social theory: this was practice theory.

Practice in social theory

There have in fact been two turns to 'practice' within social theory: the earlier work of Pierre Bourdieu and the broader movement associated particularly with Theodor Schatzki. Both were inspired, in large part, by Ludwig Wittgenstein's brilliant reflections on the failure of philosophy to grasp the dynamics of everyday thinking and acting, even in (precisely in) the attempt to 'interpret' it from the perspective of theory.[35] Yet, in the implications they draw from 'practice' to wider social thought, those turns were sharply opposed.

Bourdieu used the notion of 'practice', in part polemically, to identify those features of everyday life which, he argued, structuralist anthropology (particularly Claude Lévi-Strauss) systematically misrepresents: the duration of everyday actions in time, and their particularity, which prevent them being reduced to an abstract 'totality' or the performance of abstract functions. Most importantly, while everyday actions had for Bourdieu a 'logic', that logic was not the 'system' that could be *read off* their outcomes (the sort of system Lévi-Strauss found in myth) but the much less obvious 'system of principles of production' that *generates the conditions under which the practice itself is possible*.[36] Bourdieu rejected a method of 'reading' the social world as if it were ready for interpretation and replaced it with an investigation into the preconditions of action (the preconditions of the practice being analysed *and* the practice of the analyst herself). This insight remains radical today. Bourdieu's account of how practices are determined through pre-existing conditions (particular the notion of 'habitus') is, however, more controversial.[37] For Bourdieu, bodily practice is learned, and from there reproduced, 'below the level of consciousness'.[38] As we shall see in chapter 4, this account still has something to teach us about contemporary media culture, but it cannot capture media-related practice in general, much of which is intentional.

The more recent work on practice by Theodor Schatzki, Andreas Reckwitz and others is of wider relevance,[39] even though as social explanation it has limitations which will drive us back to Bourdieu on some points. For Schatzki, like Bourdieu, the term 'practice' achieves a theoretical, not simply descriptive, purpose, enabling a decisive move beyond old dilemmas in social theory (individual versus society, agency versus structure), dilemmas which Bourdieu also addressed. For Schatzki, practice *itself* is the site of a distinctive type of order, 'the site where understanding is structured and intelligibility articulated';[40] it is from the *organizing* properties of distinct practices (such as swimming or card-playing) that a wider 'social order' is made up. Indeed, for Schatzki, the acts of organization by which practices become distinct from each other are 'recursively' present in the organization of practice. Andreas Reckwitz's review of this approach is helpful: 'A "practice" (*Praktik*) . . . is a routinised type of behaviour which consist of several elements, interconnected to one another: forms of bodily activities, forms of mental activities, "things" and their use, a background knowledge in the form of understanding, know-how, states of emotion and motivational knowledge.'[41]

Schatzki distinguishes among the organizing work that interpretations do within a practice between (1) 'understandings', (2) 'explicit rules' and (3) 'ends, projects, beliefs'.[42] These elements contribute to the reproduction of a practice through the capacities they enact and the contexts for action they provide. Not every practice has each of these features: indeed, it is only what Schatzki calls 'integrative practices' (such as swimming, farming, cooking) that do so in their micro-rules for organizing different sub-practices. A looser type of practice that Schatzki calls 'dispersed' (such as describing, ordering) is linked only on level (1), that is, by understandings that it involves a collection of instances of the same thing. We might question what exactly are the rules of swimming anyway, and even if they are clear, how important are they to the practice as a whole, but leaving that aside, what is most important is Schatzki's point that it is the *socially* achieved patterning of practice that enables the flux of everyday activity to be *intelligible* between actors. This approach, as Ann Swidler explains,[43] dispenses with the need to explain patterns of action through some mentalist notion of 'culture' (as internal 'ideas' or 'meanings') in favour of a practically achieved coordination, what Schatzki calls the 'context-constituting hanging-together of lives'.[44]

Practice theory is therefore helpful in translating hype about a digital revolution into more concrete questions: what types of things do people *do* in relation to media? And what types of things do people *say* (think, believe) in relation to media? We wouldn't expect the organization of a media-saturated world to correspond to the organization in a 'pre-saturation' world (when audience activity could be assumed to be discrete from the rest of everyday life). But – and this is what practice theory makes clear – in order to establish what *are* the new principles by which practices related to media are demarcated, we cannot be guided simply by our instinct as media or social researchers. We must look closely at what people are doing, saying and thinking in relation to media. For an application of this, see Box 2.1 on Twitter and practice theory.

Box 2.1 Twitter and Practice Theory

Twitter is a micro-blogging platform founded in 2006. The same platform attracts and supports a number of different practices which, as forms of life, need to be distinguished. Twitter is therefore a good illustration of the value of practice theory. The success of Twitter has stimulated international imitators, for example the Sina Weibo micro-blogging platform in China.

Twitter allows blogs of no more than 140 characters; these however can easily incorporate links to other text, sound or video. It emerged first as a blogging platform with multiple advantages: for senders, because of the basic shared format and enforced brevity, tweets could be sent easily while on the move, for example, from people's mobile phones; for receivers, the brevity and sense of instantaneous thought were also benefits. This basic use of Twitter comes into its own in evolving disaster situations such as the Japan tsunami and US Hurricane Irene in 2011. The practice of re-tweeting intensifies this process of message circulation.

Prima facie, the Twitter platform could lead to a cacophony of jumbled, decontextualized messages, but from this basic starting point a number of divergent practices have developed, each linked to a particular way of defining the readership for particular Twitter accounts. First, individuals with high positions or profiles, or otherwise able to secure a regular, even if small, audience, can use Twitter as a means of *unauthorized commentary*. The consequences for institutional structures and authority are destabilizing. In fields of competition where high media attention is likely (see further chapter 6), powerful individuals with previously limited voice can start to influence events by tweeting, for example footballers tweeting of the arrival of a new player ahead of the official club announcement (Manchester United manager, Sir Alex Ferguson, has in response called tweets 'a waste of time': *Guardian*, 20 May 2011).

Second, individuals with high media status (such as celebrities) can use Twitter to maintain a constant online *presence*, whose informality and intimacy is geared to building a fan base (the English comedian Stephen Fry was an early pioneer of this, but it is now routine).

Third, groups can cohere around a particular Twitter address or hashtag, to which *commentary* (or other information) can be sent: if successful, this becomes a form of *presencing* for groups without previous identity or symbolic capital. The use of hashtags to form

> groups and coordinate high-speed action in the Arab Spring and
> many other demonstrations has become celebrated or notorious,
> depending on your point of view.
>
> A practice approach not only helps us keep these various Twitter
> uses distinct: it also stops us assuming we know what Twitter is
> 'for' without careful examination of the evidence. In the English
> summer riots of August 2011, the assumption was quickly made by
> government and others that the main use of Twitter (and Facebook)
> was to incite riotous action, leading to calls for it to be banned at
> times of instability. But the *Guardian*'s survey indicated that
> *reacting to the riots* was a much more common usage of Twitter,
> echoing debates about the Arab Spring where assumptions that
> Twitter was crucial to the mobilization in, for example, Egypt
> proved exaggerated (Lewis, Ball and Halliday 2011; Beaumont
> 2011).

Schatzki writes of the 'tissue of sociality'[45] that lies just beneath
the surface of daily life. Schatzki, however, differs fundamentally
from Bourdieu in his denial of any type of social order except that
which emerges from the *local* contexts that individual practices comprise, insisting that the only site of social order lies in the explicit
understandings, rules and ends of particular practices. Schatzki rules
out the macro-shaping role of large institutions such as media (discussed in chapters 3 and 4) because of his insistence on limiting social
order to the understandings that allow each practice locally to 'hang
together'. Here surely Schatzki goes too far. What about the articulations *between* practices which enable complex practices to emerge,
for example, in domains such as Facebook or YouTube? These may
take a recognizable form without requiring much explicit description
because of the way that our everyday practices are recursively organized through their basis in routine.[46] Similarly, what are widely known
as technologies' *affordances* shape users' shared understandings.
Actor-Network Theory, too, may provide a useful supplement here
because it is interested in how heterogeneous acts, objects and agents
get articulated together in stable forms across large scales; as Tristan
Thielmann has recently pointed out, 'ANT . . . does not predetermine
where media are to be found in a chain of action.'[47] This helps us
grasp both how large-scale 'digital formations', such as financial
markets, generate new social forms and how our everyday practices
of 'holding things together' are recursively organized.[48]

There is, as sociologist Elizabeth Shove notes, a level of social
ordering that we often miss because it is hidden in the apparently
banal need for convenience, control and comfort.[49] Shove encourages

us to look at 'complexes of practices', the order created by the *fit* of one practice with another. Phone 'apps' are a perfect example. 'Apps' and other phone functions offer an important and as yet little analysed engine of change, naturalizing a wholly new type of media/data interface. A phone 'app' with an option 'next train home' personalizes your phone in a quite powerful way; so too do the prayer time alert and Mecca-indicating compass built into the 'Qiblah phone' marketed to Muslims by a South Korean company.[50] 'Apps' which allow you to scan clothes in a shop changing room (to compare prices and check what your friend thinks)[51] are articulations of practice that enable new forms of convenience and social embedding. It is in such details that practice theory hits the ground.

The varieties of media-related practice

The value of practice theory is to ask open questions about what people are doing in relation to media. To illustrate the potential complexity, take a game of televised football. Watching a football game on television might for one person be best analysed as part of their emotional practice as a team fan; for another, perhaps that person's partner or child, it may be an obligation or pleasure of their relationship together to share the first person's passion; for another person, perhaps within the same family, this media act may matter not so much for its detailed content, but as a sign which marks one use of domestic space off from another, depending on the time of day; for someone watching in a public space, it may be part of a group solidarity; for another, it may be something done to fill in time, instantly 'putdownable' as soon as a friend rings the doorbell or the person gets the energy to go back to a task. I am not, of course, the first to point out such 'indeterminacy'.[52]

We cannot grasp what people are doing with media simply by starting out from the 'text' of, say, a televised game and the various ways people read that text (media studies' original starting point). Only in the case of the football fan is *the way s/he reads* the game's text likely to be of research interest, since it is only here that the watching of the game is a central, non-substitutable part of a wider practice. Political economy approaches are important background in all these cases but probably only important foreground in the case of the football fan, where economic pressures shape the places where televised games can be watched and even the structure of the game itself. When we turn to wider issues of coordination, people involved in a huge range of practices (from fandom to family interaction to group solidarity at a community centre or pub to just waiting for something else to do) can all be doing roughly the same thing – watching television – at the same time, but *how* the text is read is only central to understanding such forms of coordination for texts whose contents are of unusual shared importance (major sporting and political events, the climax of a soap opera or large drama serial).

In the era of digital convergence, the openness of the practice approach becomes especially important: indeed, the other media in the 'media manifold' (tweets, SMS messages, Facebook links) lead us quickly away from the original boundaries of a text, such as a televised game.

By moving media research's centre of gravity away from texts (and their production or direct reception) and towards the broader set of *practices* related to media, we get a better grip on the distinctive types of *social process* enacted *through* media-related practices,[53] practices involving not just producer and performers but also interactive audiences, audience members who would like to become performers, and non-viewing members of the public who become affected by that wider process. Such an approach has already transformed our understanding of the talk show: a huge labour process goes into constructing the encounters selected for actual broadcast, with the resulting text only one facet of that practice.[54] A similar approach is useful in grasping reality media and celebrity culture (see chapters 3 and 4). A practice approach allows us to follow practices that are related to media, but not related to any specific set of texts: for example, practices of using media sources in education; individuals' uses of media references in telling stories about themselves; the uses of media in the political, medical or legal systems, indeed in work practices everywhere (see chapter 6). A practice approach also brings into view the wider articulations of practice in systems of power. Here it is compatible with other approaches to new media, for example, Lievrouw and Livingstone's definition of new media as 'material artifacts', 'practices' and 'larger social arrangements and organization forms'.[55] There is no question here of forgetting the representational power of media: in chapters 3 and 4 we will cover different aspects of that process too.

To sum up, 'media' are best understood as a vast domain of practice that, like all practices (in Schatzki's view), are social at a basic level through the very acts that stabilize them as practices and distinguish specific practices from each other. We need to map this domain. This requires some initial, if crude, signposts. In that spirit, I want now to explore some new types of media-related practice that an older descriptive language might miss. I will start with single media-related practices and move later to more complex practices.

Searching and search-enabling

Since the internet is an unbounded informational reserve, almost any use of it, however simple, requires a search. As Matthew Hindman puts it: 'on their own, users have only two ways to find previously unknown content. First, content can be discovered by surfing away from previously known sites; and second, it can be found through online search tools.'[56]

Our dependence on search engines such as Google is no more reversible than the telephone system's early move from human operators towards automated telephone-switching devices.[57] Search is performed by crawlers which scan a certain portion of the actual internet in accordance with fixed protocols. We will discuss the impacts of search engines on the world as it appears to us in more detail in chapter 4, but for now recall Introna and Nissenbaum's aphorism: 'to exist is to be indexed by a search-engine.'[58] Search and its conditions affect social ontology.

Search is not just the operation of abstract tools; it is embedded in our practices. Even our 'favourite' default sites are the result of our earlier 'searches'. Searching extends the range of interpretative acts that belonging to an audience involves:[59] this process is open-ended, since, as Jay Bolter noted, 'web pages function as ordinary text, but they also function as places along a path.'[60] Search pathways are increasingly integrated into *how* we act: we leave the house, perhaps, for a meeting (or even leave the country on a trip) without a map, let alone details of local facilities, intending to rely on our smartphones' search capacity while we are on the move. But this new way of acting – configuring knowledge acquisition and knowledge use differently in time and space – brings with it new forms of differentiation. The vaster the internet becomes, the more salient will be the differences between peoples' search strategies and skills: here socio-economic status and education provide big advantages even if over time they can be overcome by experience.[61] In addition, many new models of news democratization depend on potential news audiences finding dispersed sources or having aggregators help them do so. If we think of the internet as an infinite informational reserve, then searching is a key practice through which people shape their distinctive conditions of action.

From searching, other practices quickly develop: practices of exchanging information by forwarding weblinks to family, friends or work colleagues, warehousing sites that collect recommendations from users so other users can narrow down their search practice (Digg, etc.), and tools for pre-ordered searches (RSS feeds and other alerts). These various *search-enabling* practices are increasingly prominent in everyday life as people seek to optimize their access to the vastly expanded flow of potentially relevant information. Their dispersed agency (*anyone* can forward a link or signal that they 'like' a post) contrasts with earlier centuries' ways of disseminating interesting material: for example, the ancient and medieval world's *florilegia* produced by groups of scholars, often in monasteries, who collected interesting quotes from otherwise obscure books into new volumes.[62] Now not only do individuals (from their computers or phones, wherever they are) make the recommendations, but system interfaces, such as Digg and reddit, enable them to recommend cumulatively. Some commentators hope that 'collaborative filtering' and other collective forms of information sorting can challenge the dominance of Google and even create new forms of social bond.[63]

Certainly search-enabling practices complicate any simple idea of individual dependence on search engines like Google. But, as Alexander Halavais points out, celebrations of 'folksonomics' and the 'social web' ignore three crucial factors. First, search-enabling practices still depend, ultimately, on 'the idea of search' and work to enhance search functionality. The underlying constraints built into search engines' workings do not disappear: indeed, they require our full sociological imagination to uncover their implications.[64] Second, the so-called social web is already inhabited by institutional predators, who know very well the potential of peer-to-peer recommendation to enhance their marketing goals. Amazon builds on quasi-social clues to push our consumption ('other readers who bought this also bought . . .'). Quasi-social prompting reaches new sophistication with the 'sparkle link' where embedded Amazon staff dedicated to specific products make adjustments so that, if you search for a related product, you are asked: 'were you actually looking for this?', that is, the product that is being pushed. In political marketing, peer-to-peer exchange of political information is certainly enhanced by search-enabling practices, particularly at times of political mobilization, but what if peer-to-peer exchange (our preferences via Digg, Delicious and so on) is itself increasingly shaped by underlying pressures from larger political and commercial actors?[65] Third, our reliance on search is increasingly serviced *in advance* by software which pushes information of potential relevance at us wherever we are, through the GPS functionality of our phones (for example, the Foursquare or MyTown applications). The prospects for such search-*bypassing* capacities are uncertain, since they bring a heavy cost: the cost of continually revealing where we are to providers and, unless we opt out, to other users. This leads us to other key practices.

Showing and being shown

If searching is about finding what's 'out there', increasingly prominent also in everyday life is a set of practices I want to call *showing*. There is no closed list of features which characterize every act of 'showing', at most what Wittgenstein calls a 'family resemblance'[66] whereby each act of showing has enough similarities to at least one other act of showing for it to belong to the extended 'family' of acts of showing. The term 'showing' helps us grasp the mass of media-related acts that make something publicly available: many of those acts were unknown in a pre-digital age.[67]

In late May 2010 when I was starting this chapter, I gathered examples of online acts of showing. One was a continuation of an old tabloid practice, the exposé of illegitimate acts by a public figure: in this case, the UK tabloid newspaper *News of the World*'s posting on its website of an undercover video of the Duchess of York (universally known as 'Fergie') apparently asking for and receiving money in return for a promise of access to her ex-husband, Prince Andrew, Queen Elizabeth's son.[68] What is striking here is, first, that, compared with earlier exposés, we *see* the act of receiving money, rather than just reading about it and, second, we see it *in a form* such that (by sending the link) we can effortlessly draw it to *others'* attention. Any online act of showing therefore entails a whole chain of re-showings.

Another example was oil giant BP's live feed from its attempt to control a disastrous leak in the Gulf of Mexico – Operation Top Kill.[69] What was I expected to learn from this 'live' footage from somewhere on the sea bed? What was I seeing? *Was* it indeed 'live' footage? These unanswered questions point to what's interesting about this act of showing: that part of BP's corporate response to the crisis was to put its own live 'stream' into the public domain, as mainstream press/TV coverage spiralled out of its control. If BP's act of showing was defensive, positive campaigns of 'showing' are frequent too, as when a year later the New York-based Human Rights Watch inspected sites in Libya for evidence of cluster ammunition used by government forces and, after their mission, showed those very weapon fragments on their website.[70]

YouTube (owned since 2006 by Google) provides a vast new space of showing where heterogeneous actors can post and discuss video material. Much of YouTube's material is itself placed there by institutional actors as a cheap and unregulated alternative to broadcasting: such acts are continuous with the production/promotion strategies of those institutions. Still other material on YouTube comprises acts of search-enabling (see above) aimed at a general, not specific audience, as when people post favourite TV clips. Most interesting are acts of showing by individuals and groups in acts of public display that previously had no practicable form. Consider these posts thrown up by my search on 27 May 2010:

- A witness video of members of the Harry Potter film cast apparently passing through the concourse of London's Kings Cross (over 136,000 views by end June 2011)
- A performance by librarian staff at University of Washington's Information School doing a cover version of a Lady Gaga song (over 800,000 views by end June 2011)
- A video of 'Lurcher' dogs with their handlers posted by Dogs Trust Salisbury, inviting new owners to adopt them (2,163 views by end of June 2011).[71]

YouTube's availability as a vast visual reserve has transformed a simple dog advertisement, an account of a celebrity sighting and a piece of office fun into acts that *coexist* in the same public space of interconnection. Whether 'doing something for YouTube' is becoming sufficiently recognizable by agents to be a 'dispersed practice' in Schatzki's term, let alone rule-bound enough to be an 'integrative practice', is an open question.

Interesting also are the diverse social contexts in which these particular acts of showing take place. *Being shown* (being put into wider circulation) is a latent dimension of almost every act today beyond the home, and often within the home. Whatever you are doing, there is usually someone around with a recording device that can be connected now or later to the internet. The work of Goffman on how situations can be 'keyed' in various ways[72] finds new relevance here: it helps us describe how the (spatial, temporal, thematic) possibilities of everyday interaction are being transformed by media devices. We often face a basic ambiguity to *where* we may be shown. Many contemporary media are characterized by this ambiguity between broadcast and closed communication.[73]

Some contexts for showing and being shown are happy ones: the now almost automatic placing of photos onto a website (Facebook, Flickr, Snapfish and countless others) after a shared holiday or party, indeed any event whatsoever. The assumption that what we do together will quickly be converted not just into images in a photo album but into an image-flow online is now integral to the management of our private and public personas: the routine act of posting photos of a shared event on Facebook links 'showing' to 'commentary' (see below).[74] Other contexts are neutral but normatively driven: the practice, built into the social networking interface, of showing our social networks via our Facebook and so on.[75] Still other acts of *showing* may have an aggressive motive: to humiliate others or triumph oneself through the act of showing, as in the exultant videos by school shooters. In past eras (and sometimes still today) heads of war victims were placed on stakes for all to see. Now perhaps there is no need: a video of an attack within minutes can be posted online or circulated by mobile phone amongst friends. In the UK, this goes by the chilling name of 'happy slapping'.[76] It is unhelpful to dismiss the media-component of 'happy slapping' as aberrant, revolting though its outputs are. For acts of 'happy slapping' are an example of how pervasive the general practice of showing has become, and how interwoven it is with continuing conflicts over territoriality, resource and identity.[77]

There are also defensive forms of showing, for example the improvised surveillance practice of pensioners in a Leicestershire neighbourhood, using cameras, a website and YouTube, that reported local drug dealing to police. I say 'defensive' since that is no doubt how those people would describe it, but such group surveillance is continuous with the overextended process of state surveillance in Britain that would be seen by many as aggressive.[78]

These multiple forms of 'showing' illustrate how social and public space is being rekeyed via media-related practices. The space of human action is now available not just to imaginative reconstruction, or occasional memory-traces, but to permanent visual tracking. Remember the Google user quoted in chapter 1 who tracked down a fugitive. Showing on a large scale regularizes mediated co-veillance in everyday life, transforming everyday action and performance into spectacle and audiencing. Showing is just one of a wider set of ways in which once-private life is being projected beyond its normal boundaries: blogging and the standard reporting on Facebook of private/public events, such as relationship break-up, are other examples.[79]

Let's move now to some originally complex (that is, multi-component) practices related to media now so routine that they can justifiably be treated as simple practices. *Presencing* is my term of convenience for individuals' and groups' acts of managing through media a continuous presence-to-others across space; *archiving*, analogously, refers to people's attempt to manage their presence (and presence-to-others) over time.

Presencing

Whether or not you are a user, it is almost impossible to be unfamiliar with the space of social networking sites. We already know a lot about how particular groups conceive such SNS: the types of narratives they want to tell there, some of the narrative constraints they impose because of fears over privacy. 'Going on [Facebook, Renren, etc.]' is a recognizable practice and its norms will depend very much on the wider culture in which it is carried out and that culture's wider framework of permission. Different platforms may have different associations, as Toshie Takahashi's recent work on Japanese users of Mixi and MySpace brings out, with MySpace associated with distant 'friends' and external networks, in part because of its late introduction into Japan from the USA.[80] But let's use the openness of the practice approach to ask a slightly different question: what is the larger family of practices of which 'going on Facebook', for example, might be a part?

That family, I suggest, is 'presencing', by which I mean a whole set of media-enhanced ways in which individuals, groups and institutions put into circulation information about, and representations of, themselves for the wider purpose of *sustaining a public presence*. The term 'public' is no doubt too simple: as Daniel Miller neatly puts it, Facebook's 'public' dimension results from 'an aggregate of private spheres'.[81] Presencing is not the same as calling up a few friends to tell them some news; nor, although the audience is unspecific, is it like putting up something on a noticeboard. That is because presencing is oriented to a permanent site in public space that is distinctively marked by the producer for displaying *that* producer's self. Whatever its basis in particular platforms (of course, people change platforms or work across multiple platforms), the act of presencing goes wider. It responds to an emerging requirement in everyday life to *have* a public presence beyond one's bodily presence, to construct an object-ification of oneself.[82] Media platforms, media skills and media use form the necessary preconditions of this practice, and may be intensively reflected upon, but presencing is not primarily a practice 'about' media. It is a project of the self: an increasingly automatic part of growing up through adolescence and, as danah boyd eloquently argues for the USA, a way for young people to have some public agency when they suffer restrictions on their ability to participate in face-to-face public space. Alternatively, in Japan it is a way for adults to moderate their relationship with distant parents towards a greater fluency and informality. In South Korea where, like Japan, internet-enabled mobile phones came early, the 'minihompy' (or mobile-device-enabled personal homepage) has become a crucial means for individuals to be 'present' to each other: 85 per cent of South Koreans use the internet for this purpose.[83] Are changing norms and expectations of presencing generating new types of political repertoire?[84] Let's hold that question until chapter 5.

Presencing may be simple self-promotion. But amongst young people not free to move as they please or in families which are dispersed (voluntarily or otherwise), presencing becomes a necessity, not a choice: a basic threshold for 'keeping in touch' or just 'hanging out', with implications for wider practices of friendship and parenting.[85] Presencing create new problems of interdependency: someone has to read what you post, you have to trust them to know where (and where not) to circulate that material, and so on. This takes us into the territory of another classic sociologist, Norbert Elias, and his work on the emergence of norms of interdependency. How do individuals establish what for them and their peers is an appropriate level of effort in sustaining their mediated presence? What shared narratives make sense of the new obligation to have a presence? What are the acceptable limits to presencing, in terms of scope, continuity and intensity, when we can never be sure who will see what we do?[86]

It remains uncertain how fundamentally new are today's practices of presencing. The scale of connection is certainly new, but remember it was once obligatory among the small elite of European societies, such as France and the UK, to be visible in 'society'. This meant attending certain dances and parties, and staging 'at homes' where others could leave their calling cards at the door to register their presence in relation to the host, enabling the host in return to record their recognition to the caller without necessarily meeting them. Proust's great novel, *In Search of Lost Time*, records, in part, the decline of that mid-nineteenth century world in favour of a mass-mediated public world with different standards.[87] Are we now seeing through social networking sites and Web-presencing the revival of something like 'society' but on a completely different scale, style, pace and rhythm? What related practices are emerging? What implications does the habit of *evaluating* each other's performances online have for power and social norms?[88]

Archiving

Archiving is presencing's equivalent in time. While the effort of presencing is directed at the difficulties of maintaining a presence in public *space* (being visible to others across social space), 'archiving' (as I use the term) is the individual's practice of managing *in time* the whole mass of informational and image traces s/he continually produces, so that, *over time*, they add up to something acceptable and perhaps even graspable as a history. Many writers note that the embedding of internet access into everyday life (both personal and institutional) has completely changed information flows and their role in social order. Giddens's insights into the role of information storage in the formation of state power remain valuable, but they were developed for an age (the 1970s) when information was stored physically, behind the literally closed doors of particular powerful institutions.[89] But now, as Bruce Bimber notes, all sorts of information persists into the present as open archive: news bulletins and newspaper content, campaign information, political communications, basic discussion. 'The past', as he puts it, 'becomes more accessible to the present', that is, for anyone with Web access.[90] Domains that were once separate – mass media and interpersonal communication – become linked by these new archiving functions: YouTube is now a cultural archive where you can search and track down a blurry extract from an old TV show you once loved and directly pass on the link to friends.[91] We come to the implications of archiving for political actors (especially groups and institutions) in chapter 6.

For now let's focus on individual practices. The desire to leave a story of one's life is universal.[92] The hyperproduction of media materials by the contemporary social actor poses new problems of archiving: who has the time or energy to manage their accumulating history of online 'presence' so that it will come in future to seem to others more than a random jumble? There are wider ethical issues here (see chapter 8); meanwhile, new types of practice may offer solutions, or at least quasi-solutions. Think of the increasingly reported act of 'life-caching', the controlled management of one's life-archive, and Facebook's recently announced Timeline feature which Mark Zuckerberg claimed will 'help you tell the story of your life'. Once, the dominant forms of archiving were the diary or the photo album, each having a particular religious or leisure context. Trans-individual contexts are emerging online for sharing archive material: photo-sharing sites from Flickr to Snapfish and countless others.[93]

As archiving photos online becomes widespread, photography, as Christensen and Røpke note,[94] becomes itself an 'integrative practice' in Schatzki's sense, a socially evolved way of combining personal memory, collective bonding and communal history production, which is increasingly tied to the spatially directed practice of presencing.

Complex media-related practices

Practices need not be, but often are, habits: habitual repetition is one way actions get stabilized as practices. Our habits are not isolated but fit together in the much larger weave of habits which make up our daily lives: pull one habit from that texture and you may disrupt the whole. That is why media habits, such as watching television, often considered in isolation (see chapter 1), change more slowly than media hype claims: they are woven into a wider set of habits. Some media-related practices are, not surprisingly, best understood as *complex articulations of many media-related practices* and sometimes of non-media-related practices too. These complex practices may either involve 'action sequences'[95] or the mutual conditioning of multiple actions. Let's consider some examples, more and less speculative.

Keeping up with the news The idea that 'keeping up with the news' might be a practice worth studying was first pursued by the Norwegian researcher Ingunn Hagen.[96] The Scandinavian sense of news consumption as a duty – with its roots in the Protestant sense of a 'duty to read' – is perhaps distinctive.[97]

At a more general level, the complex practice of keeping up with the news is of international interest and contributes to even more complex practices of narrating one's life through news or orienting oneself to a public world *through* news consumption.[98] Today's pro-liferating news interfaces mean that keeping up with the news is likely to be an articulation of many smaller practices: not just watching a prime-time TV news bulletin or listening to radio news at fixed times, but snatching a look at the news headlines on your home webpage during lunch at work, receiving an SMS update on one's phone, following up a story link in a friend's email or a blog you regularly read, picking up a free newspaper on the way home from work or college.[99] How much time we spend on each practice, how far we extend it or link it with further background news exploration will vary, possibly quite drastically. The correlation between particular news tracking practices and sociodemographic variables is a key area for new research.

The media industries' economic models and working practices are adjusting to the changing space–time distribution pattern of keeping up with the news. As dramatically illustrated by consumption of immediate news coverage of the 9/11 attacks,[100] online news consumption, often from work via office desktop computer, is now a regular part of many people's days. In Argentina, for example, recognition of this has influenced the organization of news websites, as

Pablo Boczkowski's pioneering study shows. While, prima facie, this should lead to an extension and enrichment of people's keeping up with the news, the intense distractions of the work environment may shift news consumption in the opposite direction towards a superficial if continuous awareness of basic headlines and not much more.[101] As internet-enabled phones with built-in news 'apps' become common, the changing space–time configuration of keeping up with the news may continue to change radically, but for reasons rooted in the organization of everyday practice, not civic duty in the abstract.

Commentary   Worthy of separate analysis is a complex practice I call 'commentary'. Some literary cultures have been distinguished by the richness of their practices of commentary: the Jewish tradition of cabbala is frequently cited, but the ancient world's general scarcity of textual objects meant that written manuscripts often reached people with the commentary of previous readers' (so-called 'scholiasts') embedded within them, a tradition which reaches us now via the comments written in medieval versions of Greek texts.[102] Now we are entering an age of commentary for the opposite reason: because of the almost infinite proliferation of things to read and look at, we need to send signals to help each other *select* from the flux. At the same time, and for related reasons, our ability to send comments and signals has been massively extended by digital media: we take it for granted that by emailing or uploading a link we can *point at* something interesting we have just read and so alert someone on the other side of the world. The scope of commentary as a practice has been massively enlarged.

This transforms what since the 1960s has been called 'intertextuality', as Keren Tenenboim-Weinblatt notes in a brilliant recent article. Inter-textuality is not now something latent in texts that it requires a scholar to extract; it is something we make happen every day through the practice of commentary in our work and leisure lives.[103]

Commentary is a factor of increasing importance in media economics, as organizations try to monetize the downstream hits onto other sites that their readers generate, and major industries are increasingly dependent on upstream linking from people on social networking sites.[104] But commentary is also a practice of great interest to a broader sociology of media as an *infrastructure* of commentary emerges. A practice approach that draws specifically on ANT will help us track this. Previously most people's commentary on media was lost in the ether – a shout at the television, a scrawl in a book, a remark to a friend. Now our commentary is automatically archived and made visible online. Yet such commentary takes place over multiple sites and across many particular practices. How is this complex practice of commentary being organized? How is its new organization changing how people understand the *purposes* of commentary, and its implications for their status as members of a broader media culture?

This takes us to how we are shaping our overall relations to the media manifold. Two complex practices are interesting here.

Keeping all channels open   A dominant narrative of modernity was that, even as our ability to move and transmit across space increased, the material infrastructure of our lives required us to spend more and more time confined in relatively private spaces: what Anthony Giddens called the 'sequestration of experience'.[105] And yet, as modern media have increasingly enabled *continuous* media inputs wherever we are, something different becomes possible: 'connected presence'.[106]

We can now, if we wish, be permanently open (and potentially responsive) to content from all directions.[107] Many writers see the practice (or even compulsion) of continuous connectivity as characteristic of the 'digital native' generation.[108] Being open on all channels in this way is part of the marketing promise of new portable interfaces such as the iPhone. While it is literally impossible to be open to everything, the demand to 'be available' shapes an emerging practice, recognizably different from earlier modes of media consumption based on intermittent communication and a clear distinction between mass media and interpersonal media. Keeping all channels open means permanently orienting oneself to the world beyond one's private space and the media that are circulated within it.[109]

In earlier periods of history – times of media scarcity – being more 'open to the world' required precisely the opposite configuration. In medieval Europe, it meant isolating oneself for much of the day, as in a monastery, so as to be more open to the message of God.[110] Now perhaps, within a supersaturated media landscape, a different way of opening ourselves to the world is evolving, the reverse of sequestration: a voluntary opening of as many channels of communication as possible with known others and the wider world.

Screening out   Keeping all channels open creates severe problems.[111] Such responsiveness is only possible on the basis of a considerable amount of background selection. In the pre-modern age, news of distant places was a 'luxury commodity' or at best something that reached you through chance encounters.[112] Modernity has involved an ever-increasing stream of regular news from afar, but it is only in the past two decades that the flow has become an issue to be managed in everyday life. Media studies, influenced by literary models of textual analysis, has until recently put little emphasis on what people *don't* watch/listen to/read, although there are some exceptions, for example Stewart Hoover and colleagues' study of US families' active limiting of the media their children are allowed to see.[113] Selecting out is close to a survival skill in today's media environment.

The necessity of selecting out derives not only from the volume of information and communications reaching us, but also from contradictions between the *types* of different information flow that reach us at the same time, contradictions that require extra time to resolve. As Robert Hassan notes,[114] everyday life is overridden by the instantaneity of 'network time', and yet it still takes finite amounts of our *everyday* time to open an email, click on a link, respond to an SMS text. Selecting out is increasingly (if not always intentionally) delegated to technological interfaces such as the iPhone which offer gateways to media that are the result of intense prior selection: behind these lie major commercial negotiation (it is a big deal when, say, the *Guardian* gets its content pre-selected as a phone 'app'). By choosing from a vast range of 'apps', people screen out much of the infinite media environment to create a 'chosen' interface – a customized media manifold, if you like – that is both manageable and seemingly personal.

Selecting out has considerable personal implications too. The timetabling of availability in space has always been used to provide people with periods of 'inaccessibility'. In the 1970s, it seemed as if professional circles were reducing the scope of their availability.[115] But in the early twenty-first century, as Sherry Turkle's vivid new research brings out, the pressure is in the other direction. 'Hiding out' (being online while trying to disguise this from others), or more simply avoiding using the phone for speaking, is increasingly common. Turkle quotes a 21-year-old college student: 'I don't use my phone for calls any more. I don't have the time to just go on and on.' The openness of face-to-face interaction is what gets cut: a 16-year-old school pupil tells Turkle she prefers texts to calls 'because in a call "there is a lot less boundness to the person,"' although '"later in life"' she concedes '"I'm going to need to talk to people on the phone."'[116]

Here selecting out links to wider questions of how social coordination now depends upon, but is also vulnerable to, the *systemic* overload linked with media technologies. Is the result something like a new 'crisis of control', in James Beniger's term, but deriving, not as it once did, from too little information, but from too much information?[117] If so, can we expect, as Beniger found for the nineteenth century, major *new practices* of adaptation which, as yet, are only embryonic?

Conclusion

A practice-based approach has opened up broad questions about the sorts of things people are regularly doing with media amid the proliferating complexity of the digital media era. At the start of this chapter, we distinguished between acts aimed specifically at media, acts performed through media and acts whose preconditions are media. In what followed, I have concentrated on the second and third, so as to shift our focus away from the most standard topics of media studies: reading a text, watching a programme, looking at an image. But actions, especially when repeated, become the background for other actions, so it is difficult in practice to keep these three action types separate.

Deep dynamics of practice have started to emerge: the need to keep constantly 'in touch' and in reach of information and other people, the need to maintain a public presence, the need for selection and screening out, the resulting reliance on the selective attention and inattention of others. Such webs of interdependent action, because they depend on achieved coordination, are one of our best routes to grasping how social change is occurring in and around media; they are the stuff of which, as Norbert Elias showed for early modernity, new cultural 'figurations' are made.[118] For Elias, key figurations were dances, fashion, ways of behaving at table; new figurations are emerging around us, but it may be some time before their shape is clear. We can expect, as in earlier eras of technology, more than one type of sociability to be superimposed upon another.[119] At the same time, the wider reference points and norms of social space are, in crucial respects, 'under-patterned'.[120]

A practice-based approach to media must stay close to political economy. In the digital media age, intense corporate interest in online spaces of display will be crucial to shaping how the stuff of everyday life is reconfigured. Now, for example, we perform identity and develop public or quasi-public profiles within the constraints of platforms such as Facebook: as a result, we risk a deep penetration by market logics into the very lineaments of self-reflection and self-expression, a process Sarah Banet-Weiser has called 'the branding of authenticity'.[121] This process is reinforced when images intended for limited circulation are routinely picked up in mass media stories: mainstream press routinely uses Facebook images of people taken at parties as character evidence for murder victims or alleged criminals. More deeply, the model of sociality built into networking platforms (and increasingly our networking practice) involves automatic exclusions based around certain types of nodes (and personal connection) which divert us from seeing what lies to one side of those nodes.[122]

Our understanding of media's social consequences cannot therefore stop short at the fine detail of media-related practice, in spite of Schatzki's arguments to the contrary. The Facebook example exposes once again the systemic pressures that arise from the cumulative saturation of everyday practice by media, noted earlier in relation to selecting out. I return to such systemic pressures in chapters 5 and 6. It is also important, supplementing political economy, to exploring the wider forms of social power involved in media's everyday representational practices. That is the subject of the next chapter.

3

Media as Ritual and Social Form

'New technologies often enhance "categorical" identities.'

Craig Calhoun[1]

'Symbolic boundaries ... are conceptual distinctions made by social actors to categorize objects, people, practices and even time and space. They are tools by which individuals and groups struggle over and come to agree on definitions of reality.'

Michelle Lamont and Virag Molnar[2]

'What we want to demonstrate is the fallacy of judging society according to its own standards, because its categories are part of its publicity.'

Henri Lefebvre[3]

When a young person walks up to a wall in Cairo and paints FACE-BOOK across it, what does this mean? Is it an instruction or a brand, a reference point to a place where everyone is gathering or a token for a much wider process of social transformation? This uncertainty suggests a broader problem: how do we move from the seeming infinite plurality of media-related practices considered in chapter 2 to an understanding of media's relation to power? I will address this in stages over the next four chapters.

Grasping media's relations to power is difficult and overlaps with wider issues in social theory: how do power and political order work in large, complex, porous, media-dense, globally connected societies? Increasing fragmentation of media outlets does not mean that media power disappears. Take the UK and the USA: for all the other evidence of media proliferation, decentralization of media production and a bewildering range of interfaces through which media are now available, they have a highly focused celebrity culture which is not just the result of media industry 'push' but has penetrated deep into everyday life and social norms. How do we explain this seeming contradiction?

As a starting point, let's recall Jean Baudrillard's early insight about media, that 'media ideology (or . . . the reproduction of media power) functions at the level of *form*.'[4] By 'form', Baudrillard meant social form, not programme formats. Baudrillard was interested in the most basic social form, or relation, constituted by mass media: what he called the 'social division' between media producers and media consumers,[5] a division that has been complicated in the digital media age. Developing this idea will involve drawing on the concept of 'categories'. This in turn takes us back to practice: categories are one key means through which particular practices embed and reproduce more general aspects of power. It also takes us into some important contemporary debates about the nature of social form and social order, hinted at towards the end of chapter 1. All human life needs some degree of stability and order: the question, as always, is at what price, in terms of inequalities of power.

An interest in social form – indeed the very idea that societies' *categories* of thought are intrinsic to social order – was distinctive of the classical French sociologist Emile Durkheim. We can trace this tradition into recent French debates via the work of Luc Boltanski and Laurent Thévenot. Thévenot notes 'the fruitful *and limited* heritage' of Durkheim's work with Marcel Mauss on categories of thought.[6] The limit for Thévenot is that Durkheim assumes, in a way no one would today, an 'extremely strong relation between collective cognitive categories and the collectivities to which people are assumed to belong'.[7] Boltanski and Thévenot's sociology of value, while holding on to the concept of category, places it in a radically different context from Durkheim. They see societies, indeed a world, where there are no fixed memberships, no overarching agreement on social values and no certainty who we are or whether we belong, only multiple 'regimes of justification' which compete to define *value* in the domains of social life. On the face of it, this contradicts any argument that media concentrate symbolic resources and so focus social value in systematic ways. But, as becomes clear in Boltanski's better-known work with Eve Chiapello, *The New Spirit of Capitalism*, this pluralistic approach to sociological value aims not to abandon, but to reground, critique from within the discursive resources of everyday life.

In their book *On Justification*, Boltanski and Thévenot distinguish between six regimes of justification, all of them found regularly in everyday arguments over value and justifying decision: 'domestic' worth, 'fame', 'market' worth, 'industrial' worth, 'civic' worth and 'inspiration' (based in 'creative difference'). They reject the idea that social space is shaped in advance to prioritize one regime of justification over another: indeed, the point of their approach is to recognize more rigorously the actual value-*pluralism* in everyday life. They reject a form of social critique that they identify with Bourdieu but which can be found in a great deal of 1970s' and 1980s' sociology which diagnoses power as working through the imposition, in direct and indirect ways, of a *singular* regime of value that suits the interests of power.[8] More broadly, as Peter Wagner points out, they rethink how values are generated and then compete, so providing a new basis for grounding the evolution of political community in sociological processes.[9] Strikingly for media research, one regime of justification they identify is 'fame', understood as 'visibility in public opinion',[10] but they make no mention of media.

We need to draw the lessons of this pluralistic approach to 'value' for media sociology. First, the openness of this approach to how values become embedded in everyday life does not rule out specific forms of closure. The basis, Thévenot explains, of the practical need for regimes of justification is the need 'to *commonize* [that is, make things shared] on the basis of highly personal, local experience of the world'. Contests between value regimes are resolved on the basis of which order has 'the greatest *legitimacy*'. It is an important part of Boltanski and Thévenot's connection to classic political theory that they translate legitimacy into 'fairness', but the purpose which frames legitimacy remains, as Thévenot puts it, 'the demands that weigh on human beings in society when they are called upon to "commonize" on the basis of a form of equivalency and common good'.[11] Systemic interdependencies matter here.

So what is the role of media institutions in providing common reference points and so underpinning the legitimacy of particular value regimes? It is only in Boltanski's recent book, *De La Critique*, that media institutions' symbolic power starts to be more distinctly foreshadowed, even then only by implication. As noted in chapter 1, Boltanski investigates the power to determine 'reality', that is, the version of 'reality' that takes effect for practical purposes, notwithstanding the underlying plurality, indeed partial indeterminacy, of what Boltanski calls 'world' (*monde*). Boltanski makes a key move that is potentially helpful for media sociology. He puts institutions' role of determining and certifying 'what is' into a dialectical relationship with the underlying uncertainty of value: it is *because* of such underlying uncertainty that institutions (the state, political parties) must do the work of *determining* 'reality', so far as possible. He also discusses the mechanisms through which such determinations work, including 'tests of worth' and 'tests of reality'.[12] Later, we can build on this in our analysis of media rituals and media 'reality' games.

Yet the specific reality work of media institutions remains unexplained, indeed unreferred to, by Boltanski and Thévenot (Boltanski reserves such certifying power for the state).[13] I suggest this too is related to contemporary societies' *under*determination of value. It is not that media institutions 'solve' such underdetermination by providing values around which consensus actually coalesces; rather they offer, *by default*, the most powerful, or most legitimate, available certification of value and reality. They do so, as we saw in chapter 1, in circumstances where media are just one of many institutional sectors that need, and compete, to sustain something like a common space of appearances.

To develop this, I want to return to my older work on media rituals,[14] but strengthening it in three ways: first, by making it even clearer than before that it is based on an assumption of value-pluralism, not value coherence; second, by bringing out more effectively than before how it can apply to a wide range of societies and media cultures at a time of accelerating global uncertainty about value; and third, by extending it to understand the effects not just of media's concentration of symbolic power – the power to 'determine what is' (Boltanski) – but that of other institutions too, including the corporate owners and makers of brands.[15]

The concept of category, developed first by Durkheim and Mauss and retained in Boltanski and Thévenot's pluralistic sociology of value, will be important here. *Category* is a key mechanism whereby certain types of ordered (often 'ritualized') practice reproduce power by enacting and embodying categories that serve to mark and divide up the world in particular ways. Without *some* ordering feature of practice, such as 'categories', it is difficult to connect the multiplicity of practice to the workings of power, whether in media or in any other sphere. By understanding the work of categories, we get a crucial insight into why the social world, in spite of its massive complexity, still appears to us as a *common* world.

Note that this approach to power does not rely on older, static notions of social order: the focus instead is on the open-ended processes of *ordering* (including claims about social order) that various institutions, including media, set to work *in spite of* contemporary

societies' actual value-plurality and *because of* the actual lack of any
fully achieved social order. There is, as Henri Lefebvre's work makes
clear, no contradiction – indeed, there is a close connection – between
rejecting the idea of any total social system and deconstructing the
attempts to order that pervade social and public life (see quotation
at the chapter's head).

Classification's work in social ordering, and the importance of both
registering *and* deconstructing its operations, has been emphasized
by Geoffrey Bowker and Susan Leigh Star who reject a loose post-
modernism that 'pays no attention to the work of constructing the
simulations, or the infrastructural conditions that underwrite . . . images
or events'.[16] Bowker and Star also throw down a challenge to claims
that symbolic systems cannot be sustained in a social world as complex
as ours. In fact, the argument about complexity goes the other way:
the complexity of the contemporary social world is in part *built upon*
classification. So we need to understand media institutions' role in
that classificatory work. This analysis can be framed in multiple ways:
as an extension of the ethnography of media production into broader
media worlds, as a contribution to the analysis of 'informational
power', or as part of our understanding of the 'cultural schemas'
whose legitimacy is integral to social structuration.[17] Categories can
be at work in anything from a label to the configuration of a body, a
cartoon character, brand or logo. Categories – all categories – are
both things *and* structured contents which, *as representations*, do
work in ordering the social world.

Practice and social order: a key debate

As background, let's glance back at the debate on practice theory
covered in chapter 2. For at least one theorist, Theodor Schatzki,
the point of studying practice was to *reject* the idea that there is anything like a general social order: for Schatzki, there are ordered practices, and nothing more. There is a deep tension therefore between
Schatzki's theory of practice and accounts of media as institutions of
social power and institutors of social form. One practice in which media
are engaged *is* 'constructing reality'; since media contents re-present
the world, reality construction is an irreducible part of media-related
practices, and media institutions are involved in this on a large scale,
but with what implications for practice theory? For Schatzki, a practice
approach allows us to see constructing reality as a fundamental practice in which all humans are engaged, a process that is infinitely varied,
plural and non-converging: on that interpretation, practice theory

challenges the very idea of an overall social 'order',[18] except if understood as built up bit by bit through local practices of interpretation. But whatever the abstract appeal of Schatzki's position, our world is not abstract; each of us comes to act in a pre-existing world that is the result of a history of struggles over shared resources, resources which include the power to solidify interpretations into categories that, in turn, help organize practice. The construction of what *passes for* 'reality' – as the reference point for individual lives – is not infinitely varied, and *does* converge in some striking ways; media institutions are crucial to those convergences.[19]

Grasping, on the ground, the wider orders of power that operate, in part, through social representations is difficult and not just for practice theory. To see this, let's glance further back into the history of social theory. Take Berger and Luckmann's classic statement of social constructionism that

> everyday life presents itself as a reality interpreted by men and subjectively meaningful to them as a coherent world. As sociologists we take this reality as the object of our analyses... the world of everyday life is not only taken for granted as reality by the ordinary members of society... it is a world *that originates in their thoughts and actions*, and is maintained as real by these.[20]

The everyday world, on this view, is a self-correcting 'whole' based in its members' 'thoughts and actions'. We might be tempted to update Berger and Luckmann, accept that media now contribute to the inputs of everyday life and study that expanded everyday life in a holistic way. But this would be doubly problematic: first, in assuming that everyday life does hold together as a 'whole', a premise increasingly implausible given the expanding scale on which social organization takes place; and second, in failing to consider the uneven power relations that underlie media and shape the meanings which its contents have for different audience members. As we put it in chapter 1, phenomenology without political economy is blind.

Practice theory, itself, rightly rejects the holism of social constructionism but, in versions such as Schatzki's, is sceptical about whether large-scale operations (such as media power) provide *any* useful insights for understanding the endless plurality of interpretation on the ground.[21] This generates further problems. It fails to take account of institutions' attempts to *repair* the fragility and uncertainty of the world in the interests of power. As Luc Boltanski notes, there is a danger of normalizing everyday common sense and so ignoring both the actual uncertainties of evaluation in everyday life *and* institutional strategies of building authority from particular claims to reality.[22] It also underestimates the active role of media institutions in framing the world *as if* it were a functioning whole and how such an idea gets embedded into everyday interpretation and action.

The approach which I will adopt to social order is different, insisting on how media power is effective in large societies *in spite of* the undeniable plurality of practice on the ground: the key is to understand the many ways in which power is embedded, and so effectively enacted and installed, *in* practice. There is a link back here to two classic essays in communication theory. James Carey argued that 'reality is a scarce resource', so that access to that resource (effective power over the construction of what *passes for* 'reality' in large societies) is at the root of media power. James Curran in an early essay provided a historical rider to Carey, comparing the socially integrative role of modern media institutions to that of the Catholic Church in medieval Europe. Curran argues that, to work at all, media power, like religious power, must operate through forms of consensual practice: not just domination over the means of mass communication, but also domination over what Curran calls 'the institutions of mental production' (professional culture, education) and over ritual power or magic.[23]

Our approach to media's role in social form and power will be different from older theories of ideology that focused exclusively on the automatic force of centralized messages. We need a broader understanding of how power is reproduced in the digital era. Media's role in prescribing social reality is open-ended: it is not fully determined in advance. It is based in particular material processes of power that are embedded in everyday practice; those processes are always finite and partial: they allow, at times at least, for rival prescriptive constructions of the world. But, crucially, the outputs of such processes have 'universal*izing*' effects, that is, a strategic influence over our ability to talk in generalized terms about the world: those influences get embedded in further practices that contribute to the organization of the world.[24] Understanding media power's social operations means acknowledging the actual evaluative and organizational plurality of everyday life (there is no single 'social order') while registering the universalizing force of media discourse in everyday life. It is this complexity that postmodern depictions of social reality as a play of multiple interpretations 'without any "central" coordination' completely fail to grasp.[25] The best entry point to this complexity is the concept of ritual.

Media as ritual

Rituals are enactments of power through form.[26] Media rituals, put simply, are social forms that naturalize media's consistent will-to-power, that is, media's claim to offer privileged access to a common reality to which we must pay attention. Locally, that claim may be ironized and problematized, but it remains the hook on which, for example, the very idea of 'reality TV' depends.

Background and basic concept

My first work on media was concerned to address an impasse in early 1990s audience studies over how to understand media effects. This led to my attempt in *The Place of Media Power* at a broader 'take' on the media process, asking how the uneven distribution of symbolic power that underlies the media landscape is made natural and acceptable through a society-wide process of meaning-making and belief. My fieldwork (including a study of visits to the set of the soap opera *Coronation Street*) drew on anthropology, interpreting those visits as pilgrimages. From there, I moved in *Media Rituals: A Critical Approach*[27] to look at the particular moments when the wider process of legitimating and naturalizing media power is condensed in social forms, that is, in rituals orientated not to religious or political but to media authority. This approach used social and anthropological theory to make sense of certain *rhetorics of 'the social'*, in which media institutions are heavily involved.

The concept of media rituals starts out from an appreciation of the role of symbols in social ordering. But it takes this in a direction quite opposed to traditional functionalism, foregrounding not the consensual nature of 'the symbolic' but the inherently contested nature of symbolic power. As Pierre Bourdieu argued in his essay 'On Symbolic Power':

> Durkheim has the merit of designating the *social function* ... of symbolism in an explicit way: it is an authentic *political function* [NC emphasis] which cannot be reduced to the structuralists' function of communication. Symbols ... make it possible for there to be a *consensus* on the meaning of the social world, a consensus which contributes fundamentally to the reproduction of the social order.[28]

Bourdieu here offers a politicized reading of the role of symbols,[29] and might therefore seem to revert to a Marxist deconstruction of rituals as messages that merely reproduce political ideology, but that is not the intention. A pure Marxist reading does not grasp media's ordering role at a deep enough level. If media rituals were open to deconstruction as the vehicle of ideology (as media were in pre-1989 Eastern Europe), then they would never be effective, and celebrity culture, for example, would be impossible.

Something deeper, however, is at work in media's capacities for ritual. Philip Elliott's pioneering 1982 essay on 'press rituals' began to explore this, offering as a definition of 'ritual': 'rule-governed activity of a symbolic character involving mystical notions which draws the attention of its participants to objects of thought or feeling which the leadership of a society or group hold to be of special significance.'[30] But the shadow of Marxist ideology analysis still falls heavily here, and Elliott at the end of his essay[31] seems to have been uneasy about such a reductive approach. Instead, it is better to look at the more basic mystification inherent in the *form* of media rituals, whatever their content.

The basis of media institutions' capacity for ritual lies first in the claim that, beneath society's real pressures of centralization, is a core of 'truth', a 'natural' centre that we should value as the centre of 'our' way of life, 'our' values. This is *the myth of the centre*, and while it can be appropriated exclusively by the state (as in Nazi Germany),[32] it is also open to wider definition and appropriation, for example by media institutions. This first myth is connected with a second myth, already introduced in chapter 1, that 'the media' have a privileged relationship to that 'centre', as a highly centralized system of symbolic production whose 'natural' role it is to represent or frame that 'centre': I call this *the myth of the mediated centre*.[33] In the digital media era, the struggle over what Bourdieu calls 'the means of access to the universal' is not superseded, but continues.[34]

This perspective on underlying conflicts over society's 'universals' enables us to define media rituals. *Media rituals are condensed forms of action that work with particular intensity upon category distinctions and boundaries related to the myth of the mediated centre.*[35]

In my book, *Media Rituals*, I discuss various examples of developed forms of media rituals: for example, a person crossing the floor of a talk show to reveal there a deeply private truth before 'the world' that is, on television;[36] or a person joining a reality TV programme to show some aspect of themselves. These acts, and the authority structures on which they depend, would make little sense outside of a framework through which what happens within the space of 'the media' carries more weight than anything outside. Media rituals enact, as Stewart Hoover puts it, 'media's presumed location at the center of the culture'.[37]

In media rituals, categories of thought that naturalize media power are acted out. What are these categories? First, and most important, the basic category difference between any thing, person or place 'in', 'on' or associated with the media, and any thing, person or place which is not. Like Durkheim's distinction between 'sacred' and 'profane', this difference cuts across everything in the social world; anything or any person can be 'in' the media, hence the arbitrariness of the category of 'celebrity'. (That arbitrariness and universal applicability is what, following Durkheim, makes it a *category* difference.) The difference between what is 'in' and not 'in' the media is not natural, but through continual usage constructed as natural.[38] Versions of this boundary may appear to be blurred – for example, the media producer/audience boundary – while at another level being rearticulated, as with interactive media formats such as *Pop Idol*.[39]

From that first category difference flow important secondary differences. These derive from the assumption that what is 'in' the media must have higher status than what is not, but they are distinct in their reference point. For example, the term *liveness* suggests that through media coverage we are connected to what is current for 'us', a shared reality important enough to justify its being shown as priority 'now':[40] hence the status of 'live' transmission, as an imagined direct connection to society's current 'reality'. A more explicit, but still naturalized, distinction is made in talk of the *reality* of what media present: the debates, for example, about 'reality television', or the pursuit of the 'really real' moment of 'true' emotion in the televised talk show.[41] Both categories – live and real – underpin not just ritual forms but the wider capacity of media discourse to *frame* social reality (to convince us that it is our social reality we see through the media frame) and, connectedly, to *name* the contents of social reality.[42]

These categories associated with media, like all organizing categories, are reproduced in countless different circumstances as part of what Jesus Martin-Barbero calls our 'grammars of action'.[43] Such category boundaries become automatic, unthinking: so you might say to a work colleague or partner, 'call her, she was once in that show, she might make a difference to our profile ...', and think no further of the category distinction between 'media person' and 'ordinary person' you are reproducing. In the special forms of media rituals, we see these category differences internalized in particular action forms which test out their workings and naturalize their significance, but even more important is the wider process of *ritualization* by which those categories are banally reproduced across everyday life.[44]

Before more detail on how media rituals and ritualization work in everyday practice, we must place the myth of the mediated centre in a comparative context.

The myth of the mediated centre in comparative perspective

Once there was no doubt that media institutions were the beneficiaries of a huge concentration of symbolic power and of the means to describe the world: this power was, and still sometimes is, expressed in architectural form, as Ericson, Riegert and Akers' highly original study of 'media homes' in the UK, Russia and China shows.[45] But what if that starting point is challenged by today's digital media proliferation? Media resources are diversifying; media institutions' outputs themselves now incorporate user-generated content; compared with the earlier broadcasting era, our attention is increasingly directed to the infinite space of the internet. In an age of overwhelming information flows, how can symbolic practice generate an 'ideological system' or anything beyond 'the brute flows of information'?[46] How can media institutions command enough attention and legitimacy to be the focus of media rituals any more?

The key issue here is not the fluidity of the terms of media rituals – 'liveness', for example, has shifted its reference point throughout the history of broadcasting, and most ritual terms are slippery – but their role in ongoing struggles over attention and legitimacy. First, note there is no incompatibility between an online media world and the concentration of attention required for ritual. Ken Hillis has noted how in the USA the Web *takes on* a role of social centrality, if a more distributed centrality than that of television; the simultaneity of social media (such as Twitter) allows new types of coordinated ritual practice to emerge, for example, synchronized prayers following the death of a celebrity such as Michael Jackson.[47] Second, media rituals do not require media's status (as privileged vantage points on the social and the political) to go unchallenged; indeed, as we saw in chapter 1, such status, and the continued economic viability of media institutions, is exactly at stake in the struggle to sustain something like 'the mediated centre'. Struggles by media institutions (and by other institutions that depend upon them) to sustain attention and legitimacy are real *and intensifying* in the digital media era, creating the demand, on the production side, for new forms of media ritual. The picture of the 'social' that emerges in this process is shaped by media institutions' overwhelming need to sustain *themselves* as central access points to the social in their quest for continued economic viability.[48] The resulting voicings of the social within media rituals are for that reason as likely to be dominated by a logic of entertainment as by political narratives.

A challenge to the notion of the myth of the mediated centre is that it implies a particular type of centralization – media institutions' installation as vehicles of state-driven modernization – relevant to some western countries, but perhaps not to political and social struggles under way elsewhere. The applicability of the concept to media rituals in China, Sweden, Holland, Australia, the USA and the Philippines shows the concept is not purely parochial,[49] but certainly my original account of media rituals assumed too easily, as its reference point, the nation-state, and acknowledged too little multi-nation regions.

Marwan Kraidy's recent work on Arab reality TV raises deep questions. Kraidy does not deny the existence of media rituals but insists that how we interpret their significance depends crucially on what sort of relations between media institutions and markets, state practices and religious institutions obtain in particular countries and in transnational regions such as the Middle East. The account of media's relationship to the state and modernity in my earlier book, *Media Rituals*, was too focused on liberal and neoliberal democracies. Kraidy shows that media rituals and the myth of the mediated centre are quite compatible with intensified debates *about* modernization that challenge the particular narratives of 'modernity' sustained for decades by Arab states.[50] Meanwhile, in very large countries (China), sustaining *one* 'centre', and one mediated centre, is surely so difficult that it may be to *counter*-centres that one must look for the conditions that sustain media ritual. Far from this leading to postmodern relativism, this sharpens our appreciation of the tools of political struggle in a country such as China where new forms of media-based working- class protest and more broadly scandalous 'public events' are emerging, and in the highly class-stratified Philippines where national media are particularly close to a working-class customer base that is less likely to access the transnational media followed by elites. Similarly in countries with failed states, such as Lebanon, counter-state actors may develop their own media 'centres', such as Hezbollah's Al-Manar satellite TV channel.[51] Note that there is nothing in the concept of ritual to prevent it being applied to actions that *contest* one social centre from the outside, enacting a belief in an imagined counter-centre.[52]

So it is vital to free the concept of the myth of the mediated centre (and the related concept of media rituals) from any assumption of particular institutional configurations, such as those that have dominated media studies for too long: the UK, Western Europe and North America. But that means appreciating the ability which media institutions have in many places – and not just those where modern media have developed a close relationship to the state (for example, the UK, France, Japan) – to construct themselves as *socially central*, as a central access point to some wider 'centre'. In India, the temporary 'community' generated by reality media contests, and the non-violent rivalry they spark, may prove, Aswin Punathambekar argues, important attractions in the wake of deep ethnic and political tensions. Media rituals may be relevant to the battles between old national pedagogies and global entertainment culture in Eastern Europe.[53]

Myths of a mediated centre matter, not least because nations continue to matter.[54] The persistence of the national framework is entangled with the increasingly precarious *claims* of media and other institutions to regulate social and political order. Meanwhile, national loyalties and claims to cohesion in everyday practice are part of what Craig Calhoun calls the 'prepolitical bases for [institutional] legitimacy'. Even for populations who are highly mobile, everyday habits (including media habits) can with surprising effectiveness reimpose a national frame.[55] Yet from the medieval city-state onwards, media's relations to institutional power have always worked on multiple scales,[56] so today's complexities need not surprise us.

The flexibility of media rituals

Let's return now to the concept of media ritual, leaving these important comparative questions resonating in the background.

The basic human rituals are very familiar: rituals that mark birth, death, marriage, the joining of a group, communication with the transcendent. Their subjects are linked to the basic human needs for order. Media, except when they transmit such basic rituals directly, do not fulfil such a basic human function. So how *can* a new class of rituals – media rituals – emerge at a particular point in history? How can something like a talk show or a reality TV show *be* a ritual?

Patterned action

The secular nature of media does not prevent media generating ritual: the existence of secular rituals has been accepted within anthropology for decades,[57] and new secular rituals are created all the time, for example the UK's new ritual for those acquiring British citizenship. Nor is there anything strange about the idea that media could re-present to us pre-existing rituals: a wedding, a funeral, the raising of a flag.[58] But the idea of media rituals involves much more than this: it involves the claim that certain complex practices around media have the transformative force of ritual *in their own right* and constitute a distinctive *type* of ritual based in the distinctiveness of both media institutions and of our relations to them. Media rituals are formalized, patterned actions relating to media that enact a particular way of organizing the world.

Ritual is above all *patterned action*. This is brought out clearly in anthropologist Roy Rappaport's classic definition of ritual as 'the performance of more or less invariant sequences of formal acts and utterances, not entirely encoded by the performers'.[59] Thin accounts of ritual see it merely as discourse or performance without any reference to form,[60] and ignore the role that ritual plays in enacting a world *through* form. It is this enacting of general ideas in the unarguable action-form of ritual that explains rituals' potential importance in wider social reproduction.

The strong claim that media institutions generate distinctive forms of ritual is justified, for example, by the regularity with which media organize large populations around a particular broadcast event (royal weddings; the inauguration ceremony of Nelson Mandela as president of South Africa in 1994): this is the basic principle of Dayan and Katz's foundational idea of media events.[61] It is justified by the emergence in recent decades of large media forms such as the talk show and reality media format: in each, the ability of media institutions to stand in for 'society', whether as its moral authority or as its eyes, is affirmed; on that basis, people are willing to reveal significant and often painful aspects of their lives to large audiences. Meanwhile media institutions persist and claim legitimacy for their power, based in media's underlying claim to stand in for the social, a claim that is confirmed in condensed form through the actions of media rituals.

Emile Durkheim interpreted religion as a displaced expression of our relations to the social. But my argument, while it borrows some of its shape and formulations from Durkheim,[62] does not depend on making any claims either about religion or religion's relationship to the social. Media institutions claim themselves to be our proxy for the social: an early example is *Collier's* magazine from a century ago that wrote 'news is the nerves of the modern world.'[63] But the hugeness of media's claim to speak for, and link us to, the social – 'what there is in common for us' – means that the rituals created to enact this claim may change and develop, be replaced or renewed, without losing their force.

The basis of ritual in pattern means that rituals can remain recognizable in spite of great variations, provided their basic form is preserved. Media rituals provide many examples of this. Think first of the rituals of self-disclosure through television: while the television talk show appears in countries such as the UK and USA to be declining as a TV format after three decades or so, the ritual of disclosing oneself through media is growing in new formats, such as *Pop Idol*.

Flexibility is even more marked as a feature of the reality format which has undergone multiple revisions from the early shows that tracked criminals (in Germany, UK and USA) and the early 'docu-soaps' that followed a particular slice of life for a series (in the UK, *Airport, Hotel*), to the rise of the 'game doc' (*Survivor, Big Brother, I'm A Celebrity ... Get Me Out of Here*), pedagogic shows (*What Not to Wear, The Apprentice*) and, most recently, entertainment competitions focused on 'ordinary' contestants (in the UK, *Pop Idol* and *Britain's Got Talent*; in the Middle East, *Star Academy*; in China, *Super Voice Girl*). This flexibility is enhanced, not undermined, by the ability to track content across multiple formats (websites, official and unofficial, gossip magazines, text message updates, online games, phone 'apps', Facebook groups, YouTube parodies). *Britain's Got Talent*'s website says, 'if you've not downloaded the *Britain's Got Talent*'s mobile 'app' yet, you're missing out on all the fun of the BGT buzzer.' Recent British shows, such as *The Only Way is Essex* (ITV2), have started recruiting participants via Facebook.[64] The reality media form is expandable because it is based in the belief that, at some level, media work to seek out and present shared 'reality'. Just as for Durkheim the sacred is 'contagious',[65] because it stands in for 'the social', so too reality media's claim to be 'real' is flexible enough to be embodied in almost any form.

The ambiguity of rituals' meanings is another source of flexibiilty. Ritual works by being both real and playful, both truth and fiction. The role of play in ritual is crucial for understanding, for example, contemporary reality media since, as Steven Connor notes, 'the condition of play is one in which things both are and are not, both do and do not matter.' The *Big Brother* format is a clear example of a game that claims the ability to reveal at some level the 'reality' of human interactions, as certified by psychologists.[66]

The categories of media ritual not only work within the boundaries of particular rituals; they are also reproduced in the wider hinterland of everyday practices of ritualization, a point we now explore further.

The role of categories

A category is a stable principle that enables one term to be regularly differentiated from another opposite, so 'sacred' is differentiated from 'profane' (Durkheim's theory of religious ritual) and 'media' person/thing/world is differentiated from 'ordinary' (or non-media) person/thing/world in my account of media rituals. A category is not a weak or tentative marking of difference: it is a differential definite enough to be acted out in, and transposed onto, bodily performance.

In this way, category differences can be associated with the organization of the body and multiple bodies, a link between Durkheim's work and the more recent work on gender and sexuality of Judith Butler.[67] Ritual action, organized around category differences, is a good way of *learning* such differences through the body and achieving the 'practical mastery' that Bourdieu sees as inherent to ritual practice.[68] Thus learned, category differences, and the wider ordering from which they derive, together become naturalized: confirmed in their naturalness through the seeming naturalness of the ritual action that enacts them.

The ordering role that categories play goes far beyond Schatzki's comments on the 'understandings' through which practices hold together. Categories do more than organize practices; categories ensure that practices become learned *in a form* that is obligatory, repeatable and meaningful. That is not to deny a certain looseness and improvisatory quality about ritual; but such freedom is possible precisely against the background of a clear patterned form.

Catherine Bell, a leading theorist of religion, saw 'the body invested with a "sense" of ritual' as merely the end point of a wider process of ritualization. The sense in completed ritual that certain forms of action have higher status reinforces a broader hierarchy. Ritualization's regular boundary-marking suggests a 'higher' order of things, 'a more embracing authoritative order that lies beyond the immediate situation', and applies right across social life.[69] In the same way, the (relatively exceptional) moments of media ritual are linked to, and supported by, a vast hinterland in media practice of difference-making and boundary-marking that embeds those differences and boundaries, in what gets done and thought automatically.

Think of sites where people cross from the non-media 'world' into the media 'world', such as any place where filming or media production goes on, or where non-media people expect to encounter people or things in the media (for example, celebrities); or moments where non-media people perform for the media, for example posing for a camera. In all these situations, people act out differences that reproduce in condensed form the idea that media are an access point to society's 'centre': calling out as their presence 'on air' is acknowledged; holding back, or rushing forward, at the sight of a celebrity; holding back before they enter a place connected with the media, so as to emphasize the boundary they cross by entering it.[70] In so doing, they translate category differences into the durable organization of space: *this* area for celebrities or VIPs, *that* area for 'ordinary people'. The specialness of things in 'the media world' is now the basis for a taken-for-granted brand of tourism: media tourism to TV and film locations, for example the filming sites of detective TV serials or *The Lord of the Rings*.[71] It is also the basis for the boundaries and category differences on which fully fledged media rituals (for example the moment when we enter a television studio to tell 'to the world' our private story) depend.

Media's ritual categories contribute to the ritualization of media-related practice: the category of the media person or celebrity whose special status is guaranteed by their appearance in media; the category of 'liveness' which marks out as special whatever is selected for simultaneous broadcast;[72] and the category of 'reality' itself to denote whatever media institutions authoritatively select to treat as real. Such categories, inherent in contemporary media practice, are part of what Luc Boltanski calls 'the field of determination of what is'. The *fit* of these terms with the wider *organization* of social practice (the fact that we *already do* orient our practices to media in the many ways already discussed in chapter 2) gives the ritualized categories associated with media a special force. It makes them into what Boltanski calls 'instruments of . . . representing what is, or at least what's given as relevant for the collective'; as a result, the reference points of these terms (live, real, celebrity and so on) appear to cover the social field as a whole.[73]

The basic pattern of media rituals, built upon such key categories and terms, can, in turn, generate specific applications, including games with explicit rules.[74] This is the terrain of 'gamedocs' where the presentation of 'reality' through media is structured in the form of a competition with explicit rules. One example is *The Apprentice* in its UK version (see Box 3.1).

Box 3.1 *The Apprentice*, UK

The Apprentice (UK) is a popular programme based on an improbable premise: that putting a small group of people each year through a series of highly artificial tests for the benefit of the camera, tests assessed ultimately by the programme host and entrepreneur Sir Alan Sugar, can teach a large nation such as Britain something useful about the reality of business. Its status as an entertainment programme, not a full documentary, should not lead us to forget the reality claims made on its behalf by the BBC: Jane Lush, BBC Controller of Entertainment Commissioning, said its aim was 'to bring business to those who might not have thought it was for them', while Daisy Goodwin, editorial director of the programme's production company Talkback, claimed: '[it is] the first entertainment show to have a real point – to show what it really takes to get ahead in business' (both quoted, BBC 2005). As the programme gained large audiences, the New Labour government elevated Sugar to the House of Lords and appointed him government adviser on business.

How can an entertainment show have such reality effects? Its format is grounded in the longer history of claims by media institutions to represent the social. The gamedoc form, using various rhetorics (here management and business discourses), suggests that whoever passes through its various stages will have acquired a particular type of real-world expertise (being a good cook, being an adventurous person, and in this case being someone with business talent). This rhetoric is based on the form of the game which defines particular things as success. At the end of the series, the winner is marked as someone who satisfies the values on which the game is based (what Boltanski calls a 'truth test': 2011: 103–10).

The Apprentice does more than consecrate a winner. Through its game status, it excludes from view all challenges to its rules *and* the values on which those rules are based (individual aggression, ability to withstand the verbal aggression of Sir Alan Sugar, and so on): values alternative to those asserted in the game cannot be advocated without challenging its whole structure. At times, around the margins of the game, positive claims are made that what you see in the game is 'normal': in one post-show discussion, a contestant from the first UK series justified the aggressive interviews in the series 2 episode just seen as representing 'the culture you'll be working in' (what Boltanski calls a 'reality test': 2011: 103–10). But the show itself never needs to make such positive claims because the show's norms go unopposed and are written into the game's rules. *The Apprentice* (UK version) illustrates how reality *games* are effective tools for appearing to present us with a reality, while simultaneously blocking from view other realities and protecting the shown reality from challenge. Reality TV games' resulting *narrowing* of social reality fits with the norms of the neoliberal workplace (Couldry 2010: ch. 4; Hearn 2006; McCarthy 2007; Ouellette and Hay 2008; Boltanski and Chiapello 2005), but always on the basis of the ritualized authority to present reality invested in media institutions.

For a more detailed analysis of the programme, see Couldry and Littler (2011), and, for the US *Apprentice*, Hearn (2006: 626–7).

The organizing work of media rituals does not end when the ritual is completed. Media rituals (the practice and the very idea of them) help organize other practices, *anchoring* them through the representations and categories that they authoritatively enact.[75] Ritual practices enact *new* forms of categorization and distinction that are relied upon, in turn, in organizing other practices. Such relationships between practices may not be articulated explicitly, but they are 'carried' through the bodily knowledge that people display when they perform those further practices (of imitation, retelling, rewriting). This *exemplary* role of mediated performance becomes important in chapter 4.

Let's complete our discussion by considering two dimensions of the ritualization of contemporary media: media events and celebrity culture. That will enable us to bring out some final points about how media rituals work to reproduce something *like* social order.

The banalization of media events

Media events incorporate media rituals and their changing status over the past two decades is a striking example of the dynamics of ritualization. Dayan and Katz's original theory identified in media events (televised royal weddings, state funerals, presidential inaugurations, major political meetings) a regular form based in the preplanned disruption of broadcasting schedules to reach a large national audience for coverage of events at society's 'centre'.[76] Dayan and Katz drew our attention to the larger stakes that are sometimes involved in media coverage. Their concept of the 'media event' quickly became an automatic reference point. They had taken an earlier and classically Durkheimian view of national ceremonies (Shils and Young's account of the televised coronation of Queen Elizabeth II in 1952 as 'an act of national communion'),[77] and given it hugely more sophistication. Indeed, Dayan and Katz argued that a proper appreciation of media events and their workings enabled us to see how the 'mechanical solidarity' that Durkheim a century before had regarded as in terminal decline in large modern societies was renewed when television brought whole nations together in a shared experience of 'festive' viewing.[78] The power of their account is demonstrated by how well it fitted, five years after their book's publication, with the funeral in London of Princess Diana in September 1997, broadcast to a global television audience.

Three types of processes, however, subsequently challenged the media event concept. The *first* transformation came from the increasing importance of media coverage that shared many features of media events (interruption of schedules, continuous live coverage, especially intense viewing habits) but carried none of their integrative potential. Tamar Liebes, the Israeli scholar, was the first to notice this, calling them 'disaster marathons';[79] her example was the all-channel, interruptive and open-ended coverage on Israeli TV in the aftermath of a suicide bomb attack, which tends to further split, rather than unite, the nation. A *second* transformation came from the ways in which political actors adapted to the features of media events to create a new type of symbolic politics: the most important example was the attacks on the Manhattan World Trade Centre Towers and other US targets on 11 September 2001.[80] From 9/11 onwards, any definition of media events needed to take account of disruptive events planned far from society's 'centre'. Indeed, Daniel Dayan proposed rethinking the problematic term 'terrorism' to acknowledge a strategy of mediated violence that precisely exploited its symbolic potential.[81] Elihu Katz and Tamar Liebes, in turn, concluded that monopoly coverage of disaster, war and terror now supersedes the ceremonial events that the concept 'media events' had been invented to capture.[82] A *third* transformation came from broader changes in the media landscape: a generalization of the rhetorics used to define media events *as* special and a fragmentation of the large national audiences that the original media event had assumed.[83]

Through these developments, the aspect of Dayan and Katz's original theory that was rhetorically boldest, but also theoretically the most problematic – their neo-Durkheimian insistence that media events serve to integrate nations and reinforce consensual democratic values – became both less plausible *and* less relevant to the wider phenomena that, beneath the neo-Durkheimian disguise, they had identified. As a result, a reassessment became necessary both of the initial theory of media events and of critiques (such as mine) that had rejected its neo-Durkheimian implications. As just noted, Dayan and Katz have each reassessed the concept, and now limit it to the (disappeared) features of the broadcast era.[84] Meanwhile, my own critique of Dayan and Katz's neo-Durkheimian formulations[85] must itself face the question of whether the *post*-Durkheimian concept of 'media rituals' on which that critique relied can itself withstand the very same forces of cynicism, banalization and audience fragmentation. Does the apparent decline of media events presage the decline of media rituals too?

Here we get to the heart of what is distinctive about the notion of media rituals. As we saw earlier, the definition of media rituals does not involve any claim about the *success* of a media ritual in binding its participants into actual loyalty to media institutions. The term 'media rituals', rather, identifies a social form that exploits key categories to enact a certain relation between media and their target populations, a strategic action involving media institutions and implicating their audiences and participants. Identifying such strategic action at work does not involve claiming that media rituals actually *do* hold society together. My own concept of media ritual was, on the contrary, developed against the grain of the functionalism with which many of Durkheim's followers were associated;[86] it emphasizes precisely the political contests and indeterminacies within the apparently universal language of much ritual. This is reflected in the alternative definition of media events that I offered back in 2003 as 'those large-scale event-based media-focused narratives where *the claims* associated with the myth of the mediated centre are particularly intense'.[87]

A suitably revised concept of media events can orient us in a media landscape where successful media events become rarer, yet invoking media's special relationship with society remains important. Here is the revised definition of media events which Andreas Hepp and I have proposed for a global media age: 'media events are certain situated, thickened, centering performances of mediated communication that are focused on a specific thematic core, cross different media products and reach a wide and diverse multiplicity of audiences and participants.'[88] By 'centering performances', we mean types of communicative action focused on a thematic core that attempt to articulate a relation to a social 'centre' reached through media. It is no part of this approach to assume such performances are successful, only to argue for a particular performative intent (to reproduce media institutions as privileged access points to a 'mediated center'). Indeed, it is important – particularly within a historical perspective – to allow for myths of the mediated centre that are constructed yet fail, as Brian Larkin's work on the colonial Nigerian state and its close reliance on national radio and film brings out.[89]

This new definition fits well with a digital media age that, as discussed in chapter 1, sees intensified competition for audience attention and media institutions' increasingly explicit battle for legitimacy (symbolic value) and survival (economic value). It addresses types of media production (film and increasingly television) that, because of their high cost, are particularly reliant on the generation of 'events', and forms of authority (for example, state politics) that increasingly rely on staged events to excite and orchestrate loyalty.[90] It also suggests a less absolute reading of the supposed 'disenchantment' of media events than Dayan's or Katz's latest positions allow.[91] In the political domain, there has arguably been an *increase,* not a decrease, of large-scale event-narratives – for example the Make

Poverty History narrative that accompanied the build-up to the Gleneagles G20 summit in Scotland in July 2005 – in which a variety of actors can participate. Meanwhile, distant disasters, mediated still in large part by large media institutions, increasingly generate a penumbra of user-generated content and websites where expert individuals set themselves up as privileged interpreters and witnesses exchange information and images.[92] Even in a multi-channel, internet-saturated digital environment, the subjunctive 'as-if' language that Dayan and Katz traced in the official narratives of media events can still be found, but it is dispersed among the unofficial participants. The result is very different both from the hallowed respect of early media events *and* from the general cynicism at distant spectacle that an earlier era produced.[93] Listen to these people at the G20 summit in 2005, albeit filtered through media reports: 'we wanted to be part of the message'; 'I feel proud for the first time. This is, incredibly, going to be effective ... the biggest show of solidarity I've ever seen in Edinburgh'; 'we will now force the political establishment to make a serious policy commitment to the world's poor'. In a different context – post-1989 Eastern and Central Europe – Aniko Imre has shown how versions of the *Pop Idol* format, as well as the 'event' of the *Eurovision Song Contest*, can work as sites of national spectacle, where new possibilities of national identification and group recognition are staged and contested. Similar arguments have been made for Catholic or Hindu religious institutions' use of media events – around religious drama or documentary series – to bolster their authority and national presence.[94]

Rather than media events disappearing, then, they are likely to persist as a media form, but this form must be interpreted outside of any simple neo-Durkheimian account of national or social solidarity. There is no single monolithic spectacle today, contra Guy Debord. Yet control over the central capacity, and local resources, for spectacle remains one of the most fundamental political struggles of our age.[95]

Celebrity culture

I will close the chapter by using celebrity culture to illustrate how media rituals and ritualization connect with a wider social landscape.

Celebrities, since the beginning of film, have been key ways of focusing demand; the production of celebrity, and representations of celebrity, goes back to the marketing efforts of early modernity. David Marshall has provided a definitive analysis of the production side of 'celebrity culture' and its relation to general audience demand.[96] In a digital media era, the need in newspaper and television industries to compete for news audiences, with greater intensity but on the basis of less resources, increases the temptation to cut production costs by using stories (such as celebrity gossip) that guarantee high attention. But how is celebrity culture reproduced in wider everyday practice? Think of celebrity magazines, the continual stream of news stories about celebrity and the increasingly prominent outpourings of celebrities themselves on social networking sites, Twitter feeds and so on. There is today a pervasive 'fame culture' which stretches from the most large-scale events to the most intimate practices of emotional investment.[97] How can we understand this culture?

Celebrity culture is more than a domain of internal meanings: it is *something we do*, a type of action that *organizes* behaviour and language. Here, ritual theory finds common ground with Slavoj Žižek's Lacanian theory of ideology as something we do rather than believe.[98] Celebrity culture is often treated as a 'culture' based on a convergence of belief, but it is much better understood as a convergence of ritual practice. Max Weber long ago noted the role of the 'routinization of charisma' in the reinforcement of power in large societies.[99] The fact that we all know that celebrities are 'constructions' does not undermine the category differences reproduced in our practices of *orienting ourselves towards* celebrity. It is these patterns of orientation – the fact we pick up a magazine, the fact we follow or pass on a link – that constitutes something like a social order. Karin Knorr-Cetina writes tantalizingly of a '*post*-social order', based not on positive social identifications but on certain 'unfolding structures of absences'. Whatever phrase we prefer, celebrity, I suggest, is one of those absences: answering a lack whose filling we continually pursue without any possibility of completion.[100]

Celebrity culture works through processes of ritualization: a way of acting that marks off one constructed group ('celebrities' or 'media people') from another equally constructed group ('ordinary people'). Celebrity matters as a category to media industries – over and above their investment in specific celebrities – because it condenses a call to attention towards something common and shared that 'we' need to follow. It is this vaguely consensual and ritualizing category that we act out when we turn our head, shout 'Oh my God!' and gasp at the celebrity who has suddenly entered our field of vision: listen to the sound on the Harry Potter cast-spotting video mentioned in chapter 2. In the digital media era, this also means following this category across multiple sites and platforms, including the social media domains of Facebook, Twitter and so on.

We *know* that, in most cases, celebrities are 'ordinary' but for their media profile, yet we *act* differently: buying weekend magazines that show celebrities doing 'ordinary things', flicking through those same magazines as we wait for our hair to be cut, exchanging knowledge or sightings of celebrities, using them as reference points for clothes we buy or restaurants we visit. In the UK and USA, children and young people's desire to be a celebrity is noted in recent surveys;[101] it is a disturbing undercurrent in the growing wave of school and other shootings in public places across many countries.[102] Celebrity culture requires no consensus of belief: celebrity is an open category that we reproduce in institutional, individual and social practice, through what we point out and what we do not. For a century, there has been an industry of celebrity production, but recent practice takes this to a new intensity in ways from which political power also seeks to benefit.[103] The production of 'backstage' narratives which seem to give privileged access to the 'real' working lives of media people intensifies a 'hypertrophic' celebrity culture that endlessly *reproduces* celebrity as a value.[104] The most intense embodiment of such culture is paparazzi's pursuit of celebrities in daily life: its industrial logic does not disguise the categorical trick – the presentation of '(extra) ordinary people as (extra)ordinary' – on which it is based. Take this comment from Peter Howe's book *Paparazzi*: '"Just like us" pictures can't be boring . . . the day-to-day activities that would produce dull activities if you or I were doing them become fascinating if performed by a celebrity. You simply don't expect Cameron Diaz to go to Kinko's or Jennifer Love Hewitt to pick up her own dry cleaning.'[105]

The point of the average celebrity sighting need not be the fulfilment of a deep emotional investment in the spotted celebrity; it makes enough sense *already* as the reproduction of a shared reference point, automatically recognizable by the person who hears a sighting story, a meaningful narrative act in a media culture. Through our everyday practice (for example, when we upload our own celebrity sightings to Gawkerstalker, http://gawker.com/stalker/), we make celebrities into the exemplars that media institutions need them to be. The ritualizing pressures of celebrity culture that reproduce the boundaries around celebrity in everyday practice[106] are the other side of media industries' increasing need to sustain their social centrality.

To read 'celebrity culture' as democratizing is therefore highly misleading. Thirty years ago, George Trow speculated that 'television will re-form around the idea that television *itself* is a context to which television will grant an access':[107] just substitute for 'television' here a reference to today's more networked media 'centre'. The Web's many platforms for do-it-yourself celebrity have certainly extended the scope of celebrity (take Kevin Rose, founder of the recommendation platform Digg and YouTube star) and its geographical range (think of Susan Boyle's rise to international stardom via YouTube clips of her performances on *Britain's Got Talent*). Yet none of these innovations challenge the broader hierarchies of celebrity culture: rather, as Jose van Dijk neatly puts it, they open up an 'options market', derivative of the main celebrity stock market.[108] It is equally misleading to see the rise of celebrity culture as the exclusive symptom of a social malaise external to media,[109] for that ignores the highly self-interested role of media, political and other institutions in sustaining the patterned order on which the myth of the mediated centre depends. When, in March 2011, *Big Brother* brand developer Endemol bought a 50 per cent stake in a celebrity gossip website, Holy Moly, we should not have been surprised.

Celebrity culture, with its patterns and hierarchies, therefore provides a concrete example of how media-related practices contribute to wider processes of social ordering involving large populations. Still unresolved, however, are the consequences of such ordering for wider social organization. That is the topic of the next chapter.

4

Media and the Hidden Shaping of the Social

'Narrating society, representing it to itself, is . . . what narrative systems do.'

Millie Buonanno[1]

In the last chapter, I tried to build an account of media's relations to power, from the bottom up, by examining how practices, particularly ritualized practices, contribute to social form. I did this, in the spirit of Boltanski and Thévenot, without making any assumptions about the coherence of values in society: the key linking concept was 'category', since practices are made more serviceable to power by being organized around categories and category differences. Media rituals and ritualized practice around media were explored as examples of categories at work. By the end of the chapter, we had moved from the apparently infinite proliferation of practice to an understanding of some of the key social forms constituted by contemporary media: reality TV, media events and celebrity 'culture'.

In this chapter, we explore the wider consequences of such mediated social forms for social knowledge and the organization of social life. As I noted in chapter 2, the problem of 'effects' is one of the oldest and most intractable in media research: the way forward is to avoid trying to show that what people *believe* changes as a result of *particular* media contents. We are interested instead in what people *regularly do*, and the conditions under which they are able to act. A key concept in this chapter is *naturalization*. In many varied ways, media naturalize not a coherent 'picture' of the world but certain dimensions, categorical features and 'facts' that disable alternative accounts of the world and so themselves get embedded, *by default,* in everyday actions and understandings. In this way, media contribute to the weighting of what passes for social knowledge in media-rich societies. Once again, this chapter's argument is intended to supplement, not replace, political economy approaches to media power: its focus is not media production or media economics, but the mechanisms through which media representations of the social become embedded in practice. Needless to say, we can only cover a few entry points to this vast topic.

Naturalization is not a property exclusively of media: it is an effect of all forms of power that construct a distinctive map of 'what is' (in Boltanski's phrase). Two consequences follow. First, where media maps of 'what is' *conflict* with other powerful maps (from religious or state sources, for example), then a *denaturalization* of those other maps may result: the recent role of reality television in the Middle East is a vivid example. Second, where media maps of 'what is' *coincide* with other maps (for example, those of corporate power and government in neoliberal democracies such as the UK and USA), the result is an *intensified* naturalization, or what we might call a 'hard-wiring', of certain values, distinctions and exclusions into cultural, social and political discourse.[2] Such hard-wiring converts media's apparent space of freedom into a terrain of 'durable inequality'.[3]

The distinctive nature of media power

In what follows, I offer a substantive account of media power[4] as a form of symbolic power. First, however, we must deal with some standard objections to such an account. One objection is the argument that media are precisely institutions that mediate between the various forces (economic, political, military, social, cultural, physical) that make up the world and its power struggles. On this view, there is nothing specific to say about media institutions' contribution to power. Let us call this the 'classical view' of media's contribution to social ontology: that, considered at a fundamental level, *media do not contribute anything to social ontology* but merely mediate all the forces that do. Although it has rarely been stated so baldly, only the assumption of something like this classical view can explain the absence of media from most social theory and general sociology until the late 1980s and, in some cases, even today. It is striking, for example, that John Scott's authoritative book on power makes no mention of media.[5] Meanwhile, even if in a very different way, Manuel Castells reflects this classical view in his pathbreaking work on networks' contributions to contemporary society and politics. In the 1990s,

Castells insisted that media do not have power as such (they do not determine, for example, the content of politics), but rather comprise the nodes through which power now operates.[6] In his recent work, Castells sees media institutions as in some cases potentially very powerful, but mainly in so far as, like Murdoch's News Corporation, they act as 'switches' in the space of networks through which all power now flows. Castells's work, for all its bold insistence that digital media networks usher in a new age of power, remains largely silent on how the content of media might be put to work in social life.[7]

Another objection to a substantive account of media's contribution to power, from the opposite direction, is to argue that *media have already transformed social ontology so much* that no perspective distinct from media exists: as a result, we cannot identify differences that media institutions make to power. Baudrillard formulates this in terms of 'the end of the social'. 'Outwardly', he wrote, the media 'produce more of the social, inwardly they neutralize social relations, and the social itself'.[8] In this media-saturated world, 'the social ceases to take itself as a space of reference'.[9] Baudrillard was one of the first to reflect on the emergence of reality TV, discussing the 1971 US programme *The Family*. His conclusion was apocalyptic: 'No longer is there any imperative to submit to the model, or to the gaze. "YOU are the model!" . . . "YOU are news", you are the social, the event is you, you are used, you can use your voice.'[10]

As a result, television for Baudrillard ceases to be a medium at all: 'the dissolution of TV into life, the dissolution of life into TV'.[11] Within this account – which, given the huge subsequent rise of reality TV, you can either see as brilliant prophecy or fortunate generalization – there is nothing specific to be said about the relation between media and the social because there is *no social remaining* that has not been invaded by the 'code' of television. Quite apart from the issue of whether Baudrillard's analysis has any relevance outside a few western societies (we return to comparative issues later), there is something deeply odd about his analysis. It reads like the feverish reaction of an older body of theory to an intruder: the intruder was media, and the body of theory was a sociology (and philosophy) that saw society as a real 'totality', an idea which clearly could not survive the realization that the organizing values of that 'totality' had become contaminated by feedback loops between one particular institution (media) and random sites of social experience. Whatever the reason, we learn little specific from Baudrillard about how media make a difference to the social world.

We must, in any case, reject the idea of society as a totality and focus instead on what a leading proponent of Actor-Network Theory,

John Law, calls 'the plural processes of socio-technical ordering'. There are *modes of ordering* that 'perform and embody themselves in the networks of the social'.[12] Although Law didn't consider media, there is no reason why we cannot apply this idea to what media do.[13] Indeed, if contemporary societies are witnessing a change in the nature of power and legitimacy, media are surely crucial to that transformation. Understanding how this works requires an understanding of media's distinctive form of power.

Since media involve symbols, this must start with an understanding of symbolic power. The concept of 'symbolic power' remains relatively underdeveloped. One account of 'symbolic power' can be found in John Thompson's *The Media and Modernity*. Drawing ultimately on Max Weber, Thompson valuably insists on the symbolic as a dimension of power alongside the political and the economic. But his precise definition of 'symbolic power' is less satisfactory: symbolic power is merely 'the capacity to intervene in the course of events, to influence the actions of others and indeed to create events, by means of the production and transmission of symbolic forms'.[14] This definition captures what a number of social institutions (the media, the church, educational institutions) do, but it does not capture the wider impact that certain *concentrations* of symbolic power may have.[15]

All forms of power work in a dispersed way, but symbolic power impacts upon wider society more pervasively than other forms of power (such as economic power) because the concentration of society's symbolic resources affects not just what we do but our ability to *describe* whatever 'goes on'. A strong concept of symbolic power insists that some concentrations of symbolic power (for example, the concentration from which contemporary media institutions benefit) are so great that they dominate the whole social landscape and amount to a power of 'constructing reality'.[16] A concentration of symbolic power is both a fact in its own right and a factor affecting the representation of all social facts (this one included). Effects of *mis*recognition are therefore inherent to the uneven distribution of symbolic power in the way that they are not inherent to other forms of power. Only a strong concept of symbolic power recognizes the distorting impacts that the uneven distribution of symbolic power has on social space. Understanding media institutions, I suggest, requires this strong concept of symbolic power.

Such a view of symbolic power is characteristic of Pierre Bourdieu's sociology. By contrast with Baudrillard's generalized theory of the media-driven implosion of the social, Bourdieu insisted on the possibility of describing the process of 'constructing reality' and seeing the work such constructions do in circulation: if so, 'constructing reality' for Bourdieu must mean not literally the construction of the entire reality we inhabit, but rather the production of *modes of ordering* that are applied consistently and pervasively *enough* to become for many purposes *treated as* universal reference points. Reality does not implode on this view, but universalizing descriptions and categories circulate, licensing other generalizations and constructions without effective resistance or contradiction. The result is a 'reality' that for many purposes seems consistent, orderly, unchallengeable and yet whose consistencies are based on a series of discriminations and exclusions that are largely hidden from view, without even a basic language to describe them.

Emile Durkheim argued in *The Elementary Forms of Religious Life* that religion is society's way of communing with itself. We can put to one side Durkheim's theory of religion, but keep its kernel which is the idea of the 'stimulating and invigorating effect of society' on individuals. We have already drawn upon this in chapter 3's account of media rituals and media events. Media sometimes speak with this sort of 'invigorating' power (as in media events) and, more importantly since more commonly, they speak in a way that *references* this type of power, in ritualized language that draws, implicitly, on the reference point of society. Durkheim's interest in the social went far beyond moments of exceptional social effervescence to cover 'all kinds of acts' whereby 'the feeling society has for [a person] uplifts the feeling he has for himself'.[17] He notes how certain ways of acting that are socially endorsed have a special status which derives from the work they do as representations:

> *because these ways of acting have been worked out in common*, the intensity with which they are thought in each individual mind finds resonance in all the others, and vice versa. The *representations that translate them* within each of us thereby gain an intensity that mere private states of consciousness can in no way match ... it is society that speaks through the mouths of those who affirm them in our presence; it is society that we hear when we hear them; and the voice of all itself has a tone that an individual voice cannot have.[18]

This is a fundamental insight into the workings of form, language and categories that are based in the myth of the mediated centre. Some earlier writers have registered Durkheim's point – Paddy Scannell's analysis of live television and radio, Dayan and Katz's account of media events as 'shared experiences, uniting viewers with one another and with their societies'[19] – but both accounts involve something like an organic functionalism. From a more sceptical perspective, we can follow Durkheim in believing that in everyday life we are continually faced with moments which *seem* to present us with something 'larger' than our individual selves – something that stands for the social bond that links us as members of a group or society – yet insist that such forms are indissolubly tied to the means for *representing* the social that are available in particular historical circumstances. There exist, after all, industries (media) for producing something like Durkheim's encounter with the social; their productions recall, recycle and reference the social, and those references circulate in wider life. Those modes of ordering (John Law) are doubly paradoxical: first, they are produced by very particular processes in media institutions yet lay claim to the greatest generality of application (in that they address 'society'); second, although particular, they are themselves put *into general circulation*, transcending an older model of 'socialization' carried out in discrete communities.[20] It is crucial for socially oriented media theory to understand the contradictions that result.

Media industries have evolved under a variety of local conditions as general producers of social representations. The result is not to leave social ontology untouched (the classical view), nor to destroy the social as a point of reference (Baudrillard's apocalypse), nor even (the neo-Durkheimian view of early Dayan and Katz) to rewire the social directly through the media's productions. The result, instead, is to introduce into our everyday experience of social interaction and social imagination all the power effects and exclusions inherent to the media process. Within our deepest experiences of commonality, we find at work – like the invisible worm within poet William Blake's rose – the intrinsically divisive nature of media's symbolic power, the specific division of the social between those with access to media's vast concentrations of representational power and those without such access.[21] This has key consequences for everyday agency.

Hidden injuries of media power

The organization of society around media institutions that benefit from a huge concentration of symbolic power generates a *lack* at the heart of daily life: the 'lack' constituted by living outside the world presented to us by media. While the generalizability of this statement requires more research into the workings and consequences of symbolic power in a range of countries and media cultures (a key factor here is the degree to which religious institutions constitute a rival symbolic power to media: see chapters 6 and 7), I will concentrate for the next few pages on societies where media are unquestionably a dominant force in the representation of social life.

I do not mean to deny that robust and democratically free media are an important and basic good in social organization. Development economist Amartya Sen has argued that there has never been a famine in a society with free media.[22] Strong public media institutions, where they have emerged historically, have been associated with positive ends of social engagement and education, as in 1930s' Britain with the BBC. Equally, some of the worst genocides in history have been abetted by the weak or state-dominated media: the weak press and state-controlled radio of Nazi Germany, the state-sponsored Radio-Télévision Libre des Mille Collines that incited the Rwandan genocide.[23] But thankfully these are not normal cases, and to grasp the impact of media in the majority of contemporary societies we need to look also at the more subtle (or hidden) injuries with which even mature, 'free' media can be associated under particular historical circumstances. From Tocqueville onwards, social thinkers have noted the complex balance of social good and social bad associated with powerful media institutions.[24]

Early insights

It is tempting to argue that, in societies where media institutions are crucial to daily life, lack of media resources is, quite simply, the lack of an essential resource, in which case the related injury would not be hidden at all; it would be an absence of an obvious tool for living. But this analysis, while important in certain contexts (the organization of politics: see chapter 5), does not cover a more subtle form of media-related lack. Interestingly, it is analysts of the early television age who have seen this most clearly. Neal Gabler, in his history of television and film's influence on US society, writes of 'the sanctification of the camera': by contrast, '*not* to be in the movie, *not* to be acknowledged [is] the profoundest form of failure in the entertainment state.'[25] Raoul Vaneigem, a member of the Situationist group of theorists and activists in 1960s France with whom Henri Lefebvre was closely associated, put the point most acutely: 'the mechanism of the alienating spectacle wields such force that private life reaches the point of being defined as that which is *deprived of spectacle*.'[26]

Vaneigem's formulation suggests something more subtle than that media confer a new form of prestige. Vaneigem's point is that everyday life, in mediated societies, becomes *defined* in terms of a newly perceived *lack*. Everyday life becomes defined as merely ordinary: 'merely', that is, by reference to the 'full' status assured to whatever is presented in the spectacle.

'Spectacle', as the Situationists understood it, is the everyday display – through media and otherwise – of consumer goods that affirm capitalist values. By contrast, I am applying Vaneigem's idea (that everyday life becomes defined in terms of a constitutive lack) to the more general value at the root of contemporary media's legitimacy as social institutions: the value of whatever is 'in' the media over what is not (see chapter 3). From this perspective, everyday life becomes defined by its lack of media coverage, its lack of whatever it is that makes life suitable for media coverage. We need to qualify Vaneigem's claim: there are multiple possible regimes of evaluation in everyday life. But that does not mean ignoring the weight, deriving from the coordination of media consumption across whole populations, of 'ways of acting that have been worked out in common' (Emile Durkheim).[27] I come later to the consequences of recent media proliferation.

A desire to be close to, or part of, some transcendent performance that stands in for the social is not new.[28] But the modern world's deep *embedding* of spectacle (and media presentations generally) into daily life sustains a *categorical* contrast, or gap, between the worlds that media present and the everyday flow of life. That gap continuously requires fulfilment, and yet, because it derives from the permanent division of the world implied in our relations to media, it can never be filled. This gap or lack can, perversely, be a generative force in social life.

As we saw in the last chapter, Karin Knorr-Cetina describes the role of media images in contemporary societies as 'unfolding structures of absences'. We do not need to follow Knorr-Cetina in drawing on Lacan's psychoanalysis to realize that she captures well the open-endedness of this hidden injury inherent to life in societies where vast symbolic power is concentrated in media institutions. We are implicated not so much in a desire (although sometimes the desire for media exposure is real enough) as in a *deficit* which our presence in media appears to fill: a falling short which can never be escaped unless we *redefine* everyday life entirely, that is, in accordance with alternative frames of reference. The parallel with Sennett and Cobb's famous account of the hidden injuries of class is here quite precise since the latter involve a sense of lack that requires (yet is never satisfied by) learning whatever it is that those in 'higher' class positions have. Media – or rather our whole way of living with and orienting ourselves to media – similarly induce a sense of lack that requires (but is never satisfied by) inclusion in the world constituted by media. Crucially, that lack affects different social groups differently, precisely because it suggests an offer of *social* recognition, a good that for many reasons is already unequally distributed.[29]

There are many ways of tracking this lack. One way would foreground the battle over the definition of national modernity in Brazil whose powerful media operations (especially TV Globo) create for much of the population a sense of living merely 'at the edge' of modernity. Another would note how in India, also a country of great extremes of wealth and poverty with the world's second most powerful film industry, audiences may feel at considerable distance from the worlds that Bollywood presents to them, as if they were 'written out of the film'. In France, in spite of its strong public media, much of social life is invisible in mainstream media, according to the chief editor of the Bondy Blog set up by Swiss magazine *L'Hebdo* during the Paris 2005 *banlieue* riots: 'I would challenge anybody to find 10% of the topics Bondy Blog covers anywhere in the French media.'[30]

In the UK, I began fifteen years ago to trace this lack in fieldwork that investigated people's stories of their relationship to the media world. One person I spoke to was Debbie,[31] a printing worker then in her mid-twenties, who talked to me about being in the Liverpool Dock area when by chance the then popular TV magazine programme *Richard and Judy* (specifically its weather forecast slot) was being filmed: 'you're thinking, Oh, I wonder if I'll get on telly ... I enjoyed seeing that, thinking, Oh wow! That's on telly! And I'm standing there and ... Oh Mum, quick! Put on the weather! You know I was standing up there.' For Debbie, like many other people, visiting the outside set of the longest-running British TV soap opera *Coronation Street* (then possible: it is now shut to the public) closed the gap between media and ordinary worlds, as least for a moment: 'it's not just somewhere on telly now, it's actually somewhere I've been, I've actually stood there.' Some other visitors to the *Coronation Street* set expressed the desire for media exposure more directly, for example Peter, a catering worker also then in his mid-twenties:

> I approached Granada [the TV production company] ... to be an extra [in *Coronation Street*]. But they won't let me ... I wouldn't mind, just going into the Kabin [a shop in the programme] and ordering a paper or something and then walking out, I don't want to speak or anything. Just once to be on television. On the show. I'd be happy then I think.

Peter interpreted the impact of subsequently going on a TV talk show as a member of the audience in terms of a corresponding transformation: '[I'm] totally different now from the way I used to be ... I was so quiet, I never dreamed of working in the bar ... I'm in the open now, talk to anybody.' These traces of media's hidden injuries fit with Patricia Priest's research with participants in talk shows[32] and give us a useful starting point for making sense of the worlds of celebrity and reality media in a broader way: not just as formats that are economically necessary for media industries, but as *social forms* which offer a sort of recognition through participation.

There are good reasons to take media's hidden injuries seriously. The 'desire to narrate' is, philosopher Adriana Cavarero argues, a fundamental need of human beings, not because we have some underlying authentic self there to express, but because of the singular desire of each embodied consciousness to 'look for the unity of their own identity' in story. For Cavarero, our narratable selves are, as it were, enacted on the outside, through the process of *exchanging* narratives with others.[33] The hidden injury instituted in mediated societies by our distant relation to major narrative institutions (media) is therefore not a trivial one. Every large-scale society in history has been characterized by some such hidden injury, depending on how society's narrative resources have been configured, but this injury is most salient in societies where mediatization is intense.

Attempting to satisfy this implied lack brings people into contact, often conflict, with large institutional processes with a concentrated power over narrative production. There is a real pathos to the stories of people who have gone on television to represent their lives to others and, far from being satisfied, have found themselves directly damaged by the public exposure they have received. Consider a recent account by a participant in the reality series *Castaway* (aired by the BBC in 2000) which took a group of people to the uninhabited island of Taransay in the Outer Hebrides on Britain's north-west coast to live for a year. Leaving aside the many group conflicts the year involved, Ron Copsey's main concern was at the injustice of the process of representation itself, here seen in his judgement of how another was treated:

> An incident on Taransay sticks in my mind. One of the kids stole some sweets from my room and the camerawoman demanded I be interviewed on camera. I refused, explaining that if the programme branded the child a thief, it would have devastating consequences on them. She told me that on becoming a Castaway we'd agreed that everything could be filmed: 'it's contractual,' I was informed. Her lack of concern for the child's welfare astounded me.[34]

There is a price payable for trying to satisfy the lack generated by our divided relations with media, which is to expose the entire flow of our lives to an industrial process of representation which is profoundly 'asymmetric'.[35] When people do this, they encounter the real nature of the media process that was previously masked from them. This sudden denaturalization was something I noted in my early fieldwork with protesters who for the first time in their life were represented in news.[36] Today's desire for celebrity or media exposure is much more complex than the search for objective recognition. Unless we grasp the *constructed* nature of the lack involved – and its basis in the *real* separation inherent to an institutional concentration of symbolic production – we cannot understand how acting on that lack exposes people to new injuries that are far from hidden; indeed, they are endured in full public view.

An innovation in British reality media is to incorporate characters' reactions to their media coverage into the programme itself, as with the 2011 series *The Only Way is Essex* (ITV2), which appears to have been inspired by the media feedback loop into which Jade Goody, controversial star of *Celebrity Big Brother* 2007, emerged.[37] In Box 4.1, we look in more detail at the case of Jade Goody.

Box 4.1 Jade Goody

A moving example of the working through of the hidden injuries of media power was the life-in-media of Jade Goody, a contestant in *Big Brother* (UK, 2002) who was ejected before the end of the show and subjected to a great vilification in the UK tabloid press (Holmes 2004).

Rather than withdrawing from the media machine, Goody went deeper in, succeeding with the help of skilful agents in reinventing herself as a popular celebrity, which led to her selection for *Celebrity Big Brother* in January 2007. Her racist remarks in the programme against a Bollywood celebrity, Shilpa Shetty, led to a huge furore and international political scandal when excerpted footage was circulated among the Indian diaspora via YouTube, generating a storm to which then UK Chancellor Gordon Brown had to respond during an official visit to India. Goody was forced to leave the show.

This public relations disaster led to the withdrawal of the paperback edition of her autobiography and generated a further attempt to rehabilitate her hard-won celebrity via a 'penance' trip to India. Because her main mode of self-presentation was now reality media, Goody appeared in the Indian version of *Big Brother* (*Big Boss*), during which she had to endure being told before large audiences of her diagnosis, at the age of 27, with cervical cancer. At that point, perhaps, there was no way out from her trajectory of increasing public exposure. She endured a very public period of terminal illness, leading to a public funeral in April 2009 for which the same UK politician (by then prime minister Gordon Brown) who had condemned her racism less than two years earlier sent his condolences.

The harshness that results from attempting to satisfy the lack involved in media's hidden injuries was exposed in full view in Jade Goody's life. The price Goody paid, as she put it on the last page of her 2006 autobiography, of 'let[ting] everybody see every single side of [me]' was very high: certainly high enough to raise ethical questions about media's role in daily life, to which we return in chapter 8.

For more detail, see Goody (2006), Holmes (2004), Bennett (2011: 4–5).

Eighty years ago, Walter Benjamin's lamented the loss of the personal storyteller in a world saturated by instant information.[38] More striking today is the prevalence of a model of *self*-narrativization which risks exposing people at some point to the symbolic violence[39] inherent in an industrialized mode of narrating lives (media). In attempting to *be* the story, to live within the 'spaces' generated by the media system, participants in media narratives *lose control* of the capacity to tell what is most close to them: the abstract division that underlies media power's hidden injuries becomes actualized as direct and public pain.

Yet, as part of the same process, large domains of popular culture become *driven* by the need to 'satisfy' the lack in which we are each placed by our position as 'ordinary' members of mediated societies. This lack overlaps with, but is different from, the general conflicts over recognition which characterize contemporary societies. The stratification of broader social recognition means that the desire for media-based recognition is socially stratified too, in Britain not least by class. Through reality media, however, media's hidden injuries generate 'solutions' (what Axel Honneth calls forms of 'organized self-realization')[40] that intersect with wider performative pressures in labour markets and the general rise of competitive individualism.[41]

Digital media as democratization?

But surely, you might argue, all this has been changed by the era of digital media production in which everyone can be a media producer? Indeed, hasn't the explosion of reality media itself transformed the contents of media schedules? What if we really do now see ourselves through the lens of media? Fifteen years ago being an 'ordinary person' in Britain meant, without question, having no experience of the media. One first-time protester, Louise, whom I spoke to in 1996, said: 'we're just ordinary people with no experience of the media or protests or anything'; in the words of another, Rachel, 'television's all exciting and it happens to other people.' Has everything changed now? Some would see Facebook as a hyperreal site where young people experience what Baudrillard called 'the ecstasy of communication';[42] others would say that reality media around the world have changed irrevocably people's understanding of the boundaries around the media process. The general growth of reality media across the world shows no sign of weakening even if, inevitably, some formats (such as the very successful *Big Brother* format, now ended in Britain) are tiring.[43] So what are the long-term consequences of the reality TV phenomenon for the underlying causes of media's hidden injuries?

You might argue that, as more and more people gain the experience of telling their story or performing aspects of their lives on television (still the primary shared medium), media's hidden injuries will, for those people, be cured: for them at least, television will have become something that happens *to us*. But there are plenty of reasons for scepticism. At the crudest level, there is the issue of population size. In a medium-size country (the UK, population 60 million), I do not personally know anyone who has been on reality media, nor has any friend told me they know someone who has. Elsewhere – perhaps in a country such as Norway with population just under 5 million – things may be different. But can the hidden injury of media power ever be satisfied unless the broad conditions that generate it are satisfied? This must require more than an individual appearing in media *once*. The implications of appearing in media are in any case not straightforward. Let me quote again from Debbie and her account of being part of the studio audience for a popular UK daytime talk show *Kilroy*. In recounting this, she dwelt more on the experience of watching a videotape of the programme back home than on being on the programme itself. Watching the tape shocked her:

> I thought, God, that's me, I'm on telly. God, that is so strange [short laugh] ... I couldn't remember sort of like ... being there, it just didn't

seem the same watching it on telly, it was totally different ... Or it's not like telly, it's like a sort of home video that someone's brought round that's done on a camcorder. You think, God, is that really on the telly? Is there millions of people watching it? Don't know, I honestly had to tape over it in the end, because it was making me cringe.

Debbie could not make a credible connection between the two states (being on television and being at home), and started doubting the status of the recording: was it just a piece of '*home* video' (made entirely outside the media world)? The usual gulf between media and ordinary world cannot be casually overcome; it is too deeply embedded in learned attitudes, and in the overall inequality of symbolic resources in society. And this without even considering any directly negative experience of appearing in media, such as the *Castaway* story quoted earlier.

For the growth of reality media to reverse media's hidden injuries would require a much larger transformation than tens of thousands of 'ordinary people' appearing in our television schedules. For media's hidden injuries are constituted not by any *particular* individual's absence from media, but by the whole *configuration* of mediated societies: their basis in regular separation of the spaces, times and cultural worlds of media production from those of media consumption. Reversing this geographical stratification would require an entirely new configuration of media and society. It would require most of us becoming used to being the regular sources of publicly circulated information, or at least to knowing close-to-hand those who are. It would require most of us becoming used to being storytellers in our own name, or at least storytellers represented via mediations that we can imagine influencing (a website we are involved in, a group we are active in, a network we can influence). Even more, it would require most of us becoming used to being entertained at least some of the time by the productions of those outside media institutions. Many would point to YouTube's plethora of amateur videos as the start of such a revolution. Yet, looked at overall, there is no evidence that these revolutionary conditions are generally satisfied in a society such as Britain.

If we think about the formats that have become dominant in British reality media over the past decade and ask whether people have become accustomed, through that form, to being storytellers in their own name, the evidence points mainly the other way. Whether we look at the selection of contestants, the editing process or subsequent interpretations of performance, disputes about power abound. Indeed, over the past two decades the new roles that have stabilized in reality media are not roles for individuals as authorized storytellers, but roles for the *institutional control or filtering of storytelling*. In the UK, for example, such roles include:

- the expert programme host (such as Trinny and Susannah) who judges performance and can demand that contestants accept her advice if they are to have the chance of completing the self-transformation on which the relevant show is predicated;
- the expert commentator, such as the programme psychologist or nutritionist, who judges performance from a distance during the show, without direct interaction; or
- the expert panellist who comments on performance retrospectively, as in *The Apprentice: You're Fired* which follows the main episodes in the UK series of *The Apprentice*.

By contrast, UK *Video Nation* programmes that in the early 1990s *did* create new roles for individual storytellers are a rarity.[44] UK television has been characterized by new forms of pedagogy that use 'ordinary' performance as an exemplary means to communicate to national audiences. Far from a democratization of media, 'ordinary people', in the UK at least, have during the past two decades become the *objects*, not subjects, of television's discourse: we return later to the intersection of this process with wider neoliberalism. Meanwhile, the demand for recognition in reality media seems to intensify, lending plausibility to Alberto Melucci's claim that 'the real domination is today the exclusion from the power of naming.'[45]

The same scepticism is necessary in relation to many other trends that appear to challenge the centralization of symbolic power but fall short of reconfiguring 'ordinary people's' relationship to media: user-generated content, blogs, crowd-sourcing.[46] All of them are interesting developments, but how prominent is such production in the media landscape followed by average individuals? Do any of them amount to a reconfiguration of the symbolic resources available to more than a small number of individuals, outside times of political upheaval? The potential announced by writers such as Clay Shirky of a total reconfiguration of contemporary storytelling is exciting,[47] but the preconditions for that reconfiguration have yet to be adequately specified, let alone realized.

Media and the shaping of public discourse

Our interest in this chapter is media's *hidden* shaping of the social. We began the chapter with how media power induces a sense of lack at an individual level that helps fuel reality media. Let me now turn to broader consequences across social life. I am less interested here in cases of explicit conflict where media directly challenge established power, or present the social in a way obviously at odds with most people's everyday experience. The social impact of media in unpopular totalitarian regimes is obviously based on conflict, and so not hidden; similarly in British TV of the 1950s and early 1960s, 'everyday reality' was patently constructed from the outside. This was a time when Howard Marshall, presenter of *Other People's Homes*, could report of his visit to a Newcastle slum: 'when we travel to strange places, I suppose most of us try to picture what we are going to see ... I know now my imagination totally failed me.'[48] Such class-based *naiveté* is now difficult to imagine, in Britain at least, but media's less explicit, or hidden, influences on the social remain important.

Some refer to media in general as a distorting mirror on the social,[49] but media's hidden influences may be positive. Take the gradual informalization and increased class openness of British TV and radio from the late 1960s onwards. Television and radio, as banal media for representing social life, proved powerful tools, as Scannell noted in his pioneering studies of radio, for extending the domain of 'the merely talkable about',[50] simply through their banal practice of converting other people's everyday life into a social reference point. A specific version of this argument is Josh Gamson's account of US talk shows and their ability to make lives of sexual minorities visible and 'out there': some argue online forms of self-exposure work similarly.[51] Yet, as Gamson's study brings out, the price of such exposure may be high: the confirmation of overall stereotypes and hierarchies around sexual preference, the smuggling in of other standard representations that are ambiguous, if not downright negative, in their effect. Overall, Gamson judges, the outcome of talk shows for sexual minorities was positive. This, however, is a specific and difficult case. Can we reach any conclusions about media's hidden impacts on the social more generally?

Let's take for granted the important literatures on how media reporting produces certain regular agendas or frames for public discourse: in so far as media are concerned to represent the social and its boundaries, media institutions are involved in the definition of 'insiders' and 'outsiders' in social discourse, and perhaps international political discourse also.[52] Let's also acknowledge, but put to one side for the moment, the consequences of increasing disinvestment in media production generally in many countries and the class-based narrowing of entry to media professions that results.[53] For beneath these specific processes are long-term narrative pressures *inherent* to the unequal distribution of symbolic power that are damaging enough to be considered separately among media's potential hidden injuries. Far from disappearing in the digital age, there are signs these pressures are growing.

We noted in reality media the emergence of a *pedagogic authority* for media institutions across many aspects of daily life: clothing, new relationships, marriage, home decoration, cooking, parenting, personal health management, marriage, crime prevention, recovery from unemployment (the list of programmes *seems* endless). This new authority is best understood not as the result of media institutions' intention to claim that authority for themselves in a particular territory. Most of the programmes discussed are, after all, produced not by large media with bold public ambitions, but by small independent companies that exist by selling formats to large broadcasting institutions and networks. On a transnational scale, other complexities apply: in television what Joseph Straubhaar calls 'cultural proximity' plays the main role in influencing the media people consume,[54] but such proximity often operates across a regional television market based on common language or cultural affinity (the Arab world, East Asia) with key 'media capitals' shaping media flows without any simple relationship to national authority.[55] Notwithstanding such complexities, the pedagogic authority of reality media is effective for two reasons. First, it is *necessary*, an unintended effect of media institutions needing both to trade in cheap programme formats and to find reliable ways of sustaining large populations' attention.[56] Second, it carries *legitimacy*, repackaging everyday life as media-certified 'reality' within the wider myth of the mediated centre.

Reality media are an economically effective and socially resonant *figuration* (in Elias's term) which generates narrative formats from the raw material of daily life. Reality formats are different from the long history of the human interest story and advice columns in newspapers[57] because they involve 'ordinary people' *performing* before a large audience. Reality media's pedagogy is driven by narrative concerns, not an educational intent: a regular series of claims that from *this* type of managed process emerges *that* type of outcome for the person who shows *this* sort of skill. Admittedly, the pedagogic expertise involved must itself be performed, which brings risks,[58] but it is no less authoritative for that. Media interests – the simple goal of keeping the 'reality machine' going – dictate that life-situations are found where this pedagogy can be practised without obstruction. As a result, more and more of what is presented to us as 'natural' (as slices of everyday life) takes forms shaped in advance for the exercise of that pedagogy: particular mechanisms of judgement and self-reflection, particular regular forms of self-transformation. Reality media *by default* makes the social in its own image, constricting the languages of social description and exercising a cumulative pressure that is close to a 'definitional power'.[59]

Some narratives are automatically suppressed by this process: for example, any narrative that insists that the processes of daily life are generally *not like* competitive games with easily readable results (*The Apprentice, Changing Rooms*) and readily reversible parts (*Wife Swap*); any narrative that insists that no institution or media outlet has the knowledge or authority to teach us 'how to live'. Some narratives are encouraged: those that treat social reality as easily judged, generating strong emotional responses and clear opportunities for dramatic self-transformation and spectacle.[60] The result is a practice of 'affective domination' (to quote Brenda Weber's impressive study of the US/UK make-over show) that is hardly socially neutral.[61]

As yet, we do not know how much the models and reference points offered by reality media have taken hold in wider social behaviour in particular countries: I return to the possible mechanisms involved at the end of the chapter. Reality media remain, in longer historical perspective, a relatively new figuration. Their long-term fate will depend on the degree to which such ritual forms seem to address the hidden injuries that media power induces and so draw people in on the offer of something like social recognition.

It helps, however, to look beyond the way reality media *writes over* the social world and consider other longer established forms of hidden injury that result from media. Here Bruno Latour's reading (in his iconoclastic account of 'modernity') of the hidden relation between networks and space is very helpful.[62] Once we look at media as 'technological networks' laid out *in* space, then the temptation to adopt a functionalist interpretation of how media relate to social space disappears. As Latour writes: 'technological networks are nets thrown over spaces, and they retain only a few scattered elements of those spaces. They are connected lines, not surfaces. They are by no means comprehensive, global or systematic, even though they embrace surfaces without covering them, and extend a very long way.' Latour understands ideas and information in the same way – 'reason today has more in common with a cable television network than with Platonic ideas.'[63] The aptness of Latour's metaphor reminds us that media are above all spatial – a spatial distribution of ideas and images. This gives new life to the old insight that media systematically over-access the narrative sources that they find are geographically close to them. That media do this particularly with news sources or official political sources has been known for a long time,[64] but it is not usually thought of as an inherent feature of media discourse. However, as the resources available for media production are remorselessly cut, other forms of over-accessing become important: the over-accessing of the public relations efforts of institutional actors who are outside, but close to, the media, or of the 'sources' provided *by media themselves*.[65] Such arguments can be extended when we look at the exclusionary dynamics built into new communication technologies such as GIS (geographic information systems).[66] Media are at best, in Latour's phrase, a net thrown *over* social space from specific anchoring points based in concentrations of symbolic power. We start to see here how the hidden injuries of media power go beyond individual lack and encompass systematic features of how the social world is shaped *for all of us*, making other potential 'socials' 'invisible, unthinkable, unrepresentable'.[67] This phenomenon can be followed through into a number of aspects of contemporary media culture.

Celebrity and crime

Celebrity was considered in chapter 3 from the point of view of ritualization. Celebrity is not a natural phenomenon, even if fame and admiration are features of any large society:[68] celebrity is the overdetermined outcome of populations' attention given to the types of people who are practically close to the media process.

An older diagnosis of celebrities as 'pseudo-people'[69] failed to see that celebrities are also the focus of a huge amount of popular interpretation whose resonance derives precisely from the *real* recognition deficit that is one side of media's hidden injuries. Celebrities therefore cannot be dismissed as 'nothing'. Celebrities are real people who stand in for important aspects of the social domain; they represent what Durkheim calls 'ways of acting [that] have been worked out in common'.[70] But the kernel of truth in those older critiques of celebrity lies in the exclusions inherent to the production of celebrity for which the interpretative richness of popular culture can never compensate. 'Celebrity-heavy' versions of the social world crowd out versions populated by different sorts of collective or representative actor:[71] trade unions, social movements, civil society groups. Political economy is crucial here: celebrity news is cheap to produce, certainly cheaper than sending foreign correspondents to distant wars or political movements.[72] While these are quite separate dynamics, together they reinforce the 'fit' of celebrity culture within today's changing media environment. None of this is to deny celebrity is a tool that specific players can use in social and political conflict towards their own ends (see chapter 6): we are concerned, however, with the general installation of celebrity as a reference point in public discourse.

Another important example is crime. The USA and the UK have, according to the American criminologist David Garland, become 'high crime societies' in the paradoxical sense that they are characterized not by the high incidence of crime but by the high *perception* of crime that results from the high weighting given to crime in media narratives of the social. Crime (with its ready-made official sources, vulnerable and usually ready-to-speak victims, direct link to moral pedagogy) provides a ready-to-hand source of media stories, with certain crimes being 'signal crimes' that offer media 'an index of the state of society and social order'.[73] The argument is not that media invent crime or 'construct' our experience of crime. Rather, media's regular selection of crime stories for prominence has over many decades *'institutionalized* [the] experience' of crime: we have come therefore to experience crime through media as 'close at hand', whether in practice it is close to us or not. In Garland's words, media in the USA have

> provided us with regular, everyday occasions in which to play out our emotions of fear, anger, resentment and fascination that our experience of crime provokes. This institutionalization *increases the salience of crime in everyday life*. It also attunes the public's response ... to the media through which crime is typically represented and the collective representations that these media establish over time.[74]

Government and media, popular and individual discourse become meshed together around a 'consensus' that is disconnected from the factual foundations to which it rhetorically alludes. The resulting 'make-over effect' rigidifies particular types of fact and profile in the social landscape and can be traced in the USA, UK and Holland.[75] Meanwhile, underneath the cosmetic surface alternative narratives (of impoverishment, struggle, de-socialization) are rendered invisible. The issue, then, is not only the familiar spectacularization of the social, but the subtle *de-selection* of what is just in front of us, what Nick Mirzoeff calls a logic of 'anti-spectacle'.[76]

These are hidden injuries *to the social* that flow from the accumulated concentration of symbolic power in media institutions when the media process is left to feed back upon itself. But such injuries cannot be considered in isolation from wider institutional matrices. Does media's overdetermined portrayal of crime in the USA, UK and elsewhere reflect an offensive state strategy to use crime to punish the poor (Loic Wacquant) or a defensive strategy to use crime-related action, through media, to shore up the state's own weakened legitimacy in late modernity (Garland)?[77] Since the neoliberal state is quite plausibly the site both of an exclusionary social policy and a national bureaucracy whose capacity to 'manage' everyday events is deeply reliant on media, the underlying dynamics are difficult to disentangle. We return to neoliberalism in the chapter's conclusion.

The work of search engines

The fabric and scale of the internet throws up even deeper problems of 'injury', as all public knowledge, increasingly, is accessed through the hidden practices of search engines. We discussed in chapter 2 the essential role that search engines now play in any of us finding out about the world. The question of injuries here is complex, since the filtering devices on which search engines themselves rely could not work if the Web's effectively infinite information space were absolutely 'flat': webspace *needs* to be uneven in ways that generate registrable differences if it is to be accessible to human agents at all.[78] The basic topology of the Web (its tendency to build through the accumulation of hubs and nodes with large numbers of links) constrains what we can 'see' even with the help of search engines.[79] Google's Page Rank system for evaluating what search items get ranked above others prefers the pages which have more links to them, so reinforcing a mechanism of 'preferential attachment' that ensures already popular pages become more popular.[80] Some key implications follow. Because searchers tend to spend the least time and effort in reaching a satisfactory outcome from their search (rather than spending significantly more time to get the 'best' outcome),[81] and because the volume of information (and dependence on search engines) increase exponentially, searchers are ever less likely over time to look beyond the first page of their search results.[82] As a result, any 'biases' built into Google's or any other search engine developer's algorithms, unless fully disclosed, have increasing influence on information space as it appears to users.

This has deep consequences for news, for example: not only do many news consumers now rely on search engines, homepages and RSS feeds to filter for them a personalized news,[83] but *journalists themselves* use Google to discover and track stories, and write so that their own content becomes easily searchable. The result, as a leading authority on search engines, Alexander Halavais, notes, is that there are good reasons to expect mass-media logics and search-engine dynamics to reinforce each other over time, without any need for collusion or planning: the more 'googling' becomes one of our key 'windows' on the world, the more difficult it is to see such hidden structural forces and adjust for them in practice.[84] This has implications for the *geographic* balance of 'the world' we experience which, even as it is extended in range, is pre-clustered in striking ways.[85]

There is then a major debate about the politics and ethics of search engines. According to a recent evaluation of public debate in old and new media, 'search engines might actually silence societal debate by giving more space to established actors and institutions'; far from being a space of information freedom, the internet is a market space where different types of information (driven by competing search engines) compete for attention, with all the inequalities that flow from that.[86] Leading legal theorist Lawrence Lessig goes further, arguing that the Web is less 'an architecture of innovation' than 'an architecture of control'. This control derives from multiple factors including the code from which the Web's basic architecture is built and the pre-set constraints on use and adaptation built into devices such as the iPhone that impose proprietory software and interfaces on users. Phone 'apps' represent, arguably, a key area where, as suggested in chapter 2, our experiential world is being reconfigured in a way that benefits major corporate players without those workings being open to view.[87]

If these critics of the internet's evolving architecture are right, we need, as Richard Rogers argues, much more than research on the explicit biases in content choice and presentation of websites and online portals. We also need a 'back-end information politics' that uncovers the forces that shape the hidden battles of sources to become visible in the world that appears to us online.[88] The history of media research provides here a sense of *déjà vu*: 1970s and 1980s work on the 'overdetermination' of professional news sources has now been radicalized to cover the information sources that *any of us* use. Once we take into account the role of marketers (political or commercial) in targeting 'free information' to influence our actions, then the need for a politics of information becomes acute.[89]

Conclusion

In this chapter, we have been concerned directly with media's consequences for the ontology of the social world. For much of the chapter, we have considered the hidden injuries that affect individuals and particular media's consequences for social understanding. We ended with the hidden skewing of 'what is' online, a dynamic that applies in any country. The earlier part of the chapter, however, leaves unresolved an issue of comparative analysis to which I want to return.

Much of this chapter has foregrounded neoliberal democracies such as the UK and USA where late modern media's accidental social pedagogy and the late modern state's media-focused search for legitimacy combine in a strong symbiosis of mutual interdependency between two weak institutional spheres: that symbiosis may sustain the underlying myth of the mediated centre into the foreseeable future. Under those conditions, media present us with a social world which finds its 'solutions' in a constricted politics that, in turn, relies on media for its 'factual' reference points, a social world whose history (and sources of hope) is largely reduced to the history of media's accounts of the social. The German social theorist Niklas Luhmann captures this transformation in a striking metaphor when he argues that media supply society's 'eigenvalues'.[90] In quantum mechanics, 'eigenvalues' are certain properties whose numerical 'value' remains constant, whatever the other transformations that occur to the system in which they are embedded. Through a complex set of pressures, of which reality media are among the most important, some societies risk being set by default to the settings or 'values' of social activity and social fact around which media processes tend to stabilize, given media's own competitive and performative dynamics. The result is unintended, but it has all the rigidity of ideology: an accidental ideology of the social. Could this be one hidden factor in the installation of neoliberal values as default settings in many countries' politics?[91]

But surely, you'll respond, people are capable of thinking otherwise than media propose! Of course they are, and recent studies have shown that they are specifically 'savvy' about the constructedness of reality media.[92] But, as I have emphasized, we are not concerned here with ideology in the sense of a system of false or misguided belief. We are concerned with something more difficult to shift: a patterning of action and production which limits the forms in which the social world gets presented and so narrows the reference points available for everyday talk.

If Paddy Scannell's work on mid-twentieth century UK radio's expansion of the 'merely talkable about' still has force,[93] it must help us grasp a trend in the opposite direction, a contraction of the 'merely talkable about' which limits our expectations of what there is in the social world. So, in Holland for example, talk about celebrity does not necessarily offer evidence of identification with celebrities, still less direct imitation of them, but it does offer evidence of how certain types of behaviour (not others) get legitimated and normalized.[94] Similarly in Britain and the USA, TV make-over shows do not produce a positive ideology of the body, but they do, through their normalizing practice, disable any sense of a 'valid self' which has not been bodily transformed by the 'make-over process'.[95] In such countries, new social norms are being generated, detached from formal social memberships but fine-tuned to the narrative necessities of media production. Aesthetic values (around production quality) and social networking-based recommendation and evaluation are likely to reinforce, not challenge, such entertainment-based norms.[96] No unified social system is needed to underpin the coherence of such norms; its coherence is, in part, delegated to the underlying dynamics of media industries themselves. The result is a new principle of social ontology: media's default power to shape, in Boltanski's evocative phrase, 'how things stand with what is' (ce qu'il en est de ce qui est).

But this is not the only possibility of change. Countries where a new range of media institutions is emerging, capable of challenging government and religious elites, perhaps for the first time effectively (Saudi Arabia, China), offer a very different perspective. Writing of reality media in the Arab world, Marwan Kraidy notes that 'because reality tv claims to present reality, Star Academy posits a normative world,'[97] a world to whose norms you submit by entering its projected reality as an actual or would-be contestant. Where media processes within a transregional industry generate norms at odds with existing maps of the world (for example, conservative religious and political ideologies), the resulting denaturalization transforms entertainment into a zone of unpredictable social creation. This does not rule out the possibility that the norms stabilized in such media will generate hidden injuries over the longer term; it hardly contradicts the dynamics of individual desire and injury focused on media appearance considered earlier in the chapter. Nonetheless, this opening up of public discourse by media forms in areas of intense conflict such as the Middle East deserves our close attention.

A socially oriented media theory must acknowledge both these outcomes. A similar complexity affects media's direct relation to politics, the subject of the next chapter.

5

Network Society, Networked Politics?

'The new electronic infrastructure of the world turns the whole planet into a market place for ideas . . . We are thus witness to a true revolution; power really is moving to the people.'

Walter Wriston[1]

'The [internet] does not fit well with the way people get politically socialized . . . the internet is a form of syntopia – an extension of, but still heavily integrated with, other face-to-face and mediated channels and processes.'

James Katz and Ronald Rice[2]

'Democratization is a dynamic process that always remains incomplete and perpetually runs the risk of reversal – de-democratization.'

Charles Tilly[3]

Theories of societal functioning in the early to mid-twentieth century were based on certain assumptions which are now outdated, wherever we are: assumptions of a single social system, fully integrated social values, and social processes bounded by the borders of nation-states. Contemporary social theory challenges those assumptions.[4] Bruno Latour has questioned the very idea of 'the social' as an object of analysis, proposing 'a sociology of associations' or 'associology'.[5] I have shown, however, in the first four chapters that, starting from *minimal* assumptions about social order – indeed from the explicit starting point that there is pluralism of values, no explanatory 'centre' of society, and no coherent 'centre' to media processes – we can explain many of the *centripetal* pressures in contemporary media and social life. In that sense, aspects of earlier accounts of society can be repaired, although from different premises and under starting conditions that are at least partly now transnational.

But what of the transformative potential that stems from the radically new features of digital media? What if digital media include within themselves the principles of a new social, a new politics? This has been the hope of many writers impressed by the socially distributed nature of 'Web 2.0'. Predictions of new forms of political and social connection, even radical politics, have accompanied previous waves of technological change: for the nineteenth-century European working class, for example, hopes were pinned on the political pamphlet.[6] In the past half century, accounts of the internet have been distorted by what Vincent Mosco sardonically calls the 'digital sublime'.[7] Yet, hype or no hype, we must acknowledge that the internet is potentially a major source of institutional innovation because digital communication practices, just like the newspaper two centuries ago, constitute resources with the force of institutions.[8] The events of the 2011 Arab Spring bring such debates into particular focus.

The possibility that digital media forms and infrastructures themselves constitute the means to build a different *type of* social organization – without the institutional centres taken for granted in the past 200 years – is politically inspiring. But let's remember at the outset two things. First, governments, media, corporations and even many elements in civil society have a vested interest in *avoiding* such fundamental reorganization (a power issue raised already in chapter 1); second, predictions of political and cultural change based on the features of media tend to rely on a rather thin account of social processes. This is not, *pace* Latour, because 'the social' does not exist but because an account of the 'textures' of digitally enabled social life,[9] and its resources of political engagement, remains to be developed. As we will see in the chapter's second half, there are many factors which suggest a less optimistic assessment of digital media's implications for democratic politics. Much depends on which part of the world, and which institutional matrix and cultural context, we are discussing. Understanding those factors will help us see why former Citicorp banker Walter Wriston's technoliberal claim (quoted above) – made *before* the invention of the World Wide Web – remains today as far from fulfilment as ever, and why the caution of the second and third quotes above is necessary.

While there are many competing theories (liberal, republican, deliberative or elitist) of how democracy *should* function, my argument here does not depend on taking a particular position on that issue. At most, I start out from the premise that democratization is good and that, for this purpose, as Sheldon Wolin puts it, 'democracy's idea is based on a culture that encourages members to join in common endeavours ... as the means of taking care of a specific and concrete part of the world and of its life forms.'[10]

The missing social

The internet, because of its basic networked features, has generated new possibilities for political association, mobilization and action. Sara Bentivegna sums up the democratic potentials of the internet as 'interactivity', 'co-presence', 'disintermediation', reduced costs, 'speed' and the lack of boundaries.[11] We can now meet and organize politically with people we don't know and can't see, doing so at great speed, across local, regional and even national boundaries. Some see this as the beginning of a new more conversational, less formal mode of politics;[12] others are more sceptical. On any view, there are new mechanisms of political socialization to investigate.

Three accounts of increasing complexity insist that media's role in society and political culture is changing fundamentally: Henry Jenkins's influential account of 'convergence culture', legal scholar Yochai Benkler's book, *The Wealth of Networks*, and Manuel Castells's recent book, *Communication Power*, which builds on his earlier three-volume work, *The Information Age*.[13]

Henry Jenkins starts out from (indeed, helps to clarify) the key reference point for today's media industries, that is, 'convergence': 'the flow of media across multiple platforms, the cooperation between multiple media industries, and the migratory behavior of media audiences who will go almost anywhere in search of the kinds of entertainment experiences they want.'[14] Jenkins is interested not in the basic change in media delivery systems but in changes in the 'associated protocols' of use.[15] Jenkins's account is usefully based in cultures of media use and what in chapter 2 we called 'media-related practice'. The interoperability of media interfaces – the now taken-for-granted ability, for example, to send a picture, video, weblink, song or text to anyone else – alters the *density* with which media content can circulate and so intensifies media's saturation of social interaction. New media-rich forms of social cooperation are easy in the digital media era and, as Jenkins shows well, media industries – ever more concerned to retain their audiences' loyalty and attention – are keen to stimulate that process: online audience engagement is not only easily trackable, it has become an indispensable industry resource. So a 'convergence culture' exists: certain highly engaged fans making meaning in close proximity to media industries' production and marketing interfaces. Jenkins's book provides many vivid examples of such a culture: for example, online 'spoilers' of the plot of the reality game show *Survivor*.

Jenkins's story matters a lot to the media industries; it also fits well with more emotive, more personally targeted rationales of marketing[16] and has become almost a new orthodoxy, at least within media and cultural studies. But what does it add to our wider understanding of society and politics? Jenkins offers a metaphor as to how we should understand convergence culture: *'right now* our *best* window into convergence culture comes from looking at the experience of the early settlers and first inhabitants.'[17] Certainly, early adopters provide *a* window for the types of practices Jenkins wants to foreground, but why assume that this is also the best window on *wider* convergence culture; or that there is such a thing as a general convergence *culture*? The reason cannot be because these 'early adopters' are demographically typical: as Jenkins acknowledges, they are 'disproportionately white, male, middle-class and college-educated'.[18] Nor can it be because, as fans, they are typical of wider engagement with media. Fan studies have shown that, for any media object, there is a spectrum of engagement and emotional investment, with each of us differently placed along that spectrum, depending on which object we take.[19] Yet Jenkins insists that the fan behaviours he describes are typical of something: of the 'new knowledge culture', increasingly important as other social ties break down; a new 'more democratic mode' of knowledge production that contributes to a more 'participatory form of power'; a new mode of 'creative intelligence'.[20]

What is the evidence for these claims? Perhaps Jenkins's boldest argument for why these slices of 'convergence culture' might matter is that they showcase the convergent skills we are now learning as audience members (voting, circulating, commenting, lobbying and so on), skills that we will, Jenkins claims, be deploying 'for more "serious" purposes, chang[ing] the ways religion, education, law, politics, advertising and even the military operate'.[21] But this is either a truism – all new possibilities of online social collaboration are *available* for adoption in relation to entertainment, political organizing and anywhere else – or it is a very large claim about the political field: what evidence is there to back up that large claim? Most of what Jenkins analyses as convergence culture could be described as consumer politics. Unquestionably, consumer politics has been an important form of political action both today and throughout modern history,[22] but this says nothing about consumer politics' relevance to other forms of politics, for example, contests over labour rights, political representation or the distribution of social and economic resources. The relevance of fan protests to *those* sorts of politics must be justified separately, and Jenkins's example of culture-jamming style activism around the short-lived Howard Dean campaign for the Democratic presidential nomination in 2004 is insubstantial. In addition, Jenkins's notion of 'convergence culture' is modelled exclusively on US practice, and a very particular slice of US life at that. Is there a convergence culture, Aniko Imre asks, in countries such as Eastern Europe where practices of fandom are largely imported and where American cultural forms are generally treated with suspicion?[23] The metaphor of a single 'convergence culture' to define the digital age needs at least to be treated with caution.

Yochai Benkler's important intervention in internet regulation and policy is based on an argument of more general power: that in the digital age the economics of cultural production have everywhere been fundamentally altered. In *The Wealth of Networks*, Benkler writes that:

> the high capital costs that were a prerequisite to gathering, working, and communicating information, knowledge, and culture have now been widely distributed in the society. The entry barrier they posed no longer offers a condensation point for the large organizations that once dominated the information environment. Instead, emerging models of information and cultural production, radically decentralized and based on emergent patterns of cooperation and sharing, but also of simple coordinate existence, are beginning to take on an ever-larger role in how we produce meaning.[24]

As Benkler makes clear, the reversal of the economic concentrations of industrial media production is only partial; forms of non-market 'sharing' and the alternative information infrastructure they enable will, at best, exist *alongside* market-based media structures. But that does not dim Benkler's vision of a completely new model of social storytelling; indeed he argues that 'we have an opportunity to change the way we create and exchange information, knowledge and culture.'[25] Is this, Andrew Chadwick argues, the start of a change in people's opportunities to contribute to larger political processes?[26] Potentially, but we need also to acknowledge some limits to Benkler's analysis.

First, in challenging the conventional economics of information production, Benkler makes key assumptions of his own. An explicit assumption is that '[the cost of] the mechanical means of sensing our environment, processing it, and communicating new information goods ... has drastically declined in computer networks.' This is not the end of the story for Benkler since another key form of capital, 'human communicative capacity', remains scarce if we look only at particular sites, although the internet's distributive capacity overcomes this scarcity where production and distribution tasks can be broken down into modules through what Benkler calls the 'granularity' of cultural action.[27] On a different scale, however, drastic recent changes in news production represent the withdrawal of capital from television newsrooms and press news desks.[28] Indeed, the relevance of Benkler's economic analysis depends on which 'mechanical means of sensing the environment' we are talking about. Benkler's reference to 'computer networks' suggests he mainly has in mind the economic savings in the infrastructure of the information environment, and his detailed examples bear this out.[29] But have the 'sensing' costs of the substantive information packages that people want and need – for example, foreign news or economic news – fallen in the same way? Not obviously. So the relevance of Benkler's account depends on an implicit assumption about shifting *demand* away from the types of supply typical in the last half century towards other types of supply and the assumed positive consequences of this. This is unproven. Think of political news: the demand side of new media's relationship to political information is just as important as the supply side, and much less researched.[30] We don't know yet if demand is reorienting itself to new media sources enabled by the changes in supply. Clay Shirky notes that political or social change requires much more than technological opportunity: there must be the motive for new types of media production and a relevant culture of need. Otherwise, the habits of data-sharing now evolving online will not generate real 'public and civic value'.[31]

Second, Benkler's account does not analyse in any detail people's usage of the new media landscape. An example is his discussion of internet architecture: this draws exclusively on the literature on links between websites[32] and says nothing about how such links might relate (or not) to users following those links. Benkler offers, as a spur to legal and policy reform, a vision of how things *might be*, not an account of how they are likely to be. Yet understanding the terrain of actual habitual use is crucial to analysing how technological change affects everyday culture and politics. A third problem flows from the second. Since Benkler offers no account of actual media use, he must fail also to address the wider constellations of practice and social organization built from, and around, media use. Benkler plausibly argues that the thin everyday context of individual internet use does not matter so much as we might first think. He offers two interesting cases of the 'networked public sphere'.[33] First, he describes an online campaign whereby people angry at Sinclair Broadcasting's blatantly political decision to air an anti-John Kerry documentary, *Stolen Honor*, just a month before the US 2004 presidential election were mobilized to contact local advertisers for Sinclair's local TV stations and persuade them to withdraw their ads, leading to immediate loss of revenue, a hit to Sinclair's share price and, eventually, to Sinclair pulling the programme. Second, he cites a campaign in 2002–3 (in the wake of the intensely controversial presidential election of 2000) against Diebold Electronic Systems, a manufacturer of electronic voting machines used in US elections, a campaign which involved networks of campaigners, often students, successfully protecting leaked or discovered files of incriminating data against Diebold legal threats and leading to Diebold machines being withdrawn in California. Benkler uses these cases to argue that 'the topology of the network allowed rapid emergence of a position, its filtering and synthesis, and its rise to salience. Network topology helped facilitate all these components of the public sphere, rather than undermined them.'[34]

By 'network topology', Benkler means the widespread distribution of computing skills, the quick emergence and coordination online of 'small groups that share common concerns', and mobilization of support from that base. Benkler builds a powerful case that the infrastructure of political protest has changed: the new infrastructural support for 'social production practices' creates *enough* of a context for short-term, interruptive political action, especially at election times when the legitimacy of the whole democratic process is at stake.[35] There is no doubt, as Pierre Rosanvallon argued, that in recent decades the repertoire of 'counter-democracy' has increased, that is, the politics of opposition and rejection: arguably networked publics, working as what William Dutton calls a 'fifth estate', are creating pressure towards new types of political accountability.[36] But what of the social contexts within which new projects of *positive* political action (policy promotion, advocacy, implementation) can emerge and be sustained? We need to know much more about the social and political forms that make such positive political actions possible and meaningful.

This takes us to Manuel Castells's work in communication and social theory. Castells's argument in *Communication Power* is, put simply, that in recent decades the organization of society and politics has changed radically, and from two directions: first, the emergence of *networks* which determine the distribution of resources and provide the fabric that connects people across old nation-state boundaries; second, the construction of *meaning* within those networks because power always needs to be legitimated and culturally translated. The first factor is no doubt important, but what is its relationship to the second? Castells's book rightly avoids a simple optimism or a simple pessimism. The power of networks weakens states, gives vast influence to those who control leading network nodes, and especially those who have power over the switching of context and resources from one node to another, such as Rupert Murdoch; *but* where political resistance itself forms large networks, they can mobilize quickly, interrupt everyday politics and even bring down governments. In the cultural domain, because culture is always open to multiple interpretation and reinterpretation, power is never absolute, *but* power over networks can hugely influence the messages circulated to the general population and how issues are framed, leading to bizarre misperceptions, such as the widespread US belief in the early 2000s that Saddam Hussein had a role in the 9/11 attacks. Castells's network society narrative provides a very useful account of how *spatial* flow (of meanings in media networks and resources in financial and other networks) disrupts national politics in a 'systemic dissociation between communication power and representative power';[37] his analysis of how media and finance networks converge on a global scale is particularly illuminating.

Castells does not claim to offer a comprehensive theory of power, focusing explicitly on political power[38] and spending little time on standard distinctions between types of power. Instead, he offers something more radical: a second-order theory of the forces which sustain societies *as spaces of power* within a wider global order. Building on Beck's deconstruction of national societies as power containers, Castells seeks to 'identify the sociospatial networks of power (local, national, global) that ... configure societies' from the outside. Castells draws on his well-known concept of the 'network society' – 'a social structure constructed around (but not determined by) digital networks of communication' across national borders – to claim that 'global networks' 'structure all societies'.[39] Castells rightly dismisses the notion that societies are 'based on shared values' rather than 'relational power', seeing 'relational power' as based in both 'coercive capacity and communicative resources', thereby introducing a *cultural* element to social structure: this analysis is fully compatible with the argument of chapters 3 and 4,[40] and none of what follows should be read as a rejection of the concept of networks as such.[41]

In spite of this admirable balance, Castells's account generates major uncertainties. First, how exactly does power *over* and *within* networks translate into other forms of power beyond the flow of networks, and vice versa? Castells insists that 'whoever holds power decides what is valuable' and value is generated in networks, while

also insisting on individuals' ability to interpret, use and 'repro-
gramme' the meanings that circulate in networks. While his account
of how news influences people notes the role of everyday context,
showing that people only pay attention 'to news about ... topics that
clearly relate to their lives and experiences', it leaves unresolved the
relative causal weight of context versus networks in explaining social
and political process: clearly, the context of everyday action is not
reducible to the operations of networks or people's positioning
within networks.[42] Second, while global communications networks
disseminate values that cannot be delivered within national political
processes (consider Iran's failed revolution in 2009), what contexts
and resources are needed to sustain political agency *in time*?[43] Why
were the short-term 'communities of practice' mobilized by the
Obama presidential campaign of 2008 not sustained into the battles
of the Obama presidency's first two years?[44]

Third, and more fundamentally, how exactly are societies 'configured' by communication networks? Economic power, military power,
legal authority cannot *simply* be reduced to network operations, even
if they require networks as their means: if, for example, the state's
monopoly of violence remains, as Castells notes, 'decisive', the state
must be more than 'the default network for the proper functioning
of all other [non-communication] power networks'. And then there
are crucial issues of balance: how do we weight the growth of 'mass
self-communication' (online social networks, blogs and the like)
against the constraints (of time and other resources, sheer habit) that
may block many from being permanently active online or orient them
overwhelmingly towards non-political contexts?[45] Jodi Dean argues
such communication is in everyday life coopted into corporate frames,
but even if we find that too pessimistic a generalization, the deeper
hierarchies (including class and gender) that shape political agency
must be considered.[46] What grounds *are* there for believing such
hierarchies are no longer shaping people's judgements about whether
their actions matter? Castells's examples of networked politics (the
2008 Obama presidential campaign, the decades-long growth of
global environmental politics) steer clear of everyday power struggles in the economy (rights in and to work, challenges to corporate
authority). This neglect of labour activism within debates about the
new networked politics matters when labour activism plays such a
vital role in extending democracy in countries such as China, and
when in the USA the supposed carriers of new political culture
(young people) are the least likely to be members of labour or political groups.[47] We need more insight into how non-political forms of

power (economic, legal, social) shape individuals' *own* framings of their opportunities for political action.

The notion of 'society' implicit in the hybrid concept of 'network society' remains metaphorical. Castells tries to invoke a new 'social': 'could it be that the technological and organizational transformation of the network society provides the material and cultural basis for the anarchist utopia of networked self-management *to become a social practice*?'[48]

But the implication is unclear: is the horizontal network equivalent to the social? If so, what exactly qualifies it as a *social* practice? How does it relate to other types of thick social context that we still encounter? Castells also argues that 'how people *think* about the institutions under which they live ... *define*[s] whose power can be exercised and how.'[49] But when Castells gives a detailed example of how we have come to reinterpret power (the growth of politics based on global warming), his gloss is curious: 'We had to reprogram the networks of our minds by reprogramming the networks of our communication environment.'[50] Here, the social (including the social contexts in which media contents are interpreted and put to use) is bypassed altogether, with both social networks and the processes of individual cognition collapsed into a single term: 'programming'. Castells is hardly unaware of this strange evaporation of the social; indeed, he insists in his earlier work that 'people, locales and activities lose their structural meaning' in a network society.[51] In some respects, Castells's reduction of political explanation to a confrontation between 'net' and 'self' has justification in an age of intensely individualized struggles for meaning, where political information is also individually targeted in an age of fragmenting audience and online consumer tracking.[52] Yet he leaves under-theorized the long-term contexts that *sustain* individual action: the individual cannot simply put these together him- or herself. Indeed, as Andrew Barry notes, the network metaphor 'may give little sense of ... the fissures, fractures and gaps that [the network] contains and forms'.[53] A whole set of sociological concepts (agency, social context, class, identity, value) seems to have gone missing, distilled into bland cybernetic metaphor.[54]

This foreshortening of the social is common to all three writers just discussed, and other writers too.[55] It may not be surprising to find Christakis and Fowler (medical academics who are also popular writers on connectivity) operating with a thin account of social life that draws more on biology than sociology, but it is striking when much-fêted critics of capitalism such as Hardt and Negri, while plausibly rejecting the idea of any 'unified social body', go on to invoke a new social whose features remain entirely undefined: 'What we experience [in our postmodern society] is a kind of social flesh, a flesh that is not a body, a flesh that is common, living substance ... The flesh of the multitude is pure potential, an unformed life force, and *in this sense* an element of social being, aimed constantly at the fullness of life.'[56] What is missing here, more drastically than in Castells, is a sense of the specific resources, contexts of action and historical opportunity structures required for sustained political mobilization: in short, 'social institutions'.[57] It is those same social institutions which, against all the transformative hopes surrounding past communication technologies, have ensured that their eventual outcome is to reinforce *existing* networks: the early evidence on the mobile phone and online networks is already headed in the same direction.[58] Reflecting on this, Keith Hampton and his colleagues speculate that the result of today's intensified networks may be information flows that 'again resemble the repressive, inward-looking structure of traditional village life'.[59]

The combination of internet hype and a thin account of social process generates what Evgeny Morozov calls 'the net delusion'.[60] This blocks our understanding of how the internet might contribute to the institutional structures needed for democratization. Without more sociological underpinning, the term 'network' risks becoming empty.[61] At this point, it is useful to draw on a different theorist, the late Charles Tilly, who defined democracy as 'the extent to which the state behaves in conformity to the expressed demands of its citizens' and identified three macro-conditions for the emergence of democratization in practice:

1   the integration of trust networks into public politics;
2   the insulation of public politics from categorical inequality; and
3   the reduction of major non-state power centres' autonomy from public politics.[62]

Focusing on (1) for now (I come back to (2) and (3) later), Tilly's point is not that we need more trust but, more subtly, that trust *networks* need to be integrated into wider social organization and specifically into the bargaining processes of public politics. Such integration does not require people to trust rulers more (often the opposite!) but rather to commit their 'valued enterprises' to the risks inherent in the democratic political process: they need to trust *process* more, accepting processes of 'mutually binding consultation' and the structures of judgement on which they are based.[63] That, in turn, requires a 'legible, visible totality', as Pierre Rosanvallon puts it, in which political action is assumed to take place, and a public where joint issues can be imagined and discussed.[64] This is a key link back to questions of symbolic practice and the ways in which the polity is represented.

Digital media, politics and social transformation

Recall David Easton's classic definition of politics as 'the authoritative allocation of goods, services and values'.[65] The definition is, by itself, too narrow since it does not take into account the possibility of ongoing contests over what counts as authority or the goods required to be allocated. Such contests are not abstract 'metapolitics', but the very stuff of politics. That qualification aside, Easton's definition is a good starting point for considering the conditions of politics in a digital age. Why? Because it identifies one clear dimension that we must always keep in mind: *authority*, from which follows the issue of political legitimacy.

Authority is linked to *evaluation*. If we take as our starting point French sociologists Boltanski and Thévenot's insistence that society is no longer unified by the common values that political sociology once assumed as its reference point,[66] then any transformative politics depends on actually *changing* some or all of the regimes of evaluation dominant in the organization of everyday life. A third key dimension that shapes the preconditions of politics is *framing*: the construction of the 'world' that is addressed and potentially transformed in politics.[67] Media are crucial contributors to all these contextual dimensions of politics. A strength of Castells's account is that it acknowledged these dimensions, but a problem is that network society theory says so little about the routine social domains where authority, evaluation and framing are rooted.[68] How would our account of politics and society in a digital age look if we took more seriously the role of media at this basic social level?

In one short chapter, I cannot offer a complete answer to such questions but, by reviewing the wider literature on digital media and politics, we can identify some key social factors to be incorporated into a fuller account of how digital media are changing politics. My argument will build on chapter 2's account of the complexity of media-related practice and on chapters 3 and 4's account of media's role in representing the social world. I will start by looking at the *who* of politics (what kinds of people or thing now count as political agents?); from there I move to the *what* of politics (what kinds of thing can be political in various modes: deliberation, action, decision?) and the *why* of politics (what larger contexts, or frames, make certain kinds of political agent/action possible or impossible?). We need also to look out for certain systemic side effects of the changing 'who, what and why' of politics, side effects which may shape the paths of political transformation in an age when, as Bruce Bimber notes, democracy itself 'is growing increasingly information-rich and communication-intensive'.[69]

The who and what of politics

The set of political actors has always been much larger than the official list of mainstream political institutions and their representatives. Violence or non-violent physical resistance has been one way of acting politically for those not granted the authority to speak. Such violence – by contrast with the legitimate violence of the state (Max Weber) – lies at the edges of legitimate politics: it is often not given the name of politics and called 'terrorism'. Arguments about the new digital politics are not primarily concerned with politics by violence. They concentrate instead on the claim that the digital age enables new types of legitimate political action, that is, new voices recognized as agents of political discourse.

The internet's topology, as Benkler calls it, has made possible new kinds of legitimate political actor. First there are *network actors*: distributed agents of political coordination that link multiple persons, groups and positions across space, without the need for a physical headquarters or a bounded social membership. These became increasingly prominent in the 1990s with the rise of international online networks in the NGO sector and insurgent actors such as the Zapatistas. Since the mobilization against the World Trade Organization summit at Seattle in 1999, a whole new tradition of networked political organization has emerged.[70] The internet creates new possibilities for non-formal political actors to form and build communities of practice online, challenging the boundaries of national politics. Well-designed campaign websites, such as Tescopoly.org in the UK, can name a terrain of contest, provide networking resources for local campaigns and sustain a reference point for future mobilization and long-term action; in so doing, they extend the repertoire of political action and the scale on which political action is routinely possible and, in the process, the range of political actors. National political actors such as the UK mothers' lobby group Mumsnet quickly grew online from a small local group based on an immediate community of interest.[71]

Why is this? First, the possibility of anonymous action at a distance reduces some of the barriers to action such as fear of reprisal or embarrassment. More generally, the internet as a 'network of networks' enables networked actors to link easily with each other to form larger networks. The conviviality of the internet – the ease with which informal connections can be created without reference to differences that might, face to face, constitute boundaries – is also important.[72] Lauren Langman claims the internet requires us to rethink the nature of 'political mobilization' entirely; certainly, we can't know what shape a political agent must take any more: the networked possibilities are too diverse.[73] The most radical extrapolation is legal scholar Beth Noveck's proposal that networked groups should be legally and politically recognized by governments as responsible entities capable of contributing to political decision-making. The Icelandic government's 2011 online consultation about a new constitution is perhaps the first practical application of Noveck's proposals, albeit in a country of 320,000 people.[74]

Then there are new kinds of *individual political actor*: no longer just the charismatic party or strike leader, or the authorized commentator on mainstream politics (journalists), or the silent party member or demonstrator, but the individual – without any initial store of political authority – who can suddenly acquire status as a significant political actor by acting online.

Blogging is one prominent phenomenon that has extended the scope of political 'commentary' (our term from chapter 2) but its specific implications are uncertain. Are individual bloggers genuinely new voices in politics? Some no doubt are: for example the Chinese factory workers who used their blogs on Blogcn.com to promote a strike against their distant Japanese employers, or the citizens who uploaded pictures and text to their blogs to publicize a mass protest against a proposed chemical plant in Xiamen in 2007. It may also not be coincidence that one person killed by Egyptian police in the January/February 2011 uprising was a blogger, Khaled Said. But many other bloggers are members of old-style political elites whose voices are simply now archived in print rather than heard in political backrooms.[75]

International comparison greatly complicates the analysis. In South Korea, there were in 2005 already over 15 million blogs and the related but separate citizen journalism community *OhMyNews* appeared genuinely to represent the broader population, whose self-mobilization is credited with swinging a presidential election at the last minute. In China, the number of active blog users (updating within six months) was reported as 145 million at the end of 2009:

Yin Haiqing argues that a playful relationship to mainstream political ideology prevails in the Chinese blogosphere, but this playful humour and commentary is politically challenging to an authoritarian government. In Iran, explicit contention against mainstream politics is central to a very lively individual *and group* blogosphere of considerable political significance within an authoritarian regime. In the USA and UK, the situation is complex. The percentage of US 18- to 29-year-olds blogging had *fallen* by 2009 to 15 per cent while, in the fractured space of US politics, clusters of bloggers are able to stake out and then defend new bits of political territory online, often going far beyond what formal parties or organizations can say but dragging the political spectrum towards them, if picked up by mainstream media; under these conditions, professional politicians (Sarah Palin) can for a while renounce their official status and 'return' to being a mere individual via their blogs, Facebook pages and so on. In the UK's more centred and weakly contested politics, the leading political bloggers, such as Guido Fawkes and Ian Dale, are in one sense just digital revamps of the commentators who have always hovered on the margins of political influence, but, when their stories are picked up regularly by mainstream media and political actors, they acquire some authority (Guido Fawkes's revelations against UK foreign secretary William Hague in September 2010 being one example).[76] This looks more like a reinforcement of, rather than a counter-logic to, mainstream journalism.[77]

When we consider the wider internet, the pressures towards hierarchization among individual political actors are huge. Web visibility is no accident. It depends on being picked up by search engines (which prioritize on the basis of numbers of incoming links), on personal recommendations by Web users,[78] or (increasingly) being embedded in systemic recommendations such as phone apps. The first two at least are not so different from older ways of entrenching political power, especially when those recommending certain blogs are mainstream media actors.[79] The much hyped democratic potential of Twitter is also significantly concentrated: the Web Ecology Project found that 59% of tweeters around the failed Iranian revolution of 2009 just tweeted once and the top 10% of users generated 65% of tweets.[80]

We must, however, acknowledge the growth of *latent political actors*. In Britain, for example, there are people blogging or tweeting about aspects of institutional life, not yet acknowledged as contributing to political debate but able, given a suitable political context, to emerge from the shadows: blogging doctors, teachers, policemen/women, army officers, magistrates, employees of big pharmaceutical companies, all forbidden from speaking in public about their conditions of work.[81] This domain of latent individual politics is new and only possible through the networked space of the Web. When coordinated across international borders (Wikileaks), such action may disrupt the old rule that information and trade flows tend to be closely tied together:[82] this has wider political consequences, and not necessarily good ones.[83] The result is a new *reserve* of political action.

So let's grant that the spectrum of political action has expanded in an age of 'information abundance', enabling what Bruce Bimber calls 'postbureaucratic forms of politics'. But it is not enough to identify new political actors: we also need to understand conditions whereby their actions are articulated into longer 'chains' and become recognized as part of the 'what' of politics. Mainstream political bloggers, just outside political parties, who become regular media sources, are articulated in this way, but most bloggers are not. For sure, new online networks have become visible in global politics, but with what sustained effect? Civic talk often occurs in detachment from the practice of power, while the sheer difficulty of converting an online presence into presence and legitimacy beyond a small circle makes Matthew Hindman's sobering assessment of blogs – 'the new *elite* media' – difficult to deny in countries that are working democracies. We should remember that a lot of small-scale democratic 'subactivism' lacks bridges whereby it can be linked to 'policymaking . . . in formal institutional spheres'.[84]

In principle, however, separate publics can be linked together easily online, generating 'a public of publics' around specific issues or a political crisis.[85] Let's consider some examples. Anti-globalization networks in Europe, North America and elsewhere have been a striking addition to the set of manifest, not just latent, political actors over the past decade. But how much have their actions influenced mainstream political agendas or the broader citizenry's understanding of politics? If we leave aside the work of network actors quite close to mainstream agendas (NGOs), western political agendas have, arguably, changed very little in the past two decades in spite of an undoubted extension in the range of political actors: indeed a neoliberal policy agenda has remained largely constant during that period.[86] The explanation may lie in the dimensions identified earlier: authority, evaluation, framing. Regardless of the expansion of political actors, political change requires changes in the distribution of political *authority*, which in turn must be grounded in transformations of dominant regimes of *evaluation*, which in turn depends on how the space where society's concerns and political needs get defined is itself *framed*.[87] This requires alliances across the divides of gender, age, ethnicity and class. It also, as a recent study of Indonesian politics brings out, requires the sustaining of *physical* spaces where such political agency can be visible. The difficulty of such transformations reduces the chances of even the most resourceful new political actors to wield wider political influence. Jeffrey Juris's excellent study of the anti-globalization movement brings out the resulting frustrations for those new actors. New political actors *may* emerge online: think of the US Tea Party movement. But the Tea Party had only 67,000 members (in 2010) and two crucial advantages: its campaigning worked with, not against, the grain of dominant regimes of evaluation in US society (pro-market, anti-state, pro-local action), and it benefited from rich corporate supporters.[88]

The Tea Party case foregrounds an important issue: the same forces that have transformed the basic resources of political agency (and so extended the cast list of politics) benefit *all* political institutions, including established actors. The implications of information abundance for institutional political actors are certainly complex. As Andrew Chadwick notes, 'the internet . . . offers political elites many opportunities to intensify and diversify the ways in which they sustain themselves in positions of power.'[89] But institutions must also now assume that anyone who deals with them (whether employee, customer or contractor) can blog, that leaking is easy (just press the send button on an email) and that most people have a motive to blog or leak some of the time. As a result, institutions become *porous* in new ways, while media institutions are keen to dominate new sources of news and find new ways of diverting fickle audience attention.[90] At first glance, institutional porosity might seem good for democracy, exposing established institutional authority, increasing scope for contestatory politics all round. But remember that the very same porosity affects *political* institutions as well, including the state and its agencies: in Britain, leaks of Home Office errors (lost laptops brimming with confidential data); in the USA, the circulation of soldiers' photographs of the Abu Ghraib prison's torture practice. It may be in the interests of some institutions dependent on resources from the state (for example, the police) to have such information circulating in the public domain. This increased institutional porosity therefore *may* generate new forms of individual political agency, but again the consequences of such agency always require specific analysis that draw on other dynamics: in the Abu Ghraib case, as Bennett and colleagues point out, the US press, operating on a quasi-war footing, managed to neutralize the consequences by framing the images as 'abuse', not 'torture'.[91]

In any case, individual acts of disruption tell us little about democratization for the long term. What are the chances of creating new political *institutions* with sufficient authority to transform regimes of evaluation and challenge the framing of political space? I suggest they are small: if well-established political institutions' possibilities of 'sustained performance across events and issues' becomes more difficult,[92] how much more difficult is it to establish new political institutions with the authority required for sustained programmes of radical policy action? In an age of routinized political scandal, all political authority becomes more unstable and attempts to generate new forms of political authority doubly so.

To sum up, there are clear new opportunities for collaborative social and political production online;[93] indeed the boundaries and dynamics of the 'public sphere' in Jürgen Habermas's term have been transformed as the networking of the public sphere has shifted from a slow process of institutional referral to a rapid feedback loop between multiple nodes that sometimes can move with alarming speed or, as it is put in China, like 'fire' (*huo*).[94] Possibilities of transformative political action are silently weighted towards short-term disruptive interventions and away from long-term positive projects.

The changing conditions of political engagement (the 'why' of politics)

Too many accounts of politics concentrate on institutions and neglect the level of individuals, that is, the political orientation and skills of citizens. This level is crucial to understanding whether people have *reasons* to act politically. The increasing fragility of institutional political agency has implications for the engagement of citizens who are *not yet* political agents. As Lance Bennett notes, introducing a recent study of young people's 'civic life online', we need to acknowledge a broad range of 'pathways to political engagement'. But we must also note political engagement's deep basis in contexts of empowerment or disempowerment: 'most young people simply do not believe that following and learning about various issues will translate into the power to help decide them': in this context, it remains striking that less than 50 per cent of those aged under 50 in Britain regard themselves as certain to vote in the next general election, although that figure has recently risen for the overall UK population. Apparently 'interactive' sites contribute little, for example, to young people's sense of engagement if those same young people 'do not believe' that their contributions 'are being listened to'.[95] This gap between the promise of political socialization and the reality of political (non)-participation matters. Digital media may not change this. Meanwhile traditional media remain much more important than often allowed: in the 2010 British general election, for example, television debates were universally acknowledged to be opinion-turning events, even if commentary on social networking sites amplified their effects, at least for younger and new voters.[96]

Take first the 'supply' side of political engagement. Let's put to one side any assumption that the interactivity of today's information interfaces is *itself* the same as engagement: it is not mere 'transactional' interactivity we are concerned with here but genuine possibilities of collaborative action.[97] Recall Pierre Rosanvallon's point that the implications of today's politics involve *more and more* incitements to participate in various forms of 'counter-politics' – 'the people as watchdogs, the people as veto-wielders, and the people as judges' – but *fewer and fewer* incitements to participate in forms of 'ordinary democracy', that is, sustained political action in favour of explicit political goals. It is not just that negative coalitions are easier to organize than positive coalitions.[98] Rosanvallon is concerned with a shift in the balance of incentives and disincentives that structure from below the landscape of political possibilities: although he doesn't emphasize this, *media* are crucial enablers and amplifiers of this shift. Media help negative action gather force, gain attention and generate extreme pressure on institutional actors. As regards positive political action, media destabilize the agents of constructive politics (whether established or new), framing challenges to the normal domain of 'the political' as dangerous or violent, and shortening the timescale in which new regimes of evaluation can publicly be built. The digital media landscape intensifies this asymmetry.

Turning to the 'demand' side of political engagement, what are the conditions under which today's infrastructural incitements to individual action can be converted into sustained political action? Mostly, it is large actors who dominate how the world's events are framed through their influences over the networks of media production and dissemination.[99] All the increased resources on which mass *self-*communication depends generate increased *promotional* resources also in the hands of corporations and other large actors,[100] affecting the landscape in which 'mere' individual political action is judged. The hugely increased incitements to discourse – by *anyone* – create a supersaturated environment of media *consumption* from which individuals are even less likely to select a particular theme for attention and engagement. As Danilo Zolo pointed out two decades ago, the premium on all forms of attention increases, which means that the likelihood of specifically political attention is reduced: it follows that the likelihood of positive rather than negative attention to politics is even lower. Yes, if we all stopped watching TV, we would have more time to follow the welter of political communication available online, but will that 'cognitive surplus' be enough in an age when the flow of information and opinion is effectively infinite? In an era of post-bureaucratic politics, inherited loyalties and 'interest-based political affiliation' may count for less than short-term 'event-based' loyalties, with media institutions having a vested interest in pushing the latter. Meanwhile, older patterns of citizen duty are destabilized by institutional change, leading to a sharp divide between social and civic dimensions of everyday life, particularly for young people.[101]

It is particularly important to follow the evidence, not media hype, about how people are actually using digital media. In a rich study of Argentinian news production and audiences, Pablo Boczkowski shows that a vast majority of the new audience read no blogs or online commentary and barely do more than glance at the headlines on their homepage, leaving news links unclicked.[102] Meanwhile in Denmark, a country with very high internet penetration and political efficacy, only very small numbers participate in political debate online or use social networking sites to act politically.[103] Access to the internet in itself is not enough: as Matthew Prior notes from the USA, 'people who enjoy watching entertainment more than news *and* have access to cable TV and the internet are *less knowledgeable and less likely to vote* than any other group of people.'[104] This is, in part, because there is often in the USA no regular 'civic environment' that provides a meaningful context for constructive political action (the Tea Party's negative politics being a paradoxical counter-example); it is also because of the ease of clicking *past* political knowledge on the way to online entertainment.[105]

Any strategy of transformative politics – that is, any attempt to co-ordinate new forms of discourse and action that work to transform the structures of everyday life – must also challenge the media-enhanced orders that saturate *everyday* action. Think of the increase in workplace surveillance now taken down to the smallest category of action; the ability to link such surveillance can be linked to anticipatory narratives ('targets','missions','personal goals') that organize employees' working and wider lives. The imperatives of the surveillance-saturated work environment get translated into a social, leisure and consumption environment of *co-veillance*,[106] which reproduces the pressures to generate stories, 'leaks', revelations and scandals. Mutual monitoring has always been part of social life. However, digital media support forms of mutual monitoring that are fast, extensive and increasingly continuous with institutional surveillance. Meanwhile, the intense mobility of a networked life, as Boltanski and Chiapello argue, reduces the *social* resources from which alternative values can be built and sustained collectively.[107] The constraint on transformative politics that Marx identified in 'the dull compulsion of economic life'[108] has now acquired a social and cultural dimension: what we might call *the dull compulsion of media-saturated life.*

So, on the one hand, the possibilities of *potential* political action are now greater and better resourced than in the pre-digital age. This change, because it does not depend on individual access to the new technologies, extends beyond rich countries. Websites, mobile phones, social networking sites and Twitter are now contributing to the texture of political action across the world: from the Philippines to Iran in the last decade, from Tunisia to UK Uncut this decade.[109] Yet, for reasons that are connected, *long-term* strategies of positive politics and new political institution-building are more constrained. A huge amount of 'noise' in today's augmented media environment fills in the gaps of the news cycle just as old style media did.[110] More subtly, the taking of mutual monitoring and social judgement that have always constrained people from the risks of positive politics (persuading others to change how they live) are reinforced. Networking more – and more effectively – does not stop the 'spiral of silence' against political non-conformism from turning.[111] It is this double movement – an inflation of 'counter-democracy' and reinforced constraints against 'ordinary democracy' – that is likely to shape political innovation for the foreseeable future.[112] What does it matter, against this backdrop, if mainstream *news* is being made more participatory?[113]

What are the implications of this analysis for democratization? Let's return to Tilly's three conditions of democratization. In the digital media age, Tilly's third condition (*the reduction of the autonomy of non-state power centres from public politics*) is partly enhanced. All institutions become more porous and open to media scrutiny and scandal, and so it becomes increasingly difficult for *any* institutional power centre to insulate itself from public politics: some networks (for example criminal networks) may do so, but only by not becoming public. The status of Tilly's second condition (*the openness of public politics to participants from any social category*) is unclear since it depends on the degree to which dominant regimes of evaluation already entrench categorical inequality. In some locations (where gender inequality drastically restricts entry into politics), media spectacle may provide openings for challenges to old regimes of evaluation.[114] Elsewhere, as we saw in chapter 4, the balance may be in the opposite direction. Tilly's first condition (*the integration of trust networks into public politics*) is unlikely to be enhanced in the digital media age because the increasing information saturation of politics means that there are fewer reasons to trust the institutions which underpin processes of binding consultation, and growing reasons for people to withdraw their trust from such processes. Meanwhile, more and more levels of political decision-making are pulled beyond the spaces where, until now, some democratic process existed.[115]

The potential for new democratization is at best ambiguous and partial, whereas digital media's potential to contribute towards *de*-democratization (a weakening in existing democracies' institutional infrastructure) is multiple and continuous. Then consider the continuing pressures in mainstream media towards a narrowing of political positions that political economy has long noted.[116] We must beware of celebrating 'the technical fact of communication itself . . . as an inherent good',[117] without forgetting that communication forms by themselves will not be enough to build and sustain entirely new forms of public politics.

New routes to public politics

It very much depends, however, where you stand. The constraints on a 'new politics' must, at the very least, be understood alongside the hopes. Politics are nothing without hope. Philip Howard's bleak vision of a 'thin polity' whose 'immense total supply of information is only sparingly shared among citizens' is compelling for the USA (and the UK),[118] but not for the exceptional conditions of political mobilization in the contemporary Arab world (with its particular demographics, long history of neocolonialism and authoritarianism, and increasing poverty) or indeed for China where a large and generally young mass of 'netizens' are increasingly vocal and coordinated in using digital platforms to challenge and shame government.[119] Sustained political mobilization and transformation can only ever emerge through shared perceptions of intense need: perceived gaps between available and necessary resources that are intense enough that they require coordinated action. But, in times of growing global economic and social crisis when the UN's Food and Agricultural Organization warns of increasing food riots,[120] such needs may well be emerging. Local pressures towards politicization will often be played out live on a global media stage.

Digital media offer a new infrastructure for public media and public politics, what Jeremy Gilbert calls an 'alternative media infrastructure':[121] what might a democratizing media 'infrastructure' look like? As we saw, Yochai Benkler identified the removal of key economic (and practical) obstacles to non-institutional cultural production but said too little about the dynamics of information demand. When political need exists (creating new demands for information, coordination, problem solving and mobilization), then out of media-related practice may emerge not just new sources of news and mobilization but *a new type of media user* who demands comment and information from a social pool extending far beyond institutions.[122] Such media users may become part of the media infrastructure not only through demands on other producers but through acts of 'search-enabling', 'showing', 'archiving' (see chapter 2): showing images of resistance or, as in Seoul's October 2011 mayoral elections, just voting; exchanging stories of injustice; collectively building toolkits for resistance and media archives for common use; or simply communicating across borders the experience of common struggle.[123] The revolutions (successful or halted) of the 2011 Arab Spring offer case studies of these possibilities and their limits. Social networking platforms enable, without doubt, a new *iconography* of popular politics and a new stage in the unfolding history of technology's implication in political form, extending Walter Benjamin's vision of political culture in modernity as based on reception 'in a state of distraction'.[124] Perhaps they even generated, on occasion, a *counter-myth* of the mediated centre, working against existing state/media relations. This is suggested by the idea of 'Facebook youth' that much popular and journalistic discourse saw as a key factor in the Arab Spring. An image on Twitter of a man holding a placard that reads in Arabic 'thank you Egypt's Facebook youth. Standing steadfast, we shall not leave' was perhaps a token of this possibility, but the actual role of social networking in the Arab insurrections has probably been exaggerated.[125]

Could these developments inspire political mobilization in multiple societies whose audiences all share the same basic tools for social networking? To some degree, such a transnational public sphere is already being enacted but in ways completely at odds with the capacities of existing political institutions to respond:[126] in the developing 2011 financial crisis, new social movements in Spain and Greece (*Indignados* in Spain, *Aganaktismenoi* in Greece) have emerged that echo the repertoires of the Arab Spring. But the crucial factor here is need, that is, the *demand* for politics that stems from despair. We wait to see if such pressures emerge in Britain: the riots of August 2011 may be an early warning sign. Need is the main driver of political engagement,[127] and media infrastructures, however dynamic, cannot themselves create political need. A sociology of media and politics must recognize the multiple forces of *inertia* that ordinarily (outside special conditions of need) make change difficult. New 'communities of discourse' (in Robert Wuthnow's resonant phrase) can emerge and be sustained, and digital media will play a role in that process, but *only* through multiple intersecting pressures and opportunities. 'Network society' theory does not identify the thick contexts of social interaction that long-term communities of discourse require. It remains at this stage very difficult to predict the internet's impact on international politics over the long term.[128]

It is important therefore to keep distinct: first, the emergence of new forms of popular politics (as seen in the Arab world in early 2011); second, a long-term change in the conditions of elite politics (the strength and loyalty of the armed forces to each Arab regime remains a crucial variable); third, the emergence of an entirely new political process; and finally, a move towards a greater democratization. Optimistic early readings of the Arab Spring, for example, tended to blur the first and third, while ignoring the second and fourth.[129]

I asked at the start of chapter: what notion of the social is at stake in understanding digital media's consequences for new politics? Not one that is limited to the boundaries of the nation-state: many of the resources now needed for political change are information or social capital distributed across many countries. Not one that assumes the priority of the face-to-face encounter: impossible now, when so many of our face-to-face encounters are staged, relayed, reinterpreted or bypassed online and radical new social imaginaries have been inspired by online networks.[130] We need an understanding of the social that is 'thick' enough to register the pressure of people's daily battles over resources (basic material needs, but also battles over the organization of space, time and recognition).[131] Those battles can never be reduced to networked flows *between* places, because they only condense *as* needs, *as* inequalities, in local contexts of agency. In those local contexts, further inequalities are condensed: the 'local' may, following Latour, have folded into it many resources that work on multiple scales, but that does not cancel out important inequalities in the political resources available to particular groups of situated agents. It is only from challenges to these *layered* inequalities that real possibilities of political agency emerge. Scale still matters in politics: and media institutions, digital or otherwise, remain crucial in the production of scale and so key shapers still of the possibilities of political agency.

In this chapter, we have refocused general questions about digital media platforms' consequences for politics in terms of digital media's likely consequences for situated political agency. In doing so, we have uncovered a mass of competing dynamics and a central contradiction: between increased stimuli to political contention and mistrust, and increased constraints on positive political construction. We will uncover other uncomfortable paradoxes in later chapters.

6

Media and the Transformation of Capital and Authority

If everything is mediated and, as Sonia Livingstone puts it, media 'reshap[e] relations not just among media organizations and their publics but among all social institutions – government, commerce, family, church, and so forth',[1] what are the consequences for the space of the social? The relationship media/society cannot be conceived in a linear way. Media do not have discrete 'effects' on society: for 'society' itself merely points to a whole mass of interconnecting and overlapping processes, many of which are now dependent on, or saturated with, media. I use the term 'the space of the social' not primarily in a geographical sense but to refer to the *underlying possibilities* of social organization. As in the last three chapters, questions of national differences will quickly emerge.

A crucial concept here will be that of 'field'. In his work on fields from the 1970s and 1980s, Pierre Bourdieu had theorized the plurality of social space and value. Boltanski's critiques of Bourdieu's treatment of value and social power (see chapter 1) are no reason to abandon Bourdieu's analysis of society as comprising many more or less discrete fields of competition for resources or 'capital'. Early in his career Bourdieu defined 'capital' in Marxist terms as 'accumulated labour which, when appropriated on a private, i.e. exclusive, basis by agents or groups of agents, enables them to appropriate social energy in the form of reified or living labour'.[2] By the time we reach Bourdieu's later work, 'capital' has become a more flexible concept, covering a range of possible resources. Going beyond Marx, Bourdieu distinguishes a number of fundamental types of capital (economic, social, cultural, symbolic) that work in all fields.[3] We can draw on Bourdieu's concepts of field and capital to develop our investigation of how media processes have consequences for social resources and larger forms of organization.

It is by considering media's role in particular fields of practice that we may start to make sense of Mark Fishman's apparently exaggerated claim that 'the world is bureaucratically organized for journalists.'[4] We will also get a better understanding of the significance in wider power relations of global media formats, such as *Pop Idol* and the UK show *Jamie's School Dinners*.

The mediatization debate

Two main terms have been used, historically, to point to media's general effects on social organization: 'mediatization' and 'mediation'. These terms have separate histories, which reflect different national traditions of media research. Broadly speaking, *mediatization* has been the prevalent term in Germanic- and Scandinavian-speaking countries, and *mediation* in English- and Spanish-speaking countries, although interestingly 'mediatization' is slipping into everyday Spanish usage where the phrase 'una persona mediatizada' has become equivalent to the colloquial English term 'media-savvy'.[5] But in an internationalizing field linguistic convenience must be considered at the global level.[6] Since the term 'mediation' has many meanings other than that just given (from the act of something being shown in media, to the intermediary role that money and transport, for example, play in society), there is a clear advantage in agreeing on a more distinctive term for use in media sociology. 'Mediatization' has emerged as that term,[7] and I will adopt it here. This takes us back to the debates about media's general impacts that we touched upon in chapter 3 in relation to Baudrillard: interestingly, Baudrillard himself was an early user of the term 'mediatization'.[8]

The real debate is not about terminology, but about the type of explanation at which we are aiming. Two things are generally agreed: first, that media influence now extends to 'all the spheres of society and social life'[9]; second, that, because of this pervasiveness, new types of causal complexity emerge and it is exactly these complexities that we are trying to specify. As Knut Lundby points out, there is considerable overlap between the starting points of enquiries into 'mediatization' and 'mediation'.[10] Roger Silverstone, who advocated the term 'mediation', summarized the basic complexity of media's social effects in these terms: 'processes of communication change the social and cultural environments that support them as well as the relationships that participants, both individual and institutional, have to that environment and to each other.'[11] What matters is how we grasp that complexity. For Silverstone, it was best understood as an open-ended dialectic that resists further systematization; many other scholars (indeed now the majority) have insisted on saying more specific things about how such causal complexity works, and its consequences for the way that the social is organized. It is at this more specific level where the difficulties begin.

One way of systematizing our understanding of what media do in and to the social world has been the idea that media spread the *formats* required for media performance. Pioneers of this approach were David Altheide and Robert Snow. In the late 1970s and early 1980s,[12] they offered a novel approach to media power, arguing that it derives not simply from institutional resources but from the way everyone in society interrelates with media. Seeing media as the new 'collective consciousness', they found the mechanism of this growing influence in the adoption of a 'media logic' across everyday life: 'media are powerful', they wrote 'because people have adopted a media logic.' Altheide and Snow's idea of media logic was based not in any evidence of systematic patterning of the social, but in their claims about 'the role and influence of the form and logic of major media in our lives', through 'the diffusion of media formats and perspectives into other areas of life'.[13] This emphasis on media formats was offered in contrast to earlier sociology of experience, whether Goffman's notion of the 'frames' through which we orient ourselves to the world or Simmel's notion of social forms as the constant patterns that underlie social relationships.[14] What Altheide and Snow had in mind was a rather more arbitrary *grafting* of media formats *onto* specific contexts and forms of social action.

In chapters 3 and 4, we showed that media constructions of 'reality' work in the social through the embedding in practice of specific organizing *categories*, a process which needs to be traced in multiple domains. Altheide and Snow, by contrast, tended to assert that the effect of 'mediation' (as they called it) had *already* taken place and was now pervasive.[15] They tended to blur a number of different 'logics': actual media presentation formats which may be adopted for specific purposes; the wider evaluation of media's authority and importance; people's changing definition of what is real; and desires for that media reality.[16] The basis of this diagnosis of social change in social ontology remained unclear.

If we try to explain media's social effects through a single 'media logic', various problems arise. First, do all media have a logic? Is it the same logic and, if not, what is the common 'logic' that unites their logics into an overall 'media logic' (a problem that becomes more acute with media proliferation)? Second, when media change over time (as they are doing intensively at present), do they acquire a wholly new media logic, or does something remain constant? Third, even if we *can* tie down our notion of media logic, as Altheide and Snow do, to media formats, and show *they* are pervasive in everyday life, does that capture enough of how media influence the social?

These problems persist in more recent work that retains the idea there is a media logic which, through its singularity, focuses a wider process of 'mediatization'. Thus, a leading theorist of mediatization, Stij Hjarvard, at one point[17] defines it as 'the process whereby society to an increasing degree is submitted to, or becomes dependent on, the media and their logic'.[18] But it is very difficult to see a single logic which would explain the range of general effects to which mediatization theorists claim to point. Further uncertainties arise when we look at the types of process that different theorists bundle together under the term 'mediatization'. While some still see mediatization in the sense primarily of a 'format', others use 'mediatization' to refer to 'the whole of [the] processes that eventually shape and frame media content' (surely broader?), or even two new factors: the extension of human capacities and the structural organization of social life.[19]

There is also a deeper problem with most approaches to mediatization: a lack of specificity about how they understand social ontology. On what basis do we believe that the social world is *liable* to be transformed by media materials so easily, or at least so directly? Are we to imagine the whole of social space as prey to the same media logic which spreads out without resistance or adaptation? Such claims would be fundamentally at odds with a number of important sociological approaches. To name just three: Pierre Bourdieu's field theory which insists that the space of the social is not unitary but differentiated into multiple fields of competition; Boltanski and Thévenot's insistence on value-plurality in the social world; and Norbert Elias's account of social order built up through emergent solutions to complex problems of interdependency.[20] For multiple reasons, then, it is problematic to equate mediatization with a single logic originating in media and working seamlessly across every part of social space.

How to avoid this problem? The clearest solution is provided by Friedrich Krotz. Krotz sees mediatization not as a specific process but as 'a meta-process that is grounded in the modification of communication as the basic practice of how people construct the social and cultural world'. Krotz is not concerned with whether a 'logic' is transferred from media to other social processes but more generally with 'the communicational practices associated with the media'. He identifies mediatization with a structural shift comparable to globalization and individualization: that is, the increasing involvement of media in all spheres of life so that 'media in the long run increasingly become relevant for the social construction of everyday life, society, and culture as a whole.'[21] This approach allows for 'mediatization' to encompass different types of process across different sites. As Krotz makes clear, mediatization is an overarching concept, not identifiable with any single logic operating at a specific level and indeed open to multiple such logics (if 'logic' is the right word); on this interpretation, mediatization as a term is perfectly compatible with field theory which insists upon paying attention to the 'logics' or workings of specific fields. A few years ago, I attached the term 'mediation' to a similar understanding of media's influence on social order.[22]

Mediatization, in this sense, points to the *changed dimensionality of the social world* in a media age. Through the concept of mediatization, we acknowledge media as an *irreducible* dimension of all social processes. Let's leave to one side the debate about whether mediatization can be traced back to medieval times or before, or is best understood as exclusively a modern phenomenon.[23] What matters more is how we can trace mediatization operating in different types of social process. We could explore this process by process: Elizabeth Bird, for example, looks at how non-media rituals such as weddings are increasingly filled with, and framed through, media content and media scripts.[24] Instead, because it will take us further in thinking about media's *wider* effects on social organization, I want to consider mediatization through the lens of field theory.

Media, capital and authority

Suppose we repeat our initial question – what are media's general consequences for the space of the social? – but from the starting point of Bourdieu's field theory. Bourdieu insists that we cannot analyse sociological processes without first relating them to what goes on in specific fields of practice where particular forms of capital are at stake. Bourdieu's field concept is a highly sophisticated response to the processes of *differentiation* in modernity: it is also a flexible response since Bourdieu readily acknowledges that fields are emergent phenomena and the concept should only be used if it helps us grasp the order in what particular types of people do. The best-known examples of Bourdieu's field theory in action concern non-media fields: cultural production, especially the literary field, art, politics.[25]

Over the past decade, new work has emerged on journalism as a specific field,[26] and the specific relations between the journalistic field and other fields such as medicine and economics:[27] most recently, the role of competition over symbolic capital has been investigated within the new field of online publication.[28] Some proponents of field theory might want to ignore the mediatization debate entirely on the basis that it looks for an understanding of 'media power' where it cannot be found – at the level of society as a whole rather than in the specific operations of the media field and its interrelations with other specific fields. But such a stand-off would be unhelpful.

Field theory and media's general consequences

Bourdieu himself, in his work on symbolic power completed well before he developed his field theory, showed considerable interest in the role of symbolic institutions in producing belief right across social space as a whole. Bourdieu's concern was with the church, not media. In an early essay, he suggests that some concentrations of symbolic power are so great that they dominate the whole social landscape; as a result, they seem so natural that they are misrecognized, and their underlying arbitrariness becomes difficult to see. In this way, symbolic power moves from being a merely local power (the power to construct this statement, or make this work of art) to being a general power, what Bourdieu once called a 'power of constructing [social] reality'.[29] On this strong definition (compare chapter 3), symbolic power legitimates key categories with both cognitive and social force and is defined 'in the very structure of the field in which belief is produced and reproduced'.[30] Two decades later, Bourdieu recalled this in general claims about television's symbolic weight which seem to have no anchoring in field theory. Consider this remark from *On Television and Journalism*: 'one thing leads to another, and, ultimately television, which claims to record reality, creates it instead. We are getting closer and closer to the point where the social world is primarily described – and in a sense prescribed – [*décrit–prescrit*] by television'.[31] This classic Durkheimian point would not be out of place in Altheide and Snow's writings.

A similar urge to understand media's general consequences for social space is found in work by Bourdieu's followers in field research. Patrick Champagne analyses the media's impacts on the field of contemporary politics: the journalistic field, he suggests, has a relationship with the political field so close that Champagne is tempted to refer to it as 'a journalistic-political field' or 'space'. That relationship, argues Champagne, has transformed the definition of politics in damaging ways. By a 'circular logic', both journalists and politicians 'react' to a version of public opinion which they have largely constructed, through the framing of questions for opinion polls, through the reported reactions to those polls' results and through the influence of journalists' accounts of politics.[32] I return later to the idea that politics, more than other fields, is marked by something like a media-related 'logic'. But how exactly do representations made by actors in *one* field come to have such influence on the actions and thoughts of actors in *another* field (the problem of 'cross-field effects')?[33]

Champagne here introduces the notion of 'media capital' to capture people's relative ability to influence journalistic events.[34] Either we understand Champagne to be claiming that media capital is a new basic form of capital like economic capital that applies *anywhere* (a claim he never makes as such), or we can try and fit his statement within field theory's basic assumptions, which is difficult: where is media capital acquired and exercised? In the media field or in the (political, medical, academic, etc.) field where the agent in question primarily acts? Perhaps the point of the hybrid term 'journalistic-political field' is that such questions don't matter, but, if we were to repeat this move in explaining *all* non-media fields and their relation to media, the result would be to fuse all fields into a single 'journalistic-cultural field' or to generate a whole parallel set of hybrid 'journalistic-specialist' fields (medical, political and so on) each with its own version of media capital. Either way, the field model's differentiation of the specific dynamics of particular fields would have been undermined. To be clear, the idea that many fields now depend for their operations on a media-*related* form of capital is important and plausible. The problem is how to fit this insight within conventional field theory. A potential solution comes from applying the model of Bourdieu's late work on the state.[35]

Media meta-capital and Pop Idol

Bourdieu takes over and extends Weber's notion of the state, conceptualizing the state as a monopoly of not just legitimate physical, but also legitimate *symbolic*, violence.[36] What is the resulting power that the state exercises over the rest of social space?

Bourdieu is interested in the state's pre-eminence over social definitions, for example, of legal and educational status[37]: this influence works not in one field only, but across *all* fields via the 'field of power'.[38] The concept of 'field of power' is rather undeveloped in Bourdieu.[39] The 'field of power' is the space above and beyond specific fields where the forces that vie for influence over the inter-relations *between* fields operate: the state is its main reference point. This space is not therefore best understood as a 'field' in Bourdieu's normal sense. Rather, it is a general space where the state exercises influence over the interrelations between all specific fields and so over the operation of social space itself. The state is 'the site of struggles, whose stake is the setting of the rules that govern the different social games (fields) and in particular, the rules of reproduction of those games'. More precisely, the state influences the 'exchange rate' between the fundamental types of capital at stake in each individual field (for example, economic versus cultural capital).[40] Presumably, this can include influence over what counts as 'symbolic capital' in each particular field.[41] This power of the state is, crucially, not derived from the workings of any specific field but superimposed upon them.

What if media institutions have a similar type of influence over what counts as capital in particular fields? This would be a form of 'meta-capital' through which *media* exercise power over other forms of power. It would operate only at the macro-institutional level (the level of meta-process, or 'mediatization' in Krotz's sense), and so would be quite distinct from, although linked to, media-related capital at work in specific fields. The idea would be that *the greater the whole media sector's wider meta-capital, the more likely the salience of media-related capital in any particular field.*[42] Let me emphasize once more that this implies not a simple 'media constructivism' but a realism about the materially based processes of construction that help build a social world around 'the myth of the mediated centre': indeed, the theory of media meta-capital allows us to explain more precisely *how* the myth of the mediated centre is installed and sustained across a large and highly differentiated social space.

The broad concept of media meta-capital also gives clearer theoretical shape to Bourdieu's own most interesting insights about the media. When Bourdieu discusses the increasing pressure of television on, say, the academic field,[43] he notes the obvious economic dimension (a large television audience means more books sold) but suggests that television exerts also an indirect pressure by distorting the symbolic capital properly at stake in the academic field, creating a new group of academics whose symbolic capital within the academic field rests partly on television appearances. Why suppose this shift occurs in just one field? On the contrary, it is plausibly occurring across a whole range of specialist production fields, so that we need an overarching concept to capture its consequences: '*meta*-capital'. In this way, we can address also media's influences on aspects of social life that *are not field-focused*, for example, within the general domain of media and cultural consumption, as already discussed in chapters 3 and 4.[44]

The concept of media meta-capital is also quite consistent with Bourdieu's fundamental point that capital is only *realized* by agents in specific forms in specific fields. The symbolic capital among chefs that derives from doing a successful television cookery series is *not* necessarily convertible into symbolic capital in a very different field, such as the academic field; this is because the former need involve few, if any, of the specific attributes valued *by media* in representatives of the latter. But this does not make the work of media across fields any less significant; nor does it rule out the possibility that media-based symbolic capital developed in one field can, under certain conditions, be directly exchanged for symbolic capital in another field. So in Britain recently a well-known television gardener (Alan Titchmarsh) became a popular novelist in the early 2000s: particular media domains (for example, the business-based 'reality' programme, such as *The Apprentice* and *Dragon's Den*) become sites where PR companies, politicians and business people can work together for wider promotional advantages.[45] When the media intensively cover an area of life (for example, gardening or cooking), they alter the internal workings of that sub-field and increase the ambit of media meta-capital across the social terrain. Indeed, this is one important way in which, over time, media institutions have come to benefit from a truly dominant concentration of symbolic power (in the strong sense).

Here, the specific principles of field theory/mediatization converge with the more general influences analysed in chapter 3's account of media rituals. I understand media meta-capital to extend beyond media's direct influence over capital to include a more indirect influence that works through the media's legitimation of influential *representations of*, and *categories for*, understanding the social world.[46]

Let's explore this via the example of the internationally adopted *Pop Idol/American Idol* format. If we think about its consequences in the social domain – for the time being, concentrating on the UK and US versions – it must involve more than people copying the *Pop Idol* format and its rhythms and styles in everyday life (Altheide and Snow's 'media logic' approach). First, we could look at how the authority within the show of Simon Cowell (the judge of *X-Factor, American Idol* and *Britain's Got Talent*, one of the best-paid performers in global television) is based in his capital within the broad media and creative industries field.[47] But we can't stop there; the very idea that a television show is a plausible way of judging singing talent derives from media's growing meta-capital, that is, the growing influence of media institutions over what counts as symbolic capital in many specific areas of competition. Third, and also consistent with the media meta-capital concept, the culture of support and legitimacy around the format derives from media representations and categories that circulate generally in social space within and beyond specific fields of competition and become available as reference points in everyday desires, arguments and proofs (in Boltanski and Thévenot's term). Media institutions' ability to consecrate value in a field such as popular music is naturalized through ritual formats such as *American Idol*. But the key causal mechanism in all of this is not the format itself but *the conferring and confirming of authority and category membership enacted within the format,* an enactment whose possibility depends partly on the media-related capital of its performers and partly on more general processes of categorization and the overall dynamic of media meta-capital.

What are the implications of this example for how we understand mediatization? It shows that mediatization *can* work in a very tight, almost 'logic'-like way if, as in the popular music industry, the interdependencies with the broader media production field are intense.[48] But other less 'logic'-like outcomes remain possible. In many fields other than popular music, where interdependencies with the media field are less direct, more subtle forms of mutual influence are possible. We will explore these multiple possibilities shortly for the cases of politics, education, religion and art.

Combining mediatization and field theory creates new opportunities for international comparative research. Comparing how mediatization works in different countries requires taking into account their huge international variations in institutional and field organization:[49] simply comparing media formats as they are adapted in different countries is insufficient. Some larger questions must remain unresolved at this early stage of comparative research into mediatization: under what conditions will the influence of media over symbolic capital in more and more fields lead to the increasing *convertibility* of media-related symbolic capital across social space as a whole, generating a new form of prestige or capital (truly called 'media capital')?[50] How should we understand the impact of media meta-capital on the state? The state (and the specific fields of practice within the state which generate policy) is certainly subject to media's meta-capital via the latter's operations within the political field and, in turn, politicians' executive influence over the state. But what deeper implications does this have for political authority in different countries?

There are well-known cases where political authority gets fused with media-based prestige (celebrity politicians from Ronald Reagan onwards), but it is much less clear whether this is a universal trend, or the specific outcome of local interdependencies. This links to a more fundamental uncertainty: how do economic (business), political (state) and symbolic (media) influences over the field of power – perhaps we should call *all of them* meta-capital – interpenetrate?[51] Through unstructured competition, or through a hierarchy of some sort?[52] While this larger question must remain unresolved, some interesting possibilities emerge from considering how mediatization works within different fields.

Media and the fields of politics, education, religion and art

'In our modern system of civilization, celebrity (no matter of what kind) is the lever that will move anything': so wrote the nineteenth-century English novelist Wilkie Collins in *The Moonstone*, one of the first crime novels.[53] This perceptive comment anticipates the very general role that celebrity would come to play in power relations in many countries, while grasping that this power works through the exercise of influence. 'Levers' of influence are inherently particular, even if the relevance of celebrity as prestige is general. If we translate Collins's insight into the language of the last section, celebrities are people who have acquired large amounts of media-related capital through their appearance in media which, under specific conditions, is available for use in a number of specific fields. The influence that comes from such media capital is limited, of course, by the terms which govern the currency of such media-related capital itself: negative exposure reduces the quantity of that capital, while making it more difficult to use in specific cases. Thus, when in late 2009 the golfer Tiger Woods's reputation was damaged by revelations of his extra-marital affairs, not only was his general media-related capital severely reduced (so that for a while he avoided any appearances in media) but certain uses of his broader symbolic capital in specific fields became impossible: so Andersen Consulting advertisements, which had traded on his general character, were pulled, while in sport there were fears that his image could no longer be used to promote golf's case to become a new Olympic sport.[54]

Scandal has become endemic to public life, not because people are gossiping more but (compare chapter 5) because the reputation of public figures increasingly depends on their symbolic (and particularly media-related) capital, that is, on the types of positive claims that can be made about them in media,[55] and on the leverage which the expectation of such positive coverage generates. This, too, is part of the increasing reach of media meta-capital across social space.

It is time now to follow such processes into particular fields. This will confirm that mediatization can rarely, if ever, amount to a single media-based logic but also bring out interesting differences.

The mediatization of politics

'Media democracy' is the term that German political scientist Thomas Meyer uses to capture the situation where 'the media have acquired a decisive role in the political process, above all in shaping public opinion and decision-making on political issues.'[56] The mediatization of politics is an intensely researched area. It is arguably the clearest example of a sector where *something like* a 'media logic' is at work: in the day-to-day operations of policy generation, policy implementation and public deliberation.[57] Historian Eric Hobsbawm puts the paradox sharply: 'as the [twentieth] century ended, it became evident that the media were a more important component of the political process than parties and electoral systems and likely to remain so . . . however . . . they were in no sense a means of democratic government'.[58] A 'media logic' in contemporary politics, if it exists, must cover many things: the time-cycles of politics and news,[59] the influences of media institutions over what counts as political news and policy; and more broadly, the construction of what politics *is*, the ontology of politics.

For clarity, let's limit the term 'media logic' to cover the multiple ways in which media outputs become a primary aim of political action.[60] Such a usage would seem to capture the ineluctable *force* that media have in contemporary politics, and for all actors at whatever level of politics, from incumbent presidents to local political challengers to NGOs building influence from outside formal party systems. As Richard Rogers notes in his study of Dutch NGOs' media practice, however radical their leanings, 'commercial press coverage' remains for them 'demonstrable evidence of worth'; media, then, in Boltanski and Thévenot's terms, are at the core of one contemporary 'logic of justification'.[61] But this does not mean the outcomes of this 'media logic' are simple: if all political actors are driven by this logic, then any large-scale political strategy becomes unstable, always liable to interruption by *other* actors with a similar strategy. Nor are the workings of field theory simple in the political case. If we take the concept of 'media capital' (or as I would prefer, media-*related* capital), it is clear that politicians gain capital in the political field ultimately through the quality of their media coverage, even if the instrumental uses and sources of media-related capital take many forms.[62]

It is worth stopping for a moment to ask why the interrelations between media and politics should be so intense. The reason goes back to the nature of communication. If mediatization is a process involving the modification of communication,[63] then it is clear that politics' mediatization involves the transformation of political actors' principal means of communication. In the medieval era, the scarcity of information and lack of modern media meant that the ruler directed his or her information work principally at what was *not* known, travelling incessantly to gather information and support in person. In the early twentieth century, Weber noted the links between modern communication and the speeding up of political decision-making, with implications for bureaucratic structure. Timothy Cook's study of US government in the late twentieth century brings out a more thoroughgoing saturation of politics by media when 'every branch of government is more preoccupied with, and spends more resources on, the news media today than it did 40 years ago.'[64] In the early twenty-first century, rulers, governments and politicians must deal with an incessant deluge of information and events from all directions, but with the special challenge that they must be not mere consumers of information but actors upon events: this creates massive challenges for bureaucratic process, political authority, institutional memory and individual politicians' ability to reflect on, and cope with, their jobs.[65]

If we recall once more Easton's definition of politics as the *authoritative* allocation of goods, then politics is acutely dependent on the changing means of communication-at-a-distance with large populations. Citizens' scarce attention must be competed for primarily through media. Politicians' battles to sustain their authority are closely entangled with wider contests over the myth of the mediated centre. On the face of it, this promises a more open politics with increasing numbers of actors having a stake in the very framing of politics: wider, and more open, contests for political visibility through media must surely, in some sense, be democratizing but, when we look closely, things are not so simple.

First, the digital media age, just as the age of print before it,[66] has quite radical consequences for political authority. Stories, the raw material of media coverage, can come from almost anywhere and certainly from a much wider range than the list of official political sources: for example blogs and tweets by specialist commentators or general media personalities. Stories may gain authority through simple repetition: any internet user, by re-forwarding a link, can contribute to that authority. What Jayson Harsin calls 'rumour bombs' characterize the political landscape, compelling established political actors to react and so give the rumours further legitimacy.[67] Meanwhile, unofficial commentators (for example, the expanding range of extreme right-wing commentators in the USA) may acquire new media capital through their role in regularly 'sourcing' or 'endorsing' particular types of story. But, as noted above, it is not only personal authority but also media's broader representations that are involved in the workings of media meta-capital. Since a story can come from anywhere, media institutions' ability to generate stories (and so enhance their own media-related capital) increases. Media meta-capital – media's general influence over the terms and reference points of political, social and cultural debate[68] – is increased because of the expanded space in which news gets generated. When media themselves increasingly report on how politicians are seeking, even failing, to influence media coverage of their actions (so-called 'spin'), then the inflationary cycle is complete.[69]

Digital media therefore broaden the stage on which politics is played out.[70] But this expansion of potential news sources – within a resulting accelerated news cycle – puts an even greater premium on political actors' ability to manage news: this is the second main implication of the growth of media meta-capital in the political field. The necessity for a media strategy, and the requirement to submit to something like a 'media logic', affects all political actors from traditional parties to protest groups to humanitarian NGOs.[71] Political actors are differentiated in terms of their relative power to influence news production. Justus Uitermark and Amy-Jane Gielen's study of a controversy in an Amsterdam neighbourhood over a major new mosque is illuminating.[72] The balance of media capital between local mosque spokespersons (in a catchment area inhabited by poor migrants) and local government representatives was highly unequal. This Dutch study provides rich evidence of how media meta-capital works down to the most local level of politics. The background was the intense tensions between the majority Dutch population and the Muslim minority following the murder of Theo Van Gogh in November 2005. A year later, the chair of the neighbourhood government knew the wider (mainly white Dutch) national audience that media coverage of his battle over the local mosque would give him:

> You can think, 'It's just a neighbourhood' . . . [but] there are phenomena on all kinds of levels: the family, the street, education, health, the city, the world – and all that comes together in this one neighbourhood.

So if you want to be a player in that game, you have to use the media ... The media wants a story and we have a story. We give the story.[73]

The result, he suggested, was a local 'government [that necessarily] orients itself towards the outside'.[74] All local actors' strategies were (in Uitermark and Gielen's words) 'guided or motivated by their actual or anticipated representations in the media'.[75] It is more than group memory, therefore, that perpetuates the tensions of older media controversies. Events that have previously figured in national media go on being reference points for *media* professionals: any new local incident with potential relevance to such reference points gets drawn *by virtue of that fact alone* into the potential sphere of politics. This gives advantages to political agents, such as the neighbourhood government chair, who can use effectively their potential link to national media narratives. It also gives ruling politicians a new tool of government, since media provide ready 'evidence' of the poor performance that governments seeks to manage and punish: we will see an application of this later in the UK education field, but it is equally important in authoritarian market-states such as China where Miao Di notes that the CCTV programme Focus (*Jiaodian Fantan*) has in the 2000s been used by the central government as a tool for identifying and then regulating otherwise obscured problems in local government.[76] Yet, as another recent Dutch study shows, counter-voices can strike back through forms of participatory journalism.[77] More generally, those with *automatic* capital in media narratives, such as celebrities, have a privileged role in such local narratives: think of celebrities in humanitarian appeals and celebrity-led diplomacy.[78] Some argue it is precisely such general media 'personalities' (not specialist policy-makers) who have the best chance of connecting with audiences now disenchanted with the formal political process.[79]

A third consequence of media's growing influence over the capital at stake in the political field is that *spectacle* becomes ever more central to the organization of politics. This links back to the practice of 'showing', discussed in chapter 2. Spectacle's role in politics is an old story, but its salience increases as media performance becomes increasingly the exclusive sphere where political authority is acquired and sustained. By the same token, politics and social life become prey to tactics of *counter-spectacle*: sad examples are the sensational school killings planned by lone school pupils to gain media attention. Daniel Dayan suggests a new definition of terrorist events as 'expressive events which would not exist without a certain form of publicity', a signifying act 'to whose weight and rhythm media are indispensable'. We cannot explain the increased premium on spectacular violence simply through the spread of standard media formats because violent media spectacle often works by *defeating* expectation, by disrupting media schedules, rather than through imitation of media formats.[80] A wider process of mediatization is at stake.

Is there anything in the political field that amounts to a media logic? There are three possibilities. The *first* is that the space of political values is reshaped – we might say flattened – through all political actors' shared evaluation of actions which result in positive media coverage. This requires all political actors to shape their actions towards outcomes that can be 'read' positively somewhere within mainstream media. Actions unlikely to be read positively by mainstream media become difficult to pursue, difficult even to formulate. Neoliberal politics in many countries is connected to such a flattening of political values; it connects with the increasing salience of entertainment values in politics (chapter 4) and the overall constraints on political engagement (chapter 5). A *second* possible media logic is the way the practical energies of political actors converge, in large part, around the problems of reacting to, and attempting to control, media inputs and media outcomes.[81] Christopher Foster's account of working under Tony Blair and John Major (Blair's predecessor as UK prime minister) is vivid: 'We no longer had . . . the time or the capability to be thorough enough to explain *to ourselves*, to Parliament and the public just what we were attempting, and therefore to make reasonably sure what was practical and would work.'[82] This is not a matter of value, so much as a practical shift in what politicians now do every day. Such practical shifts have a logic-like quality since they go beyond what individual actors can reflect upon and change. The *third* possibility is politics' unavoidable entanglement in ongoing contests over the myth of the mediated centre. Large political actors *must* be concerned with the maintenance of their hold on citizen attention; so too are corporate advertisers and media corporations. This tethers political institutions of all sorts to the practical demands of the media sphere.

At the level of practical values and action-logics, politics is a field where media's influence is intense, but we have identified various distinct forms that this takes. It would be misleading to portray all this as a *single* media logic, still less to expect a linear outcome for the political field as a whole. In a field of complex competition, such linear consequences are impossible.

Mediatization in education, religion and art

How does mediatization, and the spread of media meta-capital, operate outside politics? The diverse cases of education, religion and art have not much been considered from this perspective and so these thoughts will be speculative. But they illustrate the range of circumstances that the media meta-capital concept can illuminate.

Education was an area on which Bourdieu's work focused in the 1970s and was the first area where his concepts were extensively applied. We would not expect the influence of media on the education field to be as direct as in the political field: education's main aim is not to communicate with, and represent, the national population (as with politics) and so education is not dependent on mass- or distance-media for its basic communicative practice. On the face of it, there is no reason to expect that basic 'education logic' will converge with 'media logic' in the way political logic arguably does. However, wider neoliberal pressures have led some governments in the 1990s and 2000s – for example, the UK and Australia – to treat the school sector as one area where the transitions to market logic can be stimulated and managed. Education *policy* has therefore been the entry point for sociologists of education in those countries to consider media's effects on education as a field. Early studies noted the role of media pressures both in shaping basic government policy and in shaping the conflictual space where policy was debated by schools, teachers and government.[83] The transnational pressures behind neoliberal doctrines of marketization demand a reading of Bourdieu's field model and of mediatization research that takes them beyond their initial national setting.[84] Policy transitions also raise the question of 'cross-field effects' which is, as we saw, difficult for field theory, yet central if we are to understand policy macro-structures such as neoliberalism.[85] Can media's relationship to education be understood as a cross-field effect and particularly one that is illuminated by the concept of media meta-capital?[86]

There are a number of different types of media impact on education to be disentangled. Let us leave aside the role of presentational formats in teaching practice itself: the spread of basic 'media' formats, such as PowerPoint, in schools will not tell us anything distinctive about the way power is organized in education because such formats are almost universal in business too (they can just as easily be seen as the spread of a *business* logic in education, not a media logic). Another possibility would be to look at the role of IT and data management systems in school management, and such research is currently under way in Germany,[87] but that would take us into broader issues of institutional management. More relevant to an understanding of *media institutions'* relationship to the educational field is the interface between media and education that arises because governments use *media coverage* to develop, promote and monitor education policy, as noted in the research by sociologists of education just mentioned.

Such media-based effects do not involve the importation of a media logic to education; rather, mainstream national media emerge as a *space* or forum which governments use to judge and motivate educators, invite media to judge government performance (through the imposition of targets) and encourage media to showcase for judgement the exemplary cases that targets, and their related inspection regime, throw up. This is not so different from the practice of political 'showing' that we saw in the last section. Educators, in turn, may choose to respond to government or media attacks on aspects of their performance but only by exposing their whole practice to further, indeed continuous, media inspection. The result is an intensely politicized and mediatized educational field in a country such as England[88] where two types of intersecting meta-capital shape and constrain actors in that field: *the state*'s meta-capital as stipulator of educational policy (criteria and targets of success, wider goals) and *media*'s meta-capital as the arbiter of 'facts', within an intensely political struggle over the future of the education field. Both government and educators become required to 'orient [themselves] to the outside', borrowing the phrase of the Dutch local government official quoted earlier. Whether this is good for education is a matter of intense controversy, but it certainly involves a deep embedding of media pressures and media-related capital into the daily practice of education, and so goes far beyond the adoption of information technologies within the mechanics of teaching.

There is a deeper issue here about authority. Education and media converge around issues of pedagogic authority. Schools and media both teach, but in different ways: indeed the 'cultural pedagogy' of popular media is a well-established area of research.[89] Particularly interesting are cases where media celebrities use media to advocate how schools should be run. In 2004, Channel 4 showed a high-profile programme, *Jamie's School Dinners*, which challenged food quality in state schools in Britain. The programmes showed how more nutritious food could be produced on small budgets. The programme/campaign had some political impact, as a reality television format designed to enact a different 'reality' for Britain's schools and then to argue for its implementation. This example of direct media pedagogy, aimed at educators, administrators and budget-holders, illustrates that the symbolic authority on which schools rely can be challenged by the media-related capital derived from celebrity culture.

How do these themes play out in the case of *religion*? An increasing number of researchers see media as a key dynamic in shaping not merely how religion is represented, but the very practices and beliefs that today count as 'religious'.[90] Both religious and media institutions draw on a very general form of symbolic power to represent the world:[91] that is why many scholars, but surely too simply, have claimed that media in the twentieth century became the 'new religion'.[92] In principle, we could see religion's ability to describe the world and consecrate important types of authority as a distinctive type of meta-capital to set alongside that of the state and the media, but the plausibility of this varies between which countries. In some countries with very strong and authoritative religious institutions – Iran, the Philippines, perhaps the USA – this is plausible: while, in a few countries (Tibet), religious authority is in direct conflict over the constitution of the state. But, even in Iran, religious institutions are themselves increasingly reliant on media to represent their actions and aims, and increasingly vulnerable to media-based scandal, while the Catholic church, with all its global reach and power, showed itself both vulnerable to media scandal and capable of taking control of the media agenda before and during the Pope's visit to UK in 2010.

Religious institutions' ability to use media to enhance attention to, and awareness of, ritual events is well documented and flows directly from media's general reserves of symbolic power.[93] It is unclear yet whether prestige in the religious field routinely intersects with media capital so that the latter *automatically* increases the former,[94] but there are clear cases of charismatic religious leaders whose symbolic capital encompasses both media prowess and spiritual qualities, from US televangelists (Billy Graham, Benny Himm) to Islamic preachers (Yusuf Al-Qaradawi, Chérif Ousmane Haidara). Indeed, building one's own media channel or media distribution facility is a critical tool in building alternative religious authority. Blogging is increasingly a general tool for reflecting publicly on one's spirituality.[95] Indeed, religion and entertainment's shared occupation of many of the same media is a key factor in transforming religious discourse.[96] As a result, the sources of religious authority are now contested and, possibly, misrecognized.[97] We will come back to the issue of authority more generally in a moment: for more background on Ansar Dine, Chérif Ousmane Haidara's movement in Muslim North Africa, see Box 6.1.

Box 6.1 The Ansar Dine Movement in Mali

Ansar Dine is an Islamic movement in Mali, central Africa, that illustrates well the importance of media in contemporary religious transformation but also the complexity of the wider processes in which mediatization is embedded. The account here relies on the analysis of anthropologist Dorothea Schulz (2006).

Ansar Dine is the movement of the charismatic Islamic leader Chérif Ousmane Haidara. Ansar Dine is the Bamanakan (Southern Mali lingua franca) translation of the Arabic *Ansar al-Din*, meaning 'the supporters of the religion'. Founded in the mid-1980s, it attracted initially urban lower-middle classes but latterly has drawn support also in rural areas. The broad context of its growth is the economic liberalization and multi-party democracy introduced in Mali in 1991, following the rise to power of Colonel Toumani Touré. Schulz warns against interpreting Ansar Dine as another version of global political Islam and insists that we understand it instead within the complex field of social power in Mali.

Ansar Dine illustrates clearly the key role of media (here not digital media, but 'small media', the audio and video cassette, on their own and as disseminated by radio: Sreberny-Mohammadi and Mohammadi 1994) in extending religious communications and so expanding the borders of the religious field. Haidara came from a minor branch of an old religious family: for some time he has fought for influence and was kept outside the *Haut Conseil Islamique*. Haidara's use of media to disseminate his sermons was essential since it gave him a popular audience larger than members of the *Conseil* and so eventually persuaded them to allow him membership in 2000.

But, as Schulz brings out, Ansar Dine's rise also illustrates wider forces. Two key contextual factors are the weakness of the Malian state as a social authority (compare Mbembe 2001 on the 'post-colony') and the historic lack of influential religious families as sources of religious authority in Malian Islam, owing to the late conversion to Islam in the 1920s colonial era. Haidara's appeal is as much that of a general 'moral watchdog' (Schulz 2006: 137) as of a specific religious interpreter; in particular, Haidara avoids commenting on politics, except from a critical moral standpoint. Haidara also provides basic social services through Ansar Dine that the state no longer provides. This movement illustrates, then, not just mediatization but also wider battles in the field of power when competing religious and media authorities move into the space left by a weak state. Whether this amounts to an actual democratization of the social field is, Schulz notes, debatable (2006: 144–6).

The *visual arts*, by contrast, are a competitive field that is highly specialized in its focus, even if some artists have strayed at times into quasi-religious or quasi-political claims of authority (Joseph Beuys, Marina Abramovic). Given the lack of agreement about the values, reference points and basic aims of artistic practice – or indeed whether it has an external reference at all – there is no inherent reason why the art field should have any particular relation to media. Certainly, while art is an act of communication, there is no intrinsic need for it to be an act of mass or distance communication.

Yet under certain circumstances art gets close to media, as with the Young British Artists of the 1990s. The YBA are interesting as an example of how, at least for certain members of a large field, media exposure and media capital can become of overwhelming importance until, as in some of Tracy Emin's practice, media appearances become fused with art practice itself.[98]

How can we explain this? It certainly cannot be explained through the general saturation of the art world by media reference points (such as advertising)[99] because it is not a general effect across the whole artistic field. Where media does impinge intensely on artistic practice, it depends on the form of symbolic capital on which particular artists rely. In the artistic field, in its open-ended and unregulated diversity, media capital may have an intense importance for part of a field, without becoming dominant over the entire field. For certain artists among the YBA – or indeed Andy Warhol and Jeff Koons from different generations of the New York art scene – artistic logic and a narrowly defined media logic have seemed to overlap. Economic and governmental pressures may at times provide incentives to make art that meets certain media-based expectations. But there is no reason to interpret this as a general media logic at work in the artistic field.

Authority and the porosity of institutions

One emerging aspect of media's influence on social organization is the transformation of authority in a digital media age. This has broader implications for the robustness of contemporary institutions and so deserves separate treatment.

Bruce Bimber's brilliant analysis (discussed in chapter 5) shows how the digitalization of information, and the information abundance it generates, changes the basic conditions of institutional power, particularly (but not exclusively) in the political domain. Digitalization of information not only increases hugely the information resources available to institutional elites; it also transforms the *archival* access to past information and media for all sorts of actors and facilitates horizontal *communication outside elites*.[100] While this has benefits for institutional organization too,[101] a cost is that institutions become more vulnerable to the dissemination of information by non-elites, especially via media. The result is that all institutional authority becomes vulnerable to leaks, sabotage and simple informational traffic: new information flows make institutions more porous. The key actors may be NGOs with a policy agenda, rival institutions and sometimes individuals keen to use the tool of media visibility for their own ends:[102] the circulation by US soldiers of highly compromising photos from Abu Ghraib jail in Iraq is an example of the last.

In the resulting flux, institutions become vulnerable and authority unstable.[103] However, questions of authority are best understood by reference to the detailed dynamics of specific fields. In the political field, inevitably saturated by media coverage, individual political authority has, for broader reasons already noted, become increasingly reliant on media-related capital and the ability to perform personally in media. Such highly personal authority attracts scandal when things go wrong, and, even when things go right, relies less on generalized status or legitimacy and more on media-based performance.[104] The resulting difficulties for building policy or for larger-scale political organizations have been discussed in chapter 5.

The consequences of media's cross-border flows are particularly profound in the religious sphere where distinctive forms of literacy-based authority have often been central. In the digital age, the religious text becomes fluid, interactive and available for circulation far beyond the limited communities that once had controlled access to them. Theological interpretation and commentary becomes 'a communal activity', as Heidi Campbell puts it, open online to a wide range of contributors, while religious discourse circulates in the media domain in ways that are difficult for institutions to control.[105] Meanwhile, the expanding scale of digital communications enables new religious communities to form, even without face-to-face contact, around very specific religious identities.[106] New groups who are officially excluded from religious authority can use media, usually but not always the internet, to become religious interpreters for the first time: Dorothea Schulz writes of Muslim women groups in Mali who use local radio or cassettes to disseminate their alternative inflections on Islam and so challenge the gendered inequalities that shape authority in that particular religion.[107]

As a result, many now see a change in the nature of religious authority itself,[108] but this cannot be simply reduced to an effect of mediatization. In Islam, many factors coincide, including the recent growth of mass literacy and expanding disputes about the nature and direction of modernity. Those changes are too complex – and too important – to be reduced to one single media logic. In any case, Islam, as Peter Mandaville notes, has always been relatively decentralized in its authority structure.[109] Meanwhile, the changes under way in the religious field have clear precedents long before the digital age: think of the European Christian reformation's relation to the printed book.[110]

Conclusion

We have seen in this chapter how a flexible and critical use of Bourdieu's field theory, supplemented from time to time by other approaches, can make more detailed sense of the idea that contemporary societies are 'mediatized'. In politics – the field most studied to date – interdependencies with the media field are so intense that something like media logic becomes internal to *aspects of* political practice, but the result is never a single or simple media logic. In other fields, something more gradual and varied is under way, with specific issues, such as authority, becoming sites of great tension. In each case, the general idea of mediatization must be translated into more specific analysis of how capital, authority and power are being transformed by media meta-capital in particular sites. A broader paradox then emerges: that, as more and more fields of social competition become open to the dynamics of media visibility, and so in a sense 'democratized', the force of media power increases: we consider the resulting deficit of media accountability in chapter 8.

With this more nuanced understanding of media power and its workings, there is all the more reason to pursue international comparisons. In the long term, comparative research may uncover the *limits* to media meta-capital in different locations and different fields.[111] But for now only simpler forms of comparison are feasible: in the next chapter, I explore a comparative perspective on the range of media cultures across the world.

7

Media Cultures: A World Unfolding

'We are still so unclear on what to look for when we do comparative research.'

Daniel Hallin and Paolo Mancini[1]

A whole world of media-related practice is unfolding that media sociologists need to grasp. Our perspective on this world has been blocked by the overwhelming dominance of Anglophone media research and theory; accounts of US and UK media production and consumption have until now had undeserved prominence in research agendas. The sheer weight of rich work on media from elsewhere now makes that dominance absurd, yet it continues to be reinforced by the dynamics of the global publishing industry. What Asian scholars John Erni and Siew Keng Chua call a 'longing for context'[2] – no longer seeing media, society and power only through the accidental lens of how those relations have been configured in the USA and UK over the past century – is unstoppable.

To grasp this 'new' – in fact, always existing but unnoticed – world of media-related practice requires a change of thinking.[3] This world cannot be grasped synoptically from a particular privileged viewpoint:[4] to assume *that* would be to repeat the old mistake. It is an open-ended space of media development with no boundaries and much greater diversity than media research has historically recognized. As anthropologist Daniel Miller notes, many talk and write about Facebook as if it were a US phenomenon, but 'today it is a global site where over 70% of its users live outside the US.'[5]

Grasping that diversity may mean acknowledging entirely new types of social theory that come from the global South.[6] We must dispense with the assumption that the drive towards media development is naturally in the West: Dipankar Sinha calls this 'the other fundamentalism', the presumption of 'the triumph of the technocratic authority' based 'naturally' in the West, which in turn is linked to modernity's normative claim to universal applicability.[7] But modern media have no natural 'centre' anywhere, and so it is important, as Brian Larkin writes, to 'pose the question of what a theory of media would look like if it began from Nigeria rather than from Europe or the US': this would be to catch up with the Copernican revolution happening in other fields, such as economic history.[8] While the link between media institutions and modernity is fundamental (see chapter 1), we must acknowledge the many alternative modernities under construction today through digital media technologies.[9] But accumulating more accounts of media from more places will not be enough unless we can grasp the variety of everyday media practices on the ground.

The problem for a serious project of comparative media research is the conceptual one raised by Hallin and Mancini in this chapter's opening quote. Where can we look for clarification? Certainly not from what Divya McMillin calls the 'false sense of competence' that has empowered western scholars to generalize about the world from their particular location.[10] But if it is still trans-border *knowledge* at which we are aiming,[11] then some formulation is needed of the types of interrelation between society, media and power that matter. This means, however tentatively, proposing some broad frames of comparison.

One important frame of comparison concerns the institutional infrastructures in which the diverse bundle of things we call 'media' occurs. Hallin and Mancini's analysis of the social and historical interdependencies of state, market and media in *Comparing Media Systems*[12] was a huge step forward towards this goal, definitively moving beyond an older transparently western-centric literature on the development of 'the press' in different countries.[13] 'With great caution' they introduce 'three media system models':

> The Liberal model [Britain, Ireland, North America] is characterized by a relative dominance of market mechanisms and of commercial media; the Democratic Corporatist Model [northern continental Europe] by a historical coexistence of commercial media and media tied to organized social and political groups, and by a relatively active but legally limited role of the state; and the Polarized Pluralist Model [southern Europe] by integration of the media into party politics, weaker historical development of commercial media, and a strong role of the state.[14]

Hallin and Mancini's model is illuminating, but requires some adjustment. The relation of religious institutions to both state and media needs attention if the model is to be relevant to countries such as Iran, Nigeria and the Philippines, or indeed to be more effectively relevant to the USA where a counter-secular media movement has emerged in the past three decades with its own media infrastructure. It would be useful to ground Hallin and Mancini's analysis in the particular evolution of inter-field relations in different countries (compare chapter 6). In addition, as Hallin and Mancini acknowledge,[15] their model must be tested and, as necessary, adjusted for cases outside the West.

Yet however much Hallin and Mancini's model is extended and elaborated, it is a theory conceived from the standpoint of political economy. We cannot expect it to answer the questions of international comparison we would ask if (remember chapter 1) we turned the pyramid of media theory another way up. How can we begin to compare the texture of media's role in everyday life,[16] and the cultural significance that particular media-related practices have in different places, against particular contexts of power, social organization and geopolitics? The simplest route might seem to ask how media 'feel' in different places with their distinctive media institutions and media system. But the risk would be that we simply reproduce imagined national boundaries around supposed national 'media culture', and so obscure a more complex mix of commonalities and differences. Another way of working (closer to medium theory) would be to look at the different trajectories of technology introduction in different countries. It is clearly significant, as Goggin and McLelland note, that in Japan everyday internet access was primarily introduced through mobile devices rather than desktop computers, and that in East Asia camera phones were introduced much earlier than elsewhere.[17]

Alternatively, within this book's preferred standpoint of socially oriented media theory, we can develop the concept of media *cultures* within and across national borders. Media cultures derive from what people do with media. Rather than being overwhelmed with the malleability of media-related practices (production, consumption, distribution, interpretation), it is more useful to anchor our investigation in the notion of 'media cultures', whose distinctive forms are, I will argue, shaped by the dynamics of various underlying human needs. Just as (see chapter 2) forms of life related to media are shaped, in large part, by need, so too are media cultures. Inevitably, because media research historically *has been* largely nationally based, my examples will tend, in most cases, to be selected by reference to one nation or another but, as will become clear, my framework of comparison is not based in national differences. It is pressures based in broad types of human need – formed sometimes within and sometimes across national borders – that generate the communication needs[18] from which a distinctive media culture arises.

I will not therefore be interested in how certain universal types of communication need are fulfilled in similar ways everywhere (basic information needs for news, basic cultural needs for music, imagery, the transfer of cultural expression between generations). Such basic needs only generate distinctive media cultures where, under various pressures (times of revolution, circumstances of long-term cultural exclusion), they are intensified. The point is not to track minor variations in media use but to grasp the overall *span* of media cultures on a global scale and the dynamics that shape that diversity. Needless to say, no wider 'theory' of this diversity is possible. If what follows reads like a tour of a research landscape built by others, that is my intention. It is exactly to this rich *comparative* landscape that we must reorientate debates in media research.

What is a media culture?

I use the term 'media *culture*'[19] as my unit of comparison rather than media system because, as already noted, the latter term remains rooted in the political economy analysis of how resources and institutions are organized and distributed. Media system analysis remains vital, but our concern in this book is instead with our experiences of media, our ways of living with media. For this purpose, the natural unit of comparison is 'culture', meaning *not* a bounded or spatially bordered culture but *any* way in which everyday practices of sense-making hang together. Just as individual practices work, according to Schatzki, by 'hanging together' (see chapter 2), so too with larger collections of practices. The concept of 'media culture' has until recently been used either as an untheorized descriptive term (to capture the way media somehow 'feel' different in the USA, say, from France or Japan), or to capture interpretative generalities about the flow and style of media products at particular times and places.[20] I use the term 'media culture' here in a different sense to refer to collections of sense-making practices whose main resources of meaning are media. The only criterion for identifying a media culture is that its members are likely to recognize its distinctiveness, its way of 'hanging together'. When I say 'sense-making', I do not mean that media cultures are exclusively or primarily ways of making sense *of media*; I mean instead that they are ways of making sense *of the world* that work primarily *through*, or in reliance on, media.

Media cultures in this sense can be traced to various human needs that shape our ways of interacting with, and acting upon, the world. This use of the term 'media culture' is intended to support a form of international comparison that avoids 'mediacentrism'. But media cultures are not 'hard' phenomena with clear boundaries; they are fuzzy objects, identifiable (like practices themselves very often) by way of what Wittgenstein calls a 'family resemblance' (see again chapter 2). As a result, there is no way of exhaustively mapping the media cultures of the world: the point instead is to get a clear sense of the significant differences that shape their endless variety.

Media culture has from the start of Hollywood been 'translocal', based in the flow and subsequent translation of materials (media) sent from multiple places and sources. The digital media age radicalizes this since it is based on a connective space (the World Wide Web) of infinite size that can receive inputs and generate outputs from/to anywhere at all. We take translocal flows for granted, the global success of the *Harry Potter* novels being only one of the most notable recent examples. It is impossible, as Koichi Iwabuchi notes, 'to imagine a local cultural creativity outside the context of globalization' but equally unhelpful, as Kraidy and Murphy point out, to assume that 'contemporary expressions of locality' are always strongly distinct.[21]

The essential starting point for thinking about media cultures is therefore Jan Nederveen Pieterse's distinction between 'translocal' and merely 'territorial' understandings of culture. Modern forms of cultural contestation, however local their basis, are normally now framed within a transnational comparison. Take how religions (from Christianity to Islam) regard sexuality. When Freud wrote *Civilization and its Discontents* in 1929, he could assume that the politics of sexual expression and repression were resolved, if at all, within national boundaries. Now this is impossible because of global travel and global cultural flows: sexual cultures in one place are inevitably exposed to media flows from elsewhere that reflect different sexual mores.[22]

Things become even more complicated when we consider how cultures vary in the extent to which they are more, or less, open to translocal inputs. This is not a matter of 'cosmopolitanism', indeed quite the contrary. Research on middle-class, ethnically white audiences in northern Britain shows that travelling abroad a lot through work and leisure need not generate any curiosity about media and culture outside Britain, even if it provides regular casual contact with it.[23] However, everyday experience of television in the Middle East exposes people to what Marwan Kraidy calls 'a dynamic Arab *trans-national* media landscape', while, if you live in northern Nigeria, your film repertoire will be shaped by Christian films from southern Nigeria, transnational Islamic culture, the Hindu cultural reference points of Bollywood films and Hollywood![24] Factors of taste and belonging, themselves heavily stratified by class, also complicate the relation between mobility and mediatization.[25]

So how *can* we grasp what makes media cultures distinctive from one another? It cannot be, any more, their assumed connection to the territory enclosed within the borders of a particular nation – the news culture of Thailand, for example. This is not to deny that national locations are often important for distinguishing media cultures, precisely because many aspects of media infrastructure (from language reach to regulatory bodies) are in some cases still territorially bounded. Nor is it to claim that cultural loyalties are somehow more naturally 'cosmopolitan' or supra-national, for that would be to ignore the continuing role of nations as historically enduring structures of solidarity.[26] But it is to avoid developing our concept of media culture in a way that *assumes* culture's 'natural' relation to any particular territory, whether nation, region or village.

A precedent to this debate about media culture is the problem with earlier functionalist accounts of the nation and so-called 'national media', touched on in chapter 3; they failed to recognize, as Philip Schlesinger notes, 'the increasingly evident contradictions between various levels of culture and identity that are tending to decouple state and nation'.[27] It is worth remembering that classical social theory in the West already, in the nineteenth and early twentieth century, aimed to move beyond methodological nationalism.[28] Because media cultures, however local some of their features, are now composed of contents that in principle can come from, and be sent to, anywhere, a *territorial definition of media culture is incoherent*. It is better to define media cultures informally as *thickenings* of *translocal processes* – of meaning-making through media – that are more or less locally specific. Being in a place, with and through media, remains important, but it has changed its meaning fundamentally, and our descriptive language in media research needs to reflect this.[29]

If media cultures are recognizable densities in the media flux (they may be national in their distribution, but they need not be), what preconditions enable a media culture to 'thicken' – that is, to acquire a density that stably links media contents and practices and the contexts for those practices?[30] Certainly not a simple 'internal' relation that a media culture has to 'home-grown' content, or to some assumed national 'culture'. In Iran, it is *divisions* in the *ulema* (the community of religious scholars) that produce a particularly active and contentious blogosphere. Even media cultures which once seemed territorial – for example, pre-digital broadcasting cultures such as the UK until the late 1980s – were in fact divided because the same media 'offer' had different salience to different sections of highly stratified societies.[31] Recent accounts of media culture in sites as diverse as Egypt, Mexico and China all emphasize the deep fissures in what once was supposed to be a unified media culture.[32]

So what is it that generates *the variety* of media cultures? We have already considered one possibility back in chapter 3: the density that arises when various forces invest in a process of 'centring',[33] that is, the claim that media are socially central institutions. Another way of looking at variation within media cultures is via socio-economic variables: as Harindranath notes, educated television audiences in India and Britain may have more in common with each other than with less educated audiences in their own country.[34] But this might not help us understand how media use coheres into a distinctive way of life that groups would recognize as such. A different way of thinking about how media cultures become distinct is to consider how their component practices are stabilized through members' sense of what media matter to them in their daily life. What shapes how people select materials from translocal cultural flows as relevant and important for them? What are the different reasons why media matter to groups and networks of people? This takes us to the question of underlying human needs.

Media cultures seen from the perspective of needs

In a profoundly unequal world, which is also, as Susan Buck-Morss notes, 'intractably diverse',[35] only human needs are robust enough to provide a reference point by which to guide comparison. Interestingly, that is the starting point of economist Amartya Sen's attempt to think differently about global economic development; it is a good starting point also for thinking differently about media cultures on a transnational scale. This starting point was already implicit in our accounts of media as practice in chapter 2.

There is no definitive list of human needs, especially when we move from the physical to the cultural and social domains. For now – we will return to this issue in a philosophical context in chapter 8 – let's take, as given, the universal contribution of media infrastructures to basic information provision and consider instead the types of need that specific media cultures might *distinctively* fulfil.

A provisional list of such needs might include: *economic* needs; *ethnic* needs; *political* needs; *recognition* needs (linked to, but distinct from ethnic and political needs); *belief* needs; *social* needs; and *leisure* needs. 'Needs' must be understood in a broad sense, implying not a universal psychological model of individual needs but a more open-ended spectrum of human needs that emerge when we consider human 'capabilities', in Amartya Sen's term, when they become culturally embedded.[36] It is unhelpful to consider individual needs in isolation and more useful to consider the commonly experienced pressures of material and historical conditions. Similarly, historians of blogging Carolyn Miller and Dawn Shepherd use the term 'objectified social need' to make sense of how media production and consumption are shaped in an age when media forms are changing fast.[37]

Needs intersect and overlap, so a distinctive media culture may address multiple needs and gain its strength precisely from this overlap; equally, individuals may belong to more than one media culture. Media cultures may be more or less porous to each other, depending on the degree to which they share ways of making sense of media and world. The point is not to map definitively the range of human needs, but rather to orient ourselves to the *type of diversity* we can expect to find in media cultures, and therefore to the *dimensions* for comparing media cultures that might prove useful.

Let us see how far this crude template can get us in thinking about the seemingly infinite diversity of media cultures. The idea is not that a particular need defines a media culture entirely (why should things be so simple?), only that it is a plausible primary reference point by which selections and weightings of media get made by particular groups. Needless to say, this reference point is not meant to exclude, but rather to supplement, other reference points, for example historical or conjunctural accounts of media culture.

Economic needs

Media cultures may be shaped by fundamental needs in the economic domain, such as access to labour markets and other aspects of economic opportunity, because they generate distinctive needs for information and communication. Where the distribution of economic benefits is very uneven – for example, in populations some of whose members are required to relocate large distances just in order to earn enough to eat – then the needs associated with economic survival are likely to dominate other needs which would otherwise be pressing, for example, socializing or leisure. Sometimes economic needs are so acute that they do not generate any distinctive media culture at all because they render media consumption largely irrelevant to the struggle for survival. This is partly a story of the continuing global digital divide (see chapter 1): in rural Brazil, for example, poverty and poor infrastructure may put even television and radio beyond the access of most local people.[38] It is poverty that people rate most highly in terms of pressing global issues, according to a recent survey.[39] But the impact of economic need may be more subtle, where inequality forces people to seek work most or all of the time away from their families, shaping distinctive needs for information and communication technologies (ICTs).

Most studies of the media consumption of migrant populations to date have emphasized media's role in the maintenance of ethnic and cultural connection (see next section), but this underplays the role that poverty – basic economic need – plays in migration itself: whether across the US–Mexican border, or in what Simone calls the 'movement machine' of the African continent. The distinctive media-related needs of *internal* migrants have been rather neglected in media research, and yet, as Jeremy Tunstall notes, 'the biggest population movements are within the large population countries', not across national borders.[40] China has 147 million internal migrants, and Jack Qiu's recent study on the take-up of *digital* media amongst the Chinese working class challenges the obsession of media industry hype, and of much media research, with the consumption of 'high-end' information technologies and applications.[41] Qiu's research also complicates the assumption that there is a simple binary digital divide between 'information haves' and 'information have-nots'.

Once we orient our research towards how economic needs shape basic communication needs, it becomes obvious that the internet and mobile phones are not luxuries. Qiu explains why they are particularly essential to internal migrants in China and other members of the Chinese working class: unemployed workers, retirees and the 189 million 15- to 24-year-olds who live on low incomes. These groups have faced an overwhelming set of economic challenges: the need to move hundreds of miles from country to 'urban villages' (*chengzhongcun*), whether to seek family advancement or just to find work at all (one quarter of China's workforce moved out of agriculture between 1978 and 2006); the loss of employment following the privatization of many state enterprises (63 million leaving the state and collective sector between 1990 and 2004); the loss of subsidized housing through the commercialization of the housing sector in the 1990s; the rising costs and pressures associated with the privatization of care services and steeply rising tuition fees.[42] As a result, 'the changing urban conditions ... give rise to concrete everyday existential demands . . . for such indispensable needs as employment, child care and health care'.[43] As other writers on China confirm, this situation is marked by relative political isolation but intense reliance on families and friends 'back home'.[44]

This complex situation generates distinctive ICT needs – not for more broadcast media (according to Qiu, migrants' perception is that traditional media do not cater for them)[45] – but for a mobile phone, at least on a prepaid basis, and for SMS or internet chat services for instant contact with work or family networks. Evidence of a distinctive media culture lies in recent growth of an industry segment specializing in advertising and selling through text-based mobile phone services.[46] Meanwhile, the internet (for practical and entertainment purposes) is accessed in collective space (the internet café or net bar: *wangba*); chat services (QQ), rather than email, are the means for direct communication ('most [migrants] do not have an [individual] email address even after going online regularly for a year').[47] Qiu provides insight into a *collective* internet culture shaped by economic necessity. This has parallels in many other countries, for example, in Egypt, where only 0.5 per cent of the population have broadband, and in Sri Lanka, where the interconnection between radio stations (with access to the internet) and the wider population (without such access) proved crucial in the early 2000s.[48]

The distinctive economically shaped media culture of the Chinese working class can only be fully understood if traced to the labour process itself. Qiu notes the growing use of mobile phones in factories for worker surveillance, with employers tracking every SMS sent by their workers and, in a few cases, involving workers' use of new media such as blogs to gain media attention for their industrial action against a transnational employer. China has seen a huge growth of low-status employment in IT manufacture and IT service industries. For many in the Chinese working class, ICTs are the dominant context of both their work *and* leisure lives. In a media culture shaped by needs for 'work-related information', 'entertainment' and 'networking', it would be distorting to view its practices primarily through the lens of entertainment.[49]

Qiu's approach is not entirely new to media research. Since the 1980s, a few researchers on audiences have focused on how media consumption is fundamentally shaped by position in the division of labour, including the unequal division of labour in the home.[50] Indeed, the idea that, at least for the majority of the population, leisure takes largely the form that the division of labour allows goes right back to Marx.[51] There is also a great deal to be said about how all media use, including the use of computer-mediated communications, is shaped by class and specifically class's influence on educational opportunity.[52] But what is most striking about Qiu's study is its emphasis on the media needs that flow from the increasingly ICT-dependent organization of the labour market itself.

At a time of intensifying economic insecurity across the world, an orientation to the economic needs that shape media cultures is vital. Madianou and Miller's recent work on Filipina workers adds the perspective of transnational migration. Economic needs drive migration to the West of large numbers of Filipina women whose communication needs are overwhelmingly shaped by the necessity of maintaining parenting-at-a-distance through multiple platforms: Facebook, Skype, online chat, email. Again, underlying economic need and its shaping of distinctive communication needs alerts us to a distinctive configuration of media culture.

Ethnic needs

With some migrants, particularly those who move to form ethnic or cultural minorities in other countries, the need to keep in touch with home populations, and to affirm ethnic and cultural commonality, is more prominent in shaping media culture than economic necessity. What we might loosely call 'ethnic need' generates a need for distinctive media content and for whatever distribution process can enable access to that content in the distant country where migrants find themselves. There have been many studies of diasporas' distinctive media cultures. As Daniel Dayan pointed out, diasporic media use may be the purest example of the 'imagined community' since diasporic community can *only* be imagined through media, not face to face.[53]

Much work has concentrated on the need of migrants to access news and entertainment from their homeland, reinforced often by the inaccessibility of media in their adopted country due to language difficulties. Early studies focused on the use of satellite TV by migrants in Europe as their means of 'see[ing] more of what was going on in their home country'.[54] 'Ethnic' need is hardly, however, a straightforward factor and many studies report a split between first- and second-generation migrants, with the latter preferring to watch media of the country where they were born.[55] Recent work on migrants brings out how the multiplication of mediated means to keep in touch with family, friends and culture at a distance affects the balance of *where* and *how* migrants access media as means of 'place-making'. Once, the home was the principal site where media cultures shaped by ethnic needs were enacted: for example, Marie Gillespie's account of watching Bollywood and religious videos in South-Asian homes in west London in the late 1980s. But that site is just as likely now to be the internet café, or any place where an internet connection can be set up for a Skype call via mobile phone or laptop.[56] Social networking sites are increasingly important as means for diaspora to keep directly in touch: Aniko Imre illustrates this through her vivid account of the Hungarian social network, www.iwiw.hu.[57] As internet-enabled mobile phones become common, a huge amount of information is accessible in people's hands, as they move around in their locality: in this sense, as we saw in chapter 5 when considering the contagion of new forms of economic and political protest, transnational reference points may seem closer to the 'local' than national media, particularly for excluded groups. This confounds two generalized claims about the internet: that it is leading to the decline of cultural difference, and that it is merely a local 'granular space' of individual use, rather than a more complex interplay of multiple scales.[58]

The use of the internet in ethnic media cultures can be pursued in two very different directions. In one direction, the internet allows ethnic groups increasingly to differentiate their media production, providing low-cost opportunities for populations to produce their own distinctive material and archive it for public use. Latin America's indigenous population (for example, the Mapuche nation and the media of Chiloé in Chile) provides interesting cases where involvement in alternative media, far from the commercial or state mainstream, inculcates self-recognition and, potentially, political agency. In China, Wanning Sun argues that such possibilities of production remain in tension with the wider absence of political voice. The Colombian cultural theorist Jesus Martin-Barbero provides a wider rationale for these developments: 'the digitalization of heritage', he argues, 'make[s] possible the local and worldwide visibility of our heritage,' providing 'a new way for our cultures to be in the world' through media production. Such possibilities are particularly important in parts of the world where there is a history of deep ethnic conflict, as in the former Yugoslavia. But the neglect of audience research in the field of alternative media means that their implications for cultures of media *consumption* are still unclear.[59]

In another direction, the increasing complexity of media flows across borders makes it increasingly problematic to *assume* that ethnic groups have distinctive and ethnically specific media cultures. Aksoy and Robins's classic work on London Turkish migrants shows that their media use is more than national, if not exactly cosmopolitan. Under such conditions, a multiple sense of belonging can be sustained through media: the result of access to broadcasting from home may *not* be to reproduce a simple, unconflicted sense of national belonging, given the reality that migrants are not 'at home' (in Turkey) when in London or Berlin they watch satellite news bulletins aimed at a Turkish home audience. Indeed, Aksoy and Robins question whether such consumption is driven by 'ethnicity' at all; rather, they argue 'the desire for engagement with Turkish TV is entirely social.'[60] In this way, so-called 'ethnic' needs can be placed in a wider perspective of the multiple 'community horizons' that different groups develop in and through their media use.[61] We come back to social needs shortly.

Political needs

It may seem strange to talk of political needs shaping media cultures – people, after all, do not watch television because governments tell them to – but there are a number of ways in which either large-scale political strategies or demands for political recognition left unaddressed by large political structures may shape distinctive forms of media consumption and/or production. That is what I mean by saying that 'political needs' are a factor that contributes to the diversity of media cultures.

First, there are the strategies of states and other large political actors that involve media industries in nation-building. While rarely succeeding in direct terms, if we look to the context of wider political and social settlements, we can see how distinctive nationally focused media cultures emerged in earlier times of media scarcity (for example, in Britain between the 1930s and 1960s).[62] In the early twenty-first century, such strategies of concentration are more likely to be subsumed by pressures on governments to open up their territories to international media markets, but again, under particular conditions, this may result in distinctive media cultures, quite compatible for example with an explicit nationalism.[63] At least until recently, the 'yoking' of national media 'to political and social projects', as Lila Abu-Lughod puts it for the case of Egypt,[64] has shaped media landscapes and, potentially, media cultures. We must be very careful not to exaggerate the degree of intentionality or determinacy in the political strategies behind emerging types of media content, especially where production is outsourced among competing small companies. But it would be equally wrong, as noted in chapter 4, to ignore the uncanny fit between the dominance of neoliberal policy regimes (USA, UK) and the rise of TV formats that present social 'reality' focused on the competition between self-transforming individuals.

We can also consider political needs from another direction, the needs of the wider population. Cultural strategies of the state generate resistance and, under authoritarian regimes, media may be notable as sites of implicit *challenge* to established authority. It is here that Marwan Kraidy's recent study of pan-Arab reality media breaks new ground, while building on earlier work by Marc Lynch on TV talk shows as a new Arab public sphere.[65] The role of media culture in the Middle East in finding ways round heavy censorship and tight control of public space has been known since early studies of the VCR (video-cassette recorder), which had very high take-up in the Arab world.[66] Kraidy broadens the discussion from basic technology to media forms, exploring the distinctive salience that 'reality' claims and media rituals take on in contexts where the moral and political imperatives of modernity are highly charged questions, and where intense national rivalries resonate with those broader debates. Kraidy sums up the distinctive position of reality media in the Middle East eloquently:

> By luring large audiences for long periods of time, and predicating the outcome of each episode on voting, reality TV turns viewers not only into participants in controversial public events, but also into witnesses to rituals that validate alternative social and political visions. Within this changing social context, young people *recycle reality TV's participatory rituals to communicate outside of the heavily policed familial or social space*, or alternatively, for leisure, consumption and sometimes activism.... Reality TV's promise of individual transformation has some resonance in the Arab world.[67]

We have already seen in chapter 3 how Kraidy's research transforms the frame in which we understand media rituals by showing us one type of case where a media-certified 'reality' can be the focus of alignments, however unstable, *against* the state or *against* established readings of political power. As Kraidy puts it, 'by subjecting the notion of "reality" to scrutiny, reality TV made political reality [in the Arab world] more visible.'[68] This does not invalidate the idea of the myth of the mediated centre but, rather, expands our view of its political salience and contestability under different institutional conditions.

When we consider the diversity of media cultures across the world, Kraidy's study vividly suggests one way in which political needs may sometimes demand new media cultures: intense engagement with reality TV among large audiences in the Arab world and new digital forms of audience participation, such as SMS-text-based voting, are vital here. This points to a much larger range of cases where the claim to present 'reality' – alternative realities to those officially recognized previously – may resonate with large populations at times of political transformation or uncertainty. One is Eastern Europe where versions of the *Pop Idol* format enable ethnic and sexual minorities to get heard in ways that both contest and reinforce new nationalisms.[69] Other examples multiply: Chinese adaptations of the *Pop Idol* format (*Super Girl*) or the *Survivor* format (*I Shouldn't Be Alive*); the intense debates over the Malaysian adaptation of the UK format *Fame Academy* (*Akademi Fantasia*); and adaptation of the *Big Brother* format in southern Africa, where many national societies coexist in various stages of growth and tension. The potential of reality formats to open up wider debates about the 'social imaginary' has been noted by some commentators from the beginning, and it provides an important counterpoint to the more closed pedagogic form that reality TV has taken in Britain and the USA. There is a link here to a much longer history of how deep-seated political deficits are addressed by media innovations: think of the rise of political cinema in revolutionary Mexico in the early twentieth century and the more recent rise of popular cinema in northern Nigeria.[70]

A third, very different, perspective on how political needs may shape media culture is that of smaller counter-establishment actors: their overwhelming need to organize politically may sometimes generate politically shaped media cultures, for example around deterritorialized social movements such as the anti-globalization and anti-capitalism movements. Here, the implications for the study of media cultures are less clear. There is a long history of alternative political movements finding new forms of expression through media; recent history offers some distinctive examples, such as the Indymedia movement and Islamic fundamentalist websites where translocal networking has been vital to a movement's emergence and diffusion.[71] We still know too little about the broader media culture associated with these innovations because of the wider lack of audience research on alternative or radical media.[72] Indeed, some recent studies suggest that political activists may have an oppositional approach which encourages them to live at a distance from what they see as mainstream media culture.[73] Nonetheless, as conflicted ways of living with, or against, mainstream media cultures, these political cultures deserve further exploration.

What of the need for news? As I argued at the start of the chapter, the basic need for news is not a pressure that *distinguishes* media cultures since everyone needs news of some sort; indeed, this basic need for news is the start of certain debates about media injustice (see chapter 8).[74] There are undoubtedly distinctive ways of relating to news in different places. Research from Scandinavia, for example, a region with a history of high literacy levels, shows a strong sense of duty in following the news.[75] This continues today, as recent studies from Denmark and Finland show, even as multiplying news outlets displace the prime-time news bulletin or the morning newspaper as the exclusive means of keeping up with the news. In India, a country of vast variations in literacy, anthropologist Ursula Rao finds a considerable involvement of non-media professionals in the production of local news: in Lucknow, Rao reports that 'almost every man I met claimed to be a journalist' in a broader news culture sustained by networks of local 'stringers' who gather stories and pass them onto the local press. In many countries, online social networking and the connective 'reserve' of the internet is generating a new type of 'news consumption', based on individuals' routine referral of news onto others, particularly where the background is heavy authoritarian control over the circulation of news: China's growing online culture of 'citizen mobilization' is an important example of this.[76]

All these variations, however, exist within wider patterns of news use that are not fundamentally distinctive. The need for news generates a distinctive *media culture* only when under the pressure of intense political need: in such times, for example, rituals of exchange (of photos, text, video) on social networking sites intensify. Think of the recent revolutions in the Arab Spring when a new news production/consumption dynamic emerged, at least temporarily. In times of intense political change, collective news production and circulation become a media culture in which social and political needs temporarily fuse.

Recognition needs

Distinct from political needs, although they may often intersect, are broader needs for social and moral recognition in large societies where roles and status are uncertain or contradictory. Axel Honneth, its leading theorist, analyses the concept of recognition on three levels: first, basic personal care and love; second, respect for the person as a moral agent with responsibility; and third, social esteem, that is, the recognition of someone 'as a person whose capabilities are of constructive value to a concrete community'.[77] Media culture, in so far as it provides the means for individuals and groups to recognize themselves, or be recognized by others, is relevant at least to the second and third levels of recognition.

Recognition needs are relevant to both media production and media consumption. Most media cultures generate the 'gap between representation and lived experience' that a BBC representative found when she spoke to audiences who wanted to tell their own stories.[78] But if groups feel that they are not recognized or represented in the media they consume, then a broader demand for recognition builds;[79] a wider 'longing for self-representation' may give intensity to certain media forms, for example, Arab reality TV when viewed against the background of the Arab world's conflicted relationship with the USA.[80] In Britain currently, a battle is under way to save the vestiges of the local press and radio: it is such local media, as the manager of South Birmingham Community Radio puts it, that 'give the community a voice'.[81] But, given the intense concentration of resources in media institutions, recognition solutions may not come from the rare moments when one's community does obtain some coverage in mainstream media: on the contrary, stereotypical presentation in media may intensify one's sense of being *mis*recognized, as Patrick Champagne discovered in his work on working-class neighbourhoods in Lyon, southern France.[82] Recognition solutions are much more likely to come via acts of media *production*.

The growing literature on alternative and community media provides many examples of emerging media cultures that, while they may also make sense in terms of ethnic or political needs, are perhaps best understood as calls for basic recognition in societies where media opportunities are very unequally distributed. The sense of living in 'two totally different worlds' – the world in the streets around you and the world presented by media – can force people to try and create media closer to their own reality.[83] The transformation that results from *making* media in conditions of unequal recognition can be profound. Zane Ibrahim, managing director of Bush Radio in Cape Town, South Africa, a station that emerged under apartheid for a local black audience but which, post-1994, acquired a mixed audience, comments: 'One of our mandates is to demystify radio in the community; *for so long we've been spoken at, not spoken with* . . . so now, from the age of four we are teaching children, it's your radio; the airwaves belong to the people.'[84]

Newly found agency in media production may encourage a sense of political and civic agency, otherwise denied to ethnic minorities in states dominated by narrow ethnic groupings: Juan Salazar's account of the media of the Mapuche indigenous nation in Chile is valuable here.[85] Having a role in media production itself may foster a sense of *collective* action, as one activist in the DDS (Deccan Development Society) radio collective in the Indian state of Andhra Pradesh comments:

> Previously we used to bother only about our own problems. We were not keen on the problems of others. Now we are doing collective work. . . . We want to help women in other villages and expect the same from them. Before radio, we used to do a lot of good things which were not noticed by society. But now everyone knows all our activities.[86]

A researcher of participatory video in Zimbabwe comments similarly that 'participants realized they could do things, and say what they thought, knowing that they would be heard beyond their local boundaries.'[87] In Latin American societies recovering from periods of intense civil war, the mutual recognition that results from media-making may, under these special conditions, start wider processes through which memories of violence can heal.[88]

Some argue that the trans-border flexibility of the internet makes it now *the* 'primary outlet for the voices of indigenous peoples', a means by which they can build 'a global and regional constituency'.[89] The lower barriers to cultural production online have opened up some remarkable new possibilities. Sao Paolo is the tenth richest city in the world but marked by huge inequality; in one of its poorest and reputedly most dangerous *barrios*, Capao Redondo, two brothers got together to create a website to 'show the good side of Capao', providing a forum for local news, conversation and a showcase for local music and literature.[90] The impact of such a collective production is felt deeply: the *barrio* 'is making history and gaining space and a voice in society after almost one hundred years of existence', says one contributor.[91] Suburban France with its intense racial segregation provides similar cases of blogs – for example, the Bondy Blog platform sponsored by a mainstream media outlet, the Swiss magazine *L'Hebdo* – that have helped sustain a new culture of recognition.[92]

The long-term implications of such a media culture were already captured by Ananda Mitra in 2004: 'the internet has transformed popular culture by providing a virtual forum in which different communities and groups can produce a "presence" that might have been denied them in the real world.'[93] But today the word 'virtual' makes less sense since such outlets are considered by most to be part of the 'real world'. Media production closely embedded in communities, whether local or networked, generates media cultures that are distinctively rich, a 'process of "making sense" of the world and our place in it' as leading researchers of Aboriginal community media in Australia put it.[94] The role of recognition needs in driving distinctive media cultures is only just beginning to be understood. This takes us to a key area where people need recognition: religion.

Belief needs

If we take, as basic, the need to communicate about major beliefs and ritual practices, then different belief communities (not always territorially bound: for example, the globalized new age movement) may be associated with distinctive media cultures. As Daya Thussu notes, within internationalized media research, religion must be integrated into our analytic frame rather than added on as an afterthought. Indeed, if we treat religion as fundamentally 'practice' ('a constituting activity in the world' that, as such, is necessarily enmeshed in power), then the practices of religious media cultures are central to what religion *is* from the start.[95]

Religious media cultures were once a marginalized area of media studies and media sociology, in part because of a default secularism that is now outdated.[96] Yet the US Christian right has for three decades provided an important example of a movement with a distinctive media culture and its own distinctive types of output, televangelism.[97] A transnational trade in religious media has been important in global media flows for some time.[98] Meanwhile, we are learning about the role of media in sustaining other religions over recent decades: for example, the role of cassette tapes in circulating sermons in Muslim Africa or at times of political crisis in pre-revolutionary Iran in the 1970s; or the history of ritualized religious viewing of television versions of the Hindu sacred texts in India; or the Middle East's distinctive broadcasting culture every year around Ramadan.[99]

It is only recently, however, that the significance of religion to media cultures more generally has started to be understood. One entry point has been research into the meta-reflections of religious media users on mainstream media culture. Pioneering here was Stewart Hoover's work on American Christian media cultures.[100] Recently, similar insights have emerged from across the world: for example, Heidi Campbell's research into critical internet cultures in Judaism, such as Koshernet.[101] Such reflections on media are perhaps an inevitable consequence of how religion is now embedded in media culture. Often these reflections are critical, aiming to restrict or narrow down the uses of digital media culture. But, as Daniel Miller points out in his book on Trinidadian Facebook users, there are counter-examples where religious organizations have seen digital media as *particularly* suited to religious dissemination and reshaped their practice around it. Another entry point is believers' perspectives on the media mainstream as a driver to market differentiation, for example in the Middle East: examples include Samanyolu TV as an outlet of the Gulen moderate Islamic movement in Turkey, and al-Manar, the television station of the Hezbollah political movement in Lebanon. Emerging from these forms of religious media production is a distinctive vision of what media institutions can do, a vision of a media station much closer to civil society activism than to broadcasting. Lehmann and Siebzehner write of the Judaic T'shuvah movement for whom a channel such as Kol HaChesed (Voice of Charity) offers itself more as a 'family' than a broadcasting station, heavily involved in social and civil society work. Through a different logic, national television stations in the Philippines (a society with a weak state where Catholicism's philosophy of charity is strong) have, according to Jonathan Ong, become almost social centres for the poor to visit when in need.[102]

Such work raises fascinating, but as yet unanswered, questions about how far the *consumers* of such religious media differentiate their media cultures from the mainstream, or whether, as Hoover suggests, such boundaries are exaggerated and religious media cultures are not in fact hermetically sealed from the consumption of mainstream media entertainment.[103] Put another way, are the meta-reflections of believers about mainstream media contents or technologies exclusive to religious media consumers? Or are they an example of a wider and as yet unexplored set of *all* populations' meta-reflections on media values and the consequences of media's saturation of everyday culture?[104] If so, then appreciating religious media culture becomes an important way of enriching our under-standing of the spectrum of media cultures generally.

Social needs

Social needs can be said to shape media cultures where the need for general social contact, or the specific need to socialize with one's peers (at work, in a particular cultural formation, or simply those of the same age), shapes distinctive forms of media production or con-sumption. Often, media cultures are large enough to enable and encourage exchanges between distinct demographic groups but, at times of acute generational conflict, different age groups may need distinctive communication terrains. Today's mobile phone-based youth cultures are of great interest, but they must be understood always in relation to local dynamics. In the Arab region, for example, where 34 per cent of the population are under 15 years old and median age is 22, the need for distinctive media channels where youth can be in contact at a time of rapid social and cultural change is intense. Ece Algan gives a related example from a rural region of south-eastern Turkey where women are restricted in their move-ments outside the home and local youth music radio plays a fundamental role in allowing social processes as such.[105] Where sexual preferences are the object of intense regulation in public space, online communities may play a similarly essential role along lines of both age and sexuality, as Mary Gray's pioneering study of online use by queer young people in rural America shows.[106] Less dramatically, when fast-changing media resources differentiate between generations in terms of technical facility, age-segregated media cultures may emerge. But as danah boyd points out vividly for US youth, apparent 'technological context' is inseparable from deeper conditions of agency, or the lack of it: 'what is unique about the internet is that it allows [US] teens to participate in unregulated publics while located in adult-regulated physical spaces such as homes and schools.'[107] It goes without saying that social needs cannot fully be disentangled from specific types of political, ethnic and recognition need, but they nonetheless require separate treatment.

An important perspective on social needs' contribution to the range of media cultures comes from Toshie Takahashi's work on Japanese media audiences. Takahashi explores how Japan's fundamental conceptual contrast between *uchi* (literally, 'inside') and *soto* (literally, 'out') is embodied in a digital media age. *Uchi* has been defined primarily through the taken-for-granted close reciprocity of the family and, distinctively in Japan, through parallel relations of reciprocity at work.[108] Takahashi shows how traditional notions of *uchi* – 'one in which members actively reinforce their connectivity and closeness to each other in order to keep stability and security' – may no longer be actualized in the family gathered around the television typical of the pre-digital age. Even if families still sit together in front of the television, they may, Takahashi reports, be engaged in quite divergent practices (phoning, texting, surfing on a laptop and so on). At the same time, the crisis in traditional media-sustained *uchi* may be accompanied by the creation of new forms of *uchi* through media: for example, renewing old school friendship groups online and creating new local networks through community websites. Some new forms of *uchi* are explicitly translocal, whether fan groups that provide a social connection between parents and teachers at a local kindergarten or the social networks that students maintain electronically when they or their friends study abroad.[109] Takahashi's recent work explores the multiple *uchis* formed and maintained through social networking sites, particularly the Japanese platform Mixi.[110]

Takahashi's work shows, in the context of Japan's distinctive form of sociality, how media culture can take quite particular forms. Parallel insights come from South Korea's intense culture of 'internet cafés', meaning not (as in other countries) physical sites for cheap internet connection but rather online groups for common activities or enthusiasms, in which almost 80 per cent of Korean internet users participate, according to a 2006 survey.[111] Indeed, what is so far little known is how the internet's obvious networking potential is creating

new *socially* based media cultures, even in highly individualistic countries like Britain, based around the exchanging of links, television
clips, music and the like.

It is important, however, not to forget that social needs are themselves profoundly shaped by broader economic dynamics. We saw this
earlier in the chapter in the networking of the Chinese working class,
although, following Qiu's lead, we discussed it from the perspective
of economic need. The rise in unemployment in Japan and the resulting collapse of many sites of workplace *uchi* is one factor we can
possibly see behind the need for new forms of *uchi* through digital
media.[112] Japan is not the only rich country where the steeply rising
costs of housing have forced young adults to stay living at home after
education, creating distinctive needs to maintain social independence
without the possibility of spatial independence. An interesting perspective on the economic pressures underlying social needs comes
from Rosalia Winocur's work on young people's media cultures in
Mexico. Diminishing financial independence requires young people
to find new forms of personal automony within the space of the home.
As in previous generations, but even more intricately, media culture
is an essential tool in this as young people seek 'to reconcile or negotiate divergent interests without . . . leav[ing] the house to exercise
their sexual, social and cultural preferences'. This intersection of economic pressures, social needs and media affordances leads Winocur
to an important insight into how media cultures are 'thickened':

> It is not digital convergence in itself that provokes the transformations
> in the realms of society and communication, but the way in which its
> possibilities are imaginatively transposed into the diverse socio-cultural
> conditions of young people's everyday lives . . . digital convergence is
> not sustained by its technological framework, but in the *confluence of*
> *meaning that it organizes* by means of the same.[113] (my italics)

These confluences of meaning generate, as boyd points out, 'decentralized publics' with very different features, often, from formal public
spheres.[114] So it is not technological change but the intersection of
new communication technologies with underlying social needs which
generate here distinctive media cultures, confirming once again
Roger Silverstone's profound insight that media technologies are
always doubly articulated, both as practice interface and as carriers
of meaning.[115]

The emergence of social networking sites ('SNS'), particularly but
not exclusively for young users, is one of the most dramatic recent
examples of this process but only builds on the longer-term growth

of homepages and blogs.[116] What is uncertain as yet is whether there are distinctive SNS cultures emerging for different demographics and/or in different countries.[117] Data remains scarce and we would expect religious, political and socio-economic factors to be as important here as they have been in shaping the distinctive cultures that have formed around reality TV. We should be wary of seeing in the huge global growth of SNS a single universal 'culture' of self-display.[118] It is more important to hold onto the *interlocking* needs that shape media cultures in their diversity or even in some cases their apparent uniformity.

Leisure needs

You may be surprised that it is only now I reach the question of whether leisure needs shape distinctive media cultures. But we have been exploring the range of factors which *require* different ways of using media and organizing practice around media to be found. Of course, there is an endless variety of actual media tastes (from action films to history channels, from nature documentaries to continuous news updates, from music videos to celebrity magazines), but that variation need not imply any variation in the organization of media consumption or in the arrangements through which media production is organized. Some leisure needs and desires, however, are strong enough and distinctive enough to *require* different ways of organizing things: specialist sporting communities, gaming cultures, fan networks. There is no doubt that the internet has transformed the scale of such media cultures: enabling fans to exchange knowledge, excitement and skills across national borders; providing a platform for hundreds of thousands of players of indeterminate age and country to play games together 'live'.[119]

I deferred consideration of leisure needs deliberately because it was important to see how much of the terrain of media cultures can be mapped *without* focusing on leisure. On a global scale, leisure time and the ability to pay for ways of filling one's leisure are very unequally distributed. There are many parts of the global South, as Divya McMillin reminds us, where 'television is still a luxury and, if accessible, is a minor component of daily rituals.' Displacing the prominence we give to leisure needs, far from distorting our perspective on media cultures, is arguably the best way of 'putting the media in their place' in McMillin's resonant phrase.[120] The result is not to diminish our sense of media cultures' importance but to enrich it.

Indeed, the perspective of need – as broadly defined – allows us to see in a different light the interpretative work that people value in relation to media. In one of the best audience studies in recent years – but less well known in broader media studies because it is concerned with film – Martin Barker and Kate Brooks explored the weight that viewers of the film *Judge Dredd* gave to interpretative debate and argument.[121] The people they interviewed were not necessarily film fans but they certainly enjoyed swapping interpretations. Indeed, the perspective of need also illuminates other aspects of fan studies, particularly the carving out by fans of new collective territory for performance, authorship and participation.[122]

Conclusion

In this chapter, we have developed a model of the underlying factors that might be expected to shape the *open-ended* diversity of media cultures. The point was not to claim some false mastery over this unfolding terrain but instead to grasp the *types* of significant difference in media cultures to which a genuinely internationalized media research must be sensitized.

Media research must be oriented to the broad, collectively established needs that generate distinctive media cultures. Such dynamics involve much more than the market circulation of media products and media interfaces: needs for political expression or recognition are just as important and require international comparison. Still unanswered, I realize, is the question of why, when we travel to another place and experience the outputs of a different 'media system', media often *feel* different from what we are used to back home (moving from the UK to the USA, from Sweden to Iran, from Argentina to China). We could ask, for example, how do celebrity cultures vary? What creates the UK's distinctively intense celebrity culture? Attempting to answer to that would take us back to the different social forms, embedded in what are usually still national power struggles over the 'mediated centre' (see chapter 3). But such differences in content still need to be experienced, and selected from, by individuals and groups. They still need to be embedded in everyday patterns of living, driven by underlying needs not just for media but for the wider set of resources we need to live. Those are the sorts of dynamic we have explored in this chapter.

In the final chapter, we consider the implications of this comparative perspective for the ethics and justice of our lives with media.

8

Media Ethics, Media Justice

'The *News of the World* was in the business of holding others to account. It failed when it came to itself.'

Rupert Murdoch[1]

'Technology reshapes the landscape of our emotional lives, but is it offering us the lives we want to lead?'

Sherry Turkle[2]

We live *with* media, *among* media. In most parts of the world, however poor, media are part of everyday practice; the constitution of politics and the broader organization of power. For all the uncertainties about how media will develop in the next decade, our relations to contemporary media configurations help shape the social worlds we inhabit and our possibilities for due recognition within them. That is the ground we have explored in the preceding chapters, but we have yet to make explicit the normative implications of this life with media. There surely are such implications: as John Durham Peters puts it, 'we have to keep up with the world, because we are, in some complicated way, responsible to act in it, and we can only act in the present.'[3] So how should we live with media? What role should media play in the organization of our collective life? In short, can there be media ethics or media justice?

Throughout this book, I have resisted the idea that the particular – until now, highly concentrated – configuration of symbolic resources that we call 'media' is 'just there', beyond reversal or critique. In this chapter, I make explicit for the first time a *normative* horizon within which we might evaluate the media we have and imagine something different. That involves mobilizing comparative frames beyond media: what life is it good to lead? What constitutes justice, or at least specific injustice? The initial two quotations capture two dimensions of an emerging crisis in the institutional and commercial conditions for practising journalism and in the life each of us *individually* leads with, and through, digital media. There is no simple relation between those two dimensions, and in this chapter I concentrate more on the first than on the second. But, taken together, they amount to a sense widely shared that new ways of doing things with media must be found. This is what the philosopher Paul Ricoeur called a 'limit situation': it is out of such limit situations that new domains of ethical thinking are born.[4] Ricoeur's examples were the emergence of medical or legal ethics at particular points in history: will we look back on the early twenty-first century as the time when the practical necessity for an ethics of media and communication came to be realized and a permanent new domain of ethics emerged?

We cannot unthink the global scale of human interaction that media technologies have made practical, visible, imaginable. Media are historical achievements that have changed the starting conditions for all human action, just as centuries of economic development and its environmental consequences have changed the earth on which we have no choice but to live. But if media in that sense are part of our 'second nature' (as philosopher John McDowell puts it)[5] – one of the contingent facts about human life from which any consideration of ethics must start out – they do not determine a particular way of living with media or distributing the resources associated with media. Indeed, the global space that media enable presents a new challenge to ethics, transforming the scale on which ethics must be thought. Our need for media ethics is analogous to how, as Hans Jonas noted two decades ago,[6] we gradually came to see that the 'limit situation' of unplanned global environmental damage (still unresolved) made environmental ethics essential. The multiple uncertainties associated with the era of digital media may require us to think, in some respects for the first time, about the normative implications of life with media. Zygmunt Bauman, reflecting on Hans Jonas, put the challenge well: 'we seem to require now an entirely new brand of ethics. An ethics made to the measure of the enormous space-and-time distance in which we can act and on which we act even when we neither know nor intend it.'[7] In this chapter, I take up this challenge.

'Criticism of our lives is not to be prosecuted in philosophical theory, but continued in the confrontation of our lives with their own necessities', as Stanley Cavell puts it. The ultimate point of ethics is not to trap us within elaborate philosophical debate but to return us critically to the necessities that shape our lives.[8] This chapter's argument, and indeed that of this whole book, is ultimately practical. It is shaped by the need for human beings to reduce conflict on all scales up to and including the global, and other needs, too: for freedom, trust and cooperation, mutual recognition. Because I want to contribute to dialogues where no agreement over political, moral or religious principles can be assumed, I build a normative horizon for thinking about media cautiously. I avoid reliance on any particular model of democracy or democratic values: the argument must speak even to members of societies that are not recognizably democratic, and members of no society at all, precisely because of media's potential contribution to both conditions and *pre*conditions of effective democracy. Truth-seeking is a value for *all* effective forms of human organization, whether or not organized along democratic lines: without practices aimed at truth (of which media are among the most important), cooperative human activity and the fulfilment of individual capabilities are impossible. My argument's implications are, however, particularly sharp for those societies that claim to be democracies, such as the USA and the UK since, as Sheldon Wolin notes, 'it seems paradoxical to say that democracy should deliberately deceive itself.'[9]

The urgency of an ethics of media and communication systems is increasingly being recognized, including by writers closely identified with the 'digital revolution'.[10] This chapter aims to contribute to that growing debate. In the conclusion, I make explicit some underlying values that have been implicit throughout this book's argument, values which connect with a broad vision of democratic practice but do not depend for their formulation on any particular model of how democratic deliberation must be organized. Deferring those elements of this chapter's normative horizon is deliberate.

Paths not taken

A global scale implies a space of irreducible moral disagreement and diversity.[11] Media do not reduce or resolve such disagreement: on the contrary, they bring it into view. So an initial question is: how can we live *sustainably* with each other through media, even though media unavoidably expose us to our moral differences? Bruno Latour expresses the challenge with great clarity: 'An entirely new set of questions has now emerged [on the political stage]: "Can we cohabitate with you?" "Is there a way for all of us to survive together while none of our contradictory claims, interests and passions can be eliminated?" ... "What should now be simultaneously present?"'[12]

Since media affect *how* we can be 'simultaneously present' to each other, a normative perspective on media is important to the quality of our life together. That perspective must in its formulation be global, or it is worthless: Roger Silverstone affirmed this point in his work on the 'mediapolis'.[13] But this does not mean imposing one normative framework on the rest of the world, only that we always take account of the potentially global scale on which media act and enable us all to act. Given that media ethics cannot legislate away the global *lack* of moral consensus, it must instead acknowledge moral diversity, starting from premises that are normatively minimal. That is why I will develop a normative perspective on media not in terms of universal values or obligations, but rather as an exploration of some plausible conditions under which, given our mutually obvious differences, all of us who share the earth's surface can, with media's help, live well together. We need not so much a set of explicit rules about media practice as a framework of thinking that can generate shared norms and values in spite of our differences.[14]

This has major implications for the philosophical choices we make. There is a broad, if crude, choice to be made between the deontological approach to morality (so-called because of the Greek word-root for 'ought': *deont-*) and the approach known as 'ethics' (from the Greek word-root for 'way of life': *ethik-*).[15] A deontological approach asks: how *ought* I to behave in this *specific* situation? Or, perhaps, how am I rationally required to behave in this specific situation? But an ethical approach asks more broadly: 'what kind of life would it be *best* to lead?' And (given that) 'what kind of person would it be *best* to be?' The difference between the deontological and ethics traditions has been exaggerated,[16] and their focus certainly at times overlaps. Reaching a considered view on the type of life it is best to lead generates principles about the types of behaviour that should be pursued and avoided (often expressed simply in terms of 'do's and don'ts'); equally, as Paul Ricoeur notes, questions of 'ought' (moral rules) depend on a prior specification of what is 'good' (the sorts of things that humans aim for).[17] But the difference of emphasis between the two traditions is crucial in the contested and transnational situation that a normative framework for media must address.

I will place less emphasis on the Kantian tradition of moral philosophy, which is primarily concerned with what in any situation I am rationally required to do, and more on the broadly Aristotelian tradition of ethics, as developed recently by philosophers such as Bernard Williams, John McDowell and Sabina Lovibond, that asks what a good human life is. The approach I take to media justice will also draw on the latter tradition, via a different contemporary route: Amartya Sen's recent account of justice and Axel Honneth's theory of recognition.[18]

The reasons for this choice derive from the specific aims and reference points of these two traditions. Kant, writing at the height of the European Enlightenment, was concerned to discover the moral principles to which a 'good will' – *any* good will, however embodied – would assent, on pain of not contradicting itself. Kant therefore puts great emphasis on the principle of 'universalizability' which he expresses as follows: 'I ought never to act except in such a way that I could also will that my maxim should become a universal law.' *Some* idea of universalizability is important in any normative framework (norms, after all, are attempts to identify rules for all of us, not guidelines we can apply to others but evade ourselves). But Kant's aim was very specific: to find laws of absolute generality that would be compelling for any 'good will' under any circumstances. Kant, too, was looking to build a normative framework from minimal principles, but his choice of what to exclude from view was drastic: first, as the opening sentence of the *Groundwork of the Metaphysic of Morals* states, he leaves out of consideration a variety of possible goods, insisting that 'it is impossible to think of anything at all in the world . . . that could be considered good without limitation *except* a good will.' Second, Kant excludes from the considerations relevant to specifying rules for conduct all the factual conditions of everyday life which might, we would have thought, shape norms that make sense to us: '*inexperienced* in the course of the world, *incapable* of being prepared for whatever might come to pass in it, I ask myself only: can you also will that your maxim become a universal law?'[19] By contrast, ethics starts out by reflecting on the kind of life it is *possible and good* for human beings to lead. Neo-Aristotelian ethics takes as its reference point not universal law, or a 'good will' abstracted from the flow of human practice, but the types of lives – actual lives, fully embedded in the circumstances of the world – that overall it is good for human beings to lead.

The Aristotelian approach has a number of advantages for us in formulating a normative framework for media in a global age. First, it does not even attempt to specify what absolutely we *ought* to do, and so brackets out areas of disagreement (for example about obligations to God or to humanity) where we *know* there is no agreement, not least because even the definitions of 'rationality' differ between various religious and secular traditions.[20] Second, the Aristotelian approach avoids the claim that it is ever possible to specify *in advance* what one ought to do in a specific situation and seeks instead to specify the dispositions (or 'virtues') that we expect of the type of person who is likely, on balance, to live a good life and contribute to a shared good life. What actually should be done in any particular circumstance is delegated, in the Aristotelian approach, to the discretion of the person who exhibits the master-virtue of 'practical wisdom' (*phronesis*), who can weigh up the often competing impetuses of different virtues when faced with a complex factual situation. As a starting point for considering the vast and *contradictory* complexity of contemporary media practice, this seems useful. Third, as already implied, the Aristotelian approach is concerned less with the qualities of an abstract 'will', hovering above the details of everyday life, and precisely with what actual human beings in concrete circumstances do: it is concerned, in short, with *practice*. The concreteness of this approach fits well with the emphasis throughout this book on practice and the underlying needs that drive practice. Nonetheless, there is much to be learned from the Kantian tradition, which too considers virtues, and particularly from Kantian reflections on the harm that a good will must, on pain of contradiction, avoid: when I formulate the virtue of care, I draw on Onora O'Neill's concept of social virtue and Rafael Cohen-Almagor's analysis of media harm.[21]

This chapter's argument involves other choices, too, which need to be justified. You will find in what follows no discussion of Habermas, which may surprise some readers. This is for two contrasting reasons. First, the basis of Habermas's well-known work on the public sphere and norms of public discourse is his belief in the generative power of certain transcendental principles that, for Habermas, are implicit in all human discourse.[22] This extends Kant's notion of 'law' to the second-order level of laws internal to rational discourse itself. I am, however, sceptical both about the specifiability of such principles and, given their transcendental nature, their ability to generate any *specific* moral or ethical principles. As we have seen, the Aristotelian approach finds its starting points elsewhere. The second reason for not discussing Habermas here is that we are exploring the general dispositions we would expect of *anyone* who acts in relation to media. We are not directly concerned here with how media in democracy should be organized. So for similar reasons, I will not pursue the fascinating debates on whether markets offer the best macro-structure for organizing media production and distribution in a democracy;[23] in any case, for reasons already explained, I seek to avoid relying on particular notions of democracy or of how democracies work since the value of democracy *cannot* be assumed in global dialogue today. We have however already noted the continuing usefulness of Habermas's public sphere as an orientation point in considering media's interaction with actually existing or emerging democracies: see chapter 5. Nor will you find in this chapter discussion of the work of Emanuel Levinas: for reasons that there is no space to develop here, I regard Levinas's insistence that the only basis for morality is an already existing commitment to 'the other' as itself a response, equally absolute, to Kant's search for moral principles that can serve as a universal law. Once again, the ethics tradition has different starting points.[24] Finally, I will not take as my starting point any specific moral values, including cosmopolitan values or Christian humanist values,[25] because I want to see how far we can get from starting points with minimal normative content.

Our starting points in this chapter are not then so much values as facts. There is the fact, first, that media organizations, media infrastructures and what individuals and groups do in relation to media are now part of the basic template of everyday life: this raises ethical questions about our practice in and through media, questions which could not be posed before modern media. Media are one of the *ethically significant 'practices'* in which humans are involved. Our formulations of a specific ethics of media are shaped by the distinctive human needs that media can fulfil and the distinctive harms that media can cause: respectively, the need for information and the harm of misrecognition, or lack of recognition. And there is the fact, second, that particular configurations of media resources (on all scales) may leave individuals and groups without the resources they need if they are to exercise, as they choose, their 'capabilities' as human beings, as Amartya Sen puts it:[26] in particular, participating in decisions about changes in our conditions of life and exercising voice, that is, giving an account of ourselves and our lives.[27] As throughout the book, the analysis of practice remains important.

In the long run, any ethics of media and communication must be connected to a broader ethics of human life. For now, I leave those connections implicit within the neo-Aristotelian notion of 'human flourishing' (living *well* the type of life that human beings can lead in the conditions which apply to that life) that underpins the philosophical perspectives on which I will draw. Whether we look through the lens of ethics or of justice, media are not trivial. Disputes over media ethics or media justice are *the edges* where the operational and infrastructural pressures of media production *cut into* the texture of everyday life. That is why we cannot ignore them: situated at the edge of what media sociology can do, considerations of media ethics and media justice point to the changing horizon within which the 'nature' of social life gets constructed in a digital era.

Towards an ethics of media

I write of '*media* ethics' for three reasons. *First*, there is no ethics distinctive to a particular medium because media narratives – always to some degree, and emphatically now, in the digital age – are intertextual and transmedial.[28] *Second*, media ethics is broader than journalism ethics, the already part-codified rules for institutionally empowered storytellers (journalists). Such codes are important and they have ethical content, but they emerge from particular institutional circumstances; instead, I want to explore how far a *general* ethics of media can be built that is, in part at least, independent of the particular institutional contexts in which journalism now finds itself. That broader media ethics would consider the general issues that media as a human practice raises for *anyone* involved in it, whether working in an institution or not. Such an ethics would be derived from considerations of media's potential contribution to human life. *Third*, there is still a need for a *media* ethics, as distinct from a general ethics of communication. There is rightly growing interest in the latter,[29] and there is an undeniable overlap between what I will discuss under the heading of a media ethics and the concerns of a broader communicative ethics. But there remain distinctive ethical issues raised by the institutional concentration of communicative resources that we call 'media' (even still 'the media') and the deeply embedded expectations we have of such institutions and our interactions with them; those issues do not disappear just because we now receive and make media across some of the same platforms on which we speak, or present our lives, to our friends.

It follows from all this that in this chapter we will draw on general philosophical resources and cut across some of the languages and practices internal to the craft of journalism. This is the opposite of an immanent approach to journalism ethics which finds its rules within the standards evolved by journalists themselves. An eloquent argument for such an immanent approach has been made by leading journalism scholar Barbie Zelizer.[30] Zelizer traces how a certain type of normative sensibility was internal to the emergence of journalism as a field, at least in the USA; her argument, in essence, is that the idea of journalism was from the outset already philosophical, and so the embedded ethics of journalistic practice deserves to be taken on its philosophical merits from the start. While this may be plausible for aspects of North American journalism from the late nineteenth century onwards, I do not believe it is plausible for the journalism culture of, say, Britain, particularly its tabloid journalism. Indeed, journalistic cultures such as Britain's, under intense pressure from economic rationalization and market pressures, now *need* to be viewed not 'immanently' but from the outside, if their ethical potential is to be rescued.

Virtue ethics prioritizes questions of 'the good': not the good in an abstract sense ('good' for any rational being), but the good for human beings, as embodied in our practices as human beings. We get a clear sense of how neo-Aristotelian ethics might in general terms proceed from Warren Quinn:

> one tries to determine what, given the circumstances, it would be good or bad in itself to do or to aim at. These questions are referred to larger ones: what kind of life it would be best to lead and what kind of person it would be best to be. The sense of 'good' and 'best' presupposed in this noncalculative form of practical thought is very general.[31]

Ethics is based on the idea that we can come to agree certain general things about what a good life would be like without needing to pass through the seemingly more immediate question of how should I behave in this or that particular situation.

All moral and ethical thinking involves various types of generality (that is why we debate them with each other), but there is a particular type of generality in the questions virtue ethics asks that is valuable for thinking normatively about large-scale institutionally focused practices like media. We can rephrase those questions more simply as the question Socrates asked: *how should I live?* As Bernard Williams points out, this is an open question addressable to anyone:

> [Socrates' question] is anybody's question ... when the question is put before me in the Socratic way, to invite reflection, it is going to be part of the reflection, because it is part of the knowledge constituting it, that *the question can be put to anybody* ... it very naturally moves ... to the question 'how should anybody live?' That seems to ask for the reasons we all share for living in one way rather than another. It seems to ask for the conditions of the good life – the right life, perhaps, for human beings as such.[32]

This Aristotelian (in fact, Socratic) starting point for any consideration of morality looks for possible consensus around the shared conditions of human life, and certain qualities of a good life that flow from those shared conditions. Indeed, if one basic condition of human life is that it is lived not in isolation but with others, then any practical good life must involve elements that converge (things that are good *both* for you and me). The question 'how should any of us live?' is given its point by the assumption that there are shared conditions which frame *all* human life, regardless of what moral and religious beliefs people have, and that we can agree in identifying those conditions (including those we call 'human nature'). Not that all views of those shared conditions are equally acceptable: no one today would accept Aristotle's view of human nature as hierarchically structured around the 'natural' superiority of Greek men over women, non-Greeks and slaves! But that does not rule out consensus in today's completely different historical circumstances on at least *some of* the conditions we share, enough to generate further agreement on aspects of what *for all of us* would be components of a good life. In this sense, ethical reflection is a practice that moves beyond any view of human nature as fixed. Indeed, we might argue, as John McDowell does, that humans' ability to reflect on and transform their conditions of life is itself an aspect of their nature, their 'second nature'. Put another way, 'it is natural to us to participate in a history that is *more than merely* natural.'[33] And, if so, media, and our reflections on our life with media, are also part of the 'more than merely natural' conditions of human life today.

In the neo-Aristotelian approach definitive answers to the question 'how should I behave in a situation of this exact type?' are delegated, as noted earlier, to the judgements made in practice by those with the right dispositions or 'virtues'. Neo-Aristotelian ethics is guided by the eminently practical insight that right behaviour cannot be identified in advance, abstracted from the often competing requirements of specific contexts. This is what McDowell calls the principle of 'non-codifiability': the range of answers that practical ethics must generate cannot be specified or codified in advance.[34] The only answers that ethics can provide in advance are to questions posed at a different level: what is a good life for human beings in the general conditions under which human life is, as a matter of practical necessity, lived? And what are the types of disposition required in someone who will prove in the long run to have lived a good life? The neo-Aristotelian tradition is concerned not just with action but with our stable dispositions to act. The basic question for media ethics flows quite readily: 'How should we act in relation to media, so that we contribute to lives that, both individually and together, we would value on all scales, up to and including the global?' From here, virtue ethics routes all normative questions through an investigation of what stable dispositions ('virtues') each of us *need* to have in order for us to live well together, including in relation to media. Admittedly, there is a dispute in interpreting Aristotle: did he specify 'virtues' in terms of whatever will help us live well together, or merely by drawing from conventional thought about how people should act?[35] Either way, a neo-Aristotelian approach is developed in close relation to everyday practice. Neo-Aristotelian virtue ethics takes as its reference point the degree to which virtuous dispositions will contribute to 'human flourishing', that is, a good life for human beings lived individually and together.

Much of human activity, however, is not general but organized into specific types of practice. A 'practice' as defined by Alisdair MacIntyre is a coherent and complex form of cooperative human activity whose internal goods involve distinctive standards of excellence which, if achieved, extend our possibilities of human flourishing or excellence.[36] Media are surely a practice in this specific philosophical sense. What we do with media *matters* for how humans flourish overall in an era where we are dependent on the exchange of vast amounts of information through media. Media ethics in the digital age involves *all of us*, not just media professionals: indeed, as the current Wikileaks lawsuit illustrates, the set of 'professionals' in relation to media and information production is constantly expanding.[37] The digital media environment is one in which all of us have ethical responsibilities, and necessarily so, since with our computers, mobile phones and digital cameras, we are all in principle now able to 'input' the media process.[38]

We can now formulate the starting question for media ethics more precisely as follows: *what are the virtues or stable dispositions likely to contribute to us conducting the practice of media well?* – well, that is, by reference to the wider aim of contributing to a flourishing human life together.[39]

The virtues of media practice

There are at least three virtues, I suggest, which we would want anyone involved in media practice to exhibit: accuracy, sincerity and care.

Accuracy and sincerity

The first two media-related virtues flow from the discussion in Bernard Williams's book *Truth and Truthfulness* (2002). Williams was not concerned with media directly but rather with identifying the basic 'virtues of truth' or truthfulness.[40] The subtlety of Williams's argument lies in insisting on the non-negotiable importance of both accuracy and sincerity for all human social life. That does not mean that what counts as accuracy and sincerity is unaffected by historical context, and indeed Williams explains in great detail why an abstract account of ethics that ignores cumulative cultural context is useless.[41]

Yet it has never, Williams argues, been enough for people to *pretend* to care about telling the truth since, if that was all they did, we would never have a stable basis for trusting them to tell the truth. It is therefore only if truth-telling is stabilized in the form of individual *virtues* (dispositions or tendencies that we can rely upon because we regard them as characteristic of virtuous people) that a good collective life is possible.

'Accuracy' might seem too obvious to mention at all. *Of course* we want journalists and anyone else who circulates information publicly to be accurate: that is a professional requirement of journalists. But, as Williams explains, to exhibit the virtue of accuracy, it is not enough to be accurate by luck. The truth is usually complex and multi-sided and therefore difficult to reach. So the virtue of accuracy involves a commitment to make the effort, and apply the resources necessary, to ensure so far as possible that what one communicates is accurate. Indeed, accuracy would not be important enough *to be* a virtue if it were easy to achieve: it requires what Williams calls *investigative investment*, an investment we need to know others are prepared to make. The idea of investigative investment is a useful one on which we can build for the media case. We generally need people to show the virtue of accuracy, and we need this particularly in relation to the type of information that is publicly circulated. If people did *not* generally display that virtue – if we had to operate on the assumption that public information about things that are distant from us was generally false – we would lack a common basis for interaction, and human life and society would be much more difficult: in some dark periods of history, human life has had to operate on something like that basis,[42] but that is emphatically *not* a state of affairs we would choose. Williams grounds his account of accuracy not in any absolute obligation to tell the truth (in which Kant believed) or in our ability to define truth absolutely, but in a genealogy that explains how human society could only have developed at all if *something like truthfulness* could be assumed as something at which people we value seek to aim: 'every society needs there to be dispositions of this general kind and also needs them not to have a purely functional value.'[43]

So what might investigative investment mean in a media context? We have, as a basic fact, media institutions involved in activities in the domain of truth: they make claims about 'what is going on' for everyone. Achieving accuracy in such institutions is anything but simple: it involves the commitment of resources and the sustaining of an internal culture where the energy and reflection necessary to achieve accuracy are valued. If contemporary media institutions are not ones that demonstrate such investigative investment, then there is a problem. Social organization on all scales needs media institutions to sustain conditions under which those who work in and for media can be individually virtuous. Otherwise, media institutions are unlikely to contribute to a collective good life. More on that later.

If accuracy is about doing what is necessary to achieve truthfulness in specific statements, *sincerity* is the disposition to 'say what we actually believe'.[44] The disposition of sincerity refers to all the background checking and reflecting necessary to ensure that whatever one says is not just accurate in itself but fits more widely with the whole range of other things that one believes about the world. This is a more complex test since it is a commitment to truthfulness within one's wider practice. Sincerity relates to how the broader possibility of *trust* is maintained. Trust, as Williams argues, 'is a necessary condition of cooperative activity'. Since we cannot keep repeating at each moment everything we believe to be true, much in what we say must be left to implication. But, as Williams argues following Paul Grice, trust in 'conversational implicatures' is necessary to 'efficient linguistic exchange'; unless they can be relied upon, human interaction would break down.[45]

Once again, the case of institutionally produced media is distinctive. No one relies upon what they read in the paper or hear on television *in the same way* they rely upon what a close friend or family member tells them in an intimate conversation. But there are certain implications distinctive to media communication that are regularly relied upon because without them communicative exchange with media would be pointless. One implication is that media items are the output of a process aimed at truth (guided by something like the virtue of accuracy); the other is that the statements that media contain do not contradict other things (not referred to) that are also believed to be true by those issuing the statement (the virtue of sincerity). In fact, in many countries, we know that levels of trust in some parts of media are very low, but media consumption remains high and practical reliance on media is considerable, hence the controversy when a media output of any sort is proved to be faked: that is, not even aimed at truth or fitting with its producers' wider beliefs.[46] The same question can also be approached from the perspective of power. As Bernard Williams argues, drawing on Primo Levi: 'It is a very basic exercise of power over another person to induce beliefs in that person without regard to their truth or falsehood; intentionally to induce false beliefs, for instance, just because they are false.'[47]

Not to sustain the necessary conditions of accuracy and sincerity is, analogously if more indirectly, a negative exercise of power by media institutions over their audiences. It is a power that works only by *not* being accountable, precisely because we *don't* see it at work. Worse, the defenders of journalistic freedom rely too often on a confusion between the freedom of speech or communication to which individuals are entitled and the institutional licence which media corporations are given for the purpose of sustaining those very conditions of individual freedom.[48]

Recent studies of journalism practice reveal an alarming gap between the conditions under which journalists work in various countries and the conditions under which ethical action is possible. Let's leave aside more obvious cases where good journalistic ethics is in direct conflict with the demands of authoritarian power[49]and concentrate on democracies where it is generally supposed that government/ press relations work well.

Drawing on extensive interviews with UK broadsheet journalists, press agency employees and freelancers, Nick Davies argues that journalists in the UK 'work in structures which positively prevent them discovering the truth'. This result is at odds with more optimistic views of where digital journalism is heading: towards more democratization and mutualism and towards less elitism, gatewatching rather than gatekeeping, a world of empowered producers. The problem is not that journalists have changed their values, since 'for journalists the defining value [remains] honesty – the attempt to tell the truth.' The problem is that the conditions under which journalists work are not ones where that value can be consistently or reliably *acted upon*. Davies links his diagnosis to wider global trends in an age of Web-based journalism where stories from elsewhere get recycled in an unseemly form of 'churnalism', resulting in 'a global collapse of information-gathering and truth-telling'. Production imperatives – the need to get the story 'up' in the quickest possible time and maximize 'hits' in an accelerated multi-platform news environment – lead to ever greater reliance on stories sourced from other journalists. Similar concerns have fuelled the public journalism movement in the USA for over a decade. Such pressures have taken a particularly virulent form in the 2011 phone-hacking scandal engulfing the British tabloid press, particularly News Corporation's now defunct title the *News of the World*.[50]

This is not, however, just a story about the UK or the USA, still less one about evil press empires; the bigger story is about a seismic shift in the conditions of news production itself. Pablo Boczkowski in his recent study of the online Argentinian press puts the paradox starkly: we face, he says, a 'remarkable increase in the amount of news available and a perplexing decrease in the diversity of its content'. A recent ethnography of German newsrooms is even more vivid, quoting one journalist who felt his engagement with the news was being 'hollowed out' when his time was 'occupied [in] filtering, sorting and selectively elaborating on an increasing mountain of incoming information' that leaves 'little time to think'. All this amounts to a heteronomous situation which cuts journalists off from the practice they want to conduct: it is too simple to blame reduced investment in news-making resources by distant and uncomprehending owners. The undermining of journalists' time and resources for ethical reflection is related also to the frantic rush by *all* social actors to attract journalists' attention and so influence the news cycle: this is the other side of the practices of self-promotion by non-media actors considered in chapter 6. Content management systems that stem the resulting flow only increase journalists' distance from the human sources that might provoke ethical reflection: news stories, like the people who leave traces in our email boxes, become just 'stuff' to be managed. These systemic pressures derive from multiple aspects of the digital age: increased economic competition between media outlets as they seek audience attention; the dispersal of symbolic production far beyond the newsrooms' walls; and reduced resources for news-gathering. The newsroom has become in the digital age congested to a degree which undermines the conditions of ethical reflection. And yet it was the possibility of a journalism oriented towards truth that was the original purpose of a free press. Moral philosopher Onora O'Neill puts the problem thus: 'there is no case' for the press having 'a licence to spread confusion or obscure the truth'.[51]

This is where media ethics becomes a practical tool. For instead of simply repeating the mantra that journalists are required to be 'objective', a virtue ethics approach to media requires us to consider the practical conditions under which something *like* the virtues of accuracy and sincerity might be achievable in media – or not. The neo-Aristotelian approach, *because* it is practice-based and not rule-based, is more open to considering the complexities of practice than rival approaches to media ethics. Conditions which make ethical action in relation to media impossible (or unlikely) damage the roots of trust in public culture and so have fundamental implications for the possibility of living a good life together.

The virtue of care

We want each other to be disposed to care about what people believe as a result of what we say. The issues of care in communication are not limited to those which arise from the direct implications of what we say. We need to care about the consequences that follow when what we say is *circulated*, an acute issue for media. From here begins consideration of a third media-related virtue, often approached in a transnational context via the concept of *hospitality*. I will argue that it is better considered as a broader virtue of *care* exercisable on multiple scales from global to the most local and that this quality is obscured if we construe it via the territorial metaphor of hospitality.

Media's contribution to the conditions of a good collective life is not limited to the circulation of accurate information that fits with what journalists more broadly believe. As we saw in chapters 4 and 7, media also need to be considered as a key means by which mutual *recognition* is generated in social life. Media sustain a space that puts us in view of each other. Without some degree of mutual recognition as moral agents requiring respect, the chances of us living together sustainably are small: this issue becomes acute *on a global scale*. Roger Silverstone was the first to highlight this issue in his reflections on the mediapolis. Silverstone's name for the practice associated with such recognition was 'hospitality', which he calls 'the first virtue of the mediapolis'.[52] Silverstone goes on to argue hospitality is an obligation of journalists and indeed all of us in a globalized world: an obligation to listen and hear the other which follows from our own sense that we have a right to speak and be heard. The tension between 'ethical' and 'deontological' formulations runs through his argument but does not detract from its originality or boldness. In what follows, I will steer, however, towards an emphasis on dispositions, not obligations.

To how much does Silverstone's account of hospitality commit us? As Onora O'Neill points out in an essay on 'Distant Strangers',[53] the older view of hospitality (reflected in Kant) was an obligation to distant strangers seen as strictly 'temporary': a basic obligation to show no hostility to strangers who came to one's house or territory and to give them basic sustenance. This idea of hospitality was based on the normal time limits to strangers' stay within the home and on the usual territorial limits around the home, from where strangers are normally absent. This creates difficulties in the media case. Roger Silverstone wanted to argue in *Media and Morality* that global media have a duty to show 'hospitality' to *all* the others they present to the audience, and that we the audience have a duty to be open to *all* those media present to us. The metaphor suggests that somehow media become our 'home', whoever 'we' are, and that our media home must be continually open. But is the old metaphor of hospitality sufficient for the *continual* obligation of *mutual* engagement Silverstone had in mind? Indeed, is the metaphor of media as a 'home' helpful at all, given its territorial implications?[54] What if, instead of a bounded community of which 'we' and our journalists are part, the concerns raised by media 'hospitality' derive from a general challenge we face – *any* two of us concerned with what media we need – that stems from media's inherent mobility and the unpredictable human encounters media make possible?

A different approach, based on Axel Honneth's theory of recognition (encountered in chapter 4), may here be more productive. Honneth derives from Hegel the idea that the intersubjectivity of human life makes possible moral injuries: we can damage each other's 'personal integrity' by how we talk with and treat each other.[55] So, for Honneth, any notion of 'the good' has to include the absence of those moral injuries, and equally any notion of justice must cover the distribution not only of material goods but also of opportunities for recognition. A bridge to reworking these insights for the case of media is the late work of Paul Ricoeur on *'linguistic* hospitality'. Ricoeur is concerned with what he calls the 'translation ethos' so important in dealings between and within languages. For Ricoeur, such 'linguistic hospitality' is not a purely literary virtue but the basis of a wider ethics for a world of great diversity. Linguistic hospitality is a fundamental ethical disposition that involves ensuring that, when we speak and write, we keep what he calls a just distance from the language of others. *Just* distance is very close to what Silverstone, drawing on Levinas, calls 'proper distance', but it has been stripped entirely of any territorial metaphor. For Ricoeur, 'linguistic hospitality' applies *whenever* individuals meet and *whatever their territorial relations*: whether I meet you on your home territory or vice versa, or whether we meet on neutral territory. This formulation is helpful for grasping what media do when, in representing the world, they quote from, or speak for, the language – the narratives – of others. The recognition of 'diversity' that Ricoeur believes is generally necessary is not a territorially based hospitality but a capacity relevant wherever we move physically and discursively, regardless of territorial scale.[56]

This suggests that *anyone* involved in media should take due account of the impacts of their communications on those to whom those communications circulate: this point is vital in an age of user-generated content and viewer-supplied media images. We may do better to drop the word 'hospitality' entirely. Ricoeur talks of 'solicitude' and we might, more simply, speak of care.[57] If it is good to be disposed to take care about the effects of our media communications as they circulate, this derives not from any notion of territory as 'home' (with its implied exclusiveness) but from the fact of our commonly experienced *connectedness*, the common *fabric* of a mediated world, which makes all of us vulnerable to each other. This connected-ness puts media in the position where their representations can always do harm. Even if we disagree fundamentally about many specific moral issues and priorities, we may agree on one fact: that, whether we like it or not, we inhabit a world connected by a common media-based fabric, which ensures that we can harm each other through our symbolic practices. Media-based connectivity has created what Ricoeur calls a 'limit situation' from which a new set of ethical issues arises. Just as we need to show care in our use of the shared institution of language, so we need others to be disposed to show care in their use of media, because through media we can harm each other, and so, over time, damage the fabric of collective and public life.

This third media-related virtue that I am calling 'care' derives, then, from needs that arise most acutely from the circumstances of global connectivity. Unless some care is exercised by all who put images and text into mediated circulation, then *the world* will become more dangerous and productive dialogue between opposed interests and peoples more difficult: the Danish cartoon controversy of 2005 was an early warning of such dangers.[58] A media-related virtue of care has some similarities to a feminist ethics of care.[59] The latter is con-cerned with our caring relationships to particular individuals, and so seems rather distant from our relations-at-a-distance through media. Yet, if what is at issue is the particular, but large, space of communica-tion that media enable, then the concern to *sustain* that space and the interrelations it makes possible has analogies with feminist notions of care. This media-related virtue of care is not care for 'anyone' who appears before us via a television screen or the front page of a news-paper (a care of that sort is better understood as a version of a broader humanitarianism, not specifically related to media). Indeed, Roger Silverstone's argument that even audiences have general obligations to hospitality derived from the act of watching seems impossibly demanding. Instead, the virtue of care considered here means care over the consequences (of what we say and show through media) for the *common* space of communication that media make possible and for the *specific* individuals who may be damaged by a careless use of that space. Onora O'Neill, who has sought to over-come the artificial divide between ethics and deontological approaches, writes of something similar when she discusses (among the 'social virtues') 'action that sustains natural and man-made environments on which both individual lives and the social fabric depend'.[60]

This media-related virtue of care affects also, in ways to which we are only just becoming sensitive, other spaces of connectivity and representation that digital media are opening up, such as social networking sites, with their shifting boundary between public and private life.[61] And it applies to the complex space of communication that has always arisen when traditional media take fragments of everyday life and convert them into public stories for everyone to use and abuse. Perhaps the recent opportunities for user-generated content have made us more aware of the complex communication spaces in which media intervene through all their stories: everyone has a story to tell, but the versions of events circulated under the banner of media institutions carry a particular force because more or less simultaneously they enter the awareness of large numbers of people. We need the makers of media stories *and* those who source those stories (quite often ourselves) to exercise care about those stories' effects as they circulate.

The media-related virtue of care may well be in conflict with the other media-related virtues, accuracy and sincerity. Imagine (it is not difficult) a tabloid newspaper headline that screams out to its readers on the dangers or injustices that stem from the local presence of migrant workers or asylum seekers. Let us assume that the journalists involved have made appropriate efforts to check the factual accuracy and plausibility of their story; they may also, quite possibly, if asked, say that the substance of the story conforms to what they and their assumed readers sincerely believe to be true. But isn't there an additional disposition we would want those journalists to have, namely, care? Would we not want them to be disposed to consider the consequences of their story when it circulates, in *this* particular form and language and with this particular emphasis – consequences for the spaces where the specific migrant workers or asylum seekers portrayed in it interact with others? And the consequences that, longer term, regular stories *of this sort* will have on the possibility of peaceful interaction between all of us? Such issues are unlikely to be resolved by saying media professionals have an obligation not to do harm as a strict Kantian approach might suggest[62] because from other perspectives it can be argued, just as legitimately, that journalists have an obligation to make visible difficult facts. Indeed, Patricia Spyer's analysis of what happened in Indonesia when journalists agreed to *avoid* giving ethnic information in conditions of heightened inter-ethnic tension raises important questions about the generalized fear such withholding of information may itself generate.[63] But if we think about these problems as conflicts between the *multiple* virtues that are relevant to the practice of media, then such problems are amenable to resolution over time through the 'super'-virtue that Aristotle called prudence or 'practical wisdom' (*phronesis*).[64]

An ethics of media in a neo-Aristotelian approach is oriented to identifying the multiple dispositions that we would expect of those who act in and through media. There is no reason to suppose that living by those dispositions generates easy recipes for action: on the contrary, a virtue ethics of media may be a good way to *expose* the emerging contradictions in which media implicate all of us.

Media injustices

Ethics does not exhaust the normative frameworks that can be applied to media. There is also the question of justice, which applies to media in all societies, whether or not democratic, and to the relations between all the world's peoples. What can we say about whether the distribution of symbolic resources on which current media infrastructures are based is just and whether the way media operate is just? Can *anything* be said on these difficult topics?[65]

For a long time I have hesitated to write on media justice, intimidated by the vast amount of work that would seem to be required to apply existing models of justice (such as that of the American philosopher John Rawls) to the media case. I hesitated also because of doubts about the viability of what Rawls attempted to do – that is, to construct a complete and rationally compelling framework for grounding our instincts about what is just and how we can determine what is just. I hesitated finally because of the sheer lack of guidance as to how to start thinking about media justice. If you look at standard media textbooks, you will not find much consideration of media justice.

And yet for a long time some areas of media research have been motivated by an implicit concern with media justice, or at least media injustices: the growing tradition of alternative media research (also called 'radical media', 'citizens' media' and 'community media') that investigates how media practitioners fight to get heard from a position outside the media mainstream; and early fan studies which pointed out the battles of fans to have *their* cultural creations based on mass media texts recognized by the media industries. All this work is driven by a sense that there is something unjust about either the concentration of symbolic resources in large media institutions, or those institutions' lack of respect for the creativity of audiences (fan–industry relations have fortunately moved on a long way from the stand-offs of the 1980s and early 1990s). Meanwhile, in a very different mode, turn-of-the-millennium fears of a digital divide led to the United Nations summoning two World Summits on the Information Society (WSIS) in 2003 and 2005 with the aim of 'build[ing] an inclusive Information Society' whose outcomes continue to be monitored. The WSIS movement did not refer to justice in its official communiqués, and its basis was more in a long-term rights discourse, focused on the 'right to communicate'. Some US-based organizations foreground media justice explicitly: whether as 'a new vision for [media's] control, access and structure' in the words of MediaJustice or, more boldly in the words of the Center for Media Justice, to use 'media as a tool to reframe our stories'. The term 'media justice' in these initiatives seems to work either as a general term for media strategies closely focused on *other* justice issues (whether race and economic rights, or social justice more broadly) or (as with the work of www.reclaimthemedia.org) a local implementation of some of the practical principles of the WSIS; in either case, these campaigns are US focused.[66]

There is no doubting the importance of media's role in developing campaigns for social justice and, when this is informed by insights into the media forces that routinely block coverage of such issues, then it becomes plausible to argue with Robert McChesney that the 'fates of media reform and social justice research are intertwined'. But such debate falls short of an approach to media justice itself, unless it develops an explicit account of what is not only wrong, but *unjust* about a particular distribution of media resources, and why. An interesting pointer to this wider debate comes from a US community-media campaign, the Media Justice Fund, which operated in the mid-2000s and insisted on the need for 'the equitable redistribution of control of media and communication technologies'. This gets close to expressing the essential point that a just distribution of media and communication resources is, in the digital era, a constitutive element of wider justice, not merely an instrumental means towards it. Even so, as Sue Curry Jansen notes, no links exist as yet between philosophical theories of justice (or injustice) and theories of media.[67]

Approaches to injustice

What might be the philosophical resources suitable for analysing the specific questions of justice that media raise? A rare writer who examines this was Roger Silverstone in his discussion, already noted, of hospitality. Yet, when Silverstone draws on Rawls's method for formulating principles of justice, the outcome is disappointing: 'the right to speak and an obligation to listen'. The right to speak is already contained in Article 19 of the 1948 UN Universal Declaration of Human Rights which includes 'the right to seek, receive and impart information and ideas through any media and regardless of frontiers'. The obligation to listen, as it stands, seems impossibly general: who does it oblige? On what conditions? On the basis of what assumed resources? To what end? Silverstone suggests that these principles 'require ... the creation of a system of institutions of global reach, which can in their very working guarantee to maximize the basic freedoms of mediated communication, without which the mediapolis would remain unjust'.[68] This is a bold conclusion. It is left unresolved what type of institutions should be built and on what scale: what is the appropriate balance for example between people having resources to speak in their own voice and representative speech? The WSIS process in the 2000s developed this issue without reaching any final resolution.[69] Questions of media justice are clearly difficult and admit of no easy formulations.

The problem of defining what we mean by 'media justice' is entangled with other difficulties in how we think about democracy, particularly the relationship between representative and direct democracy. Democratic politics, intertwined as it is with contemporary mass media, is based on a very uneven distribution of the opportunities to speak and to control the flow of speech. A few people speak regularly (they usually have a team of people attached to them who can work to control so far as possible how their speech is presented and received), while the majority are generally listeners. Is this just? That depends on our assessment of what weight we give to those moments where non-elite people speak (and their voice appears to be heard) versus those where they do not speak at all, or at best have their voice represented by mediators (a journalist, an MP, a councillor, an NGO). Interesting new work from Australia, inspired in part by the long-standing negotiations over communications rights between Australia's white population and its indigenous Aboriginal peoples, has approached this issue by foregrounding the question of *listening,* raising questions about the effectiveness and justice of the fabric through which the speech of democracy emerges in the first place.[70] Penny O'Donnell, for example, calls for a redistribution of media resources as a way of redistributing opportunities to be heard and listened to, but this raises, as she notes, difficult issues about the status we give to media's own communicative expertise.[71] So, even as we start to give substance to issues of justice, difficult questions remain.

Where exactly might justice and injustice lie in relation to media? Rawls's theory of justice would have us first develop a full model of the deliberative processes that might generate, as Sen summarizes, 'a perfect set of *institutions* ... that determines the basic structure of a fully just society'. But, as Sen notes, we are likely to wait a very long time before perfecting that model, let alone building institutions that embody it! Instead, in a move away from Rawls's maximalist approach, Sen argues pragmatically that we can begin to fill in the conceptual space of justice by foregrounding specific cases of injustice: an approach to justice guided not by 'transcendental institutionalism' but by 'realization-focused comparison'. For Sen, the task is through comparison, first, to identify specific injustices that need correction because they involve denying to specific groups the opportunity to use the full range of their human capabilities and, second, to identify specific institutional means for correcting those injustices.[72]

For Sen, political voice is one of a number of components constitutive of human development. Free media are an essential component of justice: they contribute to the circulation of information that challenges elites, help identify threats to the security of the poor and marginalized and provide a forum for the development of new cultural values.[73] At a basic level, then, the existence of free media institutions in any polity is one of the building blocks of human development, so the absence of free media is an injustice whose remedy is the creation of those media, a point that fits with Sen's long advocacy of media's role in the aversion of famine.[74] That fundamental point, however, does not get us far in identifying whether there are any more specific forms of injustice that arise *once* free media institutions are in place. Here Sen – who does not claim to be a media specialist, even if he is rare as an economist in taking seriously media's role in economic and social development – seems to elide a free media and free communication: 'the absence of a free media *and* the suppression of people's ability to communicate with each other', he writes, 'have the effect of directly reducing the quality of life' and so contribute to injustice.[75] But, as many accounts of contemporary media at least imply, injustice is possible in the media domain *even when* formally free media institutions exist. How, building on Sen's pragmatic approach to (in)justice, can we clarify the types of media injustice that are important?

Voice is a basic capability of human beings,[76] so no account of (in)justice in relation to media can ignore completely whether the arrangement of media resources gives due recognition to that capability. No one, on the other hand, benefits if everyone speaks at once, and by analogy it is meaningless for everyone to claim the right to have their voice heard in every media outlet; or, put another way, we don't get far through the naive principle that 'everyone needs to listen to everyone', as Tanja Dreher notes.[77] So we need to think about what would be a *fair balance* between the distribution of actual opportunities to speak and be heard in one's own name, and the distribution of opportunities – sometimes as valuable – to have one's problems or injustices represented by another or by an institution. Think of the Chinese radio journalist Xinran, now living in the UK, whose regional radio programme had huge impact by telling anonymously the painful stories of abused women in China, women for whom literally speaking in their own name would have meant death, as well initially as intense pain and shame. Clearly, we cannot argue that every case of 'speaking for' is unjust simply because it involves a person not being heard in their own name: nor, going to the other extreme, is it enough to say the existence of representative media institutions solves all the issues of justice regarding media.

Useful here in bridging the gap between these two extreme positions is Leon Mayhew's book *The New Public* which considers the role in large democracies of 'rhetorical tokens': that is, the means through which political parties, NGOs and governments speak for *types* of situation and types of people. That typical speech is unavoidable in any society beyond a small village, but what is crucial is that these speech-tokens can be *redeemed* in face-to-face situations where those who have done the speaking can be challenged directly on what they said, its meaning and its consequences, and the effectiveness of those challenges can in turn be monitored.[78]

How then can we think rigorously about the justice, or injustice, of institutions, including media, that mediate between individual voice and institutional action? This deep problem is hardly superseded by the proliferation of 'mass self-communication',[79] that is, the ability of individuals and groups to 'broadcast' their voice directly without passing through the gatekeepers of media institutions. For these self-communications do not stop mass media circulating, nor do they influence the degree to which mass media are even-handed in their representation of the social world: nor, given the difficulty of becoming visible online discussed in chapter 5, do they necessarily have any wider effect beyond the momentary satisfaction of expression. However, relieved by Amartya Sen of the need to construct a large-scale theory of media justice, we can more pragmatically list some types of media injustice that might require correction.

Types of media injustice

A first type of media injustice occurs when a specific person is harmed by media and has no effective means of publicizing that harm or seeking redress for it (this type of injustice flows from the basic fact that media may do harm, just as individuals may do moral harm to each other by their speech).[80] Such injustice is endemic in virtually all societies with large-scale mass media institutions since no mechanism has yet been developed, apart from the libel laws used by the super-rich, for challenging media speech. And yet, as an academic and practical topic, this type of media injustice has been extraordinarily neglected, and media studies bear partial responsibility for this. It is, as Jan Teurlings notes, 'utterly bizarre that the television participant', for example, 'is not considered to be in need of rights' and that the huge asymmetries of television power relationships, considered back in chapter 4, are simply regarded as 'normal'.[81]

A second type of media injustice occurs when definable groups of people are not given due recognition in the outputs of a media institution or media sector that claims some representative status in relation to the wider population to which those groups belong (a channel, newspaper or website that claims only to represent a particular organization is irrelevant here). Returning to Honneth's theory of recognition, it is particular levels of moral and social recognition that matter. Many examples of this second type of media injustice can be given: from the invisibility or limited invisibility of indigenous peoples in the national media of certain countries (Chile for example), to the portrayal of disabled people in media in a country such as Australia,[82] to the general absence as speaking agents of migrant workers in the mainstream national media of countries such as Britain. Indeed, the whole domain of 'global publicity' is still, it can be argued, based on exclusion.[83] Very difficult questions arise about what would count as adequate institutional corrections to such injustice: is it enough that these groups are legally permitted and practically able to produce and circulate their own media? Or does this precisely miss the point that they are likely to remain invisible in the mainstream media that reaches the majority of the population? If so, what sort of institutional mechanisms can be created for challenging directly the speech of mainstream media, so 'redeeming', in Leon Mayhew's term, the trust normally placed in that speech? Since at present it is very difficult for direct challenges to powerful media institutions of this sort to get heard and noticed, are legal structures required that could enable class actions that could effectively demand such a process of redeeming? Ways forward may be possible in specific countries, but it is reasonable to conclude that nowhere are such solutions very advanced. Any solutions will need to be flexible enough to deal with the complexity of how representation and recognition in media culture works, while at the same time acknowledging that 'visibility' (both social and media visibility) is now a key category in social description and contemporary power.[84]

Another question arises in relation to the second type of media injustice: can we imagine it arising at the global level, as Roger Silverstone's brief account of 'media justice' seemed to imply? This is difficult, since the plurality of media-based perceptions of the world is an even more basic fact than the plurality of moral perspectives from which we started this chapter. It would be absurd for any particular group or even nation to claim as an injustice that it is not recognized in *every* media that communicates on a global scale. But that does not mean that many specific cases of injustice cannot be imagined and made plausible through specific calls for redress. Such calls may be countered by the practical argument that the most effective form of redress is to set up a competing media outlet (think of Al-Jazeera): but that does not mean there are no injustices of this sort. As yet, however, we are some way off being able to delineate what shape a claim of redress for the second type of injustice would look like on a global scale.

There is a third potential type of media injustice which arises when an individual or group wants a direct voice but is prevented by lack of access to any means of representation. All media systems are built out of an inequality of symbolic resources, what James Bohman calls the 'division of labour' in democratic discourse. But an inequality is not an injustice unless individuals' set of human capabilities is reduced as a direct result of that inequality. Until such time as we regard being visible through media as intrinsic to human life, then there will be no automatic injustice from not having access to the possibility of speaking through media. However, more specific injustices will occur when an individual or group finds that visibility in media is essential to its exercise of other basic capabilities, and such media presence is denied: cases of political voice are the most obvious specific cases of this third type of media injustice. As Matthew Hindman has cogently pointed out, the digital age's extended range of content producers does nothing to counter the inherent inequalities and hierarchies of the internet as a networked space where 'links in' – and so basic searchability – are distributed unevenly.[85]

A fourth type of media injustice might be the closure of potential public spaces of discourse which disadvantage not specific individuals but *any* individual, group or movement that wants to make public claims for resources or recognition. This relates to Lawrence Lessig's argument for the necessity of an online 'commons', but applies also to the overall space of traditional media. Here, some forms of activism (Wikileaks, the Swedish PirateBay movement) are providing important challenges to the informational asymmetries built into existing online platforms;[86] in this case, media injustice links us, by a new route, to wider questions of political power and democratic functioning.[87]

Conclusion: around the fixed point of our need . . .

We have explored some principles of media ethics (against the background of the conditions under which human beings live lives that they can value) and some types of injustice in relation to media (by reference to a broad notion of human capabilities). Those underlying accounts of what constitutes a good and possible life for human beings are typically the reference point of neo-Aristotelian approaches to ethics and values. An advantage of such approaches is that they avoid relying on the sort of substantive moral principles over which there is usually little agreement, while focusing their efforts on illuminating practical conditions of human existence that might, over time, be identified consensually. Neo-Aristotelian ethics is, in other words, oriented to the conditions of human practice. This 'minimalist' approach is useful in clarifying the dispositions we would expect of those involved in media – *regardless* of the type of state in which they live and regardless of their religious or political eschatology.

I want, however, to be more specific about the values that have motivated my argument and that emerge from this book's particular understanding of how contemporary media are shaping our world. Those values will inevitably be more contentious, but they must be made explicit if the connection between this final chapter and the rest of the book's argument is to be clear. I have deferred this connection until now in order to see how much common ground could be achieved without relying on those specific values. But, from this book's very first words (the epigraph quotation from Wittgenstein), those values have underpinned its orientation to a perspective on media, society and world that is focused around our needs as human beings. What sense emerges from my argument of the types of life with media that it would be good to lead? What are the contradictions in our current ways of living with media that generate ethical difficulty?

Following chapter 1's review of the uncertainties about the future of media and media institutions, the book's main argument began in chapter 2 with an exploration of our practices related to media and of the way they are shaped by certain basic needs for community, interaction, coordination, trust, freedom, and so forth, considered at the level of individuals and their relations with other individuals and groups. In chapter 3, we explored the role of media in the production of social forms (such as ritual) against the background of all human beings' need for some degree of stability and order; a conflict emerged between the drive of large institutions (state, corporations, media) to control resources and authority and the needs of individual and groups to be given due recognition. In chapter 4, we looked specifically at the possibilities of individuals, groups and whole societies being injured through deficits or imbalances in the operations of media institutions: here, for the first time, the question of media injustice emerged.

It is not enough, however, to consider media's relations to social organization from the perspective of individuals and groups: we also must look at the systemic issues that arise. So, in chapter 5, we considered media's implications for social and political organization on a larger scale and the massive extension of social and political action that digital media, in principle, enable. While some see a simple shift towards greater democratization, we found great uncertainty as to whether the struggle between social actors of all sizes to take advantage of that extended scope of action will result in more democracy or less. Without free media, no doubt, democracy is impossible, but it does not follow from this that 'more media' means 'more democracy': a more subtle social calculus has to be developed. Questions arose about the intensity of communication spaces, their inherent tendency, perhaps, towards domination by certain types of institutional force and the inherent constraints in media-saturated cultures on sustainable challenges to such domination.

Chapter 5 began to clarify a contradiction characteristic of the digital media era which can be summed up quite simply: we have no way any more of living together – of conducting any domain of life – *without* media but we don't yet know how to live *well* with media. Using Habermas's in some ways outdated dichotomy between 'lifeworld' and 'system', there is no lifeworld any more that is not saturated at every level by system, including the systems that are 'media', but systems are not places within which we can live. Systems' intense functional determination means that, of themselves, system spaces are incompatible with any tolerable life, a contradiction prefigured in the account of Jade Goody's life in chapter 4. The saturation of social space by media – with all the systemic commands and demands that media carry – raises therefore fundamental issues for the quality of lives we now lead.

Those contradictions arise also in relation to the resources for social order. In chapter 6, we considered the consequences of mediatization for the fields within which authority, power, capital and individual recognition are generated and fought over. The more we desire to be visible in media across all domains, the more vulnerable to a currently unaccountable form of power – media's symbolic power – all domains of social action become. In chapter 7, we internationalized our frame of reference to consider the varieties of media culture that arise when media's development is understood in the context of multiple historical trajectories and the full range of needs that shape human life. Finally, we came in this chapter to consider the possible ethics and justice/injustice of how we live with media.

In the course of this book, we have considered multiple ways of living with media and the types of systemic contradiction that emerge when we live with what Sonia Livingstone has called 'the mediation of everything'. What values might enable us to begin sorting out good from bad outcomes? We have considered some quite basic values so far in the chapter – the goods of coordination, cooperation and non-harm which generate the virtues of truthfulness and care – but, in the discussion of injustice, more substantive values emerged, such as recognition. Individuals and groups need to be recognized as moral and social agents. This is linked to the fundamental value of voice I have described elsewhere.[88] In recognizing someone as capable of contributing to the social process, we are recognizing, for example, her capacity to participate in deliberations about how life together is organized. Media play an important role in providing recognition, as Eva Illouz's pioneering work has explored, and in sustaining spaces where such specific capacities can be actualized.[89] Recognition, in turn, requires us each to be allowed some *freedom* of action within which to fulfil some of the capabilities for which we are recognized: recognition without some practical degree of freedom is empty. Yet meaningful voluntary action is impossible except against the background of various degrees of practical and ontological *security* to which media and other institutions, in their stability, contribute.

Media then, both media institutions and outputs, are involved in sustaining both immediate and underlying conditions of mutual recognition (note that, as earlier, I avoid formulating this in terms of media's practical contribution to specific forms of democracy). To sustain mutual recognition, media must be open to participation, open to criticism or challenge, worthy of trust as practices of truth-telling, and practised with care; otherwise, they can provide no basis for mutual recognition. Actual media institutions take many forms and they may well not meet these standards. As the long tradition of political economy research on media has consistently shown, there is little reason to believe that media institutions, just because they are free to compete with each other in a market, are *ipso facto* likely to contribute to these broader goods. It is interesting to find a leading philosopher such as Bernard Williams, without any background in media research, so decisively dismissing the all too common idea that the competitive freedom of media institutions such as the press in itself ensures that those institutions' outputs contribute to cultural and political freedom, as the classic liberal principle of 'the marketplace of ideas' assumes. The market system, Williams argues, while it may make outright tyranny difficult to sustain, 'does less well in sustaining the complex of attitudes and institutions that as a whole stand against tyranny'.[90] To value media freedom, then, and media's contribution to the actualization of freedom, does not mean regarding market freedoms as trumping all other values for organizing media. Media, at bottom, are *social* institutions. The acute difficulties that market forces pose for any ethical media practice of journalism can only be addressed by drawing on normative principles requiring social implementation framed beyond a narrow market-focused notion of freedom.

We cannot clarify how – individually, collectively, institutionally – we can live well together with, and through, media unless we can agree on some extrinsic aims which our practices with media should satisfy. For so long, discussions of the media we need have been dominated by polarized alternatives: media as market institutions exclusively focused on competition or national media focused on the sustaining of social order. Media institutions continue to exist with many of their former powers, but now a much wider range of individuals and groups can operate through and across them. And the mutual interactions of those individuals and groups generate, in turn, new types of ethical and social problem, as mutual co-veillance penetrates ever deeper into everyday practices of work, identity and sociality, as we leave archive trails of our lives on social networking sites and wherever we buy or observe anything.[91] It is this intense implication of our lives in media, *from all directions*, that creates systemic contradictions and a limit situation that requires us to build an ethical perspective on media. Recall here German poet Rainer Maria Rilke's prophetic words, written long before the digital media age: '... for here there is no place/ that does not see you. You must change your life.'[92]

Longer term, that ethical perspective must encompass all our communications through digital interfaces[93] but, as I have brought out in this chapter, we neglect at our peril the distinctive ethical issues that continue to be raised by *media* institutions and *media* content (such as news) produced professionally for large-scale distribution. It is, after all, principally still through mainstream media that we encounter the world's different ways of thinking about politics and morality: ways of thinking that must in some way coexist, if life on earth is not to descend into permanent war. Our shared world (what the ancient Greeks called 'oecumene', literally our 'lived space')[94] is mediated: that in itself requires us to develop a distinctive understanding of media ethics and media justice that can be applied on all scales up to the global.

The practical projects of living well, and living well with media, are inseparably intertwined with the theoretical tasks of media ethics and media theory. First, media play a crucial role in representing the facts and norms that guide our action in the world and, if they do so badly, they can injure the social fabric. A good life involves, among many other things, the existence of media that help make the world more transparent, not less, and so contribute to our ability to grasp accurately the conditions under which we, and those around us, live. In turn, an adequate debate about media ethics and justice requires, as its information base, a clear understanding of what media do in the world, that is, a media sociology grounded in a broader social theory. An ethics of media lacks moorings, if not based in an account of how media institutions shape the production and occlusion of knowledge, the formation of social power and strategic claims to social 'reality', and changing conditions of agency. The underlying point of what we have so far called 'media studies' is to study how media contribute to the conditions of knowledge and agency *in the world* and so to understand better whether media enable us to live well together.

A more adequate understanding of media's roles in the very texture of experience[95] – based in a social theory that grounds, rather than obscures, such understanding – is therefore not an academic luxury but an essential tool for living. Like any tool, it cannot operate without friction. What provides that friction? It is our critical distance, as human beings, from the expressive and systemic realities that media comprise.[96] It is important to ignore siren calls which say that our life today is a 'media life' that generates its own autonomous potentials and norms.[97] For those calls ignore two basic facts: that there are many material conditions of life apart from media and that, for many people, their stock of resources is not being significantly transformed for the better. The world is becoming more unequal and our ability to look and still not see that inequality is growing.[98] The work of media institutions is crucial to reducing that opacity, but also – sadly, many would argue – to increasing it.

We need more informed conversations about how media operate in the world and how they might operate better, about how we live with media and how that life with media might be different. It is to these conversations, likely to unfold for many years and on many continents, that this book has sought to contribute.

Notes

Preface

1 See, from various perspectives, Livingstone (1999: 61), Caldwell (2000: 15), Herring (2004), Hijazi-Omari and Ribak (2008).
2 Giddens (1990), Thompson (1995), Castells (1996), Silverstone (1994). More recently, see Beck (2000a: 12), Hardt and Negri (2000: 347–8), Urry (2000: 183).
3 Jensen (2010: 105).
4 I deal with aspects of this elsewhere: Couldry (2010: ch. 5).
5 Important recent work includes: Bagdikian (2004), Curran and Seaton (2007), Curran, Fenton and Freedman (forthcoming), Hesmondhalgh (2007), Kraidy and Khalil (2009), Mayer (2011), McChesney (2008), Mosco (2009), Schiller (2007), Chakravarty and Zhao (2008).

Chapter 1 Introduction: Digital Media and Social Theory

1 Braudel (1981: 561).
2 Rantanen (2009: 15).
3 Lazarsfeld and Merton (1969: 495).
4 Giddens (1984: 164). Compare Mann (1986: 1), Beck (2000a), Urry (2000), Touraine (2007).
5 Zielinski (2006: 7), Tomlinson (1999: 9).
6 Jensen (2010: 110). Compare Thompson (1995: 19–22), Shirky (2010: 53) and Friedrich Krotz's helpful definition of media as a distinctive modification of communication involving any of the following: 'a technology, societal institution, organizational machine, a way of setting content in a scene, and a space of experience of a [recipient]' (Krotz 2009: 23).

7   For media's relation to modernity, see Thompson (1995), Garcia Canclini (1995), Mattelart (1994). For broad histories of media, see Briggs and Burke (2005), Chapman (2005), Starr (2004). On the nature of the internet, see the definition of Chadwick (2006: 7).

8   On contemporary media as 'environment', see, for example, Press and Williams (2011: 8–16).

9   Shirky (2010: 61).

10   See, for example, Lev Manovich's account of how artistic production is changed in the era of new media by the externalization online of the resources that artists had once drawn on 'somewhere below consciousness' (2001: 127).

11   Morgan (2008: 54).

12   Thévenot (2007a: 238).

13   Innis (1991).

14   Hepp (2010: 39–40); Debray (1996: 15).

15   Proust (1983: 134–5). I quote from the C. Scott Moncrieff and T. Kilmartin translation but prefer in the text a more recent translation of the novel's overall title.

16   I wrote this passage before finding John Tomlinson's (2007: 119–20) interesting, if differently directed, discussion of the same passage.

17   Williams (1973: 295–6).

18   DeLillo (1999).

19   Quotations from Gitlin (2001: 20); Castells (2009: 55).

20   Vaidyanathan (2011); Tomlinson (2007: 95); Michael Pocock, CEO of Yell, quoted *Guardian*, 14 July 2011.

21   *Daily Mirror* reader, quoted Weaver (2007).

22   Silverstone (2002: 762).

23   Bolter and Grusin (2000: 50).

24   Gitlin (2001: ch. 1). On RFID chips, see Hayles (2009: 47); Press and Williams (2011: 202–4).

25   http://en.wikipedia.org/wiki/supersaturation, last accessed 6 January 2011: Gitlin (2001: 67) does not draw on this technical meaning.

26   Shannon and Weaver (1949). For brilliant analysis, see Kittler (2010: 43–6, 208).

27   Golding and Murdock (1991); Garnham (1990); Miège (1989); Mosco (2009); Chakravarty and Zhao (2008).

28   Kittler (1999, 2010). As Meyrowitz (2008) notes, all branches of media theory (medium theory, uses and gratifications, power theory) overlap to some degree. For 'medium theory' generally, see Meyrowitz (1994).

29   Kittler (2010: 67 and 176; 226; 44, added emphasis; 31, 42–3, 33 and 176). For commentary, see Peters (2010: 5) and the critique of Lovink (2003: 27, 22–9).

30   Thompson (1995); Giddens (1990). For related discussion, see Moores (2005), Longhurst (2005), Hesmondhalgh and Toynbee (2008).

31   Graham (2004: 23).

32   Elias (1994); Bourdieu (1993); Durkheim and Mauss (1970).

33   Mills (1959); Gouldner (1962); Splichal (2008).

34 Here, contrast an elegant defence of a broader communication theory: Jensen (2010, especially ch. 2).
35 Zielinski (2006: 269).
36 Mosco (2009: 117). Compare Sconce (2003); Curran, Fenton and Freedman (forthcoming); Palfrey and Gasser (2008: 294); Morozov (2011).
37 Marvin (1987). For important recent critiques of the myth of 'free' information, see Morozov (2011), Lanier (2011); for an example of that myth, see respected journalist commentator Jeff Jarvis's (2011) comment that 'print feels finite, digital infinite. But print is also limiting, while digital is freeing.'
38 Eisenstein (1983: 22, added emphasis).
39 Eisenstein (1983: 44, 71, 78, 85). The expansion of 'archive' capacity was a basic consequence also of writing itself (Goody 1976).
40 Febvre and Martin (1990: 170).
41 Winston (1998: 2).
42 El-Nawawy and Iskendar (2002: 68) on 1990s Iraq; on the contemporary Arab world, see Kraidy and Khalil (2009: 31).
43 Manovich (2001).
44 Berners-Lee, quoted Introna and Nissenbaum (2000: 179); on the 'information revolution' generally, see for example Bimber (2003) and the then BBC Director of Global News, Richard Sambrook (Sambrook 2006).
45 Schiller (2007); Lessig (2002).
46 Petersen (2010: 60–4); Shiels (2010). The *Guardian* (24 June 2011) reported that an FTC investigation on Google was imminent.
47 General internet penetration is stated at 78.3% (USA), 80.9% (South Korea) and 85.9% (Denmark): www.internetworldstats.com; *mobile broadband* access is however 89.8% in South Korea, according to OECD figures: www.oecd.org/document/54/0,3746,en_2649_34225_38690102_1_1_1_1,00.html (both last accessed 6 September 2011). On the UK's continuing digital divide, see Ofcom (2009a and 2009b), and globally, see ITU/UNCTAD (2007). On relative costs of a computer, see Chadwick (2006: 65).
48 Wheeler (2004) on the Middle East; Seiter (2005: 13) and Livingstone (2002) on class and children's internet use; Ofcom (2010, in 2007–11: 249–50) on class and internet access generally; Warschauer (2003: 24) and Kling (1999) on a vicious circle; Ellison, Steinfield and Lampe (2007) on social networking. For a useful recent summary of the digital divide debate, see Chadwick (2006: ch. 4).
49 CNNIC (2010) for China internet statistics; on Marathi, see Curran, Fenton and Freedman (forthcoming: ch. 2).
50 Debray (1996: 16).
51 Wuthnow (1989); Wittmann (1999).
52 Kittler (2010: 67).
53 Arnison (2002); Shirky (2010: 16).
54 Buckingham (2008: 15); Herring (2008: 87).
55 See ch. 5.

56 Shirky (2010: 156); Proust (1982: 390).
57 Beck, Giddens and Lash (1994); Fornäs (1995: 2–7); Lash (2002); McQuire (2008: 21–2).
58 Poster (1999: 17).
59 Anderson (1983); Billig (1995).
60 Jenkins (1992), Gamson (1994), Priest (1995) were important early studies on how audience and fans get involved in the media process; on 'mediation', see Martin-Barbero (1993), Couldry (2000a), Silverstone (2005); for the rapprochement between media studies and anthropology, see Dayan and Katz (1992), Ginsburg (1994), Rothenbuhler and Coman (2005).
61 E.g. Turkle (1996), Katz and Rice (2002), Livingstone (2002).
62 Compare Couldry (2000a: 184–95).
63 *Economist*, 20 April 2006, added emphasis.
64 On the USA, see Barnouw (1990 [1975]: ch. 2) and Douglas (1987: chs 5 and 9); on France, see Barbrook (1995); on the UK, see Scannell and Cardiff (1991).
65 On the need for capital, see Garnham (1990), Benkler (2006: ch. 2); on the relation of media to state, see Mattelart (1994), Barry (2001), Larkin (2008).
66 Medrich (1979) on the constant TV household; UK statistics from Ofcom (2011, in 2007–11).
67 Thompson (1990: 15); Kine (2000: 43) on early use of phone wires in the USA.
68 Contrast Beckett (2010) and Jones (2009) on the 'communities' attached to the UK's *Daily Telegraph* website and US network news channel websites, respectively.
69 Respectively, Manovich (2008: 53), Marshall (2006: 50).
70 On 'mass media', see Manovich (2008: 53), Marshall (2006: 50), McQuail (2005: 139). On Google, see Carr (2011) and Google CEO Eric Schmidt's comments following his MacTaggart Lecture, Edinburgh Television Festival, August 2011, quoted Kiss (2011).
71 On Apple and Google, see Kirwan (2010); Eric Schmidt, CEO of Google, has spoken of the new 'Gang of Four' (Google, Apple, Amazon, Facebook), quoted Waters and Edgecliffe-Johnson (2011); on the strategic use of the term 'platform', see Gillespie (2010); on Microsoft and Skype, see Arthur (2011).
72 Garrahan (2011) on Premium VOD; Castillo (2011) on Google and YouTube; Stuart (2010) on 'cloud gaming'.
73 Anderson and Wolff (2010); compare Zittrain (2008).
74 Lotz (2009a: 12–13 n. 2); Katz (2009).
75 Dawson (2007) quoted Lister et al. (2009: 229); Curtin (2009: 13).
76 Spigel and Olsson (2004); Turner and Tay (2009: 3); Lotz (2009a: 12); Curtin (2009: 18).
77 Miller (2010: 143); Ofcom (2011, in 2007–11); on China, see Miao (2011: 111).
78 Uricchio (2009: 63).

79   See Bird (2003), and for interesting reflections on the significance of this for audience research, see Ruddock (2007: ch. 7).

80   Jenkins (2006: 13).

81   Madianou and Miller (2011).

82   Gitelman (2008: 7).

83   On the era of 'plenty', see Ellis (2000); on news consumption at work, see Boczkowski (2010: ch. 5).

84   On decline in newspaper consumption, see Rantanen (2009: 115), Starr (2009); yet 65% of Finnish 15- to 29-year-olds read a newspaper compared with 24% in the USA (World Association of Newspapers 2008) and newspaper consumption among Swedish youth remains strong (Bergström and Wadbring 2008); on free papers, see Straw (2010).

85   Lotz (2009b: 95, 109); Banner, quoted Lotz (2009b: 105).

86   Pew (2008) for US television news consumption; on UK and German figures, see Couldry (2009a) discussing Ofcom (2007–2008, in 2007–11), Oemichen and Schröter (2008); on Denmark, see Linaa Jensen (2011); on European Arab migrants' news consumption, see www.media-citizenship.eu.

87   On the USA, see Miller (2010: 12–13), Curtin (2009: 13), Spigel (2004: 1) and Robinson and Martin (2009) who report television viewing as almost unchanged between 1975 and 2005; on the UK, see Ofcom (2007–2011); on Germany, see Medien Basisdaten, www.ard.de/intern/basisdaten/onlinenutzung, last accessed 20 November 2008.

88   See respectively Curtin (2009: 16), Miller (2010: 144).

89   Lotz (2009a: 9, 2); Johnson (2009).

90   Scannell (2009); Bolin (2011: ch. 5).

91   Couldry, Livingstone and Markham (2010); and see our 2006 report available from www.publicconnection.org.uk.

92   Wyatt, Thomas and Terranova (2002); Selwyn, Govard and Furlong (2005).

93   Napoli (2008: 60).

94   Halpern (2010: 26). Compare Gillespie (2011), Powell (2011), Zittrain (2008).

95   On mobile privatization, see Williams (1992: 26–31) and compare Lefebvre (1971: 100–1); on mutualization, see Rusbridger (2009) and compare Jarvis (2007), Bruns (2005), Russell (2011).

96   Christensen and Røpke (2010); Crary (1999: 1); on the bias towards entertainment, see Turner (2010), Thussu (2009), and, for important anticipation of this argument, Morley (1999).

97   On the internet's open structure, see Bolter (2001); Lessig (2002: 34ff).

98   Benkler (2006: 32–3).

99   Carroll (2007) on the *Los Angeles Times*.

100 Starr (2009: 4). In the UK, there was a 5 million drop in newspaper readership between 1992 and 2007 (National Readership Survey 2007, quoted in Brook 2007), with recent NRS surveys suggesting continuing falls (*Press Gazette*, 7 July 2011). In the USA, the percentage of the adult population reading any daily newspaper fell from 45.1% to

39.6% between 2008 and 2010, according to Newspaper Association of America data (www.naa.org, last accessed 25 June 2011).

101 Beecher (2009); Phillips (2011).
102 Rantanen (2009: 129, 132). On the uncertainty of cross-subsidy, see Starr (2009: 10–12), Fenton (2009), Massing (2009a and b), Sambrook (2010: 20–1), Lievrouw (2011: 125–32).
103 On UK TV advertising to 2010, see Bradshaw (2011) and Ofcom (2011, in 2007–11) (admittedly by August 2011 current figures looked less encouraging: Sweney 2011); globally, see Thomas (2011).
104 Smythe (1977).
105 Turow (2007); Bolin (2009: 351; compare 2011: ch. 3). A similar argument – about the fragmentation of the public sphere and communications space – can also be based on the way digital media *enhance* specialized communication (Sunstein 2001; Lievrouw 2001; anticipated by Pool (1983: 261). On fragmentation and political marketing, see Bennett and Manheim (2006), Howard (2006).
106 Compare Buonanno (2008: 26) on the likelihood that 'generalist' television will continue alongside 'narrowcast' television.
107 Compare Douglas (1987: 317) on radio in modernity.
108 Beniger (1986).
109 For more detailed discussion, see Couldry (2003a, 2006).
110 Appadurai (1996); Ong (2006).
111 Bourdieu (1977); compare Boltanski (2009).
112 Larkin (2008: ch. 2, esp. 66); see also Spitulnik (2010).
113 Jones (2009: 30, 33) on US late-night talk shows.
114 Turner (2010); compare Couldry (2009a).
115 On celebrity, see Marshall (2006: 644); on the implications of 'inter-activity', see Andrejevic (2008b). For media institutions' needs to retain our attention more generally, see Dayan (2009), Uricchio (2009: 72), Thomas (2004).
116 Feuer (1983); Bourdon (2000).
117 Hillis (2009: 58). Compare Gergen (2002: 240) on the conflict between the localism of cell phone and the general reach of mass media. Burgess and Green's survey of YouTube found that only 8% of uploaders to YouTube were media companies, although traditional media were the source of 42% of uploaded material (2009: 43–6).
118 Thomas (1971: 510–11).
119 Burgess and Green (2009: 37) on YouTube; *Press Gazette*, 11 May 2011, on WENN and Twitter; see Waters (2011), on financial value.
120 Scoble and Israel (2006); Arvidsson (2011). On the closeness of social networking sites to capital, see Palfrey and Gasser (2008: 268) and Beer (2008), criticizing boyd and Ellison (2008).
121 Turner (2009: 62) on national broadcasters; Chinese viewer, quoted Sun and Zhao (2009: 97).
122 Meyer (2003), Thompson (2001); on 'space of appearances', see Arendt (1960).
123 Sassen (2006); Turner (2007a: 288).

124   Zelizer (1993); www.bbc.co.uk 11 February 2011 (my emphasis).
125   Kellner (2003: 12), compare McNair (2006), Riegert (2007), Imre
      (2009a); Turner (2010: 22).
126   Volcic (2009) on former Yugoslavia; Sun and Zhao (2009) on China;
      Capino (2003) on the Philippines; Kraidy and Khalil (2009: 33) on the
      Arab world; Baym (2005) and the major new study by Delli Carpini
      and Williams (2011) on the USA.
127   Castells (1996); for the distinction between 'media in space' (commu-
      nication footprints) and 'spaces in media' (topologies of mediated
      communication), see Adams (2009: 1–2).
128   Giddens (1990: 14) and see geographical insights into how inequalities
      are folded into scale: Massey (1994: ch. 6); Janelle (1991); Smith (1993).
129   Beck (2000b: 11–12) compare Urry (2000: 183); Hardt and Negri (2000:
      347–8, cf. 58).
130   Held et al. (1999: 15–17).
131   Tarde (1969 [1922]: 306–7).
132   In Ficowski (1990: 179).
133   McQuire (2008: 22).
134   Giddens (1990).
135   For discussion, see Cohen (2009). The Iranian government subse-
      quently tried to block access to tributes to Neda Agha-Soltan: *Guard-
      ian*, 5 June 2010.
136   Larson and Park (1993).
137   The history of such claims is vast: see, on the telegraph, Flichy (1994: 9).
138   Jansson (2006: 100), discussing Bauman (2000). Compare Martuccelli
      (2005: 46–9, 55).
139   Poster (2006: 78) on demateralization; Sassen (2006: 344 on material
      conditions; 310 on rescaling; 10 on normative orders); Tunstall (2008:
      xiv) on national media.
140   Latour (1999: 18), and see further ch. 4 for ANT's relevance to media.
      Some geographers even reject the notion of 'scale' altogether (Marston,
      Jones and Woodward (2005); compare Thrift (2008: 17)) but this move
      has been subject to fierce attack (Leitner and Miller 2007). See, for a
      related argument, Morley (2011) and also the conclusion to ch. 5.
141   Fischer (1992) on the early telephone; Gergen (2002), Ling and Donner
      (2009) on mobile phone.
142   Urry (2007: 8–9).
143   Martuccelli (2005: 83, 58–69).
144   I write of 'human life', while acknowledging that the boundaries
      between 'human' and 'nature', and between 'human' and 'technology',
      are constructed (Strathern 1992). And yet, as Strathern points out, 'we
      still act with Nature in mind' (1992: 197, quoted Barry 2001: 11).
      Equally, we still act with 'the Human' in mind, which does not mean
      there is a simple or specifiable human 'essence' (Hayles 1999).
145   Jonas (1984), Beck (1992).
146   Silverstone (2007); Couldry (2006).
147   Compare Debray (1996: 15); Briggs and Burke (2005: 4).

148   Anthropologist Henrietta Moore (1986: 116) comments that space is not a text – 'the organization of space is not a direct reflection of cultural codes and meanings; it is, above all, a context developed through practice.'
149   Fischer (1992: 17, 85).
150   I focus here on the materiality of how representations take effect, once received. Another important issue is the materiality, and uneven distribution, of the processes whereby media representations get made and distributed: Boyd-Barrett and Rantanen (1998); Parks (2005).
151   Williams (1961: 123).
152   Couldry (2003a, 2006).
153   Boltanski (2011: 9, 34, xi) and in French translation (2009: 26, 61, 13); for p. 61, I give my slightly adjusted translation.
154   Hepp (2010: 42–3), and see earlier Martin-Barbero (1993), Couldry (2006: 13–15), Morley (2007: 200), Curran (2002: 53).
155   Thrift (2008: 183–4, 242, 250). Compare Parikka (2010).
156   Thrift (2008: 2). Other writers influenced by Gilles Deleuze go even further and dissolve all process and all subjects into pure 'immanence' (Parikka 2010: 234 n. 31), a move Thrift rightly rejects (2008: 13, 17). Parikka offers an account of how media constitute 'worlds' that is entirely non-representational, relying on an account of 'affects' that, for all its precision of language, says nothing about how media contents matter in the world. See also Clough (2009) on Deleuze's 'transcendental empiricism'.
157   Couldry (2008b) criticizing Latour (2005); Knoblauch (2011). For an exception, see Andrew Barry's reflections on the role of technology in politics which acknowledges the regulatory and constitutive role of technical 'information', although not that of broader representations of the social world (Barry 2001: ch. 7).
158   Lash (2009: 178). Compare Savage (2009: 157, 163–4). And see special issue of *European Journal of Social Theory* 12(1) in 2009.
159   Lash (2002: 18, 16).
160   For the long-established problems of functionalism in sociological explanation, see Lukes (1975). On the role of sociological explanation in everyday social order, see Boltanski (2009: 44).
161   For the philosophical basis of my approach to representation in critical realism, see Couldry (2008b): compare Downey (2008). For a powerful critique of the social constructivism about facts to which critical realism is opposed, see Boghossian (2007).
162   Barry (2001), Latour (2005).
163   The best reflections on this complexity remain Lefebvre (1971).

Chapter 2 Media as Practice

1   Larkin (2008: 3).
2   Wittgenstein (1978 [1953]: 46).

3 Pitkin (1972: 3).
4 This primary concern with action also fits with the basic emphasis of communication theory with communications as action (Jensen 2010: 5).
5 Wittgenstein (1978 [1953]: 11, 6, 88).
6 Pitkin (1972: 293). A further difficulty for my argument, and any account of media practice that follows critical realism (see ch. 1, n. 161), would follow if Wittgenstein's insights into practice *depended* on the social constructivism about facts with which Wittgenstein's work has often been associated. There is, however, no such dependence, although differing views on constructivism inform the contrast developed later in the chapter between my approach to practice and Theodor Schatzki's.
7 Knoblauch (2011).
8 Aristotle (1976: 76).
9 Krotz (2009: 22).
10 Yates (1992 [1966]).
11 Tapscott (1998); Prensky (2006).
12 Herring (2008: 72, 78, 87); Buckingham (2008: 10).
13 Hillis (2009: 25).
14 Lessig (2008), discussed by Bolin (2011: ch. 7), and compare the statement of O'Reilly (2005) that 'everyone' is now 'a content producer'; on stratification of online production, see Hargittai and Walejko (2008).
15 Lewis (1991: 49).
16 Garnham (1990); Hesmondhalgh (2007).
17 Classically challenged by Abercrombie, Hill and Turner (1981).
18 Cashmore (2006).
19 Fuller (2005: 2).
20 Manovich (2001, especially 16, 47–8).
21 Lopez Cuenca (2007/8).
22 See Parikka (2010: 61) on Deleuze's move beyond Kant's view of the world emerging from the subject.
23 Thrift interprets a practice approach differently, arguing that practices 'are not . . . the practices of actors but of the practices themselves' (2008: 8). But, while the social dimension of practice is fundamental, this need not rule out individual agency, intentionality and reflexive adjustment.
24 See Couldry (2004). Others are more cautious about such a paradigm shift (Bird 2010: 99). On agency, see Thévenot (2007b: 410).
25 Katz (1959), quoted Jensen (2010: 78).
26 On audience research, see Hall (1980); on domestic practice, see Morley (1986), Silverstone (1994), Silverstone and Hirsch (1992); for pioneering work on computer-mediated communication, see Turkle (1996).
27 Ang (1996: 70, 72).
28 Couldry (2000a: 6).
29 Alasuutaari (1999: 6); Hermes (1999).
30 Jancovich and Faire (2003: 3).

31 Michaels (1982). Thanks to Gareth Stanton for alerting me to this important source.
32 Ginsburg (1994: 13). Compare Mark Allen Peterson on the need to shift in studying media 'from word to worlds' (2003: 22).
33 Bird (2003: 2–3, added emphasis).
34 Hoover, Schofield Clark and Alters (2004).
35 Wittgenstein (1978 [1953]).
36 Bourdieu (1977: 109–10; 1990: 83).
37 As Warde notes (Warde 2005), in his later work Bourdieu gave much less emphasis to the concept of practice, preferring the concept of field.
38 Bourdieu (1990: 73).
39 Schatzki (1999); Reckwitz (2002); Schatzki, Knorr-Cetina and von Savigny (2001); Warde (2005).
40 Schatzki (1999: 12).
41 Reckwitz (2002: 249).
42 Schatzki (1999: 89).
43 Swidler (2001).
44 Schatzki (1999: 15). For Schatzki's own critical discussion of Bourdieu, see Schatzki (1999: 136–44).
45 Schatzki (1999: 202).
46 Moores (2005:9), discussing Giddens (1984). Compare Swidler (2001:78).
47 On 'affordances', see Gibson (1979); on ANT, Thielmann (2010).
48 On 'digital formations', see Latham and Sassen (2005: 10); for 'holding things together', Christensen and Røpke (2010: 246–7), and compare Tomlinson (2007: ch. 5), Shove (2007: ch. 2).
49 Shove (2007: 170).
50 Campbell (2010: 129).
51 See for example *Guardian*, 11 December 2010.
52 See Bausinger (1984), Morley (1992); for an early precedent for using televised sport as a way into the sheer diversity of practice related to media, see Nightingale, Bockardt, Ellis and Warwick (1992). For media use to mark off space, see Bengtsson (2006); for the 'putdownable' text', see Hermes (1995).
53 Peterson (2010a: 172).
54 See Gamson (1998); Grindstaff (2002); Illouz (2003).
55 Lievrouw (2011: 7), drawing on Lievrouw and Livingstone (2002).
56 Hindman (2009: 42).
57 Halavais (2009a: 56–7).
58 Introna and Nissenbaum (2000: 170).
59 Livingstone (2004).
60 Bolter (2001: 28).
61 Howard and Massanari (2007).
62 Hamesse (1999: 107ff).
63 See generally Miller and Shepherd (2008: 8); specifically on Digg, see Bennett (2011: 168–9); the phrase 'collaborative filtering' is from Papacharissi (2010: 152–7). See also Palfrey and Gasser (2008: 200), Levy (1997: 10), Halavais (2009a: ch. 8).

64   Halavais (2009a: 9, 117, 162–8).
65   Clark and van Slyke (2010), Jenkins (2006); for a pessimistic view, see Bennett and Manheim (2006), discussing Katz and Lazarsfeld (1955).
66   Wittgenstein (1978 [1953]: 32). My term 'showing' is inspired, in part, by Daniel Dayan's (2009) concept of 'monstration', but its usage is more general.
67   A longer history would include the early days of weblogs and webcams: Couldry (2003a: ch. 7); Senft (2008); Hillis (2009: ch. 5).
68   www.newsoftheworld.co.uk
69   www.bp.com/liveassets/bp_internet/globalbp/globalbp_uk_english/homepage/STAGING/local_assets/bp_homepage/html/rov_stream.html, also recycled for example on PBS Newshour's YouTube channel, www.youtube.com/pbsnewshour, last accessed 25 June 2011.
70   www.hrw.org, 15 April 2011, last accessed 25 June 2011.
71   Respectively, www.youtube.com/watch?v=tsi9HFWlA2c, www.youtube.com/watch?v=a_uzUh1VT98, and www.youtube.com/watch?v=sMQDDB0SFqw, all last accessed 25 June 2011.
72   Goffman (1974: 43–4).
73   Compare Marwick and boyd (2010: 123) on social networking sites.
74   Miller (2011: 94–5) for an example from Trinidad.
75   boyd and Ellison (2008).
76   For 'happy slapping', see e.g. *Guardian* news reports on 15 December 2005 and 27 July 2010. For school shooters videos, see Sumiala (forthcoming).
77   Rowena Davis (2008), drawing on Kintrea et al. (2008).
78   Leicester pensioners reported *Metro* 7 July 2010; on Britain's surveillance state, see House of Lords (2009).
79   On co-veillance, see Andrejevic (2008a); on everyday spectacle, see Longhurst (2005: 5), Wood and Skeggs (2008); on breaking up online, see Gershon (2010) and Ito (2010: 132–8).
80   For Japan, see Takahashi (2010b: 459–60); for cultural differences generally, see Miller (2011: 186–7); on privacy concerns and practice, see Livingstone (2008), boyd (2008), Marwick and boyd (2010).
81   Miller (2011: 175).
82   Miller (2011: 179). For something like 'presencing' in relation to organizations, see Cooren, Brummans and Charrieras (2008).
83   boyd (2008: 134–7); Takahashi (2010a: 135); Yoo (2009: 218).
84   Taylor (2007: 143–4).
85   Tomlinson (2007: 111); boyd (2008: 126). On parenting, see Madianou and Miller (2011).
86   boyd (2008: 126).
87   See especially *The Guermantes Way* and *Cities of the Plain* (Proust 1983).
88   Zittrain (2008: 219–20); Enli and Thumim (2009), discussing Beer (2008). See more generally the perspectives of Elias (1994).
89   Giddens (1974).

90 Bimber (2003: 91); compare Lev Manovich (2008: 38): 'what before was ephemeral, transient, unmappable and invisible becomes [with the web] permanent, mappable, and viewable.'

91 Burgess and Green (2009: 87).

92 Ricoeur (1992), Cavarero (2000).

93 Lury (1998) and Flichy (1994: 73ff) on photos; on today's forms of online presence, see Palfrey and Gasser (2008: 35). On life-caching, see Carter (2004); Mark Zuckerberg quoted *Guardian*, 23 September 2011.

94 Christensen and Røpke (2010: 251).

95 Wuthnow (1989: 7).

96 Hagen (1994).

97 Gilmont (1999: 237).

98 Peterson (2010b: 133); Couldry, Livingstone and Markham (2010: 65–6).

99 Compare Schrøder and Kobbernagel (2010) for Danish study.

100 Allan (2006).

101 Boczkowski (2010: ch. 2).

102 N. Wilson (2007).

103 Tenenboim-Weinblatt (2009), which uses the series *24* as an example. See Sands (2008: 72, 88, 296) for evidence that *24* worked as an 'inter-text' within the US military and judiciary during a controversial period of US politics (the height of Guantanamo Bay operations). For interesting reflections on the impact of web-searchability on criteria of literary scholarship, see Kirch (2010).

104 According to market researcher Experian Hitwise (2010: 12), entertainment industries receive 16.7% and news and media receive 10.6% of their hits this way.

105 Giddens (1991) on the sequestration of experience; compare Williams (1992) on mobile privatization.

106 Licoppe (2004).

107 Winocur (2009: 179).

108 Turkle (2011: xii); Palfrey and Gasser (2008: 5).

109 See Licoppe (2004: 147) on 'the fantasy of continuous connection'.

110 Webb (2009).

111 Here I have learnt a great deal from the ongoing research of my doctoral student Kenzie Burchell.

112 Braudel (1975: 365); Bloch (1962: 65).

113 Hoover, Schofield Clark and Alters (2004). Compare for early comments on selecting out, Morley (1986) on local news, Jennings Bryant (1993: 155), Couldry (2000b: 81). As Mansell points out (2010: 7), we cannot assume that everyone avails themselves of the most technologically sophisticated ways of managing information.

114 Hassan (2003: 41, 44).

115 Zerubavel (1981: ch. 5, esp. 141–2, 153).

116 On 'hiding out', see Turkle (2011: 146); quotes taken from Turkle (2011: 15 and 190).

117 Ling and Donner (2009: 142), discussing Beniger (1986).
118 Elias (1994: 445 on interdependence, 214–15 on figurations).
119 Flichy (1994: 168).
120 Bauman (1992: 65).
121 Banet-Weiser (forthcoming); compare Lanier (2011: Part 1).
122 Mejias (2010).

Chapter 3 Media as Ritual and Social Form

1   Calhoun (2005: 375), quoted Coleman and Ross (2010: 118).
2   Lamont and Molnar (2002: 168).
3   Lefebvre (1971: 71).
4   Baudrillard (1981: 169, original emphasis).
5   Baudrillard (1981: 169).
6   Thévenot (2007b: 409).
7   Thévenot (2007b: 410).
8   See Boltanski (2011: ch. 2).
9   Wagner (2008: 245–6).
10 Thévenot (2007b: 410).
11 Thévenot (2007b: 411 and 421 n. 3).
12 On world/monde, see Boltanski (2011: 57) and in French (2009: 93); on 'tests', see Boltanski (2011: 103–10).
13 Boltanski (2011: 34).
14 Couldry (2003a).
15 Lash and Lury (2007).
16 Bowker and Star (2000: 9–10; cf. 325).
17 See respectively for these perspectives, Peterson (2003: 195), Braman (2009: 25–6), Sewell (1996), drawing on Giddens (1984).
18 Wrong (1994).
19 As indicated in ch. 1, my approach diverges sharply here from non-representational theory (Thrift 2008).
20 Berger and Luckmann (1967: 33, added emphasis).
21 Compare also Hobart (2010).
22 Boltanski (2011: 54–5, 59–60, 90).
23 Carey (1989: 87); Curran (1982), reprinted in Curran (2002: especially 61, 58).
24 Compare Bourdieu on the 'permanent political struggle for the universalization of the means of access to the universal' (1998: 94).
25 Vattimo (1992: 7), quoted Kraidy (2009: viii).
26 Bloch (1989: 45).
27 Couldry (2000a); Couldry (2003a).
28 Bourdieu (1991: 166). Here, quite directly, Bourdieu strives to merge a Marxist and a Durkheimian perspective. For an interesting, but ultimately unconvincing, argument that this merger is impossible, see Garnham (1994).

29   Compare Israeli anthropologist Don Handelman's work on 'classification' as a means of controlling social order: Handelman (1998: xxxi).
30   Elliott (1982: 147).
31   Elliott (1982: 168–73).
32   Kershaw (1987).
33   For more detail, see Couldry (2003a: 45–6; 2006: 15–18).
34   Bourdieu (2000).
35   Compare Couldry (2003a: 29).
36   Couldry (2003a: ch. 7), drawing on Foucault (1981: 61–2) and White (1992).
37   Hoover (2006: 267).
38   Couldry (2000a: 41).
39   Ytreberg (2009, 2011).
40   Feuer (1983), Bourdon (2000), White (2004), Turner (2010:13). Compare Brunsdon and Morley (1978: 27) on 'the myth of the "nation now"'.
41   Couldry (2003a: chs 6, 7).
42   Couldry (2000a: 42–4, 50–2). On 'framing', compare Gitlin (1980: 6); on 'naming', see Freire (1972), Melucci (1996).
43   Martin-Barbero (2006: 286).
44   Bell (1992, 1997).
45   Ericson, Riegert and Akers (2010).
46   Lash (2002: 1); compare Levy (1997: 98).
47   Hillis (2009: 58); on rituals relating to Michael Jackson's death, see Sanderson and Cheong (2010).
48   Turner (2010).
49   Widestedt (2009); Reijnders, Rooijakkers and Zoonen (2007); Cui and Lee (2010); Ruddock (2007); Moore (2009); Ong (2011).
50   Kraidy (2009, noting the topic of ritual at 208). Compare Lynch (2006: 96–7) for the explosive impact of talk shows such as Al-Jazeera's Platform in the Middle East.
51   On China generally, see Lee (2000), Zhao (2008a: 11), Sun (2002: ch. 7), and specifically for political actions Qiu (2009: 222–3) and (on controversial media events) Cao (2010), Qiang (2011) and Jiang (forthcoming); on the Philippines, see Ong (2011: ch. 5); on Lebanon, see Kraidy and Khalil (2009: 98).
52   Rothenbuhler (1989).
53   On UK and France respectively, see Mattelart (1994); Scannell and Cardiff (1991); on Japan, see Chapman (2005: 53) and Kasza (1993: 87); on India, see Punathambekar (2010); on Eastern Europe, see Imre (2009a: 6–7).
54   Calhoun (2007); Turner (2009: 62).
55   On the pre-political basis of the nation, see Calhoun (2007: 3) and Appadurai (1996: 157); on everyday habits of nationalism, see Edensor (2006: 541).
56   Rantanen (2009: 32–3).
57   Moore and Myerhoff (1977).
58   Marvin and Ingle (1999).

59 Rappaport (1999: 24). Compare communication scholar Eric Rothenbuhler's definition of ritual as 'the voluntary performance of appropriately patterned behaviour to symbolically effect or participate in the serious life' (1998: 27).
60 See Wuthnow (1989: 109) discussed in Couldry (2003a: 24–5).
61 Dayan and Katz (1992).
62 For more detail, see Couldry (2000a: 14–16; 2003a: 5–9), drawing on Durkheim (1995 [1912]).
63 21 January 1911, quoted Chapman (2005: 93). Compare McLuhan (2001 [1964]).
64 On *Britain's Got Talent*, see http://talent.itv.com/2011/mobile, accessed 23 June 2011; on *The Only Way is Essex*, see Raeside (2011).
65 Durkheim (1995 [1912]: 224).
66 On ambiguity, see Bloch (1989: 130) and Connor (2005), quoted in Imre (2009a: 11); on *Big Brother*'s ambiguity, see Couldry (2002).
67 Compare Durkheim (1953) with Butler (1993).
68 Bourdieu (1977: 87–95), discussed by Bell (1992: 107–8).
69 Bell (1992: 98; 1997: 169).
70 Couldry (2000a: 111).
71 Reijnders (2011), Peaslee (2010), Couldry (2000a: Part 2).
72 Ruddock (2007: 122).
73 Boltanski (2009: 9, 34) (my translation at 34).
74 Lévi-Strauss developed a complex contrast between 'games' and 'rules' and their respectively 'disjunctive' and 'conjunctive' effects (1972: 32–3). Arguably, that distinction is subsumed in reality games such as *The Apprentice*. Thanks to Tom Malaby for pointing out this connection.
75 Swidler (2001).
76 Dayan and Katz (1992: 3–7).
77 In Shils (1975: 139).
78 Dayan and Katz (1992: viii), compare Durkheim (1984 [1893]).
79 Liebes (1998). For divisive media events, see also Mihelj (2008).
80 Liebes and Blondheim (2005).
81 Dayan (2006).
82 Katz and Liebes (2010).
83 Dayan (2010: 28–9); compare Katz and Liebes (2010: 32).
84 Dayan (2010); Katz and Liebes (2010). Compare Katz (1996).
85 Couldry (2003a: ch. 4).
86 Shils (1975).
87 Couldry (2003a: 67, added emphasis).
88 Hepp and Couldry (2009b: 12); Compare Zelizer (1993).
89 Larkin (2008: 244–53).
90 On 'political events', see, on the US state, Bimber (2003: 103), Kellner (2003) and Wolin (2008: Preview and ch. 1); on the Chinese state, Sun and Zhao (2009); and on the Israeli state, Handelman (2004). On the importance of 'events' in film reception, see Staiger (1992).
91 Compare Rothenbuhler (2010) on the revival, not decline, of media events.

92   Hakala and Seeck (2009).
93   Edelman (1988).
94   G20 attender quotes from *Guardian*, 4 July 2005: for media strategies of protesters at this event, see McCurdy (2009); for Eastern Europe, see Imre (2009a: ch. 4); on the Catholic Church's use of a series on Mother Teresa, see Buonanno (2008: 49); on Hindu TV epics in India from the 1980s onwards, see Rajagopal (2001).
95   Retort Collective (2005); Stallabrass (2006).
96   Marshall (1997).
97   Redmond (2006).
98   Žižek (1989: 32); Dean (2010).
99   Weber (1947: 364ff).
100 Knorr-Cetina's argument (2001: 527–9) draws on Lacan's psychoanalytic formulation without depending on it. Jodi Dean uses Lacan more directly and goes further, arguing that celebrity is part of a wider logic of self-publicity that constitutes a machine for 'subjectivation' based not on positive identification but on a more abstract structure of desire and drive: Dean (2002: especially 123–4). For a different approach to unlocking such paradoxes, see ch. 4.
101 For the UK, see *Times Education Supplement*, 2 November 2006 and Kay (2011) referring to a Sky Television survey that I have not been able to identify; for the USA, see Pew Research Center (2007).
102 Kellner (2008); Serazio (2010).
103 For the benefits to political legitimacy of celebrities' role in providing an interface with the political world, see Ruddock (2007: 141) and Capino (2003: 167).
104 Aslama (2009); Svec (2010); Mole (2004); Holmes (2004); Ruddock (2007: ch. 6).
105 Howe (2004: 131). On paparazzi generally, see McNamara (2011).
106 Bell (1992).
107 Trow (1981: 51).
108 On DIY-celebrity generally, see Bennett (2011: ch. 7); on celebrity's 'options market', see van Dijck (2009: 53). There is a growing literature here: on YouTube, see Burgess and Green (2009: 23), Banet-Weiser (2011); on reality media, see Holmes (2004), Grindstaff (2009), Hearn (2006), Collins (2008); on micro-celebrity, Senft (2008: 25–6), Marwick and boyd (2010). On fame and inequality generally, see Holmes and Redmond (2006: 14).
109 For example Clarke (2004: 3).

Chapter 4 Media and the Hidden Shaping of the Social

1   Buonanno (2008: 77).
2   Jim Collins noted the overlay between film values and social values through the concept of 'double referentiality' (Collins 1992).

3   Tilly (1999).
4   Compare Turner (2010: 20–1) for a helpful discussion.
5   Scott (2001).
6   Castells (1996: 312, 317).
7   An exception is Castells's adoption of 'framing' theory but, as I note in ch. 5, he describes framing effects in a strangely *asocial* fashion.
8   Baudrillard (1983a: 66).
9   Baudrillard (1983a: 71).
10   Baudrillard (1983b: 53).
11   Baudrillard (1983b: 55).
12   Law (1994: 2, 121).
13   An ANT perspective has been applied to newsrooms and TV game shows: (Hemmingway 2007; Teurlings 2007). For ANT's relevance to media generally, see Couldry (2008b and c).
14   Thompson (1995: 17).
15   Thompson recognizes this (1994: 48 n. 10), deliberately avoiding Bourdieu's concept of misrecognition.
16   Bourdieu (1991: 166). For power and entertainment, see Gray (2008).
17   Durkheim (1995 [1912]: 213).
18   Durkheim (1995 [1912]: 210, added emphasis).
19   Scannell (1996); Dayan and Katz (1992: 13).
20   Berger and Luckmann (1967: 83).
21   An early insight of Baudrillard's (1981: 169; original French edn 1969), ignored in his later work. For 'The Sick Rose', see Blake's 'Songs of Experience' (Blake 1976: 140).
22   Sen (1999).
23   For the UK, see Scannell and Cardiff (1991); for Germany, see Ekstein (1975: 310), Welch (1993); for Rwanda, see Kellow and Steeves (1998).
24   Tocqueville (1864 [1835–1840]: 135; 1961 [1835–1840]: 207).
25   Gabler (2000: 185, added emphasis). Compare Lazarsfeld and Merton (1969).
26   Quoted in Blazwick (1989: 37). Compare Lefebvre (1971: 86).
27   Durkheim (1995 [1912]: 210).
28   For historical accounts, see Altick (1978), Greenhalgh (1988), Briggs and Burke (2005: 34–6).
29   Sennett and Cobb (1972: 25). On recognition, see Honneth (2007), Illouz (2003); and Grindstaff (2009: 84) on the class differences that shape desire for celebrity in the USA.
30   On Brazil, see Straubhaar (2007: 235); on India, see Rao (2007: 73); on France, see Echchaibi (2009: 21), quoting Nordine Nabili.
31   All names are pseudonyms.
32   Priest (1995).
33   Cavarero (2000: 41, 88); and compare Butler (2005).
34   Copsey (2010).
35   Teurlings (2007: 269–70). Compare Grindstaff (2009).
36   Couldry (2000a: Part 3).

37   Raeside (2011).
38   Benjamin (1968).
39   Bourdieu (1991: 127); Couldry (2003a: 39–41).
40   Honneth (2004).
41   Honneth (2004); Ehrenberg (1998); Hearn (2006).
42   Cabrera Paz (2009).
43   The economic driver (reality media as cheap TV) that crowds out investment in more expensive TV entertainment formats affects all markets, even the richest (the USA): Mandabach (2007).
44   For discussion, see Dovey (2000: ch. 5).
45   Melucci (1996: 179).
46   On user-generated content, see Wardle and Williams (2010); on blogs, see discussion in ch. 5; on crowdsourcing, see Halliday (2010). See ch. 2 on Twitter.
47   Shirky (2010).
48   Quoted Scannell and Cardiff (1991: 142–3).
49   Brewer (2004: 45); Marcos (2000). Compare, on the blurring of dream and reality in media, Boorstin (1961), Mattelart (2000: vii).
50   Scannell (1991).
51   Gamson (1998); on online self-exposure, see Hillis (2009: ch. 5).
52   On framing, see Pan and Kosicki (1993), Cappella and Jamieson (1997) and note Bennett and Iyengar 2008's argument discussed in ch. 5 below that in political communication at least framing is breaking down; on agenda setting, see McCombs and Shaw (1993); on insiders and outsiders, Phillips and Nossek (2008: 250); Ericson, Baranek and Chan. (1991); Schlesinger and Tumber (1994), and note Sinha (2004: 12) on similar trends in international discourse.
53   The Sutton Trust (2006).
54   Straubhaar (2007).
55   On national television and regional television markets, see especially Straubhaar (2007), and for a relevant general argument, Hafez (2007). On media capitals, see Curtin (2003).
56   Turner (2010: 21).
57   LeMaheu (1988: 23–5).
58   Lunt (2009).
59   Curran (2002: 165).
60   Wood and Skeggs (2008).
61   Weber (2009: 30). Compare Matt Stahl (2004: 221) on *American Idol*'s 'tableaux of punishment and vengeance'.
62   Latour (1993). In earlier commentary (Couldry 2008b and c), I may have underestimated the potential of ANT's concepts to disrupt media's social rhetorics.
63   Latour (1993: 117–18, 119).
64   On news agencies, see Brooker-Gross (1983). More recently, see Boyd-Barrett and Rantanen (1998), Chang (1998), Paterson (2006), and for overview, Stöber (2006). On news sources generally, see Hall (1973), Hall et al. (1978).

65 On political sources, see Davis (2010); on media's sourcing from other media, see Davies (2008).
66 Adams (2009: 89–90).
67 Latour (1993: 34). Compare Bernard Stiegler on media's consequences for 'the referential milieu for psychic and collective individuation' (2009: 41).
68 Braudy (1986).
69 Boorstin (1961); compare Bourdieu (1998).
70 Durkheim (1995 [1912]: 210).
71 Schickel (1986: ix, 401).
72 Davis (2010: 129–30).
73 Innes (2004: 17).
74 Garland (2001: 158, added emphasis).
75 Miller (2008: 35) on the USA, discussed in Turner (2010: 168–9); Innes (2004) on the UK; Costera Meijer (2011) on Holland.
76 Mirzoeff (2005: 16).
77 Garland (2001: 109–10); Wacquant (2009: 299–303).
78 Halavais (2009a: 59–60).
79 Barabasi (2003).
80 Huberman (2001), discussed in Halavais (2009a: 63–7).
81 Halavais (2009a: 69).
82 Spink et al. (2002).
83 Carlson (2007).
84 Halavais (2009a: 104, 116). Compare Introna and Nissenbaum (2000), Vaidyanathan (2011: 7, 80).
85 See the book by Bibliothèque Nationale chief Jean Jeanneney (2007), and compare Vaughan and Zhang (2007), Halavais (2000).
86 Gerhards and Shäfer (2010: 156); and on the internet as a 'market of markets', see Introna and Nissenbaum (2000: 177).
87 See especially Lessig (2002: 268). Compare Zittrain (2008: 3) on 'tethered appliances' and Gillespie (2011) and Powell (2011) on the power struggle behind phone 'apps'.
88 Rogers (2004: 4). For similar calls, see Lanier (2011).
89 On news sources, see Hall (1980), compare recently Coleman and Ross (2010: ch. 3); for the shaping of political news sources, see Howard (2006), Bennett and Iyengar (2008).
90 Luhmann (1999: 37). Compare Bourdieu's (2005: 137) better-known concept of social knowledge as 'doxa'.
91 Couldry (2010: ch. 4). See generally Turner (2010: 25, 68).
92 Hill (2007), Andrejevic (2008b: 39), Teurlings (2010).
93 Scannell (1988).
94 Duits and van Ronondt Vis (2009: 35).
95 Weber (2009: 14). For make-over shows' longer history in both reality TV and the beauty pageant, see Banet-Weiser and Portwood-Stacer (2006).

96   Carpentier (2009) on audiences' rejection of user-generated video content because it looked 'banal'; Halavais (2009b) on the biases of online recommendation.
97   Kraidy (2009: 359).

Chapter 5 Network Society, Networked Politics?

1   Wriston (1992: 176).
2   Katz and Rice (2002: 150).
3   Tilly (2007: xi)
4   E.g. Martuccelli (2005), Urry (2000 and 2007), Sassen (2006), Layder (2005).
5   Latour (2005).
6   Marvin (1987) on electricity and the telephone; Douglas (1987: 23) on hopes that radio would bring world peace. On the pamphlet, see Thompson (1963: 805).
7   Mosco (2004).
8   Chadwick (2006: 3).
9   Martuccelli (2005: 46–9).
10   Wolin (2008: 288); compare Tilly (2007: 59).
11   Bentivegna (2002: 54–6). Compare Coleman and Blumler (2009: 12–13), Bennett (2003).
12   Clark and van Slyke (2010); Coleman (2005); Mutz (2008).
13   Jenkins (2006); Benkler (2006); Castells (1996, 1997, 1998, 2009).
14   Jenkins (2006: 2).
15   Jenkins (2006: 13–14).
16   Arvidsson (2011).
17   Jenkins (2006: 23, added emphasis).
18   Jenkins (2006: 23).
19   Abercrombie and Longhurst (1998); Harrington and Bielby (1995).
20   Jenkins (2006: 27, 29, 4); Jenkins (2006: 235), discussing Pierre Levy (1997).
21   Jenkins (2006: 4).
22   Littler (2008), Micheletti (2010), Mukherjee and Banet-Weiser (forthcoming).
23   Imre (2009a: 10).
24   Benkler (2006: 32–3).
25   Benkler (2006: 121, 23); Benkler (2006: 473, cf. 162–5).
26   Chadwick (forthcoming).
27   Benkler (2006: 52, 105–6).
28   Fenton (2009).
29   Benkler (2006: chs 2 and 3).
30   Delli Carpini (2000).
31   Shirky (2010: 157–9, 175).
32   Benkler (2006: ch. 6).
33   Benkler (2006: 219–34).
34   Benkler (2006: 246).

35 Benkler (2006: 210, 246, 237, 219).
36 Rosanvallon (2008); Dutton (2009).
37 Castells (2009: 298).
38 Castells (2009: 5).
39 Castells (2009: 18); Castells (2009: 24, 53).
40 Castells (2009: 13–15). These arguments are broadly similar to the arguments against functionalism and for a cultural supplement to political economy in chs 1 and 3 above.
41 On which, see Monge, Heiss and Margolin (2008).
42 Castells (2009: 28, 42, 126); Castells (2009: 205). There is an underlying ambiguity over what constitutes a node within a network (Hepp 2008).
43 Compare McDonald (2006: 218) on the lack of attention to time in network theory generally.
44 See generally Castells (2009: 364–412, 406) on 'communities of practice', quoting Wenger (1998).
45 Castells (2009: 417, 427); Castells (2009: 196).
46 Dean (2002, 2010); and on broader constraints, see Pateman (1970), Croteau (1995), LeBlanc (1999).
47 On labour activism in China, see Zhao (2008b: 310–15), Qiu (2009: 193–5); on the general neglect of labour activism, see Lovink and Rossiter (2011); on US youth, see Rainie, Purcell and Smith (2011).
48 Castells (2009: 346, added emphasis).
49 Castells (2009: 417, added emphasis).
50 Castells (2009: 339).
51 Castells (1996: 477).
52 On the net versus the self, see Castells (1996: 3). On individualization, see Touraine (2007) and Barry Wellman's often-quoted phrase that 'the person has become the portal' (Wellman 2000); on online consumer tracking, see Bennett and Manheim (2006), Howard (2006), Turow (2007), Bennett and Iyengar (2008).
53 Barry (2001: 15). Compare ch. 4 above and Mejias (2010).
54 Compare Martuccelli (2005: 81–2) on how in Castells the notion of flow replaces any substantive account of social life.
55 See Wagner (2008: 244–5) for deeper historical roots of political theory's neglect of the social; and Calhoun (2007: 8) for the neglect of solidarity in contemporary accounts of the post-national.
56 Hardt and Negri (2005: 191, added emphasis). Compare Christakis and Fowler (2010).
57 Turner (2005: 136).
58 Matei and Ball-Rokeach (2003); Gergen (2002); Ling and Donner (2009); Livingstone (2009a: 95); Choi (2006).
59 Hampton, Lee and Ja Her (forthcoming).
60 Morozov (2011: xvii).
61 Lovink and Rossiter (2011).
62 Tilly (2007: 13, 23).
63 Tilly (2007: 74).

64   On 'totality', see Rosanvallon (2008: 308); on the 'public', see Dayan (2001: 746).
65   Easton (1965), quoted Delli Carpini and Keater (1996: 12).
66   Boltanski and Thévenot (2006); Thévenot (2007b); see also Touraine (2007).
67   Boltanski (2009).
68   Compare Postill (2008) on 'network society' theory's failure to address the complexity of everyday sociality.
69   Bimber (2003: 9).
70   Keck and Sikkink (1998); Castells (1996); Lievrouw (2011: ch. 6, esp. 168–71). More generally on distributed agents, see Bach and Stark (2005: 45) and on new possibilities of political agency, see Sassen (2006: 374–5), Bennett (2003: 15), Lievrouw (2011: ch. 6), Baym (2010: ch. 4).
71   On Tescopoly.org, see Couldry (2009b). On Mumsnet, see Coleman and Blumler (2009: 127–34), Chadwick (forthcoming). In a recent survey, a majority of US citizens thought the internet has facilitated group communication and impact on society at large, but there was little support for the idea that the internet has made it easier to *create* groups: Rainie, Purcell and Smith (2011: 12–13).
72   On the reduction of embarrassment, see Chadwick (2006: 202); on the 'network of networks' see Terranova (2004: 41), Lievrouw (2011: 9); on conviviality, see Lim and Kann (2008).
73   Langman (2005: 45).
74   Noveck (2009); *Guardian*, 10 June 2011.
75   Qiu (2009: 193–4) on Chinese factory workers and Qiang (2011: 202) on Xiamen protests; *Guardian*, 25 June 2010 on Khaled Said; for sceptical views on blogging as politics, see Meikle (2009: ch. 4), Matheson (2004), Singer (2005).
76   Yoo (2009: 221) on South Korea; Allan (2006: 129–34) on 9/11 blogs; Haiqing (2007) and Qiang (2011) on Chinese blogs; Khiabany and Sreberny (2009: 204, 206) on Iran; Lenhart et al. (2010) and Harsin (2010) on US bloggers; Davis (2009) on the UK. More generally on international comparison, see Goggin and McLelland (2009), Russell and Echchaibi (2009).
77   Lowrey and Latta (2008).
78   Compare ch. 4, and see especially Hindman (2009), Gerhards and Schäfer (2010).
79   For the interrelation between the strategies of political actors and media actors in influencing what issues and debates are easily 'visible' online, see Rogers (2004).
80   http://webecologyproject.org, quoted Sambrook (2010: 92).
81   Couldry (2009b).
82   Briggs and Burke (2005: 19). As Rantanen notes, political actors are also now less dependent on national *supplies* of news (Rantanen 2009: 41).
83   Benkler (2011).

84   Bimber (2003: 21); Latour (2007) on 'chains'; Noveck (2009: 37), Eliasoph (1998) on civic talk; Hindman (2009: 102) on blogs as elite media; Bakardjeva (2009: especially 103) on subactivism.

85   Bohman (2004: 152).

86   Leys (2001), Crouch (2000).

87   Boltanski (2009).

88   Lim and Padawangi (2008) on Indonesia; Juris (2008); Chinni (2010) and Monbiot (2010) on the Tea Party.

89   Chadwick (2006: 202). Compare Bimber (2003: 99–108), Hindman (2009: 139), Braman (2009: 315).

90   On the history of gossip in media, see Thompson (1997) and the pioneering insights of Gabriel Tarde (1969 [1922]).

91   Bennett, Johnson and Livingston (2008). On the circulation of the Abu Ghraib images, see Anden-Papadopoulos (2009) and Russell (2011: 16–18).

92   Bimber (2003: 107).

93   Leadbeater (2007); Chadwick (forthcoming).

94   Habermas (1989 and 1996). On *huo* or 'information cascade', see Qiang (2011).

95   Rosenau (1990: 10) on the neglect of the individual perspective on politics; Bennett (2008: 3, 5, 19), compare Livingstone (2009a: 137) and Earl and Schussman (2008: 89); on UK propensity to vote and disengagement, see Hansard (2011: 66) and compare Leighton (2011: 23–4); Livingstone (2007: 180) and Manovich (2001: 55) on the limits of interactivity.

96   Coleman (2011).

97   Xenos and Foot (2008: 65–7). Compare Manovich (2008) on 'closed' versus 'open' interactivity.

98   Rosanvallon (2008).

99   Castells (2009: chs 2 and 4).

100 Hindman (2009: 139).

101 Zolo (1992) and Thomas (2004) on attention; Shirky (2010) on cognitive surplus; Bimber (2003: 103) on event-based loyalties; Bennett (2008: 11–14) on decline of the 'dutiful citizen model'.

102 Boczkowski (2010: 164); Linaa Jensen (2011: Table 4). Compare Bolton (2006) who notes that only 1% of Australians access alternative news providers.

103 4% and 10% respectively (Linaa Jensen 2011). On the 'perceived worthwhileness' of keeping up with the news in Denmark, see Schrøder and Larsen (2009).

104 Prior (2002: 145, added emphasis). On the general pull of entertainment, see Dahlgren (2009: 125), Morley (1999), Turner (2010).

105 Papacharissi (2010: 110) and Dean (2010) on the lack of a civic environment; on the ease of 'clicking past', see Prior (2002: 145) and Starr (2009: 8); on the general pull of entertainment, see Dahlgren (2009: 125), Morley (1999), Turner (2010).

106 Andrejevic (2008a).

107 Boltanski and Chiapello (2005).
108 Marx (1973).
109 Castells et al. (2007) on mobile media and politics generally; http://
     webecology.com on Iran, last accessed 25 June 2011; Beaumont (2011)
     on the Arab world; www.ukuncut.org.uk, last accessed 18 November
     2011.
110 Sambrook (2010: 93).
111 Noelle-Neumann (1974).
112 For this contrast, see Rosanvallon (2008). For other negative or cau-
     tious assessments of how new media affect politics, see Papacharissi
     (2010), Dahlgren (2009: 200), Davis (2010: 113); Howard (2006: 186);
     Heikkila et al. (2010).
113 And maybe it isn't becoming more participatory! For positive views,
     see Clark and van Slyke (2010) and Russell (2011). For sceptical views,
     see Gans (2003: ch. 5), Wardle and Williams (2010), Ornebring (2008),
     Anderson (2010). Ofcom (2010, in 2007–11: 271) report that, apart
     from photosharing and social networking, all other forms of user-
     generated content excited 'relatively low levels of interest' among UK
     internet users.
114 See Kraidy (2009) on reality TV in the Middle East.
115 Fraser (2007).
116 Curran and Seaton (2007), Bagdikian (2004), Baker (2002). For a
     useful overview of 'ownership and control in the new media', see Press
     and Williams (2011: ch. 2).
117 Ross (1991: 35), quoted Hassan (2003: 134).
118 Howard (2006: 186).Compare, on the USA, Wolin (2008: ch. 13) and,
     on the UK, Davis (2010) and Marquand (2004).
119 Anderson (2011) on the Arab world; Qiang (2011) on China.
120 *Guardian*, 'UN Warns of food riots in developing world as drought
     pushes up prices', 28 May 2011.
121 Gilbert (2008: 96). On the new logic of 'public media', see Aufderheide
     and Clark (2009: 1). For fascinating reflections on the digital media
     infrastructure's potential for engaging young people in civic action, see
     Rheingold (2008).
122 Leadbeater (2007); Tapscott and Williams (2008).
123 Idle and Nunns (2011); *Korea Times*, 26 October 2011, www.
     koreatimes.co.kr/www/news/nation/2011/10/117_97371.html.
124 Benjamin (1968: 240).
125 Previously found at http://twitpic.com/3whvv3g, last accessed 15 May
     2011. Thanks to my Arabic-speaking colleague Kay Dickinson for
     discussion of this image and its embedded text. For balanced assess-
     ments of the role of SNS in the Arab spring, see Beaumont (2011),
     Zuckerman (2011).
126 Fraser (2007) and Bohman (2007) for contrasting views of the trans-
     national public sphere.
127 Pattie, Seyd and Whiteley (2004).
128 Bremner (2010).

129 McDonald (2011); Hardt and Negri (2011).
130 Marcos (2000).
131 Geertz (1971).

Chapter 6 Media and the Transformation of Capital and Authority

1 Livingstone (2009a: x), compare Livingstone (2009b).
2 Bourdieu (1983: 241). Bolin (2011: 135) questions whether Bourdieu's use of Marx on capital is accurate.
3 Bourdieu and Wacquant (1992: 98).
4 Fishman (1980: 51), quoted Meikle (2009: 29).
5 Thanks to Klaus Zilles for this insight.
6 Compare Livingstone (2009a: ix).
7 Lundby (2009a) brings together the latest debates; another term used has been 'mediazation' (Thompson 1995: 49). 'Mediatization' has increasingly become an automatic claim in wider sociology (Lash and Lury 2007: 9; Urry 2007: 9) without explicit theorization. For a subtle discussion of 'mediatization' and culture, see Fornäs (1995: 210–21).
8 Discussed in Lundby (2009b: 10), quoting the original French 1976 edition of Baudrillard (1993).
9 Mazzoleni (2008).
10 Lundby (2009b).
11 Silverstone (2005: 189).
12 Altheide and Snow (1979); Snow (1983); Altheide (1985).
13 Snow (1983: 11); Altheide and Snow (1979: 237); Altheide (1985: 9).
14 Altheide (1985: 13–14).
15 Altheide and Snow (1979: 12, 60); Altheide (1985: 35–6).
16 Snow (1983: 151–2).
17 By 2011, however, this was not his position: see Hjarvard (2011).
18 Hjarvard (2009: 160). Compare Hjarvard (2006: 5) and Andrea Schrott's (2009: 47) definition of 'mediatization . . . as a social process of media-induced social change that functions by a specific mechanism . . . the institutionalization of media logic in social spheres'.
19 See respectively Mazzoleni (2008), quoted Lundby (2009b: 8) and Schulz (2006: 90).
20 Bourdieu (1993); Boltanski and Thévenot (2006); Elias (1994).
21 Krotz (2009: 26, 27, 24).
22 Couldry (2008a). Hepp (2009a: 149) reads my earlier argument on media meta-capital (Couldry 2003b) as, in effect, an argument about mediatization in Krotz's sense.
23 Contrast Krotz (2009) and Hjarvard (2011).
24 Bird (2010: 91–6).
25 Bourdieu (1993 and 1996b); Champagne (1990).
26 Bourdieu (1998); Marlière (1998); Benson and Neveu (2005).

27   Champagne and Marchetti (2005); Duval (2005).
28   O'Neil (2009: 63).
29   Bourdieu (1990: 166).
30   Bourdieu (1977: 88).
31   Bourdieu (1998: 22); French version is Bourdieu (1996c: 21).
32   Champagne (1990: 261 and 277; 264; 39). For a broadly similar position, see Champagne and Marchetti (2005: 43).
33   Lingard, Rawolle and Taylor (2005).
34   Champagne (1990: 237, 239, 243).
35   For a fuller if much earlier version of what follows, see Couldry (2003b).
36   Bourdieu (1996a); Weber (1947).
37   Bourdieu (1996a: 40–5; 1990: 239–41).
38   Bourdieu (1990: 229).
39   Bolin (2009: 352–3).
40   See, respectively, Bourdieu in Wacquant (1993: 42, added emphasis); Bourdieu (1996a: 265); Bourdieu in Wacquant (1993: 23).
41   The concept of 'symbolic capital' in Bourdieu generally means any type of capital (economic, cultural, and so on) that happens to be legitimated or prestigious in a particular field. For example, Bourdieu (1986: 132, 133; 1990: 230).
42   Champagne argues something similar, but without using the term 'meta-capital' (Champagne 2005: 54).
43   Bourdieu (1998).
44   See Lahire (1999) for the argument that much of everyday life is *not* embedded in particular fields of competition.
45   Boyle and Kelly (2010).
46   This is consistent with how Bourdieu himself uses the term 'meta-capital' in relation to the state.
47   Bennett (2011: 130).
48   Compare Strömback and Esser (2009: 213–14).
49   Compare Hallin and Mancini's comparative theory of media systems (2004).
50   See Champagne (1990: 237, 243), Couldry (2003b).
51   Compare Hallin (2005).
52   Compare Bolin (2011: ch. 2; 2009). Bolin's approach to the difficulties raised by Bourdieu's concept of field of power is more focused on explaining the dynamics of media production.
53   Collins (1994 [1868]: 434).
54   Reported BBC Radio 4 *Today* programme, 12 December 2009.
55   Thompson (2001).
56   Meyer (2003: xv).
57   For key work, see Mazzoleni and Schulz (1999), Benson (2006), Davis (2007), Riegert (2007), Strömback and Esser (2009), Thompson (2001), Fairclough (2000).
58   Hobsbawm (1995: 581–2).
59   Cook (2005).
60   On which see Meyrowitz (1985: ch. 6).

61 Rogers (2004: 173).
62 Davis and Seymour (2010).
63 Krotz (2009: 25).
64 On medieval era, see Braudel (1975: 372–3), Bloch (1962: 62); on the early twentieth century, see Weber in Gerth and Mills (1991: 215); on the late twentieth century USA, see Cook (2005: 122).
65 See respectively Foster (2005), Cook (2005: 113, 137), Braman (2009: 319), Davis (2010: 65–6).
66 Briggs and Burke (2005: 18–19).
67 Harsin (2010).
68 Compare note 46 above and the relevant main text discussion.
69 Coleman and Blumler (2009: 58).
70 Contrast Meyer (2003: 91) on the narrow confines of the televisual public sphere in the twentieth century.
71 Cottle and Nolan (2007) on humanitarian NGOs.
72 Uitermark and Gielen (2010).
73 Jaap van Gils, quoted Uitermark and Gielen (2010: 1331).
74 Uitermark and Gielen (2010: 1331).
75 Uitermark and Gielen (2010: 1340).
76 Miao (2011: 109).
77 Costera Meijer (2011).
78 Chouliaraki (forthcoming); Cooper (2008).
79 Ruddock (2007: 141) on Boris Johnson, MP (currently Mayor of London).
80 On spectacle in politics, see generally Boorstin (1961), Debord (1983) and, for its recent intensification, Kellner (2003; 2009); on school killings, see Serazio (2010), Kellner (2008); on the links between 'terrorism' and spectacle, see Dayan (2006: 15, 19, my translation).
81 Cook (2005).
82 Foster (2005: 1–2).
83 See respectively Gewirtz, Dickson and Power (2004) and Blackmore and Thorpe (2003) on Education Action Zones in the UK and the implementation of 'sclf-managing schools' in the Australian state of Victoria.
84 Lingard, Rawolle and Taylor (2005) on education.
85 Lingard, Rawolle and Taylor (2005: 769); compare Rawolle and Lingard (2008).
86 Rawolle (2010).
87 Breiter, Schulz and Welling (2011).
88 Educational powers in Scotland and Wales are largely separate from those in England.
89 Giroux (2000).
90 Hoover (2006); Hjarvard (2006).
91 Meyer (2006: 307–8).
92 E.g. Goethals (1997).
93 Hepp and Krönert (2009) on Catholic World Youth Day. Compare generally Dayan and Katz (1992).

94   Lundby (2006) discusses the election of the Bishop of Oslo from this perspective.
95   On televangelists, see Hoover (1988), Thomas (2008); on Islamic preachers, see Kraidy and Khalil (2009: 73); on Ansar Dine, see Schulz (2006); on religious blogging, see Cheong, Halavais and Kwon (2008).
96   Meyer and Moors (2006: 19); de Witte (2009: 13) quoted in Asamoah-Gyadu (2009: 165).
97   Thomas (2008: 95).
98   Stallabrass (2000).
99   Here I disagree with Lash and Lury's account of the YBA (2007).
100 Bimber (2003: 91).
101 Latham and Sassen (2005: 16).
102 Thompson (2005: 31), and, more generally, Boyer (2010: 253).
103 Bimber 2003; compare Turner (2007b: 117).
104 Howard (2006: 193).
105 On the religious text, see Ess (2010: 15); on commentary, see Stolow (2006), Mandaville (2003), Campbell (2010: 154); on the resulting issues for institutional control, see Meyer and Moors (2006: 11).
106 Howard (2009: 138).
107 Schulz (2006: 140).
108 Turner (2007b); Meyer and Moors (2006: 8); Hoover and Kaneva (2009: 8).
109 Mandaville (2007: 102).
110 Wuthnow (1989).
111 Thanks to Sigurd Allern for making this point to me.

Chapter 7 Media Cultures: A World Unfolding

1   Hallin and Mancini (2004: 17).
2   Erni and Chua (2005: 9).
3   For eloquent calls for that internationalization, see Curran and Park (2000), Thussu (2009), Wang (2011), Goggin and McLelland (2009).
4   See Connell (2007: 59–60) for a trenchant analysis of similar problems in globalization theory; compare Harindranath (2003: 155).
5   Miller (2011: x).
6   Connell (2007).
7   Sinha (2004); see Appadurai (1996: 1) on modernity and 'universality'.
8   On Nigeria, see Larkin (2008: 253); for the Copernican revolution elsewhere, see Pomeranz (2000), and much earlier in anthropology, Goody (1976).
9   Kraidy (2010: xvi, 210–11).
10 McMillin (2007: 9).
11 As it must be: see Connell (2007: 226–7).
12 Hallin and Mancini (2004).

13 Siebert, Peterson and Schramm (1956).
14 Hallin and Mancini (2004: 10–11).
15 Hallin and Mancini (2004: xiv, 1).
16 Silverstone (1999: 2); Martuccelli (2005: 46–9).
17 Goggin and McLelland (2009: 9–10).
18 On communication need, see Herring (2008: 72). As Nick Stevenson (1999: 33) notes, 'the politics of communication needs have long been neglected.'
19 In this section, I draw on the joint work Andreas Hepp and I have developed (Hepp and Couldry 2009a; Couldry and Hepp forthcoming). Many thanks to Andreas for agreeing to my publishing this development of our work here.
20 Kellner (1995); Stevenson (2002).
21 Iwabuchi (2007: 78), compare Kraidy (2005); Kraidy and Murphy (2008: 340). According to Bloomsbury, the last English language instalment of the Harry Potter saga (*Harry Potter and the Deathly Hallows*) sold as many copies overseas as in the UK: quoted *Guardian*, 19 September 2007.
22 Nederveen Pieterse (1995); Freud (1991 [1927]).
23 Savage, Bagnall and Longhurst (2005).
24 Kraidy (2010: 27, added emphasis); Larkin (2008: 201).
25 On taste and belonging, see Jansson (2009: 259); on class, see Straubhaar (2007: 243–4).
26 Calhoun (2007); Skey (2011).
27 Schlesinger (2000: 100), discussing Deutsch (1966).
28 Chernilo (2007).
29 On 'thickening', see Löfgren (2001); on the origins of the idea of 'trans-local' media cultures, see Hepp (2008) and compare Morley (2000).
30 Compare Winocur (2009: 184).
31 Khiabany and Sreberny (2009: 211); compare Hannerz (1992) on culture as based in 'non-sharing'.
32 Abu-Lughod (2005); Garcia Canclini (1995); Qiu (2009). For the metaphor of 'fissures', see Garcia Canclini (1995: 63), discussed in Connell (2007: 161); and compare Rodriguez (2001).
33 Hepp and Couldry (2009a: 12).
34 Harindranath (2003).
35 Buck-Morss (2003: 93).
36 Maslow (1943) on the psychological model; Sen (1992: 109–12; 1999: 147–8, 153–4). Since we are only concerned here to suggest a new way of thinking about the open-ended *diversity* of the media culture spectrum, no formal definition of 'needs' is necessary. But the difference here from earlier communications research that correlated types of media use with individual psychological needs, for example, Uses and Gratifications research, should be clear: for criticisms of that earlier approach, see Morley (1992: 52–6), Elliott (1974).
37 Miller and Shepherd (2008); compare Schrøder and Kobbernagel (2010: 116 n. 1).

38 Straubhaar (2007: 128).
39 BBC Global News (2011).
40 Simone (2006: 143); Tunstall (2008: 355).
41 Qiu (2009: 4).
42 Qiu (2009: 12, 91, 89, 10, 14).
43 Qiu (2009: 10).
44 Mallee (2000); Lee (2000).
45 Qiu (2009: 14, 169).
46 Qiu (2009: 68, 70–1). According to Qiu, China has 360 million users of prepaid mobile phone facilities (2009: 74–5).
47 Qiu (2009: 99).
48 On Egypt, see Sakr 2009: 173–4; on Sri Lanka and India, see Slater and Tacchi (2004); Tacchi (2008). Compare earlier work on 'working-class cosmopolitanisms', Werbner (1999).
49 Qiu (2009: 188–91, 193–4, 233).
50 Morley (1986); Lembo (2000); Modleski (1986).
51 Lodziak (1987: 135). For the origins of this approach, see Kracauer (1995: 325).
52 Livingstone (2002); Livingstone and Bovill (2001); Livingstone and Bober (2004).
53 Dayan (1998), commenting on Anderson (1983).
54 Hargreaves and Mahdjouh (1997) on Maghreb migrants in France, compare Moores (1993) on South Asian and Naficy (2001) on Iranian migrants.
55 Gillespie (1995); Hargreaves and Mahdjouh (1997); Mainsah (2009) on Cameroonian migrants in Norway.
56 For recent accounts, see Moores and Metykova (2009), Imre (2009b), Hepp (2009b). Compare Gillespie (1995).
57 Imre (2009b).
58 For these two positions, see Rifkin (2001) and Serres (2001).
59 Sun (2002: 134); Martin-Barbero (2009: 154, 155). On Chile, see Rodriguez (2003), Salazar (2010); on the former Yugoslavia, Gavrilovic (2009). For the neglect of audience research for alternative media, see Downing (2003a).
60 Aksoy and Robins (2003: 95, 101).
61 Hepp, Bozdag and Suna (forthcoming).
62 For the early part of that history, see Scannell and Cardiff (1991).
63 Volcic (2009).
64 Abu-Lughod (2005: 10).
65 Lynch (2006).
66 Boyd, Straubhaar and Lent (1989: ch. 3).
67 Kraidy (2010: 208, added emphasis).
68 Kraidy (2010: 198).
69 Imre (2009a: 123–9).
70 Cui and Lee (2010) and Miao (2011: 100–2) on *Super Girl*, and Fung (2009) on *I Shouldn't Be Alive*; Maliki (2008), discussed in Turner (2010: 58–63) on Malaysia; Jacobs (2007) on southern Africa's *Big*

Brother; Martin-Barbero (1993: 163–5) on Mexico; Larkin (2008) on Nigeria. Taylor (2004) develops the concept of 'social imaginary'.

71 On anti-globalization movements, see Juris (2008), della Porta, Kriesi and Rucht (1999), Bailey, Cammaerts and Carpentier (2008). On Indymedia, see Allan (2006: ch. 7), Atton (2004: ch. 2), Bennett (2003), Downing (2003b), Kidd (2003), Skinner et al. (2010). On Islamic fundamentalist sites, see Khatib (2010). See generally on radical media Downing (2001) and, on translocal networking, see especially Skinner et al. (2010: 192).

72 An exception is Rauch (2007).

73 McCurdy (2009); Gerbaudo (2010). See, generally, Melucci (1996) on the option of withdrawing from media culture as a form of resistance.

74 See Garnham (1999b), developing Sen's capabilities approach for the case of media, and Zimmermann (2006) for useful discussion of the relation of Sen's approach to qualitative sociology. And see my discussion of Bernard Williams's work in ch. 8 below.

75 Hagen (1994). Compare Hallin and Mancini (2004: 146–7) for a historic perspective on newspaper reading in Scandinavia.

76 Schrøder and Kobbernagel (2010) on Denmark; Heikkila et al. (2010) on Finland; Rao (2010: 104; quotation at 110) on India; Spitulnik Vidali (2010) on news referral as a practice; Xiao (2011: 219) on 'citizen mobilization' in China.

77 Honneth (2007: 138–9).

78 Rose (2000: 181) of the BBC Community Programmes Unit, quoted in Kidd (2010: 298–9).

79 Compare Qiu (2009: 169).

80 Kraidy (2010: 195).

81 Goldsmiths Leverhulme Media Research Centre (2010: 34).

82 Champagne (1999).

83 Barker-Plummer and Kidd (2010).

84 Quoted Bosch (2010: 79, added emphasis). Compare, on the earlier history of Bush radio, Browne (2005: 135–7).

85 Salazar (2010).

86 Quoted Pavarala and Malik (2010: 108).

87 Matewa (2010: 126).

88 Rodriguez (2011) on Colombia; Rocha (2007).

89 Alia (2003: 48) on the Aboriginal People's TV Network in North America.

90 Sá (2007).

91 Quoted Sá (2007: 130).

92 Echchaibi (2009).

93 Mitra 2004: 492, quoted by Sá (2007: 127).

94 Meadows et al. (2010: 178).

95 Thussu (2009: 23–4); on religion as practice, see Morgan (2008: 8), quoting Talal Asad. For general perspectives on religious needs and media, see Knoblauch (2008), Hoover and Lundby (1997), Meyer and Moors (2006), Sumiala-Seppänen, Lundby and Salokangas (2006).

96   Berger (2005).
97   Hoover (1988).
98   Lundby and Dayan (1999); Thomas (2008: 45).
99   On the use of the cassette, see Hirschkind (2006) on Egypt, Schulz (2006) on Mali, Sreberny-Mohammadi and Mohammadi (1994) on Iran. See Mankekar (1999: 202), Rajagopal (2001), Mitra (1993) on Hindu mythical serials; Kraidy and Khalil (2009) on Ramadan TV in the Middle East.
100   Hoover, Schofield Clark and Alters (2004); Hoover (2006: ch. 5).
101   Campbell (2010: 120).
102   Miller (2011: 89–91) on the Elijah Muslims in Trinidad; Campbell (2010: 103) on Samanyola TV; Kraidy and Khalil (2009) on al-Manar; Lehmann and Siebzehner (2006) on Kol HaChesed; Ong (2011: chs 5 and 7) on the Philippines.
103   Hoover (2006: 272–3; 2008: 41).
104   Compare Seiter (1999).
105   Pasquier (2005) on youth media and peer cultures; Castells et al. (2007) on youth and mobile media; Algan (2005) on Turkey; Arab statistics taken from Kraidy and Khalil (2009: 57)
106   Gray (2009).
107   boyd (2008: 136).
108   Takahashi (2010a: 80).
109   Takahashi (2010a: 96–8, 129–31, 137–9).
110   Takahashi (2010b).
111   Yoo (2009: 219).
112   Takahashi (2010a: 60–1; 122–4).
113   Quotations respectively from Winocur (2009: 181, 184).
114   boyd (2008: 136).
115   Silverstone (1994).
116   Chandler (1998); Hodkinson (2007); Livingstone (2008).
117   For one interesting study on a Turkish confession site itiraf.com, see Ogan and Cagiltay (2006).
118   I therefore disagree with Jose Cabrera Paz's claim that 'what unites us with an ever more common logic . . . and in this we do become irreducibly global – is the logic to make of our lives an interactive spectacle to see and be seen in the techno-networks' (Cabrera Paz 2009: 138).
119   Klinger (2006: 233) on film fans; Condry (2009) on fansubbing; and online fandom generally, see Jenkins (2006), Helleksen and Busse (2006), Booth (2010). For 'massively-many' online games (so-called MMPORG), see the proceedings of the Digital Games Research Association, www.digra.org, last accessed 25 August 2011.
120   McMillin (2007: 156, 192).
121   Barker and Brooks (1998).
122   The pioneers here were Bacon-Smith (1992) and Jenkins (1992). For more recent work, see Hills (2002), Gray, Sandvoss and Harrington (2007). For the particular importance of interpretative work in media culture, see Harris (1998: 43, 45).

Chapter 8 Media Ethics, Media Justice

1 Signed statement by Rupert Murdoch printed full page in UK newspapers, 16 July 2011.
2 Turkle (2011: 17). For another recent perspective on the consequences of digital media for our overlapping work and emotional lives, see M. Gregg (2011).
3 Peters (2001: 722).
4 Ricoeur (2007: 35–6).
5 McDowell (1994: 84).
6 Jonas (1984: 1). For discussion, see Couldry (2006: 136–7).
7 Bauman (1995: 280).
8 Cavell (1964), quoted by Pitkin (1972: 34). Compare on Google Vaidhyanathan (2011: 211).
9 Wolin (2008: 263).
10 Turkle (2011); Lanier (2011).
11 Compare Ess (2010: chs 4 and 6) for useful reflections on how, ethically, to address this diversity.
12 Latour (2004: 40).
13 Silverstone (2007).
14 Compre Ess (2009: 197).
15 For helpful discussion, see Ricoeur (2007).
16 O'Neill (1996).
17 Ricoeur (2007; 1992: 197, 238–9).
18 Sen (2009); Honneth (2007).
19 Kant (1997: 15, 7, 16, added emphasis).
20 MacIntyre (1988: chs 18–20).
21 O'Neill (1996); Cohen-Almagor (2001).
22 Habermas (1968).
23 Baker (2002); Christians et al. (2009).
24 For more positive readings of Levinas's work for general and media ethics, see Bauman (1992), Pinchevski (2005) and Silverstone (2007).
25 For a broadly Christian humanist approach to media ethics, see Christians, Ferré and Fackler (1993).
26 Sen (1992).
27 On voice, see Couldry (2010).
28 Hepp (2010).
29 Hayles (2009). Compare Jensen (2010).
30 Zelizer (2011).
31 Quinn (1995:186).
32 Williams (1985: 20, adjusted emphasis).
33 Lovibond (2002: 63 and 25, adjusted emphasis), drawing on McDowell (1994: 84).
34 McDowell (1998: 50–73, especially 65, 73).
35 Swanton (2003: 9, 87).
36 MacIntyre (1981: 175).

37 Benkler (2011).
38 Sontag (2004). Compare Russell (2011) on the emergence of a 'networked news public'.
39 On the issue of 'the human', see ch. 1, n. 144.
40 Williams (2002: 44).
41 Williams (2002: 24).
42 For a period where a disposition towards truthfulness could not be relied upon, see Snyder (2009, 2010) on the terrible history of Eastern Europe during the Second World War.
43 Williams (2002: 124,106, 63, 35).
44 Williams (2002: 44).
45 Williams (2002: 88 and 2002: 97, 99) quoting Grice (1989).
46 See the 1998 scandal over Carlton Communications' reality TV programme *The Connection* on Colombian drug-running and the disputes over the selection process on *Britain's Got Talent* in 2011.
47 Williams (2002: 146).
48 Nordenstreng (2010); compare Ronald Dworkin (2010) on recent USA Supreme Court decision that gives general corporations the right of freedom of speech.
49 See, e.g., de Burgh (2003) on China.
50 Davies (2008: especially 28, 12, 154). Compare Boczkowski (2010: 33, 77, 109); Czarniawska (2010); Boyer (2010); Phillips, Couldry and Freedman (2009). For more optimistic views, Deuze and Dimoudi (2002), Deuze (2003), Bruns (2005). On US public journalism, Glasser (1999). The scandal over 'phone-hacking' at News International newspapers in the UK, particularly the *News of the World*, has been extensively covered in all English newspapers from February 2011 onwards. See in particular News International's statement on 8 April 2011 available from http://guardian.co.uk/media/2011/apr/08/news-international-statement-news-of-the-world. For the long-term impact of News International on British public life, see Harris (2011).
51 Boczkowski (2010: 6); Boyer (2010: 6, 254–6 and 253) on Germany, and compare the US press authority Charles Lewis's vision of the 'hollowing out' of the mainstream US press (Lewis 2008). On heteronomy, see Phillips (2011), drawing on Bourdieu (2005); on content management systems, see Boczkowski (2010) and Quandt (2008). For a broader philosophical perspective, see O'Neill (2002: 93).
52 Silverstone (2007: 136).
53 O'Neill (2000: 186).
54 Silverstone's use of Derrida's extended notion of hospitality as visitation does not escape this problem (Silverstone 2007: 149–51; Derrida 2002). See Kogen (2009) for an interesting reflection on how Silverstone's onerous obligations might be reconciled with models of how individuals react to news about distant others, and Wright (forthcoming) for a lively critique of the notion of 'proper distance'.
55 Honneth (2007: 130).

56 Ricoeur (2007: 31, 35). Compare Frosh (forthcoming) who also extends Silverstone's notion of 'proper distance' away from dyadic relations and towards overlapping relations between the self and multiple others.

57 Ricoeur (2007).

58 Eide, Kunelius and Phillips (2008); Ess (2010: 104–9).

59 Held (2006).

60 O'Neill (1996: 203).

61 Turkle (2011); Hayles (2009); Ess (2010).

62 See Cohen-Almagor (2001: 95, 97, 100).

63 Spyer (2006).

64 Aristotle (1976: book 6).

65 Note there is a potential link between questions of justice and virtue, since acting justly is itself a virtue for Aristotle (1976: book 5), but I will not pursue this, since the priority is to clarify what injustice in relation to media might comprise. There are also problems with Aristotle's particular conception of justice as an individual virtue, which is maladapted for considering societal justice/injustice.

66 On alternative media, see Atton (2002), Downing (2001), Rodriguez (2001); on fandom and injustice, see Jenkins (1992), Bacon-Smith (1992); on WSIS, see http://www.itu.int/wsis/docs/geneva/official/poa.html#c3, para B4, last accessed 25 August 2011, and www.itu.int/wsis/implementation/index.html, last accessed 25 August 2011. On the right to communicate, see D'Arcy (1977). On Media justice campaigns, see www.mediajustice.org/ and http://centerformediajustice.org/home/about/our-framework/, both last accessed 25 August 2011. For a specific study of MediaJustice, see Klinenberg (2005).

67 McChesney (2007: 220), quoted in Jansen (2011: 7); Media Justice Fund (2007: 4), quoted N. Gregg (2011: 83); Jansen (2011: 2).

68 Silverstone (2006: 144–9), quotations from 149. See also Hamelink (2000: ch. 4).

69 Nordenstreng (2010); Goggin (2009).

70 See special issue of the journal *Continuum* 23(4) (2009).

71 O'Donnell (2009: 514).

72 Sen (2009). Note that Sen continues to see Rawls's (1971) approach to justice as relevant to 'process aspects' of justice and liberty (Sen 2009: 299–301).

73 Sen (2009: 336–7). For discussion of Sen's interest in voice, see Couldry (2010: ch. 5).

74 Sen (1983); compare Sen (2009: ch. 4).

75 Sen (2009: 335–6).

76 Couldry (2010: 105).

77 Dreher (2009: 452).

78 Mayhew (1997). For related discussion, see Couldry (2010: 100–3).

79 Castells (2009: 55).

80 O'Neill (2002).

81 Teurlings (2007: 273).

82 Salazar (2010); Goggin and Newell (2005).
83 Kunelius and Nossek (2008: 264).
84 Brighenti (2007, especially 339) and Thompson (2005). See Imre (2009a: 101) for an interesting example of ambivalence in how minorities are represented in popular culture.
85 Bohman (2000: 48), compare Bourdieu (1992: 118) on the 'de facto division of labour of social production with regard to major varieties of experience'; Hindman (2009).
86 On justice and the digital public sphere, see Lessig (2002), and in political theory Fraser (2005); for traditional media, see Ginsburg (2008: 141). On 'pirate activism', see Stalder (2011).
87 There is potentially still another type of media injustice: the environmental side-effects of media processes. As Toby Miller and Rick Maxwell (Maxwell and Miller 2011) have pointed out, the environmental costs of the systematic *overproduction* of equipment, chemicals and unwanted detritus that our media-saturated life requires are high, and those costs are distributed with massive inequality. This is a long-term debate that has barely started, but it takes us far beyond the scope of media ethics and media injustice.
88 Honneth (2007); Couldry (2010).
89 On recognition, see Illouz (2003). On capabilities, see Sen (1992) and, in relation to media, Garnham (1999b), Mansell (2002).
90 Williams (2002: 213–19, quoting 217).
91 On co-veillance, see Andrejevic (2008a); compare Zittrain (2008: 219–20); Vaidhyanathan (2011: 111); compare on 'participatory surveillance', Albrechtslund (2008). On archives and their ethics, see Palfrey and Gasser (2008), Turkle (2011), Howard (2006: 187).
92 Rilke (1987: 60–1).
93 Hayles (2009); Stiegler (2009).
94 See the important current research project at the Open University, UK: *Oecumene: Citizenship after Orientalism*: www.oecumene.eu.
95 Silverstone (1999: 9).
96 For similar insistence on critical distance from our relations to media, see Tomlinson (2007: 97), Martin-Barbero (2006: 28).
97 Deuze (2011).
98 Dorling (2010).

References

Abercrombie, N. and Longhurst, B. (1998) *Audiences: A Sociological Theory of Performance and Imagination*. London: Sage.

Abercrombie, N., Hill, S. and Turner, B. (1981) *The Dominant Ideology Thesis*. London: Allen & Unwin.

Abu-Lughod, L. (2005) *Dramas of Nationhood: The Politics of Television in Egypt*. Chicago: University of Chicago Press.

Adam, B. (2004) *Time*. Cambridge: Polity.

Adams, P. (2009) *Geographies of Media and Communication*. Malden, MA: Wiley-Blackwell.

Aksoy, A. and Robins, K. (2003) 'Banal Transnationalism: The Difference that Television Makes', in K. Karim (ed.), *The Media of Diaspora*. London: Routledge, pp. 89–104.

Alasuutaari, P. (ed.) (1999) *Rethinking the Media Audience*. London: Sage.

Albrechtslund, A. (2008) 'Online Social Networking as Participatory Surveillance', *First Monday* 13, 3 March.

Aldridge, J. and Cross, S. (2008) 'Young People Today: News Media, Policy and Youth Justice', *Journal of Children and Media* 2(3): 203–18.

Algan, E. (2005) 'The Role of Turkish Local Radio in the Constitution of a Youth Community', *The Radio Journal* 3(2): 75–92.

Alia, V. (2003) 'Scattered Voices, Global Vision: Indigenous Peoples and the New Media Nation', in K. Karim (ed.), *The Media of Diaspora*. London: Routledge, pp. 36–50.

Allan, S. (2006) *Online News*. Maidenhead: Open University Press.

Almond, G. and Verba, S. (1963) *The Civic Culture*. Princeton: Princeton University Press.

Altheide, D. (1985) *Media Power*. Beverly Hills: Sage.

Altheide, D. and Snow, R. (1979) *Media Logic*. Beverly Hills: Sage.

Altick, R. (1978) *The Shows of London*. Cambridge, MA: Harvard University Press.

Anden-Papadopoulos, K. (2009) 'US Soldiers Imaging the Iraq War on YouTube', *Popular Communication* 7(1): 17–27.

Anden-Papadopoulos, K. and Pantti, M. (ed.) (forthcoming) *Amateur Images and Global News*. Bristol: Intellect.

Anderson, B. (1983) *Imagined Communities*. London: Verso.

Anderson, C. (2010) 'Analyzing Grassroots Journalism on the Web: Reporting and the Participatory Practice of Online News Gathering', in C. Rodriguez, D. Kidd and L. Stein (eds), *Making Our Media*, vol. I. Creskill, NJ: The Hampton Press, pp. 47–70.

Anderson, C. and Wolff, M. (2010) 'The Web is Dead. Long Live the Internet', *Wired*. www.wired.com/magazine/2010/8/ff_webrip/all/, last accessed 4 July 2011.

Anderson, P. (2011) 'On the Concatenation in the Arab World', *New Left Review* 68: 5–15.

Andrejevic, M. (2008a) *I-Spy*. Kansas City: Kansas University Press.

Andrejevic, M. (2008b) 'Watching Television without Pity: The Productivity of Online Fans', *Television & New Media* 9(1): 24–46.

Ang, I. (1996) *Living Room Wars*. London: Routledge.

Appadurai, A. (1996) *Modernity at Large*. Minneapolis: University of Minnesota Press.

Aristotle (1976) *Nicomachean Ethics*, trans. J. Thomson. Harmondsworth: Penguin.

Arnison, M. (2002) 'Crazy Ideas for Webcasting'. www.purplebark.net/maffew/cat/webcast.html, last accessed 3 September 2011.

Arthur, C. (2011) 'Microsoft Makes Grab for Phones in Bid to Catch up with Google', *Guardian*, 11 May.

Arvidsson, A. (2011) 'Towards a Branded Audience: On the Dialectic between Marketing and Consumer Agency', in V. Nightingale (ed.), *The Handbook of Media Audiences*. Malden, MA: Wiley-Blackwell, pp. 269–85.

Asamoah-Gyadu, J. (2009) 'African Traditional Religion, Pentacostalism and the Clash of Spiritualities in Ghana', in S. Hoover and N. Kaneva (eds), *Fundamentalisms and the Media*. London: Continuum, pp. 161–78.

Aslama, M. (2009) 'Playing House: Participants' Experience of *Big Brother* Finland', *International Journal of Cultural Studies* 12(1): 81–96.

Atton, C. (2001) *Alternative Media*. London: Sage.

Atton, C. (2004) *An Alternative Internet*. Edinburgh: Edinburgh University Press.

Aufderheide, P. and Clark, J. (2009) *The Future of Public Media: FAQ*. Washington, DC: American University.

Bach, J. and Stark, D. (2005) 'Recombinant Technology and New Geographies of Association', in R. Latham and S. Sassen (eds), *Digital Formations*. Princeton: Princeton University Press, pp. 37–53.

Bacon-Smith, C. (1992) *Enterprising Women: Television Fandom and the Creation of Popular Myth*. Philadelphia: University of Pennsylvania Press.

Bagdikian, B. (2004) *The New Media Monopoly*. New York: Beacon Press.

Bailey, O., Cammaerts, B. and Carpentier, N. (2008) *Understanding Alternative Media*. Maidenhead: Open University Press.

Bakardjeva, M. (2009) 'Subactivism: Lifeworld and Politics in the Age of the Internet', *The Information Society* 25(2): 91–104.

Baker, C. (2002) *Media Markets and Democracy*. Cambridge: Cambridge University Press.

Banet-Weiser, S. (2011) 'Branding the Post-Feminist Self: Girls' Video Promotion and YouTube', in M. Kearney (ed.), *Mediated Girlhood*. New York: Peter Lang, pp. 277–94.

Banet-Weiser, S. (forthcoming) *Authentic™: The Politics of Ambivalence in a Brand Culture*. New York: New York University Press.

Banet-Weiser, S. and Portwood-Stacer, L. (2006) '"I Just Want to Be Me Again!" Beauty Pageants, Reality Television and Post-feminism', *Feminist Theory* 7(2): 255–72.

Barabasi, A.-L. (2003) *Linked*. Harmondsworth: Penguin.

Barbrook, R. (1995) *Media Freedom*. London: Pluto.

Barker, M. and Brooks, K. (1998) *Knowing Audiences: Judge Dredd*. Luton: University of Luton Press.

Barker-Plummer, B. and Kidd, D. (2010) 'Closings and Openings: Media Restructuring and the Public Sphere', in K. Howley (ed.), *Understanding Community Media*. Newbury Park: Sage, pp. 318–27.

Barnouw, E. (1990 [1975]) *Tube of Plenty*. New York: Oxford University Press.

Barry, A. (2001) *Political Machines*. London: Athlone Press.

Baudrillard, J. (1981) 'Requiem for the Media', in *For a Critique of the Political Economy of the Sign*. St Louis: Telos Press, pp. 164–84.

Baudrillard, J. (1983a) *In the Shadow of the Silent Majorities*. New York: Semiotext(e).

Baudrillard, J. (1983b) *Simulations*. New York: Semiotext(e).

Baudrillard, J. (1993) *Symbolic Exchange and Death*. London: Sage.

Bauman, Z. (1992) *Intimations of Postmodernity*. London: Routledge.

Bauman, Z. (1995) *Life in Fragments*. Oxford: Blackwell.

Bauman, Z. (2000) *Liquid Modernity*. Cambridge: Polity.

Bausinger, H. (1984) 'Media, Technology and Daily Life', *Media, Culture and Society* 6(4): 343–52.

Baym, G. (2005) '*The Daily Show*: Discursive Integration and the Reinvention of Political Journalism', *Political Communication* 22: 259–76.

Baym, N. (2010) *Personal Connections in the Digital Age*. Cambridge: Polity.

BBC (2005) 'Sir Alan Sugar Confirmed for BBC Two's Apprentice', press release, 18 May, available from www.bbc.co.uk/print/pressoffice/pressreleases/, last accessed 25 March 2011.

BBC Global News (2011) *The World Speaks 2011*. London: BBC.

Beaumont, P. (2011) 'Friends, Followers and Countrymen', *Guardian*, 25 February.

Beck U. (1992) *Risk Society*. London: Sage.

Beck, U. (1997) *The Reinvention of Politics*. Cambridge: Polity.

Beck, U. (2000a) 'The Cosmopolitan Perspective: Sociology of the Second Age of Modernity', *British Journal of Sociology* 51(1): 79–105.

Beck, U. (2000b) *What is Globalization?* Oxford: Blackwell.

250 **References**

Beck, U., Giddens, A. and Lash, S. (1994) *Reflexive Modernization*. Cambridge: Polity.

Beckett, C. (2010) *The Rise of Networked Journalism*. London: Polis.

Beecher, E. (2009) Contribution to plenary discussion: 'Journalism Practice and the Changing Newsroom', Journalism in the 21st Century Conference, Melbourne University, 16–17 July 2009.

Beer, D. (2008) 'Social Network(ing) Sites . . . Revisiting the Story So Far', *Journal of Computer-Mediated Communication* 13(2): 516–29.

Bell, C. (1992) *Ritual Theory, Ritual Practice*. New York: Oxford University Press.

Bell, C. (1997) *Ritual: Perspectives and Dimensions*. New York: Oxford University Press.

Bengtsson, S. (2006) 'Framing Space: Media and the Intersection of Work and Leisure', in J. Falkheimer and A. Jansson (eds), *Geographies of Communication*. Göteborg: Nordicom, pp. 189–204.

Beniger, J. (1986) *The Control Revolution*. Cambridge, MA: Harvard University Press.

Benkler, Y. (2006) *The Wealth of Networks*. New Haven: Yale University Press.

Benkler, Y. (2011) *A Free Irresponsible Press: Wikileaks and the Battle over the Soul of the Networked Fourth Estate*. http://benkler.org/Benkler_Wikileaks_current.pdf, last accessed 19 July 2011.

Benjamin, W. (1968) *Illuminations,* trans. H. Zohn. New York: Schocken Books.

Bennett, J. (2011) *Television Personalities*. London: Routledge.

Bennett, L. (2003) 'Communicating Global Activism: Strengths and Vulnerabilities of Networked Politics', *Information Communication and Society* 6(2): 143–68.

Bennett, L. (2008) 'Changing Citizenship in a Digital Age', in L. Bennett (ed.), *Civic Life Online*. Cambridge, MA: MIT Press, pp. 1–24.

Bennett, L. and Iyengar, S. (2008) 'A New Era of Minimal Effects? The Changing Foundations of Political Communication', *Journal of Communication* 58: 707–31.

Bennett, L., Johnson, R. and Livingston, S. (2008) *When the Press Fails*. Chicago: Chicago University Press.

Bennett, W. L. and Manheim, J. (2006) 'The One-Step Flow of Communication', *Annals of American Academy of Social and Political Science* 608: 213–32.

Benson, R. (2006) 'News Media as "Journalistic Field": What Bourdieu Adds to New Institutionalism and Vice Versa', *Political Communication* 23(2): 187–202.

Benson, R. and Neveu, E. (eds) (2005) *Bourdieu and the Journalistic Field*. Cambridge: Polity.

Bentivegna, S. (2002) 'Politics and New Media', in L. Lievrouw and S. Livingstone (eds), *Handbook of New Media*, 1st edn. London: Sage, pp. 50–61.

Berger, P. (2005) 'The Desecularization of the World: A Global Overview', in P. Berger (ed.), *The Desecularization of the World*. Grand Rapids: Eerdmans Publishers, pp. 1–15.

Berger, P. and Luckmann, T. (1967) *The Social Construction of Reality*. Harmondsworth: Penguin.

Bergström, A. and Wadbring, I. (2008) 'The Contribution of Free Dailies and News on the Web: Is Readership Strictly Decreasing among Young People?'. Paper presented to Nordic Media in Theory and Practice Conference, UCL, 7–8 November, http://reutersinstitute.politics.ox.ac.uk/fileadmin/documents/nordic_media_papers/Bergstrom_Wadbring.pdf, last accessed 23 June 2011.

Billig, M. (1995) *Banal Nationalism*. London: Sage.

Bimber, B. (2003) *Information and American Democracy*. Cambridge: Cambridge University Press.

Bird, S. E. (2003) *The Audience in Everyday Life*. London: Routledge.

Bird, S. E. (2010) 'From Fan Practice to Mediated Moments: The Value of Practice Theory in the Understanding of Media Audiences', in B. Brauchler and J. Postill (eds), *Theorising Media and Practice*. New York/Oxford: Berghahn Books, pp. 85–104.

Biressi, A. and Nunn, H. (2008) 'The Kidnapped Body and Precarious Life: Reflections on the Kenneth Bigley Case', *Continuum* 22: 222–38.

Blackmore, J. and Thorpe, S. (2003) 'Media/ting Change: The Print Media's Role in Mediating Education Policy in a Period of Radical Reform in Victoria, Australia', *Journal of Education Policy* 18(6): 577–95.

Blake, W. (1976) *Selected Poems of William Blake*. Chicago: Signet Books.

Blazwick, I. (ed.) (1989) *A Situationist Scrapbook*. London: ICA/Verso.

Bloch, M. (1962) *Feudal Society*, vol. I. London: Routledge & Kegan Paul.

Bloch, M. (1989) *Ritual History and Power*. London: The Athlone Press.

Boczkowski, P. (2010) *News at Work: Imitation in an Age of Information Abundance*. Chicago: Chicago University Press.

Boghossian, P. (2007) *Fear of Knowledge: Against Relativism and Constructivism*. Oxford: Oxford University Press.

Bohman, J. (2000) 'The Division of Labour in Democratic Discourse', in S. Chambers and A. Costain (eds), *Deliberation, Democracy and the Media*. Lanham, MD: Rowman and Littlefield, pp. 47–64.

Bohman, J. (2004) 'Expanding Dialogue: The Internet, the Public Sphere and Prospects for Transnational Democracy', in N. Crossley and J. Roberts (eds), *After Habermas*. Oxford: Blackwell, pp. 131–55.

Bohman, J. (2007) *Democracy Across Borders*. Cambridge, MA: MIT Press.

Bolin, G. (2009) 'Symbolic Production and Value in Media Industries', *Journal of Cultural Economy* 2(3): 345–61.

Bolin, G. (2011) *Value and the Media*. Aldershot: Ashgate.

Boltanski, L. (2009) *De La Critique*. Paris: Gallimard.

Boltanski, L. (2011) *On Critique*. Cambridge: Polity.

Boltanski, L. and Chiapello, E. (2005) *The New Spirit of Capitalism*. London: Verso.

Boltanski, L. and Thévenot, L. (2006). *On Justification*. Princeton: Princeton University Press.

Bolter, J. (2001) *Writing Space*, 2nd edn. Mahwah, NJ: Lawrence Erlbaum.

Bolter, R. and Grusin, D. (2001) *Remediation*. Cambridge, MA: MIT Press.

Bolton, T. (2006) 'News on the Net: A Critical Analysis of the Potential of Online Alternative Journalism to Challenge the Dominance of Mainstream News Media', *Scan* (web journal) 3(1), http://scan.net.au/scan/journal/display.php?journal_id=71, last accessed 18 November 2011.

Boorstin, D. (1961) *The Image: Or, Whatever Happened to the American Dream?* London: Weidenfeld and Nicholson.

Booth, P. (2010) *Digital Fandom*. New York: Peter Lang.

Bosch, T. (2010) 'Theorizing Citizens' Media: A Rhizomatic Approach', in C. Rodriguez, D. Kidd and L. Stein (eds), *Making Our Media*, vol. I. Cresskill, NJ: The Hampton Press, pp. 72–87.

Bourdieu, P. (1977) *Outline of a Theory of Practice*. Cambridge: Cambridge University Press.

Bourdieu, P. (1983) 'The Forms of Capital', in J. Richardson (ed.), *Handbook of Theory and Research for the Sociology of Education*. New York: Greenwood Press, pp. 241–58.

Bourdieu, P. (1986) 'The Production of Belief: Contribution to an Economy of Symbolic Goods', in R. Collins et al. (eds), *Media, Culture and Society: A Critical Reader*. London: Sage, pp. 131–63.

Bourdieu, P. (1990) *The Logic of Practice*. Cambridge: Polity.

Bourdieu, P. (1991) *Language and Symbolic Power*. Cambridge: Polity.

Bourdieu, P. (1992) (with Terry Eagleton) 'Doxa and Common Life', *New Left Review* 191: 111–21.

Bourdieu, P. (1993) *The Field of Cultural Production*. Cambridge: Polity.

Bourdieu, P. (1996a) *The State Nobility*. Cambridge: Polity.

Bourdieu, P. (1996b) *The Rules of Art*. Cambridge: Polity.

Bourdieu, P. (1996c) *Sur La Télévision*. Paris: Liber.

Bourdieu, P. (1998) *On Television and Journalism*. London: Pluto.

Bourdieu, P. (2000) *Pascalian Meditations*. Stanford: Stanford University Press.

Bourdieu, P. (2005) 'The Political Field, the Social Science Field and the Journalistic Field', in R. Benson and E. Neveu (eds), *Bourdieu and the Journalistic Field*. Cambridge: Polity, pp. 29–47.

Bourdieu, P. and Wacquant, L. (1992) *Invitation to Reflexive Sociology*. Cambridge: Polity.

Bourdon, J. (2000) 'Live Television is Still Alive', *Media, Culture and Society* 22(5): 531–56.

Bowker, G. and Leigh Star, S. (2000) *Sorting Things Out*. Cambridge, MA: MIT Press.

Boyd, D. (2008) 'Why Youth ♥ Social Network Sites: The Role of Networked Publics', in D. Buckingham (ed.), *Youth, Identity and Digital Media*. Cambridge, MA: MIT Press, pp. 119–42.

Boyd, D. and Ellison, N. (2008) 'Social Network Sites: Definition, History and Scholarship', *Journal of Computer-Mediated Communication* 13(1): 210–30.

Boyd, D., Straubhaar, J. and Lent, J. (1989) *Videocassette Recorders in the Third World*. New York: Longman.

Boyd-Barrett, O. and Rantanen, T. (eds) (1998) *The Globalization of News*. London: Sage.

Boyer, D. (2010) 'Making (Sense of) News in the Era of Digital Information', in S. E. Bird (ed.), *The Anthropology of News and Journalism: Global Perspectives.* Bloomington, IN: Indiana University Press, pp. 241–56.

Boyle, R. and Kelly, L. (2010) 'The Celebrity Entrepreneur on Television: Profile, Politics and Power', *Celebrity Studies* 1(3): 334–50.

Bradshaw, T. (2011) 'Media watchdog to investigate "opaque" TV advertising', *Financial Times*, 17 March.

Braman, S. (2009) *Change of State: Information, Policy, Power.* Cambridge, MA: MIT Press.

Braudel, F. (1975 [1949]) *The Mediterranean and the Mediterranean World in the Age of Philip II.* London: Fontana.

Braudel, F. (1981) *Civilization and Capitalism*, vol. I. London: Collins.

Braudy, L. (1986) *The Frenzy of Renown: Fame and its History.* New York: Oxford University Press.

Breiter, A., Schulz, A. and Welling, S. (2011) 'Schools as Mediatised Translocal Network Organizations'. Paper presented to Mediatized Worlds Conference, University of Bremen, 14–15 April.

Bremner, I. (2010) 'Democracy in Cyberspace', *Foreign Affairs* (Nov./Dec.): 86–92.

Brewer, J. (2004) *A Sentimental Murder.* New York: Farrar, Strauss, Giroux.

Briggs, A. and Burke, P. (2005) *A Social History of the Media*, 2nd edn. Cambridge: Polity.

Brighenti, A. (2007) 'Visibility: A Category for the Social Sciences', *Current Sociology* 55(3): 323–42.

Brook, S. (2007) 'Paper Readership Dips 5m in 15 years', *Guardian*, 21 December.

Brooker-Gross, S. (1983) 'Spatial Aspects of Newsworthiness', *Geografisker Annaler* 65B: 1–9.

Browne, D. (2005) *Ethnic Minorities, Electronic Media and the Public Sphere: A Comparative Study.* Creskill, NJ: The Hampton Press.

Bruns, A. (2005) *Gatewatching.* New York: Peter Lang.

Brunsdon, C. and Morley, D. (1978) *Everyday Television: "Nationwide".* London: BFI.

Bryant, J. (1993) 'Will Traditional Media Research Paradigms be Obsolete in the Era of Intelligent Communication Networks?', in P. Gaunt (ed.), *Beyond Agendas.* Westport, CN: Greenwood Press, pp. 149–67.

Buckingham, D. (2008) 'Introducing Identity', in D. Buckingham (ed.), *Youth, Identity and Digital Media.* Cambridge, MA: MIT Press, pp. 1–22.

Buck-Morss, S. (2003) *Thinking Past Terror.* London: Verso.

Buonanno, M. (2008) *The Age of Television.* Bristol: Intellect.

Burgess, J. and Green, J. (2009) *YouTube.* Cambridge: Polity.

de Burgh, H. (2003) 'Great Aspirations and Conventional Repertoires: Chinese regional television journalists and their work', *Journalism Studies* 4(2): 225–38.

Butler, J. (1990) *Gender Trouble.* New York: Routledge.

Butler, J. (1993) *Bodies That Matter.* New York: Routledge.

Butler, J. (2005) *Giving an Account of Oneself*. New York: Fordham University Press.

Butsch, R. (2008) *The Citizen Audience*. London: Routledge.

Cabrera Paz, J. (2009) 'Techno-Cultural Convergence: Wanting to Say Everything, Wanting to Watch Everything', *Popular Communication* 7: 130–9.

Caldwell, J. (2000) 'Introduction: Theorising the Digital Landrush', in J. Caldwell (ed.), *Electronic Media and Technoculture*. New Brunswick, NJ: Rutgers University Press, pp. 1–34.

Calhoun, C. (1995) *Critical Social Theory*. Cambridge: Polity.

Calhoun, C. (2005) 'Community without Propinquity', *Sociological Inquiry* 68(3): 373–97.

Calhoun, C. (2007) *Nations Matter*. London: Routledge.

Callon, M. and Latour, B. (1981) 'Unscrewing the Big Leviathan: How Actors Macro-structure Reality and How Sociologists Help Them to Do So', in Karin Knorr-Cetina and Alvin Cicourel (eds), *Advances in Social Theory and Methodology*. London: Routledge & Kegan Paul, pp. 277–303.

Campbell, H. (2010) *When Religion Meets New Media*. London: Routledge.

Cao, K. (2010) *Media Incidents: Power Negotiation on Mass Media in Time of China's Social Transition*. Konstanz: UVK.

Capino, J. (2003) 'Soothsayers, Politicians, Lesbian Scribes: The Philippino Movie Talk Show', in L. Parks and S. Kumar (eds), *Planet TV: A Global Television Reader*. New York: New York University Press, pp. 262–74.

Cappella, J. and Jamieson, K. H. (1997) *Spiral of Cynicism: The Press and the Public Good*. New York: Oxford University Press.

Carey, J. (1989) *Communications as Culture*. Boston: Unwin Hyman.

Carlson, M. (2007) 'Order Versus Access: News Search Engines and the Challenge to Traditional Journalistic Roles', *Media, Culture and Society* 29(6): 1014–30.

Carpentier, N. (2009) 'Participation is Not Enough: The Conditions of Possibility of Mediated Participation Practices', *European Journal of Communication* 24(4): 407–20.

Carr, D. (2011) 'The Evolving Mission of Google', *New York Times*, 21 March 2011, Business section 1, 6.

Carroll, J. (2007) 'John S. Carroll on Why Newspapers Matter', www.niemanwatchdog.org/index.cfm?fuseaction=ask_this. views&askthisid=00203, last accessed 24 December 2007.

Carter, M. (2004) 'Coming Soon to Your Living Room', *Guardian*, 26 July.

Cashmore, E. (2006) *Celebrity/Culture*. London: Routledge.

Castells, M. (1996) *The Rise of the Network Society*. Oxford: Blackwell.

Castells, M. (1997) *The Power of Identity*. Oxford: Blackwell.

Castells, M. (1998) *End of Millennium*. Oxford: Blackwell.

Castells, M. (2009) *Communication Power*. Oxford: Oxford University Press.

Castells, M., Fernandez-Ardevol, M., Qiu, J. and Sey, A. (2007) *Mobile Communication and Society*. Cambridge, MA: MIT Press.

Castillo, M. (2011) '#YouTube Goes on Demand with Hollywood Blockbusters', 26 April, www.cbsnews.com/8301-504943_162-20057503-10391715.html.

Cavarero, A. (2000) *Relating Narratives*. London: Routledge.

Cavell, S. (1964) 'Existentialism and Analytic Philosophy', *Daedalus* 93: 946–74.

Chadwick, A. (2006) *Internet Politics*. Oxford: Oxford University Press.

Chadwick, A. (forthcoming) 'Recent Shifts in the Relationship between Internet and Democratic Engagement in Britain and the US: Granularity, Informational Exuberance and Political Learning', in E. Arviza, M. Jensen and L. Jorba (eds), *Digital Media and Political Engagement Worldwide*. Cambridge: Cambridge University Press.

Chakravarty, P. (2008) 'Labor in or as Civil Society? Workers and Subaltern Publics in India's Information Society', in P. Chakravarty and Y. Zhao (eds), *Global Communications: Towards a Transcultural Political Economy*. Lanham, MD: Rowman and Littlefield, pp. 285–307.

Chakravarty, P. and Zhao, Y. (2008) 'Introduction: Toward a Transcultural Political Economy of Global Communications', in P. Chakravarty and Y. Zhao (eds), *Global Communications: Towards a Transcultural Political Economy*. Lanham, MD: Rowman and Littlefield, pp. 1–22.

Champagne, P. (1990) *Faire L'Opinion*. Paris: Editions Minuit.

Champagne P. (1999) 'The View from the Media', in P. Bourdieu et al., *The Weight of the World*. Cambridge: Polity, pp. 46–59.

Champagne, P. (2005) 'The "Double Dependency": The Journalistic Field between Politics and Markets', in R. Benson and E. Neveu (eds), *Bourdieu and the Journalistic Field*. Cambridge: Polity, pp. 48–63.

Champagne, P. and Marchetti, D. (2005) 'The Contaminated Blood Scandal: Reframing Medical News', in R. Benson and E. Neveu (eds), *Bourdieu and the Journalistic Field*. Cambridge: Polity, pp. 113–34.

Chandler, D. (1998) 'Personal Homepages and the Construction of Identities on the Web', www.aber.ac.uk/media/Documents/short/webident.html, last accessed 18 July 2011.

Chang, T.-K. (1998) 'All Countries Not Created Equal to be News: World System and International Communication', *Communication Research* 25(5): 528–63.

Chapman, J. (2005) *Comparative Media History*. Cambridge: Polity.

Cheong, P. and Gong, J. (2010) 'Cyber Vigilantism, Transmedia Collective Intelligence, and Civic Participation', *Chinese Journal of Communication* 3(4): 471–87.

Cheong, P., Halavais, A. and Kwon, K. (2008) 'The Chronicles of Media: Understanding Blogging as a Religious Practice', *Journal of Media and Religion* 7: 107–31.

Chernilo, D. (2007) 'A Quest for Universalism: Reassessing the Nature of Classical Social Theory's Cosmopolitanism', *European Journal of Social Theory* 10(1): 17–35.

Chinni, D. (2010) 'Tea Party Mapped: How Big is it and Where is it Based?', 21 April. www.pbs.org/newshour/rundown/2010/04, last accessed 15 July 2011.

Choi, J. (2006) 'Living in *Cyworld*: Contextualising Cy-ties in South Korea', in A. Bruns and J. Jacobs (eds), *Use of Blogs*. New York: Peter Lang, pp. 173–86.

Chouliaraki, L. (forthcoming) 'Humanitarianism and Celebrity: The Theatre of Pity', *Communication and Critical/Cultural Studies* 9(1).

Christakis, N. and Fowler, J. (2010) *Connected*. New York: Harper Collins.

Christensen, T. and Røpke, I. (2010) 'Can Practice Theory Inspire Studies of ICTS in Everyday Life?', in B. Brauchler and J. Postill (eds), *Theorising Media and Practice*. New York/Oxford: Berghahn Books, pp. 233–56.

Christians, C., Ferré, J. and Fackler, M. (1993) *Good News: Social Ethics and the Press*. New York: Longman.

Christians, C., Glasser, T., McQuail, D., Nordenstreng, K. and White, R. (2010) *Normative Theories of the Media*. Chicago: University of Illinois Press.

Clark, J. and van Slyke, T. (2010) *Beyond the Echo Chamber*. New York: The New Press.

Clarke, N. (2004) *The Shadow of a Nation: How Celebrity Destroyed Britain*. London: Phoenix Books.

Clough, P. (2009) 'The New Empiricism: Affect and Sociological Method', *European Journal of Social Theory* 12(1): 43–61.

CNNIC (2010) *26th Statistical Report on Internet Development in China*. China Internet Network Information Centre, July. www.cnnic.net.cn/uploadfiles/pdf/2010/8/24/93145.pdf, last accessed 26 July 2011.

Cohen, R. (2009) 'Iran: the Tragedy and the Future', *New York Review of Books*, 13 August, 7–10.

Cohen-Almagor, R. (2001) *Speech, Media and Ethics: The Limits of Free Expression*. Basingstoke: Palgrave.

Coleman, S. (2005) 'The Lonely Citizen: Indirect Representation in an Age of Networks', *Political Communication* 22: 197–214.

Coleman, S. (2008) 'Doing IT for Themselves: Management versus Autonomy in Youth e- Citizenship', in L. Bennett (ed.), *Civic Life Online*. Cambridge, MA: MIT Press, pp. 189–206.

Coleman, S. (ed.) (2011) *Leaders in the Living Room: The Prime Ministerial Debate of 2010*. Oxford: Reuters Institute for the Study of Journalism.

Coleman, S. and Blumler, J. (2009) *The Internet and Democratic Citizenship*. Cambridge: Cambridge University Press.

Coleman, S. and Ross, K. (2010) *The Media and the Public*. Malden, MA: Wiley-Blackwell.

Collins, J. (1992) 'Genericity in the Nineties: Eclectic Irony and the New Sincerity', in J. Collins (ed.), *Film Theory Goes to the Movies*. New York: Routledge, pp. 242–64.

Collins, S. (2008) 'Making the Most Out of 15 Minutes: Reality TV's Dispensable Celebrity', *Television and New Media* 9(2): 87–110.

Collins, W. (1994 [1868]) *The Moonstone*. Harmondsworth: Penguin.

Condry, I. (2009) 'Anime Creativity: Characters and Premises in the Quest for Cool Japan', *Theory, Culture & Society* 26(2–3): 139–63.

Connell, R. (2007) *Southern Theory*. Cambridge: Polity.

Connor, S. (2005) 'Playstations, or, Playing in Earnest', *Static* 1(1), http://static.londonconsortium.com/issue01/connor_playstations.html, last accessed 18 July 2011.

Cook, T. (2005) *Governing the News*. Chicago: Chicago University Press.

Cooper, A. (2008) *Celebrity Diplomacy*. Boulder, CO: Paradigm.

Cooren, F., Brummans, B. and Charrieras, D. (2008) 'The Coproduction of Organizational Presence: A Study of Médécins Sans Frontières in Action', *Human Relations* 61(10): 1339–70.

Copsey, R. (2010) 'My Castaway Hell', *Guardian*, G2 section, 12 August.

Corner, J. (1997) 'Television in Theory', *Media, Culture and Society* 19(2): 247–62.

Costera Meijer, I. (2011) 'Living in the Media Polis: Is Participatory Journalism an Answer to Changing Civic Engagement?' Paper presented to ICA Conference, Boston, 26–30 May.

Cottle, S. and Nolan, D. (2007) 'Global Humanitarianism and the Changing Aid-Media Field', *Journalism Studies* 8(6): 862–78.

Couldry, N. (1999) 'Remembering Diana: The Geography of Celebrity and the Politics of Lack', *New Formations* 36: 77–91.

Couldry, N. (2000a) *The Place of Media Power*. London: Routledge.

Couldry, N. (2000b) *Inside Culture*. London: Sage.

Couldry, N. (2001) 'The Hidden Injuries of Media Power', *Journal of Consumer Culture* 1(2): 155–78.

Couldry, N. (2002) 'Playing for Celebrity: *Big Brother* as Ritual Event', *Television & New Media* 3(3): 283–94.

Couldry, N. (2003a) *Media Rituals: A Critical Approach*. London: Routledge.

Couldry, N. (2003b) 'Media Meta-Capital: Extending the Range of Bourdieu's Field Theory', *Theory and Society* 32(5/6): 653–77.

Couldry, N. (2004) 'Theorizing Media as Practice', *Social Semiotics* 14(2): 115–32.

Couldry, N. (2006) *Listening Beyond the Echoes*. Boulder, CO: Paradigm Books.

Couldry, N. (2008a) 'Mediatization or Mediation? Alternative Understandings of the Emergent Space of Digital Storytelling', *New Media & Society* 10(3): 373–92.

Couldry, N. (2008b) 'Form and Power in an Age of Continuous Spectacle', in D. Hesmondhalgh and J. Toynbee (eds), *Media and Social Theory*. London: Routledge, pp. 161–76.

Couldry, N. (2008c) 'Actor Network Theory and Media: Do They Connect and On What Terms?', in A. Hepp et al. (eds), *Cultures of Connectivity*. Creskill, NJ: The Hampton Press, pp. 93–110.

Couldry, N. (2009a) 'Does "the Media" have a Future?', *European Journal of Communication* 24(4): 437–50.

Couldry, N. (2009b) 'New Online News Sources and Writer-gatherers', in N. Fenton (ed.), *New Media, Old News*. London: Sage, pp. 138–52.

Couldry, N. (2010) *Why Voice Matters: Culture and Politics after Neoliberalism*. London: Sage.

Couldry, N. and Hepp, A. (forthcoming) 'Media Cultures in a Global Age: A Transcultural Approach to an Expanded Spectrum', in I. Volkmer (ed.), *Handbook of Comparative Research*. Malden, MA: Wiley-Blackwell.

Couldry, N. and Littler, J. (2011) 'Work, Power and Performance: Analyzing the "Reality" Game of *The Apprentice*', *Cultural Sociology* 5(2): 263–79.

Couldry, N., Livingstone, S. and Markham, T. (2010) *Media Consumption and Public Engagement*. Basingstoke: Palgrave Macmillan. Revised paperback edn (original edn 2007).

Crary, J. (1999) *Suspensions of Perception*. Cambridge, MA: MIT Press.

Crisp, R. (1996) 'Modern Moral Philosophy and the Virtues', in R. Crisp (ed.), *How Should One Live?* Oxford: Oxford University Press, pp. 1–18.

Croteau, D. (1995) *Politics and the Class Divide*. Philadelphia: Temple University Press.

Crouch, C. (2000) *Living with Post-Democracy*. London: Fabian Society.

Cui, L. and Lee, F. (2010) 'Becoming Extra-ordinary: Negotiation of Media Power in the Case of *Super Girls Voice* in China', *Popular Communication* 8(4): 256–72.

Curran, J. (1982) 'Communications, Power and Social Order', in M. Gurevitch et al. (eds), *Culture, Society and the Media*. London: Routledge, pp. 202–35.

Curran, J. (2002) *Media and Power*. London: Routledge.

Curran, J. and Park, M.-J. (2000) 'Beyond Globalization Theory', in J. Curran and M.-J. Park (eds), *De-westernizing Media Studies*. London: Routledge, pp. 3–18.

Curran, J. and Seaton, J. (2007) *Power Without Responsibility*, 4th edn. London: Arnold.

Curran, J., Fenton, N. and Freedman, D. (forthcoming) *Misunderstanding the Internet*. London: Bloomsbury.

Curran, J., Iyengar, S., Brink Lund, A. and Salovaara-Moring, I. (2009) 'Media System, Public Knowledge and Democracy', *European Journal of Communication* 24(1): 5–26.

Curtin, M. (2003) 'Media Capital: Towards the Study of Spatial Flows', *International Journal of Cultural Studies* 6(2): 202–28.

Curtin, M. (2009) 'Matrix Media', in G. Turner and T. Tay (eds), *Television Studies After TV*. London: Routledge, pp. 9–19.

Czarniawska, B. (2010) 'Cyberfactories: Where Production and Consumption Merge'. Keynote to Danish SMID Conference, Koldingfjord, Denmark, 2 December.

Dahlgren, P. (2009) *Media and Political Engagement*. Cambridge: Cambridge University Press.

Dalton, R. (2000) 'Value Change and Democracy', in S. Pharr and R. Putnam (eds), *Disaffected Democracies*. Cambridge, MA: Harvard University Press, pp. 252–69.

D'Arcy, J. (1977) 'Direct Broadcast Satellites and the Right to Communicate', in L. S. Harns (ed.), *The Right to Communicate: Collected Papers*. Honolulu: University of Hawaii Press.

Davies, N. (2008) *Flat Earth News*. London: Chatto and Windus.

Davis, A. (2007) *The Mediation of Power*. London: Routledge.

Davis, A. (2009) 'Elite News Sources, New Media and Political Journalism', in N. Fenton (ed.), *New Media, Old News*. London: Sage, pp. 121–37.

Davis, A. (2010) *Political Communication and Social Theory*. London: Routledge.

Davis, A. and Seymour, E. (2010) 'Generating Forms of Media Capital Inside and Outside a Field: The Strange Case of David Cameron in the UK Political Field', *Media, Culture and Society* 32(5): 739–59.

Davis, R. (2008) 'A Thin Line between Love and Hate', *Guardian*, 14 October.

Dawson, M. (2007) 'Little Players, Big Shows: Format, Narration and Style on Television's New Smaller Screens', *Convergence* 13(3): 231–50.

Dayan, D. (1998) 'Particularistic Media and Diasporic Communication', in T. Liebes and J. Curran (eds), *Media, Ritual and Identity*. London: Routledge, pp. 103–13.

Dayan, D. (2001) 'The Peculiar Public of Television', *Media, Culture and Society* 23(5): 743–65.

Dayan, D. (2006) 'Terrorisme, Performance, Représentation: Notes sur un genre discursive contemporain', in D. Dayan (ed.), *La Terreur Spectacle*. Brussels: De Boeck, pp. 11–22.

Dayan, D. (2009) 'Sharing and Showing: Television as Monstration', in E. Katz and P. Scannell (eds), '*The End of Television?' Annals of the American Academy of Political and Social Science* 625: 19–31.

Dayan, D. (2010) 'Beyond Media Events: Disenchantment, Derailment, Disruption', in N. Couldry, A. Hepp and F. Krotz (eds), *Media Events in a Global Age*. London: Routledge, pp. 23–31.

Dayan, D. and Katz, E. (1992) *Media Events: The Live Broadcasting of History*. Cambridge, MA: Harvard University Press.

Dean, J. (2002) *Publicity's Secret*. Ithaca: Cornell University Press.

Dean, J. (2010) *Democracy and Other Neoliberal Fantasies*. Durham, NC: Duke University Press.

Debord, G. (1983) *Society of the Spectacle*. Detroit: Black and Red.

Debray, R. (1996) *Media Manifestos*. London: Verso.

DeLanda, M. (2005) *Intensive Science and Virtual Philosophy*. London: Continuum.

DeLillo, D. (1999) *Underworld*. London: Picador.

Delli Carpini, M. (2000) 'Gen.com: Youth, Civic Engagement, and the New Information Environment,' *Political Communication* 17(4): 341–9.

Delli Carpini, M. and Keater, S. (1996) *What Americans Know About Politics and Why It Matters*. New Haven: Yale University Press.

Delli Carpini, M. and Williams, B. (2011) *After the Broadcast News*. Cambridge: Cambridge University Press.

Derrida, J. (2002) *On Cosmopolitanism and Forgiveness*. London: Routledge.

Deutsch, K. (1966) *Nationalism and Social Communication*, 2nd edn. Cambridge, MA: MIT Press.

Deuze, M. (2003) 'The Web and its Journalisms: Considering the Consequence of Different Types of News Media Online', *New Media & Society* 5(2): 203–30.

Deuze, M. (2011) 'Media Life', *Media, Culture and Society* 33(1): 137–48.

Deuze, M. and Dimoudi, C. (2002) 'Online Journalists in the Netherlands: Towards a Profile of a New Profession', *Journalism* 3(1): 85–100.

Dorling, D. (2010) *Injustice: Why Social Inequality Persists*. Bristol: Policy Press.

Douglas, S. (1987) *Inventing American Broadcasting 1899–1922*. Baltimore: The Johns Hopkins University Press.

Dovey, J. (2000) *Freakshow*. London: Pluto.

Downey, J. (2008) 'Recognition and the Renewal of Ideology Critique', in D. Hesmondhalgh and J. Toynbee (eds), *Media and Social Theory*. London: Routledge, pp. 59–74.

Downing, J. (2001) *Radical Media*. Newbury Park: Sage.

Downing, J. (2003a) 'Audiences and Readers of Alternative Media: Absent Lure of the Virtually Unknown', *Media, Culture and Society* 25 (5): 625–46.

Downing, J. (2003b) 'The Independent Media Center Movement and the Anarchist Socialist Tradition', in N. Couldry and J. Curran (eds), *Contesting Media Power*. Boulder, CO: Rowman and Littlefield, pp. 243–58.

Dreher, T. (2009) 'Listening Across Difference: Media and Multiculturalism beyond the Politics of Voice', *Continuum* 23(4): 445–58.

Duits, L. and Ronondt Vis, P. van (2009) 'Girls Make Sense: Girls, Celebrities and Identities', *European Journal of Cultural Studies* 12(1): 41–58.

Durkheim, E. (1953) 'Individual and Collective Representations', in *Sociology and Philosophy*. London: Cohen and West, pp. 1–34.

Durkheim, E. (1984 [1893]) *The Division of Labour in Society*, trans. W. Halls, 2nd edn. Basingstoke: Macmillan.

Durkheim, E. (1995 [1912]) *The Elementary Forms of Religious Life*, trans. K. Fields. New York: Free Press.

Durkheim, E. and Mauss, M. (1970) *Primitive Classification*. London: Cohen and West.

Dutton, W. (2009) 'The Fifth Estate Emerging Through the Network of Networks', *Prometheus: Critical Studies in Innovation* 27(1): 1–15.

Duval, J. (2005) 'Economic Journalism in France', in R. Benson and E. Neveu (eds), *Bourdieu and the Journalistic Field*. Cambridge: Polity, pp. 135–55.

Dworkin, R. (2010) 'The Decision that Threatens Democracy', *New York Review of Books*, 13 May.

Earl, J. and Schussman, A. (2008) 'Contesting Cultural Control: Youth Culture and Online Petitioning', in L. Bennett (ed.), *Civic Life Online*. Cambridge, MA: MIT Press, pp. 71–95.

Easton, D. (1965) *A Systems Analysis of Political Life*. New York: John Wiley.

Echchaibi, N. (2009) 'From the Margins to the Center: New Media and the Case of *Bondy Blog* in France', in A. Russell and N. Echchaibi (eds), *International Blogging*. New York: Peter Lang, pp. 11–28.

Edelman, M. (1988) *Constructing the Political Spectacle*. Chicago: University of Chicago Press.

Edensor, T. (2006) 'Reconsidering National Temporalities: Institutional Times, Everyday Routines, Serial Spaces and Synchronicities', *European Journal of Social Theory* 9(4): 525–45.

Ehrenberg, A. (1998) *La Fatigue d'être soi*. Paris: Odile Jacob.

Eide, E., Kunelius, R. and Phillips, A. (eds) (2008) *Transnational Media Events: The Mohammed Cartoons and the Imagined Clash of Civilizations*. Nordicom: Göteborg.

Eisenstein, E. (1983) *The Printing Revolution in Early Modern Europe.* Cambridge: Cambridge University Press.

Ekstein, M. (1975) *The Limits of Reasons: The German Democratic Press and the Collapse of Weimar Democracy.* Oxford: Oxford University Press.

Elias, N. (1994 [1939]) *The Civilizing Process.* Oxford: Blackwell.

Eliasoph, N. (1998) *Avoiding Politics.* Cambridge: Cambridge University Press.

Elliott, P. (1974) 'Uses and Gratifications Research: A Critique and a Sociological Alternative', in J. Blumler and E. Katz (eds), *The Uses of Mass Communications.* Beverly Hills: Sage, pp. 249–68.

Elliott, P. (1982) 'Press Performance as Political Ritual', in H. Christian (ed.), *The Sociology of Journalism and the Press.* Keele: Keele University Press, pp. 141–77.

Ellis, J. (2000) *Seeing Things.* London: IB Tauris.

Ellison, N., Steinfield, C. and Lampe, C. (2007) 'The Benefits of Facebook "Friends": Social Capital and College Students' Use of Online Social Network Sites', *Journal of Computer-Mediated Communication* 12(4): 1142–68.

El-Nawawy, M. and Iskendar, A. (2002) *Al-Jazeera.* Boulder, CO: Westview Press.

Enli, G. and Thumim, N. (2009) 'Socializing and Self-Representation Online: Exploring Facebook'. Paper presented to Mediatized Stories pre-conference at *Transforming Audiences 2*, University of Westminster, 2 September.

Ericson, R., Baranek, P. and Chan, J. (1991) *Representing Order.* Milton Keynes: Open University Press.

Ericson, S., Riegert, K. and Akers, P. (2009) 'Introduction', in S. Ericson and K. Riegert (eds), *Media Houses: Architecture, Media and the Production of Centrality.* New York: Peter Lang, pp. 1–17.

Erni, J. and Chua, S. K. (2005) 'Introduction: Our Asian Media Studies?', *Asian Media Studies.* Malden, MA: Blackwell.

Ess, C. (2010) *Digital Media Ethics.* Cambridge: Polity.

Experian Hitwise (2010) *Getting to Grips with Social Media*, October. Available from www.hitwise.com/uk/resources/reports, last accessed 23 September 2011.

Fairclough, N. (2000) *New Labour New Language.* Cambridge: Polity.

Febvre, L. and Martin, H.-J. (1990 [1958]) *The Coming of the Book.* London: Verso.

Fenton, N. (ed.) (2009) *New Media, Old News.* London: Sage.

Feuer, J. (1983) 'The Concept of Live Television', in E. Kaplan (ed.), *Regarding Television.* Los Angeles: American Film Institute, pp. 12–22.

Ficowski, J. (ed.) (1990) *Letters and Drawings of Bruno Schulz with Selected Prose.* New York: Fromm.

Fischer, C. (1992) *America Calling.* Berkeley: University of California Press.

Fishman, M. (1980) *Manufacturing the News.* Austin, TX: Texas University Press.

Fiske, J. (1987) *Television Culture.* London: Methuen.

262　**References**

Flichy, P. (1994) *Dynamics of Modern Communication*. London: Sage.
Foot, P. (2000) *Natural Goodness*. Oxford: Oxford University Press.
Fornäs, J. (1995) *Cultural Theory and Late Modernity*. London: Sage.
Foster, C. (2005) *British Government in Crisis*. Oxford: Hart Publishing.
Foucault, M. (1979) *Discipline and Punish: The Birth of the Prison*. Harmondsworth: Peregrine.
Foucault, M. (1981) *The History of Sexuality*, vol. I. Harmondsworth: Penguin.
Fraser, N. (2005) 'Reframing Global Justice', *New Left Review*, new series 36: 69–90.
Fraser, N. (2007) 'Transnationalizing the Public Sphere', *Theory, Culture & Society* 24(4): 7–30.
Freire, P. (1972) *Pedagogy of the Oppressed*. Harmondsworth: Penguin.
Freud, S. (1991 [1927]) 'Civilization and its Discontents', in *Civilization, Society and Religion*. Harmondsworth: Penguin.
Frosh, P. (forthcoming) 'Phatic Morality: Television and Proper Distance', *International Journal of Cultural Studies*.
Fuller, M. (2005) *Media Ecologies*. Cambridge, MA: MIT Press.
Fung, A. (2009) 'Globalizing Televised Culture: The Case of China', in G. Turner and T. Tay (eds), *Television Studies After TV*. London: Routledge, pp. 178–89.
Gabler, N. (2000) *Life: The Movie*. New York: Vintage Books.
Gamson, J. (1994) *Claims to Fame: Celebrity in Contemporary America*. Berkeley: University of California Press.
Gamson, J. (1998) *Freaks Talk Back*. Chicago: Chicago University Press.
Gans, H. (2003) *Democracy and the News*. New York: Oxford University Press.
Garcia Canclini, N. (1995) *Hybrid Cultures*. Minneapolis: University of Minnesota Press.
Garfinkel, H. (1984) [1967] *Studies in Ethnomethodology*. London: Routledge & Kegan Paul.
Garland, D. (2001) *The Culture of Control*. Oxford: Oxford University Press.
Garnham, N. (1990) *Capitalism and Communication*. London: Sage.
Garnham, N. (1994) 'Bourdieu, the Cultural Arbitrary and Television', in C. Calhoun, E. Lipuma and M. Postone (eds), *Bourdieu: Critical Perspectives*. Cambridge: Polity, pp. 178–92.
Garnham, N. (1999a) *Emancipation, the Media and Modernity*. Oxford: Oxford University Press.
Garnham, N. (1999b) 'Amartya Sen's "Capabilities" Approach to the Evaluation of Welfare and its Application to Communications', in A. Calabrese and J.-C. Burgelman (eds), *Communication, Citizenship and Social Policy*. Boulder, CO: Rowman and Littlefield, pp. 113–24.
Garrahan, M. (2011) 'Cinemas in Threat over Home Screenings', *Financial Times*, 13 April.
Gavrilovic, L. (2009) 'Serbian Minority/Refugees on the Internet: In the Midst of Denial and Acceptance of Reality', in G. Goggin and M. McLelland (eds), *Internationalizing Internet Studies*. London: Routledge, pp. 145–60.

Geertz, C. (1971) *The Interpretation of Cultures*. Chicago: Chicago University Press.

Gerbaudo, P. (2010) 'Navigating the Rebel Archipelago: Orientation, Space and Communication in the "Autonomous" Scene'. PhD thesis, University of London, June.

Gergen, K. (2002) 'The Challenge of Absent Presence', in J. Katz and M. Aakhus (eds), *Perpetual Contact*. Cambridge: Cambridge University Press, pp. 227–41.

Gerhards, J. and Schäfer, M. (2010) 'Is the Internet a Better Public Sphere? Comparing Old and New Media in the USA and Germany', *New Media & Society* 12(1): 143–60.

Gershon, I (2010) *Break up 2.0: Disconnecting Over New Media*. Ithaca: Cornell University Press.

Gerth, H. and Mills, C. (1991) *From Max Weber*. London: Routledge.

Gewirtz, S., Dickson, M. and Power, S. (2004) 'Unravelling a "Spun" Policy: A Case Study of the Constitutive Role of "Spin"', *Journal of Education Policy* 19(3): 3121–338.

Gibson, J. (1979) *The Ecological Approach to Visual Perception*. Boston, MA: Houghton-Mifflin.

Giddens, A. (1974) *The Nation-State and Violence*. Cambridge: Cambridge University Press

Giddens, A. (1984) *The Constitution of Society*. Cambridge: Polity.

Giddens, A. (1990) *The Consequences of Modernity*. Cambridge: Polity.

Giddens, A. (1991) *Modernity and Self-Identity*. Cambridge: Polity.

Gilbert, J. (2008) *Anticapitalism and Culture*. Oxford: Berg.

Gillespie, M. (1995) *Television Ethnicity and Cultural Change*. London: Routledge.

Gillespie, T. (2010) 'The Politics of "Platforms" ', *New Media & Society* 12(3): 347–64.

Gillespie, T. (2011) 'The Private Governance of Digital Content, or how Apple Intends to Offer You "Freedom from Porn"'. Presentation to *Platform Politics* Conference, Anglia Ruskin University, 11–13 May.

Gillmor, D. (2004) *We the Media*. Sebastopol: O'Reilly Media.

Gilmont, J.-F. (1999) 'Protestant Reformations and Reading', in G. Cavallo and R. Chartier (eds), *A History of Reading in the West*. Cambridge: Polity, pp. 213–37.

Ginsburg, F. (1994) 'Culture/Media: A Mild Polemic', *Anthropology Today* 10(2): 5–15.

Ginsburg, F. (2008) 'Rethinking the Digital Age', in D. Hesmondhalgh and J. Toynbee (eds), *The Media and Social Theory*. London: Routledge, pp. 127–44.

Ginsburg, F., Abu-Lughod, L. and Larkin, B. (eds) (2002) *Media Worlds*. Berkeley: University of California Press.

Giroux, H. (2000) *Stealing Innocence: Youth, Corporate Power and the Politics of Culture*. New York: St Martin's Press.

Gitelman, L. (2008) *Always Already New*. Cambridge, MA: MIT Press.

264 References

Gitlin, T. (1980) *The Whole World is Watching*. Berkeley: University of California Press.

Gitlin, T. (2001) *Media Unlimited*. New York: Metropolitan Books.

Glasser, T. (1999) (ed.) *The Idea of Public Journalism*. New York: Guilford Press.

Goethals, G. (1997) 'Escape from Time: Ritual Dimensions of Popular Culture', in S. Hoover and K. Lundby (eds), *Rethinking Media Religion and Culture*. Thousand Oaks: Sage, pp. 117–32.

Goffman, E. (1974) *Frame Analysis*. Harmondsworth: Penguin.

Goggin, G. (2009) 'The International Turn in Internet Governance: A World of Difference?' in G. Goggin and M. McLelland (eds), *Internationalizing Internet Studies*. London: Routledge, pp. 48–61.

Goggin, G. and McLelland, M. (2009) 'Internationalising Internet Studies: Beyond Anglophone Paradigms', in G. Goggin and M. McLelland (eds), *Internationalizing Internet Studies*. London: Routledge, pp. 3–17.

Goggin, G. and Newell, C. (2005) *Disability in Australia*. Sydney: University of New South Wales Press.

Golding, P. and Murdock, G. (1991) 'Culture Communications and Political Economy', in J. Curran and M. Gurevitch (eds), *Mass Media and Society*, 2nd edn. London: Arnold, pp. 15–32.

Goldsmiths Leverhulme Media Research Centre (2010) *Meeting the News Needs of Local Communities*. www.mediatrust.org, last accessed 2 August 2010.

Goody, J. (1976) *The Domestication of the Savage Mind*. Cambridge: Cambridge University Press.

Goody, J. (2006) *Jade: My Autobiography*. London: Harper Collins.

Gouldner, A. (1962) '"Anti-Minotaur": The Myth of a Value-Free Sociology', *Social Problems* 9: 199–213.

Graham, S. (2004) 'Beyond the "Dazzling Light": From Dreams of Transcendence to the "Remediation" of Urban Life', *New Media & Society* 6(1): 16–25.

Gray, J. (2008) *Television Entertainment*. London: Routledge.

Gray, J., Sandvoss, C. and Harrington, C. (eds) (2007) *Fandom*. New York: New York Universities Press.

Gray, M. (2009) *Youth, Media and Queer Visibility in Rural America*. New York: New York University Press.

Greenhalgh, P. (1988) *Ephemeral Vistas*. Manchester: Manchester University Press.

Gregg, M. (2011) *Work's Intimacy*. Cambridge: Polity.

Gregg, N. (2011) 'Media is not the Issue: Justice is the Issue', in S. Curry Jansen, J. Pooley and L. Taub-Pervizpour (eds), *Media and Social Justice*. New York: Palgrave Macmillan, pp. 1–26.

Grice, P. (1989) *Studies in the Way of Words*. Cambridge, MA: Harvard University Press.

Grindstaff, L. (2002) *The Money Shot*. Chicago: Chicago University Press.

Grindstaff, L. (2009) 'Self-Serve Celebrity: The Production of Ordinariness and the Ordinariness of Production in Reality TV', in V. Mayer, M. Banks and J. Caldwell (eds), *Production Studies*. New York: Routledge, pp. 71–86.

Habermas, J. (1968) 'On Systematically Distorted Communication', in P. Connerton (ed.), *Critical Sociology*. Harmondsworth: Penguin.

Habermas, J. (1989) *The Structural Transformation of the Public Sphere*. Cambridge, MA: MIT Press.

Habermas, J. (1996) *Between Facts and Norms*. Cambridge: Polity.

Hafez, K. (2007) *The Myth of Media Globalization*. Cambridge: Polity.

Hagen, I. (1994) 'The Ambivalences of Television News Viewing', *European Journal of Communication* 9(2): 193–220.

Haiqing, Y. (2007) 'Blogging Everyday Life in Chinese Internet Culture', *Asian Studies Review* 31(4): 423–33.

Hakala, S. and Seeck, H. (2009) 'Crisis and Web-enabled Agency in Practice: The Cases of Sukellus.fi and Thairy.net', in U. Kuvikuru and L. Nord (eds), *After the Tsunami*. Göteborg: Nordicom.

Halavais, A. (2000) 'National Borders on the Worldwide Web', *New Media & Society* 2(1): 7–28.

Halavais, A. (2009a) *Search Engine Society*. Cambridge: Polity.

Halavais, A. (2009b) 'Do Dugg Diggers Digg Diligently? Feedback as Motivation in Collaborative Moderation Systems', *Information Communication and Society* 12(3): 444–59.

Hall, S. (1973) 'The "Structured Communication" of Events'. Stencilled Occasional Paper No. 5. Birmingham: Centre for Contemporary Cultural Studies.

Hall, S. (1980) 'Encoding/Decoding', in S. Hall, D. Hobson, A. Lowe and P. Willis (eds), *Culture, Media, Language*. London: Unwin Hyman, pp. 128–38.

Hall, S., Critcher, C., Jefferson, T., Clarke, J. and Roberts, B. (1978) *Policing the Crisis*. London: Macmillan.

Halliday, J. (2010) 'The Power to Put News on the Map', *Guardian*, Media section, 16 August.

Hallin, D. (2005) 'Field Theory, Differentiation Theory and Comparative Media Research', in R. Benson and E. Neveu (eds), *Bourdieu and the Journalistic Field*. Cambridge: Polity, pp. 224–43.

Hallin, D. C. and Mancini, P. (2004) *Comparing Media Systems*. Cambridge: Cambridge University Press.

Halpern, S. (2010) 'The iPad Revolution', *New York Review of Books*, June 10: 22–6.

Hamelink, C. (2000) *The Ethics of Cyberspace*. London: Sage.

Hamesse, J. (1999) 'The Scholastic Model of Reading', in G. Cavallo and R. Chartier (eds), *A History of Reading in the West*. Cambridge: Polity, pp. 103–19.

Hampton, K., Lee, C.-J. and Ja Her, E. (forthcoming) 'How New Media Affords Network Diversity: Direct and Mediated Access to Social Capital through Participation in Local Settings', *New Media & Society*.

Handelman, D. (1998) *Models and Mirrors*, 2nd edn. Cambridge: Cambridge University Press.

Handelman, D. (2004) *Nationalism and the Israeli State*. Oxford: Berghahn.

Hannerz, U. (1992) *Cultural Complexity*. New York: Columbia University Press.

266   References

Hansard Society, The (2008) *5th Audit of Political Engagement*, www.hansard society.org.uk, last accessed 5 September 2011.

Hansard Society, The (2011) *8th Audit of Political Engagement*, www.hansardsociety.org.uk/blogs/publications/archive/2011/04/08/audit-of-political-engagement-8.aspx, last accessed 5 September 2011.

Hardt, M. and Negri, T. (2000) *Empire*. Cambridge, MA: Harvard University Press.

Hardt, M. and Negri, T. (2005) *Multitude*. Harmondsworth: Penguin.

Hardt, M. and Negri, T. (2011) 'Arabs are Democracy's New Pioneers', *Guardian*, 25 February.

Hargittai, E. (2007) 'The Social, Political, Economic and Cultural Dimensions of Search Engines: An Introduction', *Journal of Computer-Mediated Communication* 12(3): 769–77.

Hargittai, E. and Walejko, G. (2008) 'The Participation Divide: Content Creation and Sharing in the Digital Age', *Information Communication & Society* 11(2): 239–56.

Hargreaves, A. and Mahdjouh, D. (1997) 'Satellite Television Viewing Among Ethnic Minorities in France', *European Journal of Communication* 12(4): 459–77.

Harindranath, R. (2003) 'Reviving "Cultural Imperialism": International Audiences, Global Representation and the Transnational Elite', in L. Parks and S. Kumar (eds), *Planet TV: A Global Television Reader*, New York: New York University Press, pp. 155–68.

Harrington, L. and Bielby, D. (1995) *Soap Fans*. Philadelphia: Temple University Press.

Harris, C. (1998) 'A Sociology of Television Fandom', in C. Harris, and A. Alexander (eds), *Theorising Fandom*. Creskill, NJ: The Hampton Press, pp. 41–54.

Harris, J. (2011) 'When Will It End?' *Guardian*, G2 section, 19 July.

Harsin, J. (2010) 'That's Democratainment: Obama, Rumor Bombs, and Primary Definers', *Flow TV*, http://flow.org/2010/10/thats-democratainment/, last accessed 19 November 2011.

Hassan, R. (2003) *The Chronoscopic Society*. New York: Peter Lang.

Hayles, N. K. (1999) *How We Became Posthuman*. Chicago: University of Chicago Press.

Hayles, N. K. (2009) 'RFID: Human Agency and Meaning in Information-Intensive Environments', *Theory, Culture & Society* 26(2–3): 47–72.

Hearn, A. (2006) '"John, a 20-year-old Boston Native with a Great Sense of Humour": On the Spectacularization of the "Self" and the Incorporation of Identity in the Age of Reality Television', in D. Marshall (ed.), *The Celebrity Culture Reader*. London: Routledge, pp. 618–33.

Heikkila, H., Ahva, L., Antio, H., Siljmaki, J. and Valtonen, S. (2010) 'A Cause for Concern: News and Politically Oriented Everyday Talk in Social Networks'. Paper presented to *Cultural Research and Political Theory: New Intersections* pre-conference, ICA Singapore, June 22–6.

Held, V. (2006) *The Ethics of Care*. New York: Oxford University Press.

Held, D., McGrew, A., Goldblatt, D. and Perraton, J. (1999) *Global Transformation*. Cambridge: Polity.

Helleksen, K. and Busse, K. (eds) (2006) *Fan Fiction and Fan Communities in the Age of the Internet*. London: Routledge.

Hemmingway, E. (2007) *Into the Newsroom*. London: Routledge.

Hepp, A. (2008) 'Translocal Media Cultures: Networks of the Media and Globalization', in A. Hepp, F. Krotz, S. Moores and C. Winter (eds), *Connectivity, Networks and Flow*. Cresskill: Hampton Press, pp. 33–58.

Hepp, A. (2009a) 'Differentiation: Mediatization and Cultural Change', in K. Lundby (ed.), *Mediatization*. New York: Peter Lang, pp. 135–154.

Hepp, A. (2009b) 'Localities of Diasporic Communicative Spaces: Material Aspects of Translocal Mediated Networking', *The Communication Review* 12(4): 327–48.

Hepp, A. (2010) 'Researching "Mediatized Worlds": Non-Mediacentric Media and Communication Research as a Challenge', in N. Carpentier et al. (eds), *Media and Communication Studies: Interventions and Intersections*. Tartu: Tartu University Press, pp. 37–48.

Hepp, A. and Couldry, N. (2009a) 'What Should Comparative Media Research be Comparing? Towards a Transcultural Approach to "Media Cultures"', in D. K. Thussu (ed.), *Transnationalising Media Studies*. London: Routledge, pp. 32–47.

Hepp, A. and Couldry, N. (2009b) 'Media Events in Globalized Media Cultures', in N. Couldry, A. Hepp and F. Krotz (eds), *Media Events in a Global Age*. London: Routledge, pp. 1–20.

Hepp, A. and Krönert, V. (2009) 'Religious Media Events: The Catholic "World Youth Day" as an Example of the Mediatization and Individualization of Religion', in N. Couldry, A. Hepp and F. Krotz (eds), *Media Events in a Global Age*. London: Routledge, pp. 265–82.

Hepp, A., Bozdag, C. and Suna, L. (forthcoming) 'Mediatized Migrants: Media Cultures and Communicative Networking in the Diaspora', in L. Fortunati, R. Pertierra and J. Vincent (eds), *Migrations, Diaspora and Information Technology in Global Societies*. London: Routledge.

Herman, E. and McChesney, R. (1997) *The Global Media*. London: Cassell.

Hermes, J. (1995) *Reading Women's Magazines*. London: Sage.

Hermes, J. (1999) 'Media Figures in Identity Construction', in P. Alasuutaari (ed.), *Rethinking the Media Audience*. London: Sage, pp. 69–85.

Herring, S. (2004) 'Slouching Towards the Ordinary: Current Trends in Computer-Mediated Communication', *New Media & Society* 6(1): 26–36.

Herring, S. (2008) 'Questioning the Generational Divide: Technological Exoticism and Adult Constructions of Online Youth Identity', in D. Buckingham (ed.), *Youth, Identity and Digital Media*. Cambridge, MA: MIT Press, pp. 71–92.

Hesmondhalgh, D. (2007) *The Cultural Industries*, 2nd edn. London: Sage.

Hesmondhalgh, D. and Toynbee, J. (2008) 'Why Media Studies Needs Better Social Theory', in D. Hesmondhalgh and J. Toynbee (eds), *The Media and Social Theory*. London: Routledge, pp. 1–24.

268 References

Hijazi-Omari, H. and Ribak, R. (2008) 'Playing with Fire: On the Domestication of the Mobile Phone among Palestinian Teenage Girls in Israel', *Information Communication & Society* 11(2): 149–66.

Hill, A. (2007) *Reality TV*. London: Routledge.

Hillis, K. (2009) *Online a Lot of the Time*. Durham, NC: Duke University Press.

Hills, M. (2002) *Fan Cultures*. London/New York: Routledge.

Hindman, M. (2009) *The Myth of Digital Democracy*. Princeton: Princeton University Press.

Hirschkind, C. (2006) 'Cassette Ethics: Public Piety and Popular Media in Egypt', in B. Meyer and A. Moors (eds), *Religion, Media, and the Public Sphere*. Bloomington: Indiana University Press, pp. 29–51.

Hjarvard, S. (2004) 'From Bricks to Bytes: The Mediatization of a Global Toy Industry', in I. Bondjeberg and P. Golding (eds), *European Culture and the Media*. Bristol: Intellect, pp. 43–63.

Hjarvard, S. (2006) 'The Mediatization of Religion: A Theory of the Media as an Agent of Religious Change'. Paper presented to 5th international conference on Media Religion and Culture, Sigtuna, Sweden, 6–9 July.

Hjarvard, S. (2009) 'Soft Individualism: Media and the Changing Social Character', in K. Lundby (ed.), *Mediatization*. New York: Peter Lang, pp. 159–77.

Hjarvard, S. (2011) 'Mediatization: The Challenge of New Media'. Keynote address to *Mediatized Worlds* Conference, University of Bremen, 14–15 April 2011.

Hobart, M. (2010) 'What Do We Mean by "Media Practices"?', in B. Brauchler and J. Postill (eds), *Theorising Media and Practice*. New York/Oxford: Berghahn Books, pp. 55–76.

Hobsbawm, E. (1995) *Age of Extremes: The Short Twentieth Century*. London: Abacus.

Hodkinson, P. (2007) 'Interactive Online Journals and Individualization', *New Media & Society* 9(4): 625–50.

Holmes, S. (2004) '"All You've Got to Worry About is the Task, Having a Cup of Tea and Doing a Bit of Sunbathing": Approaching Celebrity in *Big Brother*', in S. Holmes and D. Jermyn (eds), *Understanding Reality Television*. London: Routledge, pp. 111–35.

Holmes, S. and Redmond, S. (2006) 'Introduction: Understanding Celebrity Culture', in S. Holmes and S. Redmond (eds), *New Directions in Celebrity Culture*. London: Routledge, pp. 1–16.

Honneth, A. (2004) 'Organized Self-Realization: Some Paradoxes of Individualization', *European Journal of Social Theory* 7(4): 463–78.

Honneth, A. (2007) *Disrespect*. Cambridge: Polity.

Hoover, S. (1988) *Mass Media Religion*. Newbury Park: Sage.

Hoover, S. (2006) *Religion in the Media Age*. London: Routledge.

Hoover, S. (2008) 'Audiences', in D. Morgan (ed.), *Key Words in Religion, Media and Culture*. London: Routledge, pp. 31–43.

Hoover, S. and Kaneva, N. (eds) (2009) *Fundamentalisms and the Media*. London: Continuum.

Hoover, S. and Lundby, K. (eds) (1997) *Rethinking Media, Religion and Culture*. New Delhi: Sage.

Hoover, S., Schofield Clark, L. and Alters, D. (2004) *Media, Home and World*. London: Routledge.

House of Lords, The (2009) *Surveillance: Citizens and the State*. Select Committee on the Constitution, vol. I. House of Lords Paper 18-I, February.

Howard, P. (2006) *New Media Campaigns and the Managed Citizen*. Cambridge: Cambridge University Press.

Howard, R. (2009) 'The Vernacular Ideology of Christian Fundamentalism on the World Wide Web', in S. Hoover and N. Kaneva (eds), *Fundamentalisms and the Media*. London: Continuum, pp. 126–41.

Howard, P. and Massanari, A. (2007) 'Learning to Search and Searching to Learn: Income, Education and Experience Online', *Journal of Computer-Mediated Communication* 12: 846–65.

Howe, P. (2004) *Paparazzi*. New York: Artisan Books.

Huberman, B. (2001) *The Laws of the Web*. Cambridge, MA: MIT Press.

Hursthouse, R. (1999) *Virtue Ethics*. Oxford: Oxford University Press.

Idle, N. and Nunns, A. (2011) *Tweets from Tahrir*. London: OR Books.

Illouz, E. (2003) *Oprah Winfrey and the Glamor of Misery*. New York: Columbia University Press.

Imre, A. (2009a) *Identity Games*. Cambridge, MA: MIT Press.

Imre, A. (2009b) 'National Intimacy and Post-Socialist Networking', *European Journal of Cultural Studies* 12(2): 219–33.

Innes, M. (2004) 'Crime as a Signal, Crime as a Memory', *Journal of Crime, Conflict and the Media* 1(2): 15–22.

Innis, H. (1991 [1951]) *The Bias of Communication*. Toronto: University of Toronto Press.

Introna, L. and Nissenbaum, H. (2000) 'Shaping the Web: Why the Politics of Search Engines Matters', *The Information Society* 16: 169–85.

Ito, M. (2010) *Hanging Out, Messing Around and Geeking Out* (with multiple authors). Cambridge, MA: MIT Press.

ITU/UNCTAD (2007) *World Information Society Report*, www.itu.int/osg/spu/publications/worldinformationsociety/2007/report.html, last accessed 5 September 2011.

Iwabuchi, K. (2007) 'Contra-flows or the Cultural Logic of Uneven Globalization? Japanese Media in the Global Agora', in D. Thussu (ed.), *Media on the Move*. London: Routledge, pp. 67–83.

Jacobs, S. (2007) '*Big Brother*, Africa is Watching', *Media, Culture and Society* 29(6): 851–68.

Jancovich, M. and Faire, L., with Stubbings, S. (2003) *The Place of the Audience: Cultural Geographies of Film Consumption*. London: BFI.

Janelle, D. (1991) 'Global Interdependence and its Consequences', in S. Brunn and T. Leinbach (eds), *Collapsing Space and Time*. London: Harper Collins, pp. 49–81.

Jansen, S. Curry (2011) 'Introduction: Media, Democracy, Human Rights and Social Justice', in S. Curry Jansen, J. Pooley and L. Taub-Pervizpour (eds), *Media and Social Justice*. New York: Palgrave Macmillan, pp. 1–26.

Jansson, A. (2006) 'Textual Analysis: Mediatizing Mediaspace', in J. Falkheimer and A. Jansson (eds), *Geographies of Communication*. Göteborg: Nordicom, pp. 87–103.

Jansson, A. (2009) 'Mobile Belongings: Texturation and Stratification in Mediatization Processes', in K. Lundby (ed.), *Mediatization: Concept, Changes, Consequences*. New York: Peter Lang, pp. 243–62.

Jarvis, J. (2007) 'The Pro-am Approach to News Gathering', *Guardian*, 22 October.

Jarvis, J. (2011) 'Is the Writing on the Wall?' *Guardian*, Media section, 27 June.

Jeanneney, J.-C. (2007) *Google and the Myth of Universal Knowledge*. Chicago: University of Chicago Press.

Jenkins, H. (1992) *Textual Poachers*. New York: Routledge.

Jenkins, H. (2006) *Convergence Culture*. New York: New York University Press.

Jensen, K.-B. (2010) *Media Convergence*. London: Routledge.

Jiang, M. (forthcoming) 'Chinese Internet Events', in A. Esarey and R. Kluver (eds), *The Internet in China*. New York: Berkshire Publishing.

Johnson, V. (2009) 'Everything is Old Again: Sport TV, Innovation and Tradition for a Multi-Platform Era', in A. Lotz (ed.), *Beyond Prime Time*. London: Routledge, pp. 114–37.

Jonas, H. (1984) *The Imperative of Responsibility*. Chicago: Chicago University Press.

Jones, J. (2009) 'I Want my Talk TV – Network Talk Shows in a Digital Universe', in A. Lotz (ed.), *Beyond Prime Time*. London: Routledge, pp. 14–35.

Juris, J. (2008) *Networking Futures: The Movements against Corporate Globalization*. Durham, NC: Duke University Press.

Kant, I. (1997 [1785]) *Groundwork of the Metaphysic of Morals*, trans. M. Gregor. Cambridge: Cambridge University Press.

Kasza, G. (1993) *The State and the Mass Media in Japan 1918–1945*. Berkeley: University of California Press.

Katz, E. (1959) 'Mass Communication Research and the Study of Popular Culture: An Editorial Note on a Possible Future for this Journal', *Studies in Public Communication* 2: 1–6.

Katz, E. (1996) 'And Deliver us from Segmentation', *Annals of the American Academy of Political and Social Science* 564: 22–33.

Katz, E. (2009) 'Introduction: The End of Television', in E. Katz and P. Scannell (eds), *'The End of Television?' Annals of the American Academy of Political and Social Science* 625: 6–18.

Katz, E. and Lazarsfeld, P. (1955) *Personal Influence*. Glencoe: Free Press.

Katz, E. and Liebes, T. (2010) '"No More Peace!" How Disaster, Terror and War have Upstaged Media Events', in N. Couldry, A. Hepp and F. Krotz (eds), *Media Events in a Global Age*. London: Routledge, pp. 32–43.

Katz, J. and Rice, R. (2002) *Social Consequences of Internet Use*. Cambridge, MA: MIT Press.

Kay, J. (2011) 'Why the Rioters should be Reading Rousseau', *Financial Times*, 17 August.

Keck, M. and Sikkink, K. (1998) *Activists Beyond Borders*. Ithaca: Cornell University Press.

Kellner, D. (1995) *Media Culture*. London: Routledge.

Kellner, D. (2003) *Media Spectacle*. London: Routledge.

Kellner, D. (2008) *Guys and Guns Amok*. Boulder, CO: Paradigm.

Kellner, D. (2009) 'Barack Obama and Celebrity Spectacle', *International Journal of Communication* 3: 715–31.

Kellow, C. and Steeves, L. (1998) 'The Role of Radio in the Rwandan Genocide', *Journal of Communication* 48(3): 107–28.

Kershaw, I. (1987) *The Hitler Myth*. Oxford: Oxford University Press.

Khatib, L. (2010) 'Communicating Islamic Fundamentalisms', in D. Thussu (ed.), *International Communication: A Reader*. London: Routledge, pp. 279–94.

Khiabany, G. and Sreberny, A. (2009) 'The Internet in Iran: The Battle over an Emerging Virtual Public Sphere', in G. Goggin and M. McLelland (eds), *Internationalizing Internet Studies*. London: Routledge, pp. 196–213.

Kidd, D. (2003) 'Indymedia.org: A New Communications Commons', in M. McCaughey and M. Ayers (eds), *Cyberactivism*. New York: Routledge, pp. 47–69.

Kidd, J. (2010) 'Capture Wales Digital Storytelling: Community Media Meets the BBC', in C. Rodriguez, D. Kidd and L. Stein (eds), *Making Our Media*, vol. I. Cresskill, NJ: The Hampton Press, pp. 293–308.

Kine, R. (2000) *Consumers in the Country*. Baltimore: The Johns Hopkins University Press.

Kintrea, K., Bannister, J., Pickering, J., Reid, M. and Suzuki, N. (2008) 'Young People and Territoriality in British Cities', www.jrf.org.uk, last accessed 22 October 2008.

Kirch, S. (2010) 'Poets Haunted by Poets', *New York Review of Books* (8 April): 75–8.

Kirwan, P. (2010) 'Apple v. Google: The New Frontier', *Guardian*, Media section, 9 August.

Kiss, J. (2011) 'Google Crashes TV's Party', *Guardian*, Media section, 29 August.

Kittler, F. (1999) *Gramophone, Film, Typewriter*. Stanford: Stanford University Press.

Kittler, F. (2010) *Optical Media*. Cambridge: Polity.

Klein, N. (2000) *No Logo ®*. London: Flamingo.

Klinenberg, E. (2005) 'Channeling into the Journalistic Field: Youth Activism and the Media Justice Movement', in R. Benson and E. Neveu (eds), *Bourdieu and the Journalistic Field*. Cambridge: Polity, pp. 174–94.

Kling, R. (1999) 'Can the "Net-Generation Internet" Effectively Support "Ordinary Citizens"?', *The Information Society* 15: 57–63.

Klinger, B. (2006) *Beyond the Multiplex*. Berkeley: University of California Press.

Knoblauch, H. (2008) 'Spirituality and Popular Religion in Europe', *Social Compass* 55(2): 141–54.

Knoblauch, H. (2011) 'Communication Culture, Communicative Action and Mediatization'. Keynote address, *Mediatized Worlds* Conference, University of Bremen, 14–15 April.

Knorr-Cetina, K. (2001) 'Post-Social Relations: Theorizing Sociality in a Post-Social Environment', in G. Ritzer and B. Smart (eds), *The Handbook of Social Theory*. London: Sage, pp. 520–37.

Kogen, L. (2009) 'Why the Message Should Matter: Genocide and the Ethics of Global Journalism in the Mediapolis', *Journal of International Communication* 15(2): 62–78.

Kracauer, S. (1995) *The Mass Ornament*. Cambridge, MA: Harvard University Press.

Kraidy, M. (2005) *Hybrid Cultures*. Philadelphia: Temple University Press.

Kraidy, M. (2009) 'Reality TV, Gender and Authenticity in Saudi Arabia', *Journal of Communication* 59: 345–66.

Kraidy, M. (2010) *Reality Television and Arab Politics*. Cambridge: Cambridge University Press.

Kraidy, M. and Khalil, J. (2009) *Arab Television Industries*. London: Palgrave/BFI.

Kraidy, M. and Murphy, P. (2008) 'Shifting Geertz: Towards a Theory of Translocalism in Global Communication Studies', *Communication Theory* 18: 335–55.

Krotz, F. (2009) 'Mediatization: A Concept with which to Grasp Media and Societal Change', in K. Lundby (ed.), *Mediatization*. New York: Peter Lang, pp. 19–38.

Kuipers, G. (forthcoming) 'Cultural Globalization as the Emergence of a Transnational Cultural Field: Transnational Television and National Media Landscapes in Four European Countries', *American Behavioral Scientist*.

Kunelius, R. and Nossek, H. (2008) 'Between the Ritual and the National: From Media Events to Moments of Global Public Spheres', in E. Eide, R. Kunelius and A. Phillips (eds), *Transnational Media Events: The Mohammed Cartoons and the Imagined Clash of Civilizations*. Nordicom: Göteborg, pp. 252–73.

Lahire, B. (1999) 'Champ, Hors-champ, Contre-champ', in B. Lahire (ed.), *Le Travail Sociologique de Pierre Bourdieu – Dettes et Critiques*. Paris: La Découverte/Poche, pp. 23–58.

Lamont, M. and Molnar, V. (2002) 'The Study of Boundaries in the Social Sciences', *Annual Review of Sociology* 28: 167–95.

Langman, L. (2005) 'From Virtual Public Spheres to Global Justice: A Critical Theory of Internetworked Social Movements', *Sociological Theory* 23(1): 42–74.

Lanier, J. (2011) *You Are Not a Gadget*, updated edn. London: Penguin.

Larkin, B. (2008) *Signal and Noise: Media, Infrastructure and Urban Culture in Nigeria*. Durham, NC: Duke University Press.

Larson, W. and Park, H.-S. (1993) *Global Television and the Politics of the Seoul Olympics*. Boulder: Westview Press.

Lash, S. (2002) *Critique of Information*. London: Sage.

Lash, S. (2009) 'Afterword: In Praise of the *A Posteriori*: Sociology and the Empirical', *European Journal of Social Theory* 12(1): 175–87.

Lash, S. and Lury, C. (2007) *Global Culture Industry*. Cambridge: Polity.

Latham, R. and Sassen, S. (2005) 'Introduction: Digital Formations: Constructing an Object of Study', in R. Latham and S. Sassen (eds), *Digital Formations*. Princeton: Princeton University Press, pp. 1–34.

Latour, B. (1993) *We Have Never Been Modern*. London: Prentice Hall.

Latour, B. (1999) 'On Recalling ANT', in J. Law and J. Hassard (eds), *Actor Network Theory and After*. Oxford: Blackwell, pp. 15–25.

Latour, B. (2004) 'From Realpolitik to Dingpolitik, or How to Make Things Public', in B. Latour and P. Weibul (eds), *Making Things Public: Atmospheres of Democracy*. Cambridge, MA: MIT Press, pp. 14–43.

Latour, B. (2005) *Reassembling the Social*. Oxford: Oxford University Press.

Latour, B. (2007) 'From Associations to Modes of Existence'. Keynote address to British Sociological Association Conference, University of East London, 13 April.

Law, J. (1994) *Organizing Modernity*. Oxford: Blackwell.

Layder, D. (2005) *Emotions and Social Theory*. London: Sage.

Lazarsfeld, P. and Merton, R. (1969) 'Mass Communication, Popular Taste and Organised Social Action', in W. Schramm (ed.), *Mass Communications*, 2nd edn. Urbana: University of Illinois Press, pp. 494–512.

Leadbeater, C. (2007) *We-think*. London: Profile Books.

LeBlanc, R. (1999) *Bicycle Citizens: The Political World of the Japanese Housewife*. Berkeley: University of California Press.

Lee, C. K. (2000) 'Pathways of Labour Insurgency', in E. Perry and M. Sedden (eds), *Chinese Society: Change, Conflict, and Resistance,* 2nd edn. London: Routledge, pp. 71–92.

Lefebvre, H. (1971) *Everyday Life in the Modern World*. London: Allen Lane.

Lehmann, D. and Siebzehner, B. (2006) 'Holy Pirates: Media, Ethnicity and Religious Renewal in Israel', in B. Meyer and A. Moors (eds), *Religion, Media and the Public Sphere*. Bloomington: Indiana University Press, pp. 91–111.

Leighton, D. (2011) *Back to the Future*. Demos report. www.demos.org, February, last accessed 25 August 2011.

Leitner, H. and Miller, B. (2007) 'Scale and the Limitations of Ontological Debate: A Commentary on Marston Jones and Woodward', *Transactions of the British Institute of Geographers* 32(1): 116–25.

LeMaheu, D. (1988) *A Culture for Democracy*. Oxford: Clarendon Press.

Lembo, R. (2000) *Thinking Through Television*. Cambridge: Cambridge University Press.

Lenhart, A., Purcell, K., Smith, A. and Zickhur, K. (2010) *Social Media and Mobile Use among Teens and Young Adults*, www.pewinternet.org/Reports/2010/Social-Media-and-Young-Adults.aspx, last accessed 7 November 2011.

Lessig, L. (2002) *The Future of Ideas*. New York: Vintage.

Lessig, L. (2008) *Remix*. London: Penguin.

274 References

Lévi-Strauss, C. (1972) *The Savage Mind*. London: Weidenfeld and Nicholson.

Levy, P. (1997) *Cyberculture*. Minneapolis: University of Minnesota Press.

Lewis, C. (2008) 'Seeking New Ways to Nurture the Capacity to Report', *Nieman Reports*, www.nieman.harvard.edu/reports/article/100060/Seeking-New-Ways-to-Nurture-the-Capacity-to-Report.aspx, last accessed 2 March 2011.

Lewis, J. (1991) *The Ideological Octopus*. London: Routledge.

Lewis, P., Ball, J. and Halliday, J. (2011) 'Twitter Study Casts Doubt on Ministers' Post-Riot Plans', *Guardian*, 25 August.

Leys, C. (2001) *Market-Driven Politics*. London: Verso.

Licoppe, C. (2004) '"Connected" Presence: The Emergence of a New Repertoire for Managing Social Relationships in a Changing Communication Technoscape', *Society and Space* 22: 135–56.

Liebes, T. (1998) 'Television's Disaster Marathons', in T. Liebes and J. Curran (eds), *Media Ritual Identity*. London: Routledge, pp. 71–86.

Liebes, T. and Blondheim, M. (2005) 'Myths to the Rescue: How Live Television Intervenes in History', in E. Rothenbuhler and M. Coman (eds), *Media Anthropology*. Thousand Oaks: Sage, pp. 188–98.

Lievrouw, L. (2001) 'New Media and "Pluralization of Lifeworlds": A Role for Information in Social Differentiation', *New Media & Society* 6(1): 9–15.

Lievrouw, L. (2011) *Alternative and Activist New Media*. Cambridge: Polity.

Lievrouw, L. and Livingstone, S. (2002) 'Introduction', in L. Lievrouw and S. Livingstone (eds), *Handbook of New Media*, 1st edn. London: Sage, pp. 1–15.

Lim, M. and Kann, M. (2008) 'Politics: Deliberation, Mobilization and Networked Practices of Agitation', in K. Varnelis (ed.), *Networked Publics*. Cambridge, MA: MIT Press, pp. 77–107.

Lim, M. and Padawangi, R. (2008) 'Contesting *alun-alun*: Power Relations, Identities and the Production of Urban Space in Bandung, Indonesia', *International Development and Planning Review* 30(3): 307–26.

Linaa Jensen, J. (2011) 'Old Wine in New Bottles: How the Internet Mostly Reinforces Existing Patterns of Political Participation and Citizenship'. Paper presented to the ICA Conference, Boston, 26–30 May.

Ling, R. and Donner, J. (2009) *Mobile Communication*. Cambridge: Polity.

Lingard, B., Rawolle, S. and Taylor, S. (2005) 'Globalizing Policy Sociology in Education: Working with Bourdieu', *Journal of Education Policy* 20(6): 759–77.

Lister, M., Dovey, J., Giddings, S., Grant, I. and Kelley, K. (2009) *New Media: A Critical Introduction*, 2nd edn. London: Routledge.

Littler, J. (2008) *Radical Consumption*. Milton Keynes: Open University Press.

Livingstone, S. (1999) 'New Media, New Audiences', *New Media & Society* 1(1): 59–66.

Livingstone, S. (2002). *Young People and New Media*. London: Sage.

Livingstone, S. (2004) 'The Challenge of Changing Audiences: Or, What is the Audience Researcher to Do in the Internet Age?' *European Journal of Communication* 19(1): 75–86.

Livingstone, S. (2007) 'The Challenge of Engaging Youth Online: Contrasting Producers' and Teenagers' Interpretations of Websites', *European Journal of Communication* 22(2): 165–94.

Livingstone, S. (2008) 'Taking Risky Opportunities in Youthful Content Creation: Teenagers' Use of Social Networking Sites for Intimacy, Privacy and Self-Expression', *New Media & Society* 10(3): 393–412.

Livingstone, S. (2009a) *Children and the Internet*. Cambridge: Polity.

Livingstone, S. (2009b) 'On the Mediation of Everything', *Journal of Communication* 59(1): 1–18.

Livingstone, S. and Bober, M. (2004) *UK Children Go Online*. London: London School of Economics, http://eprints.lse.ac.uk/388/, last accessed 18 November 2011.

Livingstone, S. and Bovill, M. (2001) *Families and the Internet*. London: London School of Economics, http://eprints.lse.ac.uk/21164/, last accessed 18 November 2011.

Lodziak, K. (1987) *The Power of Television*. London: Frances Pinter.

Löfgren, O. (2001) 'The Nation as Home or Motel? Metaphors and Media of Belonging', *sociologisk årbok* 2001: 1–34.

Longhurst, B. (2005) *Cultural Change and Ordinary Life*. Milton Keynes: Open University Press.

Lopez Cuenca, A. (2007/8) 'Digital Communities of Representation: From Wittgenstein to Brazilian Motoboys', *Glimpse* 9(10): 45–52.

Lotz, A. (2009a) 'Introduction', in A. Lotz (ed.), *Beyond Prime Time*. London: Routledge, pp. 1–13.

Lotz, A. (2009b) 'National Nightly News in the On-Demand Era', in A. Lotz (ed.), *Beyond Prime Time*. London: Routledge, pp. 94–113.

Løvheim, M. (2009) 'Blogs as Self-Representation: A Gendered Perspective on Agency, Authenticity, and Negotiations of Public and Private'. Paper presented to Mediatized Stories pre-conference at *Transforming Audiences 2*, University of Westminster, 2 September.

Lovibond, S. (2002) *Ethical Formation*. Cambridge, MA: Harvard University Press.

Lovink, G. (2003) *Dark Fiber*. Cambridge, MA: MIT Press.

Lovink, G. (2012) *Networks Without a Cause: A Critique of Social Media*. Cambridge: Polity.

Lovink, G. and Rossiter, N. (2011) 'Urgent Aphorisms: Notes on Organized Networks for the Connected Multitudes', available from http://nedrossiter.org/?p=136, last accessed 24 February 2011.

Lowrey, W. and Latta, J. (2008) 'The Routines of Blogging', in C. Paterson and D. Domingo (eds), *Making Online News*. New York: Peter Lang, pp. 185–97.

Luhmann, N. (1999) *The Reality of the Mass Media*. Cambridge: Polity.

Lukes, S. (1975) 'Political Ritual and Social Integration', *Sociology* 29: 289–305.

Lundby, K. (2006) 'Contested Communication: Mediating the Sacred', in J. Sumiala-Seppänen, K. Lundby and R. Salokangas (eds), *Implications of the Sacred in (Post)Modern Media*. Göteborg: Nordicom, pp. 43–62.

Lundby, K. (ed.) (2009a) *Mediatization*. New York: Peter Lang.

Lundby, K. (2009b) 'Media Logic: Looking for Social Interaction', in K. Lundby (ed.), *Mediatization*. New York: Peter Lang, pp. 101–19.

Lundby, K. and Dayan, D. (1999) 'Mediascape Missionaries? Notes on Religion as Identity in a Local African Setting', *International Journal of Cultural Studies* 2(3): 398–417.

Lunt, P. (2009) 'Television, Public Participation and Public Service: From Value Consensus to the Politics of Identity', in E. Katz and P. Scannell (eds), *'The End of Television?' Annals of the American Academy of Political and Social Science* 625: 128–38.

Lury, C. (1998) *Prosthetic Culture*. London: Routledge.

Lynch, M. (2006) *Voices of the New Arab Public*. New York: Columbia University Press.

Ma, E. (2000) 'Rethinking Media Studies: The Case of China', in J. Curran and M.-J. Park (eds), *De-westernizing Media Studies*, London: Routledge, pp. 21–34.

MacIntyre, A. (1981) *After Virtue*. London: Duckworth.

MacIntyre, A. (1988) *Whose Justice? Which Rationality?* Notre Dame: University of Notre Dame Press.

Madianou, M. and Miller, D. (2011) *Migration and New Media*. London: Routledge.

Mainsah, H. (2009) *Ethnic Minorities and Digital Technologies: New Spaces for Constructing Identity*. PhD thesis, University of Oslo, April.

Maliki, J. (2008) 'Cultural Identity and Cultural Representation on Reality TV: An Analysis of *Akademi Fantasia*'. Unpublished MPhil thesis, University of Queensland, Australia.

Mallee, H. (2000) 'Migration, *hukou* and Resistance in Reform China', in E. Perry and M. Sedden (eds), *Chinese Society: Change, Conflict, and Resistance*, 2nd edn. London: Routledge, pp. 136–57.

Mandabach, C. (2007) 'How America Stopped Laughing', *Guardian*, Media section, 4 June.

Mandaville, P. (2003) 'Communication and Diasporic Islam: A Virtual Ummah?', in K. Karim (ed.), *The Media of Diaspora*. London: Routledge, pp. 135–47.

Mandaville, P. (2007) 'Globalization and the Politics of Religious Knowledge: Pluralizing Authority in the Muslim World', *Theory, Culture & Society* 24(2): 101–15.

Mankekar, P. (1999) *Screening Culture, Viewing Politics*. Durham, NC: Duke University Press.

Mann, M. (1986) *The Sources of Social Power*, vol. I. Cambridge: Cambridge University Press.

Manovich, L. (2001) *The Language of New Media*. Cambridge, MA: MIT Press.

Manovich, L. (2008) 'The Practice of Everyday (Media) Life', in G. Lovink and S. Niederer (eds), *Video Vortex Reader: Responses to YouTube*. Amsterdam: Institute of Network Cultures, pp. 33–43.

Mansell, R. (2002) 'From Digital Divides to Digital Entitlements in Knowledge Societies', *Current Sociology* 50(3): 407–26.

Mansell, R. (2010) 'Power, Media Culture and New Media', available from http://eprints.lse.ac.uk/36165/1/Power_media_culture_and_new_media_ (LSERO).pdf, last accessed 27 June 2011.

Marcos, Subcommandante (2000) 'La Droite Intellectuelle et le fascism libéral', *Le Monde Diplomatique* (August) 1: 14–15.

Marlière, P. (1998) 'The Rules of the Journalistic Field: Pierre Bourdieu's Contribution to the Sociology of the Media', *European Journal of Communication* 13(2): 219–34.

Marquand, D. (2004) *Decline of the Public*. Cambridge: Polity.

Marres, N. (2009) 'Testing Powers of Engagement: Green Living Experiments, the Ontological Turn and the Undoability of Involvement', *European Journal of Social Theory* 12(1): 117–33.

Marshall, D. (2006) 'New Media, New Self: The Changing Power of Celebrity', in D. Marshall (ed.), *The Celebrity Culture Reader*. London: Routledge, pp. 634–44.

Marshall, P. D. (1997) *Celebrity and Power*. Minneapolis: University of Minnesota Press.

Marston, S., Jones, J. and Woodward, K. (2005) 'Human Geography without Scale', *Transactions of the Institute of British Geographers* 30: 416–32.

Martin-Barbero, J. (1993) *Communication, Culture and Hegemony*. London: Sage.

Martin-Barbero, J. (2006) 'A Latin American Perspective on Communication/Cultural Mediation', *Global Media and Communication* 2(3): 279–97.

Martin-Barbero, J. (2009) 'Digital Convergence in Cultural Communication', *Popular Communication* 7: 147–57.

Martuccelli, D. (2005) *La Consistance du Social*. Rennes: Rennes University Press.

Marvin, C. (1987) *When Old Technologies Were New*. Oxford: Oxford University Press.

Marvin, C. and Ingle, D. (1999) *Blood Sacrifice and the Nation*. Cambridge: Cambridge University Press.

Marwick, A. and boyd, d. (2010) 'I Tweet Honestly, I Tweet Passionately: Twitter Users, Context Collapse, and the Imagined Audience', *New Media & Society* 13(1): 114–33.

Marx, K. (1973) *Capital*, vol. I. Harmondsworth: Penguin.

Maslow, A. (1943) 'A Theory of Human Motivation', *Psychological Review* 50: 370–96.

Massey, D. (1994) *Space, Place, and Gender*. Cambridge: Polity.

Massing, M. (2009a) 'The News About the Internet', *New York Review of Books*, 13 August.

Massing, M. (2009b) 'A New Horizon for the News', *New York Review of Books*, 24 September.

Matei, S. and Ball-Rokeach, S. (2003) 'The Internet in the Communication Infrastructure of Urban Residential Communities: Macro- or Meso-Linkage?', *Journal of Communication* 53(4): 642–57.

278 **References**

Matewa, C. (2010) 'Participatory Video as an Empowerment Tool for Social Change', in C. Rodriguez, D. Kidd and L. Stein (eds), *Making Our Media*, vol. I. Creskill, NJ: The Hampton Press, pp. 115–30.

Matheson, D. (2004) 'Weblogs and the Epistemology of the News: Some Trends in Online Journalism', *New Media & Society* 6(4): 443–68.

Mattelart, A. (1994) *The Invention of Communication*. Minneapolis: University of Minnesota press.

Mattelart, A. (2000) *Networking the World 1794–2000*. Minneapolis: University of Minnesota Press.

Maxwell, R. and Miller, T. (2011) 'Old, New and Middle-Aged Convergence', *Cultural Studies* 25(4–5): 585–603.

Mayer, V. (2011) *Below the Line: Producers and Production Studies in the New Television Economy*. Durham, NC: Duke University Press.

Mayhew, L. (1997) *The New Public*. Cambridge: Cambridge University Press.

Mazzoleni, G. (2008) 'Media Logic', in W. Donsbach (ed.), *The International Encyclopedia of Communication*, vol. VII. Malden, MA: Blackwell, pp. 2930–2.

Mazzoleni, G. and Schulz, W. (1999) '"Mediatization" of Politics: A Challenge for Democracy?' *Political Communication* 16: 247–61.

Mbembe, A. (2001) *On the Postcolony*. Berkeley: University of California Press.

McCarthy, A. (2007) 'Reality Television: A Neoliberal Theater of Suffering', *Social Text* 25: 93–110.

McChesney, R. (2007) *Communication Revolution*. New York: New Press.

McChesney, R. (2008) *The Political Economy of Media*. New York: Monthly Review Press.

McCombs, M. and Shaw, D. (1993) 'The Evolution of Agenda-setting Research: 25 Years in the Marketplace of Ideas', *Journal of Communication* 43(2): 58–67

McCurdy, P. (2009) '"I Predict a Riot": Mediation and Political Contention: Dissent!'s media Practices at the 2009 Gleneagles G8 summit'. Unpublished PhD thesis, London School of Economics, March.

McDonald, K. (2006) *Global Movements: Action and Culture*. Oxford: Blackwell.

McDonald, K. (2011) 'The Old Culture of Rigid Ideologies is Giving Way to Individual Activism', *Sydney Morning Herald* 18 February.

McDowell, J. (1994) *Mind and World*. Cambridge, MA: Harvard University Press.

McDowell, J. (1998) *Mind, Value and Reality*. Cambridge, MA: Harvard University Press.

McLuhan, M. (2001 [1964]) *Understanding Media*. London: Routledge.

McMillin, D. (2007) *International Media Studies*. Oxford: Blackwell.

McNair, B. (2006) *Cultural Chaos*. London: Routledge.

McNamara, K. (2011) 'The Paparazzi Industry and New Media: The Evolving Production and Consumption of Celebrity News and Gossip Websites', *International Journal of Gultural Studies* 14(5): 515–30.

McQuail, D. (2005) *McQuail's Mass Communication Theory*, 5th edn. London: Sage.

McQuire, S. (2008) *The Media City*. London: Sage.

Meadows, M., Forde, S., Ewert, J. and Foxwell, K. (2010) 'Making Spaces: Community Media and Formation of the Democratic Public Sphere in Australia', in C. Rodriguez, D. Kidd and L. Stein (eds), *Making Our Media*, vol. I. Cresskill, NJ: The Hampton Press, pp. 163–81.

Media Justice Fund (2007) *Media Justice or Media Control*. Knoxville, TN: Appalachian Community Fund. Previously published at www.fex.org/assets/262_appalachainfscconvening.pdf.

Medrich, R. (1979) 'Constant Television: A Background to Daily Life', *Journal of Communication* 29(3): 171–76.

Meikle, G. (2009) *Interpreting News*. Basingstoke: Palgrave.

Mejias, U. (2010) 'The Limits of Networks as Models for Organizing the Social', *New Media & Society* 12(4): 603–17.

Melucci, A. (1996) *Challenging Codes*. Cambridge: Cambridge University Press.

Meyer, B. (2006) 'Impossible Representations: Pentecostalism, Vision and Video Technology in Ghana', in B. Meyer and A. Moors (eds), *Religion, Media, and the Public Sphere*. Bloomington: Indiana University Press, pp. 290–312.

Meyer, B. and Moors, A. (2006) 'Introduction', in B. Meyer and A. Moors (eds), *Religion, Media, and the Public Sphere*. Bloomington: Indiana University Press, pp. 1–28.

Meyer, T. (2003) *Media Democracy*. Cambridge: Polity.

Meyrowitz, J. (1985) *No Sense of Place*. New York: Oxford University Press.

Meyrowitz, J. (1994) 'Medium Theory', in D. Crowley and D. Mitchell (eds), *Communication Theory Today*. Cambridge: Polity, pp. 50–77.

Meyrowitz, J. (2008) 'Power, Pleasure, Patterns: Intersecting Narratives of Media Influence', *Journal of Communication* 58: 641–63.

Miao, D. (2011) 'Between Propaganda and Commercials: Chinese Television Today', in S. Shirk (ed.), *Changing Media, Changing China*. Oxford: Oxford University Press, pp. 91–114.

Michaels, E. (1982) *TV Tribes*. PhD dissertation presented to University of Texas, available from http://astro.temple.edu/~ruby/wava/eric/index.html, last accessed 7 July 2011.

Micheletti, M. (2010) *Political Virtue and Shopping*. Basingstoke: Palgrave.

Miège, B. (1989) *The Capitalization of Cultural Production*. New York: International General.

Mihelj, S. (2008) 'National Media Events: From Displays of Unity to Enactments of Division', *European Journal of Cultural Studies* 11(4): 471–88.

Miller, C. and Shepherd, D. (2008) 'Blogging as Social Action: A Genre Analysis of the Weblog', available from http://blog.lib.umn.edu/blogosphere/blogging_as_social_action_a_genre_analysis_of_the_weblog.html, last accessed 7 July 2011.

Miller, D. (2011) *Tales from Facebook*. Cambridge: Polity.

Miller, D. and Slater, D. (2000) *The Internet: An Ethnographic Approach*. Oxford: Berg.

Miller, R. K. and Associates (2008) *Consumer Use of the Internet and Mobile Web*. New York.

Miller, T. (2008) *Makeover Nation*. Lawrence, KS: Kansas University Press.

Miller, T. (2010) *Television Studies: The Basics*. London: Routledge.

Mills, C. Wright (1958) *The Sociological Imagination*. Harmondsworth: Penguin.

Mirzoeff, N. (2005) *Watching Bablyon*. London: Routledge.

Mitra, A. (1993) *Television and Popular Culture in India*. London: Sage

Mitra, A. (2004) 'Voices of the Marginalized on the Internet: Examples from a Website for Women of South Asia', *Journal of Communication* 54(3): 492–510.

Modleski, T. (1986) *Studies in Entertainment*. Bloomington: Indiana University Press.

Mole, T. (2004) 'Hypertrophic Celebrity', *M/CJournal* 7(5), http://journal.media-culture.org.au/0411/08-mole.php, last accessed 26 July 2011.

Monbiot, G. (2010) 'The Tea Party Movement is Deluded and Inspired by Billionaires', *Guardian*, 25 October.

Monge, P., Heiss, B. and Margolin, D. (2008) 'Communication Network Evolution in Organization Communities', *Communication Theory* 18(4): 449–77.

Moore, C. (2009) 'Liminal Places and Spaces: Public/Private Considerations', in V. Mayer, M. Banks and J. Caldwell (eds), *Production Studies*. New York: Routledge, pp. 125–39.

Moore, H. (1986) *Space, Text and Gender*. Cambridge: Cambridge University Press.

Moore, S. and Myerhoff, B. (eds) (1977) *Secular Ritual*. Assen/Amsterdam: Van Gorcum.

Moores, S. (1993) 'Satellite Television as Cultural Sign: Consumption, Embedding and Articulation', *Media, Culture and Society* 15(4): 621–39.

Moores, S. (2005) *Media/Theory*. London: Routledge.

Moores, S. and Metykova, M. (2009) 'Knowing How to Get Around: Place, Migration and Communication', *The Communication Review* 12(4): 313–26.

Moran, A. (2009) 'Reasserting the National? Programme Format, International Television and Domestic Culture', in G. Turner and T. Tay (eds), *Television Studies After TV*. London: Routledge, pp. 149–58.

Morgan, D. (2008) 'Introduction', in D. Morgan (ed.), *Key Words in Religion, Media and Culture*. London: Routledge, pp. 1–19.

Morley, D. (1986) *Family Television*. London: BFI.

Morley, D. (1992) *Television, Audiences and Cultural Studies*. London: Routledge.

Morley, D. (1999) 'Finding Out About the World from Television: Some Problems', in J. Gripsrud (ed.), *Television and Common Knowledge*. London: Routledge, pp. 136–58.

Morley, D. (2000) *Home Territories*. London: Routledge.

Morley, D. (2007) *Media Modernity and Technology: The Geography of the New*. London: Routledge.

Morley, D. (2011) 'Communications and Transport: The Mobility of Information, People and Commodities', *Media, Culture and Society* 33(5): 743–59.

Morozov, E. (2011) *The Net Delusion*. London: Allen Lane.

Mosco, V. (2004) *The Digital Sublime*. Cambridge, MA: MIT Press.

Mosco, V. (2009) *The Political Economy of Communication*, 2nd edn. London: Sage.

Mukherjee, R. and Banet-Weiser, S. (eds) (forthcoming) *Commodity Activism*. New York: New York University Press.

Mutz, D. (2008) 'Is Deliberative Theory a Falsifiable Theory?' *Annual Review of Political Science* 11: 512–38.

Naficy, H. (2001) *An Accented Cinema: Exilic and Diasporic Filmmaking*. Princeton: Princeton University Press.

Napoli, P. (2008) 'Hyperlinking and the Forces of "Massification"', in J. Turow and L. Tsui (eds), *The Hyperlinked Society*. Ann Arbor: University of Michigan Press, pp. 56–69.

Nederveen Pieterse, J. (1995) 'Globalization as Hybridization', in M. Featherstone, S. Lash and R. Robertson (eds), *Global Modernities*. London: Sage, pp. 45–68.

Neuman, W. Russell (1991) *The Future of the Mass Media*. Cambridge: Cambridge University Press.

Nightingale, V., with Bockardt, V., Ellis, B. and Warwick, T. (1992) 'Contesting Domestic Territory: Watching Rugby League on Television', in A. Moran (ed.), *Stay Tuned: The Australian Broadcasting Reader*. Sydney: Allen Unwin, pp. 156–65.

Noelle-Neumann, E. (1974) 'The Spiral of Silence: A Theory of Public Opinion', *Journal of Communication* 24: 43–51.

Nordenstreng, K. (2010) 'Free Flow Doctrine in Global Media Policy', in R. Mansell and M. Raboy (eds), *Handbook on Global Media and Communication Policy*. Malden, MA: Wiley-Blackwell.

Noveck, B. (2009) *Wiki Government*. New York: Brookings Institution Press.

O'Donnell, P. (2009) 'Journalism, Change and Listening Practices', *Continuum* 23(4): 503–18.

Oemichen E. and Schröter, C. (2008) 'Medienübergreifende Nutzungsmuster: Struktur- und Funktionsverschiebungen', *Media Perspektiven* 8: 394–405.

Ofcom (2007) *New News Future News,* June, www.ofcom.org.uk, last accessed 5 September 2011.

Ofcom (2007–2011) *Communications Market Reports*, www.ofcom.org.uk, last accessed 5 September 2011.

Ofcom (2009a) *Digital Britain Final Report*, http://webarchive. nationalarchives.gov.uk and www.culture.gov.uk/images/publications/ digitalbritain-finalreport-jun09.pdf, last accessed 5 September 2011.

Ofcom (2009b) 'UK Consumers Embrace Digital Communications', 17 December, www.ofcom.org.uk/consumer/2009/12/uk-consumers-embrace-digital-communications/, last accessed 5 September 2011.

Ogan, C. and Cagiltay, K. (2006) 'Confession, Revelation, and Storytelling: Patterns of Use on a Popular Turkish Website', *New Media & Society* 8(5): 801–23.

O'Neil, M. (2009) *Cyberchiefs: Autonomy and Authority in Online Tribes*. London: Pluto.

O'Neill, O. (1996) *Towards Justice and Virtue*. Cambridge: Cambridge University Press.

O'Neill, O. (2000) 'Distant Strangers, Moral Standing and Porous Boundaries', in *Bounds of Justice*. Cambridge: Cambridge University Press, pp. 186–202.

O'Neill, O. (2002) *A Question of Trust*. Cambridge: Cambridge University Press.

Ong, A. (2006) *Neoliberalism as Exception*. Durham, NC: Duke University Press.

Ong, J. (2011) *The Mediation of Suffering: Classed Moralities of Television Audiences in the Philippines*. Unpublished PhD thesis, University of Cambridge, October.

O'Reilly, T. (2005) 'Design Patterns and Business Models for the Next Generation of Software', http://oreilly.com/pub/a/oreilly/tim/news/2005/09/30/what-is-web-20.html, last accessed 3 September 2011.

Ornebring, H. (2008) 'The Consumer as Producer – Of What?', *Journalism Studies* 9(5): 771–85.

Ouellette, L. and Hay, J. (2008) *Better Living Through Reality TV*. Malden: Blackwell.

Palfrey, J. and Gasser, U. (2008) *Born Digital*, rev. edn. New York: Basic Books.

Pan, Z. and Kosicki, G. (1993) 'Framing Analysis: An Approach to News Discourse', *Political Communication* 10(1): 55–75.

Papacharissi, Z. (2010) *A Private Sphere: Democracy in a Digital Age*. Cambridge: Polity.

Parikka, J. (2010) *Insect Media: An Archaeology of Animals and Technology*. Minneapolis: University of Minnesota Press.

Parks, L. (2005) *Cultures in Orbit: Satellites and the Televisual*. Durham, NC: Duke University Press.

Pasquier, D. (2005) 'Le Culture Comme Activité Social', in E. Maigret and E. Macé (eds), *Penser Les Médiacultures*. Paris: Armand Colin, pp. 103–20.

Pateman, C. (1970) *Participation and Democratic Theory*. Cambridge: Cambridge University Press.

Paterson, C. (2006) 'News Agency Dominance in International News on the Internet'. Papers in International and Global Communication No. 01/06. Centre for International Communication Research, Leeds University. Available online from http://ics.leeds.ac.uk/papers/cicr/exhibits/42/cicrpaterson.pdf, accessed 5 February 2011.

Pattie, C., Seyd, P. and Whiteley, P. (2004) *Citizenship in Britain*. Cambridge: Cambridge University Press.

Pavarala, V. and Malik, K. Kumar (2010) 'Community Radio and Women: Forging Subaltern Counterpublics', in C. Rodriguez, D. Kidd and L. Stein (eds), *Making Our Media: Global Initiatives Toward a Democratic Public Sphere*, vol. I, Creskill, NJ: The Hampton Press, pp. 95–113.

Peaslee, R. (2010) '"The Man from New Line Knocked on the Door": Tourism, Media Power and Hobbiton/Matamata as a Boundaried Space', *Tourist Studies* 10(1): 57–73.

Peters, J. D. (2001) 'Witnessing', *Media, Culture and Society* 23: 707–23.

Peters, J. D. (2010) 'Introduction: Friedrich Kittler's Light Shows', in F. Kittler, *Optical Media*. Cambridge: Polity, pp. 1–17.

Petersen, C. (2010) 'Google and Money!', *New York Review of Books*, 9 December: 60–4.

Peterson, M. (2003) *Anthropology and Mass Communication*. New York/ Oxford: Berghahn Books.

Peterson, M. (2010a) 'Getting the News in New Delhi: Newspaper Literacies in an Indian MediaSpace', in S. E. Bird (ed.), *The Anthropology of News and Journalism: Global Perspectives*. Bloomington, IN: Indiana University Press, pp. 168–81.

Peterson, M. (2010b) '"But It is My Habit to Read the *Times*": Meta-Culture and Practice in the Reading of Indian Newspapers', in B. Brauchler and J. Postill (eds), *Theorising Media and Practice*. New York/Oxford: Berghahn Books, pp. 127–45.

Pew Research Center (2007) 'How Young People View their Lives, Futures and Politics', Washington, DC: Pew Research Center.

Pew Research Center (2008) *Biennial News Consumption Survey*, August, www.pewinternet.org, last accessed 5 September 2011.

Pharr, S. and Putnam, R. (eds) (2000) *Disaffected Democracies*. Cambridge, MA: Harvard University Press.

Phillips, A. (2011) 'Transparency and the New Ethics of Journalism', in P. Lee-Wright, A. Phillips and T. Witschge, *Changing Journalism*. London: Routledge, pp. 135–48.

Phillips, A. and Nossek, H. (2008) 'Ourselves and Not Others: Minority Protest and National Frames in Press Coverage', in E. Eide, R. Kunelius and A. Phillips (eds), *Transnational Media Events: The Mohammed Cartoons and the Imagined Clash of Civilizations*. Göteborg: Nordicom, pp. 235–52.

Phillips, A., Couldry, N. and Freedman, D. (2009) 'An Ethical Deficit? Accountability, Norms and the Material Conditions of Contemporary Journalism', in N. Fenton (ed.), *New Media, Old News*. London: Sage, pp. 51–68.

Pinchevski, A. (2005) *By Way of Interruption: Levinas and the Ethics of Communication*. Pittsburgh: Duquesne University Press.

Pitkin, H. (1972) *Wittgenstein and Justice*. Berkeley: University of California Press.

Pomeranz, K. (2000) *The Great Divergence*. Princeton: Princeton University Press.

Pool, I. de Sola (1983) *Technologies of Freedom*. Cambridge, MA: Harvard University Press.

della Porta, D., Kriesi, H. and Rucht, D. (eds) (1999) *Social Movements in a Globalizing World*. London: Macmillan.

Poster, M. (1999) 'Underdetermination', *New Media & Society* 1(1): 12–17.

Poster, M. (2006) *Information Please*. Durham, NC: Duke University Press.

Postill, J. (2008) 'Localizing the Internet beyond Communities and Networks', *New Media & Society* 10(3): 413–31.

Powell, A. (2011) 'Openness and Enclosure in Mobile Internet Architecture'. Presentation to *Platform Politics* Conference, Anglia Ruskin University, 11–13 May.

Prensky, M. (2006) *Don't Bother Me Mum – I'm Learning!* St Paul MN: Paragon House.

Press, A. and Williams, B. (2011) *The New Media Environment*. Malden, MA: Wiley-Blackwell.

Priest, P. (1995) *Public Intimacies: Talk Show Participants and Tell-All TV*. Cresskill, NJ: The Hampton Press.

Prior, M. (2002) 'Efficient Choice, Inefficient Democracy?', in L. Cranor and S. Greenstein (eds), *Communications Policy and Information Technology: Promises, Problems, Prospects*. Cambridge, MA: MIT Press, pp. 143–79.

Prior, M. (2008) 'Are Hyperlinks Weak Ties?', in J. Turow and L. Tsui (eds), *The Hyperlinked Society*. Ann Arbor: University of Michigan Press, pp. 250–67.

Proust, M. (1982) *Remembrance of Things Past*, vol. I, *Swann's Way*, trans. C. Scott Moncrieff and T. Kilmartin. Harmondsworth: Penguin.

Proust, M. (1983) *Remembrance of Things Past*, vol. II, *The Guermantes Way* and *The Cities of the Plain*, trans. C. Scott Moncrieff and T. Kilmartin. Harmondsworth: Penguin.

Punathambekar, A. (2010) 'Reality TV and Participatory Culture in India', *Popular Communicaion* 8(4): 241–55.

Putnam, R. (2000) *Bowling Alone*. New York: Simon & Schuster.

Qiang, X. (2011) 'The Rise of Online Public Opinion and its Political Impact', in S. Shirk (ed.), *Changing Media, Changing China*. Oxford: Oxford University Press, pp. 202–24.

Qiu, J. (2009) *Working-Class Network Society*. Cambridge, MA: MIT Press.

Quandt, T. (2008) 'News Tuning and Content Management: An Observation Study of Old and New Routines in German Online Newsrooms', in C. Paterson and D. Domingo (eds), *Making Online News*. New York: Peter Lang, pp. 77–98.

Quinn, W. (1995) 'Putting Rationality in its Place', in R. Hursthouse, G. Lawrence and W. Quinn (eds), *Virtues and Reasons*. Oxford: Oxford University Press, pp. 181–208.

Raeside, J. (2011) 'Virtual Reality', *Guardian*, 1 June.

Rainie, L., Purcell, K. and Smith, A. (2011) 'The Social Side of the Internet', Pew Internet and American Life Project, 18 January, www.pewinternet.org, last accessed 14 March 2011.

Rajagopal, A. (2001) *Politics after Television: Hindu Nationalism and the Reshaping of the Public in India*. Cambridge: Cambridge University Press.

Rantanen, T. (2009) *When News Was New*. Malden: Wiley-Blackwell.

Rao, S. (2007) 'The Globalization of Bollywood: An Ethnography of Non-Elite Audiences in India', *The Communication Review* 10: 57–76.

Rao, U. (2010) 'Empowerment Through Local News-Making: Studying the Media/Public Interface', in S. E. Bird (ed.), *The Anthropology of News and Journalism: Global Perspectives*. Bloomington, IN: Indiana University Press, pp. 100–15.

Rappaport, R. (1999) *Ritual and Religion in the Making of Humanity*. Cambridge: Cambridge University Press.

Rauch, J. (2007) 'Activists as Alternative Communities: Rituals of Consumption and Interaction in an Alternative Media Audience', *Media, Culture and Society* 29(6): 994–1013.

Rawls, J. (1972) *A Theory of Justice*. Oxford: Oxford University Press.

Rawls, J. (1996) *Political Liberalism*. Cambridge: Cambridge University Press.

Rawolle, S. (2010) 'Understanding the Mediatisation of Educational Policy as Practice', *Critical Studies in Education* 51(1): 21–39.

Rawolle, S. and Lingard, B. (2008) 'The Sociology of Pierre Bourdieu and Researching Education Policy', *Journal of Education Policy* 23(6): 729–40.

Reckwitz, A. (2002) 'Toward a Theory of Social Practices', *European Journal of Social Theory* 5(2): 243–63.

Redmond, S. (2006) 'Intimate Fame Everywhere', in S. Holmes and S. Redmond (eds), *Framing Celebrity*. London: Routledge, pp. 27–43.

Reijnders, S. (2011) *Media Tourism*. Aldershot: Ashgate.

Reijnders, S., Rooijakkers, G. and Zoonen, L. van (2007) 'Community Spirit and Competition in *Idols*: Ritual Meanings of a Television Talent Quest', *European Journal of Communication* 22(3): 275–93.

Retort Collective, The (2005) *Afflicted Powers*. London: Verso.

Rheingold, H. (2008) 'Using Participatory Media and Public Voice to Encourage Civic Engagement', in L. Bennett (ed.), *Civic Life Online*. Cambridge, MA: MIT Press, pp. 97–118.

Ricoeur, P. (1992) *Oneself as Another*. Chicago: Chicago University Press.

Ricoeur, P. (2007) *Reflections on the Just*. Chicago: Chicago University Press.

Riegert, K. (ed.) (2007) *Politicotainment*. New York: Peter Lang.

Rifkin, J. (2001) 'Quand les marchés s'effacent contre les réseaux', *Le Monde Diplomatique* (September): 22–3.

Rilke, R. (1987) *The Selected Poetry of Rainer Maria Rilke*, trans. Stephen Mitchell. New York: Picador Classics.

Robins, K. (1999) 'New Media and Knowledge', *New Media & Society* 1(1): 18–24.

Robinson, J. and Martin, S. (2009) 'Of Time and Television', in E. Katz and P. Scannell (eds), '*The End of Television?*' *Annals of the American Academy of Political and Social Science* 625: 74–86.

Rocha, L. (2007) 'Media Against Terrorism in the Peruvian Andes', *Media Development* (March): 27–31.

Rodriguez, C. (2001) *Fissures in the Mediascape*. Creskill, NJ: The Hampton Press.

Rodriguez, C. (2003) 'The Bishop and his Star: Citizens' Communication in Southern Chile', in N. Couldry and J. Curran (eds), *Contesting Media Power*. Boulder, CO: Rowman and Littlefield, pp. 177–94.

Rodriguez, C. (2011) *Citizens' Media against Armed Conflict: Disrupting Violence in Colombia*. Minneapolis: University of Minnesota Press.

Rogers, R. (2004) *Information Politics on the Web*. Cambridge, MA: MIT Press.

Rosanvallon, P. (2008) *Counter-Democracy*. Cambridge: Cambridge University Press.

Rose, M. (2000) 'Through the Eyes of the *Video* Nation', in J. Izod, R. Kilborn and M. Hibberd (eds), *From Grierson to the Docu-soap*. Luton: University of Luton Press, pp. 173–84.

Rosen, J. (2006) 'The People Formerly Known as the Audience', http://journalism.nyu.edu/pubzone/weblongs/pressthink/2006/06/27/ppl_frmr_p.html, last accessed 8 March 2011.

Rosenau, J. (1990) *Turbulence in World Politics*. Princeton: Princeton University Press.

Rosenberg, S. (2007) 'The Blog Haters Have Barely Any Idea What They are Raging Against', *Guardian*, 28 August.

Ross, A. (1991) *Strange Weather*. London: Verso.

Rothenbuhler, E. (1989) 'The Liminal Fight: Mass Strikes as Ritual and Interpretation', in J. Alexander (ed.), *Durkheimian Sociology: Cultural Studies*. Cambridge: Cambridge University Press.

Rothenbuhler, E. (1998) *Ritual Communication*. Thousand Oaks: Sage.

Rothenbuhler, E. (2010) 'Media Events in the Age of Terrorism and the Internet', *Journalism Si Communicare* V(2): 34–41.

Rothenbuhler, E. and Coman, M. (eds) (2005) *Media Anthropology*. Newbury Park: Sage.

Ruddock, A. (2007) *Investigating Audiences*. London: Sage.

Ruggie, J. (1993) 'Territoriality and Beyond: Problematizing Modernity in International Relations', *International Organization* 47(1): 139–74.

Rusbridger, A. (2009) 'First Read: The Mutualized Future is Bright: But We Will Need Some Help – from Government and Others – to Get There', 19 October, www.cjr.org/reconstruction/the_mutualized_future_is_brigh.php, last accessed 9 July 2011.

Russell, A. (2011) *Networked: A Contemporary History of News in Transition*. Cambridge: Polity.

Russell, A. and Echchaibi, N. (eds) (2009) *International Blogging*. New York: Peter Lang.

Sá, L. (2007) 'Cyberspace Nationhood: The Virtual Construction of Capao Redondo', in C. Taylor and T. Putnam (eds), *Latin American Cyberculture and Cyberliterature*. Liverpool: Liverpool University Press, pp. 123–39.

Sakr, N. (2009) 'Fragmentation or Consolidation? Factors in the Oprahization of Social Talk on Multi-Channel Arab TV', in G. Turner and T. Tay (eds), *Television Studies After TV*. London: Routledge, pp. 168–77.

Salazar, J. (2010) 'Making Culture Visible: The Mediated Constitution of a Mapuche Nation in Chile', in C. Rodriguez, D. Kidd and L. Stein (eds), *Making Our Media*, vol. I. Creskill, NJ: The Hampton Press, pp. 29–46.

Sambrook, R. (2006) 'How the Net is Transforming News', 20 January, http://news.bbc.co.uk/1/hi/technology/4630890.stm/, last accessed 31 January 2011.

Sambrook, R. (2010) *Are Foreign Correspondents Redundant? The Changing Face of International News*. Oxford: Reuters Institute.

Sanderson, J. and Cheong, P. (2010) 'Tweeting Prayers and Communicating Grief over Michael Jackson Online', *Bulletin of Science Technology & Society* 30(5): 328–40.

Sands, P. (2008) *Torture Team*. London: Allen Lane.

de Santis, H. (2003) 'Mi programa as su programa: Tele/visions of a Spanish language diaspora in North America', in K. Karim (ed.), *The Media of Diaspora*. London: Routledge, pp. 63–75.

Sassen, S. (2006) *Territory Authority Rights*. Princeton: Princeton University Press.

Savage, M. (2009) 'Contemporary Sociology and the Challenge of Descriptive Assemblage', *European Journal of Social Theory* 12(1): 155–74.

Savage, M., Bagnall, G. and Longhurst, B. (2005) *Globalization and Belonging*. London: Sage.

Scannell, P. (1988) 'Radio Times: The Temporal Arrangements of Broadcasting in the Modern World', in P. Drummond and R. Paterson (eds), *Television and its Audiences*, London: British Film Institute, pp. 15–31.

Scannell, P. (1996) *Radio, Television and Modern Life*. Oxford: Blackwell.

Scannell, P. (2002) 'History Media and Communication', in K.-B. Jensen (ed.), *A Handbook of Media Communication Research* London: Routledge.

Scannell, P. (2009) 'The Dialectic of Time and Television', in E. Katz and P. Scannell (eds), *'The End of Television?'* Annals of the American Academy of Political and Social Science 625: 219–35.

Scannell, P. and Cardiff, D. (1991) *A Social History of British Broadcasting*, vol. I. Oxford: Blackwell.

Schatzki, T. (1999) *Social Practices: A Wittgensteinian Approach to Human Activity and the Social*. Cambridge: Cambridge University Press.

Schatzki, T., Knorr-Cetina, K. and von Savigny, E. (eds) (2001) *The Practice Turn in Contemporary Theory*. London: Routledge.

Schickel, R. (1986) *Intimate Strangers*. New York: Fromm.

Schiller, D. (2007) *How to Think About Information*. Urbana and Chicago: University of Illinois Press.

Schlesinger, P. (2000) 'The Nation and Communicative Space', in H. Tumber (ed.), *Media Power, Professionals and Policies*. London: Routledge, pp. 99–115.

Schlesinger, P. and Tumber, H. (1994) *Reporting Crime*. Oxford: Oxford University Press.

Schrøder, K. and Kobbernagel, C. (2010) 'Towards a Typology of Cross-media News Consumption: A Qualitative-Quantitative Synthesis', *Northern Lights* 8: 115–38.

Schrøder, K. and Larsen, B. (2009) 'The Shifting Cross-Media News Landscape: Challenges for News Producers', *Journalism Studies* 11(4): 524–34.

288   **References**

Schrott, A. (2009) 'Dimensions: Catch-all Label or Technical Term', in K. Lundby (ed.), *Mediatization*. New York: Peter Lang, pp. 41–62.

Schulz, D. (2006) 'Morality, Community, Publicness: Shifting Terms of Public Debate in Mali', in B. Meyer and A. Moors (eds), *Religion, Media, and the Public Sphere*. Bloomington: Indiana University Press, pp. 132–51.

Schulz, W. (2004) 'Reconsidering Mediatization as an Analytical Concept', *European Journal of Communication* 19(1): 87–101.

Scoble, R. and Israel, S. (2006) *Naked Conversations: How Blogs are Changing the Way Businesses Talk with Customers*. New York: John Wiley.

Sconce, J. (2003) 'Tulip Theory', in A. Everett and J. Caldwell (eds), *New Media: Theories and Practices of Digitextuality*. New York: Routledge, pp. 179–96.

Scott, J. (2001) *Power*. Cambridge: Polity.

Seiter, E. (1999) *New Media Audiences*. Oxford: Oxford University Press.

Seiter, E. (2005) *The Internet Playground*. New York: Peter Lang.

Selwyn, N., Govard, S. and Furlong, J. (2005) 'Whose Internet is it Anyway? Exploring Adults' (Non)Use of the Internet in Everyday Life', *New Media & Society* 7(1): 5–26.

Sen, A. (1983) *Poverty and Famines*. Oxford: Oxford University Press.

Sen, A. (1992) *Inequality Reexamined*. Oxford: Oxford University Press.

Sen, A. (1999) *Development as Freedom*. Oxford: Oxford University Press.

Sen, A. (2009) *The Idea of Justice*. London: Allen Lane.

Senft, T. (2008) *Camgirls*. New York: Peter Lang.

Sennett, R. and Cobb, J. (1972) *The Hidden Injuries of Class*. Cambridge: Cambridge University Press.

Serazio, M. (2010) 'Shooting for Fame: Spectacular Youth, Web 2.0 Dystopia and the Celebrity Anarchy of Generation Mashup', *Communication Culture and Critique* 3(3): 416–34.

Serres, M. (2001) 'Entre Disneyland et les Ayatollahs', *Le Monde Diplomatique* (September): 6.

Sewell, W. (1996) 'Historical Events as Transformations of Structures: Inventing Revolution and the Bastille', *Theory & Society* 25: 841–81.

Shannon, C. and Weaver, W. (1949) *The Mathematical Theory of Communication*. Urbana: University of Illinois Press.

Shiels, R. (2010) 'Google and Verizon's Online Vision for "Open Internet"', 10 August, www.bbc.co.uk/news/technology-10920871.

Shils, E. (1975) *Center and Periphery*. Chicago: Chicago University Press.

Shirky, C. (2010) *Cognitive Surplus*. London: Allen Lane.

Shove, E. (2007) *Comfort, Cleanliness and Convenience: The Social Organization of Normality*. Oxford: Berg.

Siebert, F. S., Peterson, T. and Schramm, W. (1956) *Four Theories of the Press*. Urbana: Illinois University Press.

Silverstone, R. (1994) *Television and Everyday Life*. London: Routledge.

Silverstone, R. (1999) *Why Study the Media?* London: Sage.

Silverstone, R. (2002) 'Complicity and Collusion in the Mediation of Everyday Life', *New Literary History* 33(5): 745–64.

Silverstone, R. (2005) 'Media and Communication', in C. Calhoun, C. Rojek and B. Turner (eds), *The International Handbook of Sociology*. London: Sage, pp. 188–208.

Silverstone, R. (2007) *Media and Morality*. Cambridge: Polity.

Silverstone, R. and Hirsch, E. (eds) (1992) *Consuming Technologies*. London: Routledge.

Simone, A. (2006) 'Intersecting Geographies? ICTS and Other Virtualities in Urban Africa', in M. Fisher and G. Downey (eds), *Frontiers of Capital*. Durham, NC: Duke University Press, pp. 133–59.

Singer, J. (2005) 'The Political J-blogger: "Normalising" a New Media Form to Fit Old Norms and Practices', *Journalism* 6(2): 173–98.

Sinha, D. (2004) 'Religious Fundamentalism and its "Other": A Snapshot View from the Global Information Order', in S. Saha (ed.), *Religious Fundamentalism in the Contemporary World*. Lanham, MD: Lexington Books, pp. 1–19.

Skey, M. (2011) *National Belonging and Everyday Life*. Basingstoke: Palgrave.

Skinner, D., Uzelman, S., Langlois, A. and Dubois, F. (2010) 'IndyMedia in Canada: Experiments in Developing Glocal Media Commons', in C. Rodriguez, D. Kidd and L. Stein (eds), *Making Our Media*, vol. I. Creskill, NJ: The Hampton Press, pp. 183–202.

Slater, D. and Tacchi, J. (2004) *Research on ICT Innovations for Poverty Reduction*. New Delhi: UNESCO, http://eprints.qut.edu.au/4398/, last accessed 18 November 2011

Smith, N. (1993) 'Homeless/Global', in J. Bird et al. (eds), *Mapping the Futures*. London: Routledge, pp. 92–107.

Smythe, D. (1977) 'Communications: Blindspot of Western Marxism', *Canadian Journal of Political and Social Theory* 1(3): 1–27.

Snow, R. (1983) *Creating Media Culture*. Beverly Hills: Sage.

Snyder, T. (2009) 'Holocaust: The Ignored Reality', *New York Review of Books*, 16 July: 14–16.

Snyder, T. (2010) *Bloodlands: Europe between Hitler and Stalin*. London: Bodley Head.

Sontag, S. (2004). 'What Have We Done?' *Guardian*, 24 May.

Spigel, L. (2004) 'Introduction', in L. Spigel and J. Olsson (eds), *Television After TV*. Durham, NC: Duke University Press, pp. 1–34.

Spigel, L. and Olsson, J. (eds) (2004) *Television After TV*. Durham, NC: Duke University Press.

Spink, A., Jansen, B., Wolfram, D. and Saracevic, T. (2002) 'From e-Sex to e-Commerce: Web Search Changes', *IEEE Computer* 35(3): 107–9.

Spitulnik, D. (2010) 'Personal News and the Price of Public Service: An Ethnographic Window into the Dynamics of Production and Reception in Zambian State Radio', in S. E. Bird (ed.), *The Anthropology of News and Journalism: Global Perspectives*. Bloomington, IN: Indiana University Press, pp. 182–93.

Spitulnik Vidali, D. (2010) 'Millennial Encounters with Mainstream Television News: Excess, Void and Points of Engagement', *Journal of Linguistic Anthropology* 20(2): 372–88.

Splichal, S. (2008) 'Why Be Critical?' *Communication, Culture and Critique* 1(1): 20–30.

Spyer, P. (2006) 'Media and Violence in an Age of Transparency: Journalistic Writing in War-torn Maluku', in B. Meyer and A. Moors (eds), *Religion, Media, and the Public Sphere*. Bloomington: Indiana University Press, pp. 152–65.

Sreberny-Mohammadi, A. and Mohammadi, A. (1994) *Small Media, Big Revolution*. Minneapolis: University of Minnesota Press.

Stahl, M. (2004) 'A Moment Like This: *American Idol* and Narratives of Meritocracy', in C. Washburne and M. Darno (eds), *Bad Music*. London: Routledge, pp. 212–32.

Staiger, J. (1992) *Interpreting Films*. Princeton: Princeton University Press.

Stalder, F. (2011) 'The Pirate Bay and Wikileaks: Platforms for Radical Politics of Access and their Politics'. Paper presented to *Platform Politics* Conference, Anglia Ruskin University, May 12–13.

Stallabrass, J. (2000) *High Art Lite*. London: Verso.

Stallabrass, J. (2006) 'Spectacle and Terror', *New Left Review* 37: 87–108.

Starr, P. (2004) *The Creation of the Media*. New York: Basic Books.

Starr, P. (2009) 'Goodbye to the Age of Newspapers (Hello to a New Era of Corruption)', *The New Republic*, 4 March, www.tnr.com/print/article/goodbye-the-age-newspapers-hello-new-era-corruption, last accessed 19 July 2011.

Stevenson, N. (1999) *The Transformation of Media*. London: Longman.

Stevenson, N. (2002) *Understanding Media Culture*, 2nd edn. London: Sage.

Stiegler, B. (2009) 'Teleologies of the Snail: The Errant Self Wired to a Wimax Network', *Theory, Culture & Society* 26(2–3): 33–45.

Stöber, B. (2006) 'Media Geography: From Patterns of Diffusion to the Complexity of Meanings', in J. Falkheimer and A. Jansson (eds), *Geographies of Communication*. Göteborg: Nordicom, pp. 29–44.

Stolow, J. (2006) 'Communicating Authority, Consuming Tradition: Jewish Orthodox and Outreach Literature and its Reading Public', in B. Meyer and A. Moors (eds), *Religion, Media, and the Public Sphere*. Bloomington: Indiana University Press, pp. 73–90.

Strathern, M. (1992) *After Nature*. Cambridge: Cambridge University Press.

Straubhaar, J. (2007) *World Television: From Global to Local*. Newbury Park: Sage.

Straw, W. (2010) 'Hawkers and Public Space: Free Commuter Newspapers in Canada', in B. Beaty, D. Briton, G. Filax and R. Sullivan (eds), *How Canadians Communicate III*. Athabasca: Athabasca University Press, pp. 79–93.

Strömback, J. and Esser, F. (2009) 'Shaping Politics: Mediatization and Media Interventionism', in K. Lundby (ed.), *Mediatization*. New York: Peter Lang, pp. 205–24.

Stuart, K. (2010) 'Cloud Gaming Means the Sky's the Limit for Any PC', *Guardian*, 24 November.

Sumiala, J. (forthcoming) 'You Will Die Next', in K. Anden-Papadopoulos and M. Pantti (eds), *Amateur Images and Global News*. Bristol: Intellect.

Sumiala-Seppänen, J., Lundby, K. and Salokangas R. (eds) (2006) *Implications of the Sacred in (Post)modern Media*. Göteborg: Nordicom.

Sun, W. (2002) *Leaving China: Media, Migration and Transnational Imagination*. Lanham, MD: Rowman and Littlefield.

Sun, W. (2009) *Maid in China*. London: Routledge.

Sun, W. and Zhao, Y. (2009) 'Television Culture with "Chinese Characteristics": The Politics of Compassion and Education', in G. Turner and T. Tay (eds), *Television Studies After TV*. London: Routledge, pp. 96–104.

Sunstein, C. (2001) *Republic.com*. Princeton: Princeton University Press.

Sutton Trust, The (2006) *The Educational Backgrounds of Leading Journalists*. www.suttontrust.com/research/the-educational-backgrounds-of-leading-journalists, last accessed 10 August 2010.

Svec, H. (2010) '"The Purpose of These Acting Exercises": The Actors' Studio and the Labours of Celebrity', *Celebrity Studies* 1(3): 303–18.

Swanton, C. (2003) *Virtue Ethics*. Oxford: Oxford University Press.

Sweney, M. (2011) 'TV Advertising Still Needs an X-factor', *Guardian*, Media section, 29 August.

Swidler, A. (2001) 'What Anchors Cultural Practices', in T. Schatzki, K. Knorr Cetina and E. von Savigny (eds), *The Practice Turn in Contemporary Theory*. London: Routledge, pp. 74–92.

Tacchi, J. (2008) 'Voice and Poverty', *Media Development* (January): 12–16.

Takahashi, T. (2010a) *Audience Studies: A Japanese Perspective*. London: Sage.

Takahashi, T. (2010b) 'MySpace or Mixi? Japanese Engagement with SNS (social networking sites) in the Global Age', *New Media & Society* 12(3): 453–75.

Tapscott, D. (1998) *Growing Up Digital: The Rise of the Net Generation*. New York: McGraw Hill.

Tapscott, D. and Williams, A. (2008) *Wikinomics*. New York: Penguin.

Tarde, G. (1969 [1922]) *Communication and Social Opinion*. Chicago: Chicago University Press.

Taylor, C. (1985) *Philosophy and the Human Sciences. Philosophical Papers, vol. II*. Cambridge: Cambridge University Press.

Taylor, C. (2004) *Modern Social Imaginaries*. Durham, NC: Duke University Press.

Taylor, C. (2007) 'Cultures of Democracy and Citizen Efficacy', *Public Culture* 19(1): 117–50.

Tenenboim-Weinblatt, K. (2009) '"Where is Jack Bauer When You Need Him?" The Uses of Television Drama in Mediated Political Discourse', *Political Communication* 26: 267–387.

Terranova, T. (2004) *Network Culture*. London: Pluto.

Teurlings, J. (2007) *Dating Shows and the Production of Identities: Institutional Practices and Power in Television Production*. PhD thesis, University of Amsterdam.

Teurlings, J. (2010) 'Media Literacy and the Challenges of Contemporary Media Culture: On Savvy Viewers and Critical Apathy', *European Journal of Cultural Studies* 13(3): 359–73.

Thévenot, L. (2007a) 'A Science of Life Together in the World', *European Journal of Social Theory* 10(2): 233–44.

292 **References**

Thévenot, L. (2007b) 'The Plurality of Cognitive Formats and Engagements: Moving between the Familiar and the Public', *European Journal of Social Theory* 10(3): 409–23.

Thielmann, T. (2010) 'Conference Introduction Remarks', Media in Action Conference, University of Seigen, 17 June.

Thomas, A. (2011) 'Global TV Advertising Market Looks Forward to Bumper 2012', 2 June, http://blogs.informatandm.com/, last accessed 26 July 2011.

Thomas, G. (2004) 'The Cultural Contest for our Attention in Observations on Mediality, Property and Religion', in W. Schweiker and C. Mathewes (eds), *Having: Property and Possessions in Religion and Social Life*. Grand Rapids, MI: William B. Eerdmans, pp. 272–95.

Thomas, K. (1971) *Religion and the Decline of Magic*. Harmondsworth: Penguin.

Thomas, P. (2008) *Strong Religion, Zealous Media*. New Delhi: Sage.

Thompson, E. P. (1963) *The Making of the English Working Class*. Harmondsworth: Penguin.

Thompson, J. (1990) *Ideology and Modern Culture*. Cambridge: Polity.

Thompson, J. (1995) *The Media and Modernity*. Cambridge: Polity.

Thompson, J. (1996) 'Tradition and Self in a Mediated World', in P. Heelas, S. Lash and P. Morris (eds), *Detraditionalization*. Oxford: Blackwell, pp. 89–108.

Thompson, J. (1997) 'Scandal and Social Theory', in J. Lull and B. Hinerman (eds), *Media Scandals*. Cambridge: Polity, pp. 34–64.

Thompson, J. (2001) *Political Scandals*. Cambridge: Polity.

Thompson, J. (2005) 'The New Visibility', *Theory, Culture & Society* 22(6): 31–51.

Thrift, N. (2008) *Non-Representational Theory*. London: Routledge.

Thussu, D. (2009) 'Why Internationalize Media Studies and How?', in D. Thussu (ed.), *Internationalizing Media Studies*. London: Routledge, pp. 13–31.

Tilly, C. (1999) *Durable Inequality*. Berkeley: University of California Press.

Tilly, C. (2007) *Democracy*. Cambridge: Cambridge University Press.

Tocqueville, A. de (1961 [1835–1840]) *Democracy in America*, vol. I. New York: Schocken.

Tocqueville, A. de (1864 [1835–1840]) *Democracy in America*, vol. II. Cambridge: Sever and Francis.

Tomlinson, J. (1999) *Globalization and Culture*. Cambridge: Polity.

Tomlinson, J. (2007) *The Culture of Speed*. London: Sage.

Touraine, A. (2007) 'Sociology after Sociology', *European Journal of Social Theory* 19(2): 184–93.

Trow, G. (1981) *Within the Context of No Context*. Boston: Little Brown & Company.

Tunstall, J. (2008) *The Media Were American*. New York: Oxford University Press.

Turkle, S. (1996) *Life on the Screen*. London: Weidenfeld and Nicholson.

Turkle, S. (2011) *Alone Together*. New York: Basic Books.

Turner, B. (2005) 'Classical Sociology and Cosmopolitanism: A Critical Defence of the Social', *British Journal of Sociology* 57(1): 133–51.

Turner, B. (2007a) 'The Enclave Society: Towards a Sociology of Immobility', *European Journal of Social Theory* 10(2): 287–303.

Turner, B. (2007b) 'Religious Authority and the New Media', *Theory, Culture & Society* 24(2): 117–34.

Turner, G. (2009) 'Television and the Nation: Does this Matter Any More?', in G. Turner and T. Tay (eds), *Television Studies After TV*. London: Routledge, pp. 54–64.

Turner, G. (2010) *Ordinary People and the Media*. London: Sage.

Turnock, R. (2000) *Interpreting Diana*. London: BFI.

Turow, J. (2007) *Niche Envy*. Cambridge, MA: MIT Press.

Uitermark, J. and Gielen, A.-J. (2010) 'Islam in the Spotlight: The Mediatization of the Politics in an Amsterdam Neighbourhood', *Urban Studies* 47(6): 1325–42.

Uricchio, W. (2009) 'Contextualising the Broadcast Era: Nation, Commerce and Constraint', in E. Katz and P. Scannell (eds), *'The End of Television?' Annals of the American Academy of Political and Social Science* 625: 60–73.

Urry, J. (2000) *Sociology Beyond Societies*. London: Sage.

Urry, J. (2007) *Mobilities*. Cambridge: Polity.

VSS (2005) *Communications Industry Forecast 2005–9*. New York.

Vaidhyanathan, S. (2011) *The Googlization of Everything (and Why We Should Worry)*. Berkeley: University of California Press.

van Dijk, J. (1999) *The Network Society*. London: Sage.

van Dijck, J. (2009) 'Users Like You? Theorizing Agency in User-Generated Content', *Media, Culture and Society* 31(1): 41–58.

Vattimo, G. (1992) *The Transparent Society*. Cambridge: Polity.

Vaughan, L. and Zhang, Y. (2007) 'Equal Representation by Search Engines? A Comparison of Websites across Countries and Domains', *Journal of Computer-Mediated Communication* 12(6): 888–909.

Vickers, A. (2001) 'Reality Text', *Guardian*, Online section, 24 May.

Virilio, P. (1999) *Open Sky*. London: Verso.

Volcic, Z. (2009) 'Television in the Balkans: The Rise of Commercial Nationalism', in G. Turner and T. Tay (eds), *Television Studies After TV*. London: Routledge, pp. 115–24.

Wacquant, L. (1993) 'From Ruling Class to Field of Power: An Interview with Pierre Bourdieu on *La Noblesse d'Etat*', *Theory, Culture & Society* 10(3): 19–44.

Wacquant, L. (2003) 'On the Tracks of Symbolic Power: Prefatory Notes to Bourdieu's "State Nobility"', *Theory, Culture and Society* 10(3): 1–17.

Wacquant, L. (2009) *Punishing the Poor*. Durham, NC: Duke University Press.

Wagner, P. (2008) *Modernity as Experience and Interpretation*. Cambridge: Polity.

Wang, G. (ed.) (2011) *De-Westernizing Communication Research*. London: Routledge.

294   References

Warde, A. (2005) 'Consumption and Theories of Practice', *Journal of Consumer Culture* 5: 131–53.

Wardle, C. and Williams, A. (2010) 'Beyond User-Generated Content: A Production Study Examining the Ways in which UGC is Used at the BBC', *Media, Culture and Society* 32(5): 781–99.

Warschauer, M. (2003) *Technology and Social Inclusion*. Cambridge, MA: MIT Press.

Waters, R. (2011) 'Google Throws Full Weight at Facebook', *Financial Times*, 29 June.

Waters, R., Edgecliffe-Johnson, A. and Menn, J. (2011) 'The Crowded Cloud', *Financial Times*, 4 June.

Weaver, M. (2007) 'Woman Found Canoeist Photo via Google', *Guardian*, 6 December.

Webb, D. (2009) *Privacy and Solitude in the Middle Ages*. London: Hambleden Continuum.

Weber, B. (2009) *Makeover TV: Selfhood, Citizenship and Celebrity*. Durham, NC: Duke University Press.

Weber, M. (1947) *The Theory of Social and Economic Organization*. New York: Free Press.

Webster, J. (2005) 'Beneath the Veneer of Fragmentation: Television Audience Polarization in a Multichannel World', *Journal of Communication* 55(2): 366–82.

Welch, D. (1993) *The Third Reich: Politics and Propaganda*. London: Routledge.

Wellman, B. (2001) 'Physical Place and Cyber Place: The Rise of Networked Individualism', *International Journal of Urban and Regional Research* 25: 227–52.

Welsch, W. (1999) 'Transculturality – The Changing Forms of Cultures Today', in Bundesminister für Wissenschaft und Verkehr and Internationales Forschungszentrum für Kulturwissenschaften (eds), *The Contemporary Study of Culture*. Wien: Turia & Kant, pp. 217–44.

Wenger, E. (1998) *Communities of Practice*. Cambridge: Cambridge University Press.

Werbner, P. (1999) 'Global Pathways: Working Class Cosmopolitans and the Creation of Transnational Ethnic Worlds', *Social Anthropology* 7(1): 17–35.

Wheeler, D. (2004) 'Blessings and Curses: Women and the Internet Revolution in the Arab World', in N. Sakr (ed.), *Women and Media in the Middle East*. London: IB Tauris, pp. 138–61.

White, M. (1992) *Tele-advising*. Chapel Hill: University of North Carolina Press.

White, M. (2004) 'The Attractions of Television: Reconsidering Liveness', in N. Couldry and A. McCarthy (eds), *MediaSpace: Place, Scale and Culture in a Media Age*. London: Routledge, pp. 75–92.

Widestedt, K. (2009) 'Pressing the Centre of Attention: Three Royal Weddings and a Media Myth', in M. Jönsson and P. Lundell (eds), *Media and Monarchy in Sweden*. Göteborg: Nordicom, pp. 47–58.

Williams, B. (1985) *Ethics and the Limits of Philosophy*. London: Fontana/Collins.

Williams, B. (2002) *Truth and Truthfulness: An Essay in Genealogy*. Princeton: Princeton University Press.

Williams, R. (1961) *The Long Revolution*. Harmondsworth: Penguin.

Williams, R. (1973) *The Country and the City*. London: The Hogarth Press.

Williams, R. (1992) *Television: Technology and Cultural Form*. London: Fontana.

Wilson, N. (2007) 'Scholiasts and Commentators', *Greek, Roman and Byzantine Studies* 47: 39–70.

Wilson, T. (2007) *Understanding Media Users*. Malden, MA: Wiley-Blackwell.

Winocur, R. (2009) 'Digital Convergence as the Symbolic Medium of New Practices and Meanings in Young People's Lives', *Popular Communication* 7: 179–87.

Winston, B. (1998) *Media Technology and Society*. London: Routledge.

de Witte, M. (2009) *Spirit Media: Charismatics, Traditionalists and Mediation Practices in Ghana*. PhD thesis, Free University of Amsterdam.

Wittgenstein, L. (1978 [1953]) *Philosophical Investigations*. Oxford: Blackwell.

Wittmann, R. (1999) 'Was There a Reading Revolution at the End of the Eighteenth Century?', in G. Cavallo and R. Chartier (eds), *A History of Reading in the West*. Cambridge: Polity, pp. 284–312.

Wolin, S. (2008) *Democracy Inc.* Princeton: Princeton University Press.

Wood, H. and Skeggs, B. (2008) 'Spectacular Morality: "Reality" Television, Individualization and the Remaking of the Working Class', in D. Hesmondhalgh and J. Toynbee (eds), *Media and Social Theory*. London: Routledge, pp. 177–93.

Woolard, C. (2010) Speech to MeCCSA Conference, London School of Economics and Political Science, 6 January.

World Association of Newspapers (2008) *Youth Media DNA: Decoding the Media and News Consumption of Finnish Youth 15–29*, www.hssaatio.fi/en/images/stories/files/Final_YouthMediaDNAReport_October19.pdf, last accessed 23 June 2011.

Wright, J. (forthcoming) 'Listening to Suffering: What Might "Proper Distance" Have to Do with Media News?', *Journalism: Theory, Practice and Criticism*.

Wriston, W. (1992) *The Twilight of Sovereignty*. New York: Scribners.

Wrong, D. (1994) *The Problem of Order*. New York: Free Press.

Wuthnow, R. (1989) *Communities of Discourse*. Cambridge, MA: Harvard University Press.

Wyatt, S., Thomas, G. and Terranova, T. (2002) '"They Came, They Surfed, They Went Back to the Beach": Conceptualizing Use and Non-Use of the Internet', in S. Woolgar (ed.), *Virtual Society?* Oxford: Oxford University Press, pp. 71–92.

Xenos, M. and Foot, K. (2008) 'Not Your Father's Internet: The Generation Gap in Online Politics', in L. Bennett (ed.), *Civic Life Online*. Cambridge, MA: MIT Press, pp. 57–70.

Yates, F. (1992 [1966]) *The Art of Memory*. London: Pimlico.

296 References

Yoo, S. (2009) 'Internet, Internet Culture, and Internet Communities of Korea: Overview and Research Directions', in G. Goggin and M. McLelland (eds), *Internationalizing Internet Studies*. London: Routledge, pp. 217–36.

Ytreberg, E. (2009) 'Extended Liveness and Eventfulness in Multi-platform Reality Formats', *New Media & Society* 11(5): 467–85.

Ytreberg, E. (2011) 'The Encounter between Media Professionals and "Ordinary People" in Event-Based Multi-Platform Formats'. Paper presented to the ICA Conference, Boston, 26–30 May.

Zelizer, B. (1993) *Covering the Body: The Kennedy Assassination, the Media and the Shaping of Collective Memory*. Chicago: Chicago University Press.

Zelizer, B. (2011) 'Journalism in the Service of Communication', *Journal of Communication* 61(1): 1–21.

Zerubavel, E. (1981) *Hidden Rhythms*. Berkeley: University of California Press.

Zhao, Y. (2008a) 'Neoliberal Strategies, Socialist Legacies: Communication and State Transformation in China', in P. Chakravarty and Y. Zhao (eds), *Global Communications: Towards a Transcultural Political Economy*. Lanham, MD: Rowman and Littlefield, pp. 23–50.

Zhao, Y. (2008b) *Communication in China*. Lanham, MD: Rowman and Littlefield.

Zielinski, S. (2006) *Deep Time of the Media*. Cambridge, MA: MIT Press.

Zimmermann, B. (2006) 'Pragmatism and the Capability Approach: Challenges in Social Theory and Empirical Research', *European Journal of Social Theory* 9(4): 467–84.

Zittrain, J. (2008) *The Future of the Internet and How to Stop It*. New Haven: Yale University Press.

Žižek, S. (1989) *The Sublime Object of Ideology*. London: Verso.

Zolo, D. (1992) *Democracy and Complexity*. Cambridge: Polity.

Zuckerman, E. (2011) 'The First Twitter Revolution?', *Foreign Policy*, 14 January, www.foreignpolicy.com/articles/2011/01/14/the_first_twitter_revolution, last accessed 24 January 2012.

Index